SURVEY
OF
SOCIAL
SCIENCE

GOVERNMENT AND POLITICS SERIES

Volume 5
1809-2222

Separation of Powers: Political Philosophy—Z

Edited by
FRANK N. MAGILL

Consulting Editor
JOSEPH M. BESSETTE
CLAREMONT MCKENNA COLLEGE

SALEM PRESS
Pasadena, California   Englewood Cliffs, New Jersey

Library of Congress Cataloging-in-Publication Data
Survey of social science: government and politics series /
edited by Frank N. Magill; consulting editor Joseph M.
Bessette.
    p.   cm.
Includes bibliographical references and index.
   1. Political science—Encyclopedias. 2. United States—
Politics and government—Encyclopedias. I. Magill,
Frank Northen, 1907-   . II. Bessette, Joseph M.
JA61.S88   1995
320'.03—dc20
ISBN 0-89356-745-0 (set)   95-30408
ISBN 0-89356-750-7 (volume 5)   CIP

CONTENTS

GOVERNMENT AND POLITICS

SURVEY
OF
SOCIAL
SCIENCE

SEPARATION OF POWERS: POLITICAL PHILOSOPHY

Field of study: Political philosophy

Separation of powers is a system for dividing governmental authority so that no one person or group of political officials may exercise all the political power the government possesses. The most common division attempts to separate legislative, executive, and judicial powers into three distinct branches of government.

Principal terms

CHECKS AND BALANCES: political arrangement whereby each branch of government has oversight of one or more of the other branches to ensure that none oversteps its constitutional authority

CONSTITUTION: organic law that sets up the system of government for a society. Constitutions establish the amount of power the government will have and how that power is allocated among the different branches of government

EXECUTIVE: head of government who usually oversees the daily administration of government

JUDICIARY: branch of government responsible for interpreting the laws of the state

LEGISLATURE: branch of government responsible for deliberating and passing laws

PRESIDENTIAL SYSTEM: system of government most closely associated with separation of powers

Overview

Separation of powers is most closely associated with the political writings of the French philosopher Baron de Montesquieu, the English philosopher John Locke, and the government of the United States of America. The seventeenth century ushered in a period of major political change. Many accepted practices and beliefs were challenged during the seventeenth and eighteenth centuries. One of the central beliefs that was challenged was the notion that governments were determined by divine right.

As political thinkers began to question the authority of the divine right of kings, new theoretical foundations had to be developed for governmental systems. One of the most enduring beliefs that emerged from this period is the belief in natural or human rights. With this development political theorists began writing about governments being created to protect the natural rights of citizens. As these principles became more widely accepted, the old forms of government—primarily monarchy and aristocracy—became increasingly difficult to defend.

Popular government gradually became more common. The American and French revolutions signaled this change of political vision. As nations turned more and more of their political powers over to a larger percentage of their population, the abuse of power took on new characteristics. By the late eighteenth and nineteenth centuries political historians and theorists started focusing their attentions on tyranny by the majority and how to keep popular government from infringing on the citizens' rights.

One of the institutional devices utilized to protect citizens' rights was written constitutions that set limits on the government's powers. Constitutions that not only limit the powers of government but also allocate those powers to different branches of government establish a system of separation of powers. Within such a constitutional system it is customary for different branches of government (usually consisting of the legislative, executive, and judicial branches) to each perform a different political function for the government.

To ensure a reasonable degree of autonomy for each branch of government there is usually some effort made to provide for different methods of selection for the members of the different branches of government. For example, members of Congress are elected by the voting public, the president is selected by a group called the electoral college (the makeup of this group is determined by presidential elections), and judges are recommended by the president but must be confirmed by the Senate. The president and members of Congress are elected for set numbers of years, but judges receive lifetime appointments.

Each branch of government performs specific governmental functions; each also serves as a check on the others. The Constitution of America was the first and continues to be the oldest constitutional document to establish separation of powers. The political system established by the U.S. Constitution sets up three distinct functional areas for the government. Article 1 of that document establishes the legislative branch. Article 1 states: "All legislative authority herein granted shall be vested in the Congress of the United States." It then enumerates the nature and extent of the legislative grant of authority.

The United States Congress has a degree of separation of powers within it as well. The U.S. Congress is bicameral, consisting of a House of Representatives and a Senate, with most of the legislative chores being shared by both chambers. Still there are some legislative tasks that are assigned to only one of the chambers. The Senate, for example, is the only legislative body granted the power to ratify treaties drafted by the president.

Some of the shared responsibilities of the two houses of Congress are set up so each chamber performs a particular part of the responsibility. The best example of this would be the impeachment and removal of government officials for violating the law or public trust. The U.S. Constitution states that government officials can be removed from office for committing "high crimes and misdemeanors." The House of Representatives is responsible for the preliminary investigation to determine if there is enough evidence to warrant a trial (this is the impeachment process). If the House determines that there is enough evidence to justify a trial, it determines what specific areas of the law may have been violated. The actual trial then takes place in the Senate.

Article 2 of the U.S. Constitution states that the executive authority shall be exercised by the president of the United States. The president of the United States has a wide range of responsibilities for overseeing both domestic and foreign policy affairs of the state. The president is the chief administrator of the American government, the commander in chief of the armed services, and the person responsible for drafting all of the nation's treaties.

The judicial branch of government, established in Article 3 of the Constitution, has the responsibility for settling cases and controversies related to law and equity. Judges have lifetime appointments, which permit them to function independently of the more popular branches of government. The United States judiciary also has the final word on questions relating to constitutional interpretation (this power is referred to as judicial review).

The sharing of governmental functions that is reflected in separation of powers reflects a strong lack of trust in elected and appointed government officials. In dividing governmental functions and powers, the Framers intended that no one group would exercise too much authority over the lives of the regular citizens. Suspicion of political power is one of the hallmarks of a system of separation of powers.

Applications

Separation of powers creates distinct but not isolated political units. The powers each branch of government enjoys are distinct from those of the other branches, yet there are important areas where the different branches overlap and must cooperate. The workings of the American political system provide some good illustrations of this point.

One of the best examples is how legislation is passed. The Constitution was cited above as stating that all legislative powers are to be vested in Congress. Despite this claim, the president has an important role in both the development and passage of legislation. An example of the president's role in developing a legislative agenda may be found with President Theodore Roosevelt in the early part of the twentieth century. The Constitution requires that the president, from time to time, inform Congress about the state of the union. Many of the early American presidents viewed this responsibility as a mere formality and placed little importance on exercising this function.

President Theodore Roosevelt used this address as an opportunity not only to describe the state of the union but also to suggest a legislative agenda for Congress to follow during its legislative session, as was his explicit duty, so described in the Constitution. Since then, most presidents not only have reported on the state of the union but also have mapped out a legislative initiative they expect Congress to act on over the course of the coming year.

Presidential initiatives have been developed to the point that Congress not only expects the president to set the legislative agenda for the legislative terms but also relies on the president to sponsor key bills and submit them for Congress's consideration. It has become commonplace for textbooks to refer to the legislative process as one where the president proposes and the Congress disposes. It is important to keep in mind that this procedure is followed only because Congress permits it to work that way. There is nothing in the Constitution that grants the president authority to set Congress' political agenda.

The courtesy that Congress extends to the president of letting the president set the legislative agenda does not guarantee that the legislation passed during that session of Congress will be what the president desires. Separation of powers prohibits anyone who is not a member of Congress from formally introducing legislation. The president's legislative proposals, therefore, must be introduced in Congress by a member of either the House or the Senate. Once these presidential bills have entered the legislative process, the president's control over them is limited.

Members of Congress often will introduce competing legislative proposals. While there is no guarantee that Congress will pass any particular legislative proposal, the bills that do finally get passed by Congress are usually a compromise between what the president requested and what the different members of Congress wanted.

The only official role that the president performs in the legislative process is his constitutional role of signing or vetoing all final bills. If the president signs a bill that has passed both houses of Congress, the bill becomes law. If the president does not approve of the bill, he can veto it. A presidential veto may be overruled by a two-thirds vote in both houses of Congress. Congress' power to override a presidential veto means that the president's authority to thwart the will of Congress is limited. A two-thirds majority in Congress can pass any legislation it desires regardless of the president's wishes.

The constitutional statement that all legislative authority is vested in Congress actually means that a two-thirds majority of both houses of Congress can pass any legislation it desires provided that the legislation remains within constitutional limits. It is the job of the courts to determine if Congress or any other part of the government has overstepped its constitutional authority.

The government's powers are separated, but they are not isolated. Separation of powers permits a degree of functional specialization, but it is the areas of overlapping and shared responsibility that permit the different branches to check and balance one another. Separation of powers is a system of government founded on distrust between and among the different branches of government.

Context

The historical development of separation of powers is usually traced back to Aristotle's idea of a mixed regime. Aristotle (384-322 B.C.E.) was the first political philosopher to describe a political system that utilized a shared system of power. Aristotle thought that his mixed regime would serve to stabilize government. Most modern advocates of separation of power consider stability to be an important political end as well. Aristotle's mixed regime included a tripartite division of governmental functions. The historical and intellectual path that leads from Aristotle's mixed regime to modern systems of separation of powers is not as clear or precise as might be desired.

Two modern political philosophers who are most closely identified as promoting separation of powers are John Locke and Baron de Montesquieu. Their political writings had a strong influence on America's constitutional designers. One of the documents that most thoroughly describes and defends separation of powers is the

Federalist Papers. This collection of editorials was written by Alexander Hamilton, James Madison, and John Jay to convince New Yorkers to ratify the proposed Constitution in 1788. These papers have outlived their original historical purpose; they are now viewed as one of the most authoritative statements on general workings of separation of powers.

For about the last two hundred years, the main competing forms of democratic government have been a parliamentary system and a presidential system. The main theoretical difference between these two systems is that the parliamentary system places all of its political powers in the hands of parliament and a presidential system utilizes separation of powers. It must be noted that the parliamentary system has proven to be the more popular system during these two centuries.

The complicated mechanisms involved in a system of separation of powers is, no doubt, one of the main reasons for the greater popularity of parliamentary systems. Nations that have evolved from a monarchical system to a democratic system (Great Britain, for example) seem to find a parliamentary system convenient for making that transition.

Many of President Woodrow Wilson's academic writings called for breaking down our system of separation of powers. He, like many other reformers, desired a democratic system that placed fewer obstacles in the way of the majority will. There have been a number of reform movements that demonstrated hostility toward the checks and balances that are facilitated by our system of separation of powers. These reformers have tended to ignore the need to protect minority rights. Parliamentary systems do make it easier for simple majorities to control policy formation. One of the chief attributes of a presidential system is that it provides better safeguards for minority interests.

The guiding principles of separation of powers appear to be twofold. First, they permit governmental officials to specialize in one of the three governmental areas: They either execute, legislate, or adjudicate. Second is the principle that reflects political suspicion. James Madison definitely stated this principle in Federalist No. 51, where he claims: "Ambition must be made to counteract ambition."

Separation of powers should be considered one of the least utopian of all theoretical perspectives on government. It is firmly rooted in an understanding of human nature that recognizes the limits of both human ability and generosity.

Bibliography

Aristotle. *The Politics.* Translated by Carnes Lord. Chicago: The University of Chicago Press, 1984. The starting point for political systems that attempt to balance political interests and functions.

Carey, George. "The Separation of Powers." In *Founding Principles of American Government*, edited by George Graham, Jr., and Scarlett Graham. Bloomington: Indiana University Press, 1977. Description of separation of powers in general, with a thorough history of the historical development of separation of powers.

Eidelberg, Paul. *The Philosophy of the American Constitution: A Reinterpretation of the Intentions of the Founding Fathers.* New York: Free Press, 1968. Makes a strong case for the American system of separation of powers.

Hamilton, Alexander, James Madison, and John Jay. *The Federalist Papers.* Edited by Clinton Rossiter. New York: New American Library, 1961. No. 9 provides the overall theoretical guideline for separation of powers, and Nos. 47-51 describe the Framers' theory of separation of powers.

Locke, John. *Second Treatise of Government.* Edited by Richard H. Cox. Arlington Heights, Ill.: Harlan Davidson, 1982. One of the major modern works on the principle of separation of powers.

Montesquieu, Baron de. *The Spirit of the Laws.* Translated by Thomas Nugent. New York: Hafner Press, 1949. The most detailed modern defense of the theoretical importance of separation of powers.

Donald V. Weatherman

Cross-References

Aristotle's Political Philosophy, p. 83; Checks and Balances in U.S. Government, p. 216; Constitutional Law in the United States, p. 439; Government Powers, p. 772; Locke's Political Philosophy, p. 1142; Montesquieu's Political Philosophy, p. 1228; Political Philosophy, p. 1505; Polity, p. 1545; Separation of Powers: Presidential Government, p. 1815.

SEPARATION OF POWERS: PRESIDENTIAL GOVERNMENT

Field of study: Types of government

Separation of powers, or the division of the executive, legislative, and judicial functions, is manifested in presidential government in that the president is elected separately from the legislature. This is unlike the fusion of powers of a parliamentary government, in which the people elect a legislature that then elects the executive.

Principal terms

EXECUTIVE FUNCTION: function of executing the laws of a government, carried out by a person typically called the "president" in a presidential system and the "prime minister" in a parliamentary system

JUDICIAL FUNCTION: function performed by the courts; they determine whether individual behaviors conform to the laws and call on the executive to enforce its judgments on the law

JUDICIAL REVIEW: U.S. Supreme Court power to declare acts of the other national government branches to be out of conformity with the Constitution and therefore unconstitutional

LEGISLATIVE FUNCTION: lawmaking function, performed by the U.S. Congress; Congress makes the laws that the executive administers

Overview

Separation of powers, or the splitting of government functions into categories and institutions (the executive, legislative, and judicial), is a distinguishing characteristic of nearly all presidential governments. The people elect the president directly and separately from the legislature, unlike what happens under the fusion of powers of a parliamentary government, in which the people elect a legislature that then elects the executive.

The notion of separation of powers is associated with the political philosopher Montesquieu, who analyzed the British government in the eighteenth century (when the British monarch still had political power, but was balanced by the increasingly independent Parliament). The influential Montesqueiu's statement that, "When the legislative and the executive powers are united in the same person, or in the same body of magistrates, there can be no liberty," was quoted directly by James Madison, a principal Framer of the Constitution, in his famous Federalist No. 47.

The clearest manifestations of the doctrine of separation of powers occurs in the U.S. Constitution, which names and describes the separate powers, in the first three articles. Article 1 establishes the legislative branch by creating the Congress; Article 2 establishes the executive branch by creating the presidency; and Article 3 establishes the judicial branch by creating the Supreme Court.

The Framers of the Constitution wrote a constitution for a representative rather than a direct democracy. The Framers' dislike of the British monarchy is reflected in the Constitution's measures to prevent excessive concentrations of power. Still, the Framers wrote the Constitution to replace the Articles of Confederation, which they believed were too weak. The Articles of Confederation did not concentrate power enough for government to be effective. The Framers thus sought a balance; the creation of a central government that would be powerful but not too powerful. They provided it with substantial powers while including important limits. While regularly scheduled elections provide the main check in our government, the Framers thought this might not be sufficient and they added protections in the form of separate institutions.

Separation of powers has three elements, the first of which is the separation of the functions of government into the executive, legislative, and judicial branches, as previously described. The second element is the requirement that no individual hold office in more than one branch at the same time. One cannot be a U.S. president and a senator, or a senator and a federal judge, or a president and a supreme court justice at the same time. It is not a question of having too much work to do; it is a question of having too much power in the system. Any person who were to hold offices in more than one branch would be too powerful. The third element of the separation of powers is the intention to prevent any single group from controlling more than one branch. Voters in the United States elect members of three branches of the federal government differently. The methods of election were even more diverse under the original Constitution (in which state legislatures rather than the people elected senators). Different election methods theoretically prevent any one political faction from taking over all three branches at the same time.

In the United States, the people directly elect members of the House of Representatives every two years, but elect the president indirectly through the electoral college. The president appoints federal judges and the Senate confirms them. The people elect senators to staggered six-year terms with no more than one-third of the Senate being changed in any one election. A large and single-minded majority might elect a sympathetic majority in the House of Representatives and one of their number as president in a single presidential election year, but they would still not alter more than one-third of the Senate. Since Supreme Court justices serve life terms, this faction could not control the Court until it also controlled two-thirds of the Senate so that the faction might impeach unsympathetic justices. The whole process would require an overwhelming and long-lasting majority. The fact that the Framers went to such a degree to prevent this single-faction political dominance indicates they understood the danger of simple majority rule.

As a further restraint against dictatorship, the Framers created an overlapping system of checks and balances. Congress passes the laws, but the president may veto them. The veto is in turn subject to a congressional override by a two-thirds vote in both houses. Neither house of Congress can pass laws or override vetoes without the agreement of the other. The Supreme Court may declare acts of Congress or the president unconstitutional. The justices, however, are appointed by the president, who in turn needs the consent of the Senate to do so. The president may be removed by a process of impeachment that requires action in both houses. The president and the executive bureaucracy administer the laws, but they can only do so with funds appropriated by Congress. There are even checks between the two legislative chambers, and their duties are not precisely identical. The Senate confirms some presidential appointments and ratifies treaties, while all revenue measures (taxes) must originate in the House. The House, which is the power most answerable to the people, controls the money.

Checks and balances keep the separation of powers from being entirely separate. While Congress has the main legislative power, the president is exercising a legislative power when vetoing a bill. The president also uses the threat of a veto to persuade Congress to amend bills before passage. The president has the main executive power, but the Senate is performing an executive function when it confirms or denies presidential appointments. The court has the main judicial power, but the president acts as a judge when pardoning someone convicted of a federal crime. The Congress behaves as a court in cases of impeachment. The Supreme Court legislates when it interprets laws. The more checks there are, the less separation occurs. Checks and balances create intermixing of power between the separated institutions, which diminishes the amount of separation. Still, separation of powers would not be effective without checks and balances, because the checks oblige the different branches of government to cooperate. The Framers also intended that the separately empowered institutions would have an interest or motivation in keeping other institutions from abusing their powers.

Applications

Separation of powers and checks and balances are part of the political scene, as shown by conflicts between the president and Congress over budgets and by the impeachment proceeding initiated against President Richard Nixon. Nearly all cases of judicial review involve an assertion by the Supreme Court that an act of the Congress or the president is unconstitutional and is therefore invalid. From the first declaration in *Marbury v. Madison* in 1803 to the late twentieth century, the Court avoided challenging the other two branches and only declared slightly more than one hundred congressional enactments unconstitutional. The acts struck down, however, have often involved separation of powers. In the case of President Nixon, the Court ruled that the president must obey a congressional subpoena.

Two cases serve as examples regarding separation of powers. In *INS v. Chada*, the Court struck down the legislative veto (a provision in which the Congress sought to have some administrative agencies submit proposed regulation changes to it for approval). The Court argued that the Congress was encroaching on executive areas. A comparable ruling came in *Bowsher v. Synar* when the Court found the portion of the Gramm-Rudman Balanced Budget Act, which that would have created the office of a congressionally controlled appointee to exercise an executive power, was unconstitutional.

The Court also invalidated presidential actions, as in *Youngstown Sheet and Tube Co. v. Sawyer*, sometimes referred to as the "Steel Seizure" case. President Harry S Truman seized a steel company to stop a strike that threatened to disrupt military production during the Korean War. While the Court has generally supported the president in foreign affairs, it found no constitutional authority for the president to undertake his action in that case. Perhaps the most significant invalidation of a presidential action came in *United States v. Nixon*, in which Nixon sought to keep tape-recorded conversations with his aides out of the hands of the Congress and the courts. Nixon said executive privilege meant the tapes were his alone. In this, Nixon adopted an extreme view of complete separation, but the Court rejected this in an eight-to-zero opinion in which even three justices that Nixon had appointed voted with the others against him. The Court acknowledged an executive privilege existed, but insisted it could not be asserted when the Court needed the information as part of a criminal investigation. This case makes clear that separation is not an absolute power, but must be limited by various checks and balances.

Although separation of powers and checks and balances are helpful for fostering a democratic government, they are not essential for democracy. Democratic Britain lacks separation of powers and has fewer checks and balances. Britain concentrates all political power in the legislature. While Britain has a monarch, the monarchy lost political power long ago. Britain has two chambers to its legislature (called Parliament), but only one has real power. One chamber, the House of Commons, consists of more than 650 voting members, who serve as long as the majority maintains popular support (but not longer than five years). The members' positions are apportioned across the country according to population. The Commons selects a majority party leader who is traditionally chosen by the British monarch to serve as prime minister. The other chamber, the House of Lords, is an unelected chamber, consisting of more than 1,000 voting members. Some have inherited their positions and others are selected by the monarch to serve a lifetime term. As an unelected body, the Lords do not select the prime minister, nor can they block any bill indefinitely, although they may delay enactment. The Commons has key powers; it appoints the prime minister, enacts laws, and makes the rules that provide for the appointment of judges. Separation of powers and of checks and balances also necessitates a written constitution; such a constitution is lacking in Britain. The British parliamentary system seems to stand at the opposite end of the spectrum from the American presidential system in that the British use a fusion of powers rather than a separation of powers to achieve critical functions. The British also separate the chief of state (monarch) from the active political leader (prime minister). In the United States, both chief of state and head of government are combined in the single office of the president. Some observers have suggested that the American combination of these functions is somewhat inconvenient in that criticism of the president becomes, in the minds of many, an unpatriotic act; one seems to be attacking the chief of state personally. In the British system, one can revere the monarch as the chief of state and still engage in spirited criticism of the chief political leader of the government.

A more important distinction is how the governmental executive functions are carried out. Presumably, under fusion of powers, the legislature should be extremely powerful since it has the right to change a prime minister at any time. The British experience in the last half of the twentieth century has not borne this out, however, largely as a result of its dominant two-party system. The House of Commons has been weakened because the majority party members consider themselves obliged to maintain tight party discipline in order to keep the prime minister in office. Each majority party member in the Commons knows that if he or she votes against the prime minister on an important piece of legislation, he or she is not only bringing down the leader of the party but also he or she is forcing a new election. This prospect is a powerful deterrent to voting against the prime minister and imposes tight party discipline. Such discipline is absent in the U.S. Congress, where Congress members often vote against a president of their own party.

The British prime minister has great power over the Commons in that the prime minister essentially decides all legislative matters and merely submits them to Commons for ratification. The House of Commons lacks the permanent standing committees of the U.S. Congress that give congresspersons such a powerful voice in shaping legislation. Nevertheless, the prime minister's executive power is not as great as it seems. The prime minister needs the support of powerful members of the House of Commons.

Context

Separation of powers is a distinguishing and enduring characteristic of presidential government. Some call for abandoning the presidential system and its separation of powers because it is said to lead to gridlock. Gridlock, however, may simply be taken to mean that the American people have not fully made up their mind on an issue. Separation of powers was designed to block a narrow majority from imposing its will on others. Although it is disheartening to see important legislation stall while Congress and the president bicker, the operation of separation of powers continues to prevent simple majorities from deciding what will be the law for all. It is the Supreme Court's power of judicial review that functions to police the boundaries between the separated powers. Other democratic systems, such as parliamentary governments, are able to operate without separation of powers or checks and balances, but it is not clear that they are superior for this reason.

Bibliography

Anastaplo, George. *The Constitution of 1787: A Commentary*. Baltimore: The Johns Hopkins University Press, 1989. Excellent explanation of the constitutional system of separation of powers.

Diamond, Martin. *The Founding of the Democratic Republic*. Itasca, Ill.: F. E. Peacock, 1981. Separation of powers is thoughtfully examined in this philosophical examination of the founding of the United States.

Dragnich, Alex N., Jorgen S. Rasmussen, and Joel C. Moses. *Major European*

Governments. 8th ed. Monterey, Calif.: Brooks/Cole, 1991. Examination of the governments of Britain, France, Germany, and Russia from an institutional perspective.

Hamilton, Alexander, James Madison, and John Jay. *The Federalist Papers*. Edited by Clinton Rossiter. New York: New American Library, 1961. Best statement of the intentions of the Framers' intentions for both separation of powers and checks and balances is found in Nos. 47 through 51.

Lowi, Theodore. *The Personal President: Power Invested, Promise Unfulfilled*. Ithaca, N.Y.: Cornell University Press, 1985. Deals with separation of powers as a part of explaining the American presidency. Lowi and Neustadt (below) offer contrasting views.

Neustadt, Richard C. *Presidential Power, the Politics of Leadership*. New York: John Wiley, 1960. Classic treatment of the American presidency and its relationship with the Congress.

Richard L. Wilson

Cross-References

The British Parliamentary System, p. 146; Cabinet Government, p. 184; Checks and Balances in U.S. Government, p. 216; Comparative Government, p. 384; Congress, p. 412; The Constitution of the United States, p. 425; Constitutional Law in the United States, p. 439; Intergovernmental Relations, p. 942; Judicial Review, p. 1012; Legislative Body Types, p. 1091; Legislative Functions of Government, p. 1098; Mexico: Politics and Government, p. 1179; Montesquieu's Political Philosophy, p. 1228; Parliamentary Government, p. 1377; The Presidency in the United States, p. 1590; Separation of Powers: Political Philosophy, p. 1809.

SLAVERY AND U.S. POLITICAL HISTORY

Field of study: Politics

From the 1840's to 1861, a principal issue in American politics was the question of whether the institution of slavery should extend into the western territories of the United States. The political battle between Northerners and Southerners regarding slavery led to the outbreak of the American Civil War in 1861.

Principal terms

ABOLITIONIST: one who supported the immediate ending of slavery

COMPROMISE OF 1850: most controversial compromise between the North and South regarding slavery. California was admitted as a free state, popular sovereignty was applied to New Mexico and Utah, and a new fugitive slave law was enacted

KANSAS-NEBRASKA ACT: act of Congress that repealed the Missouri Compromise line and established the doctrine of popular sovereignty for Kansas and Nebraska territories

MISSOURI COMPROMISE LINE: dividing line between free and slave territories in the Louisiana Purchase. The Missouri Compromise line was established by Congress in the Missouri Compromise of 1820

POPULAR SOVEREIGNTY: doctrine that the residents of each territory should decide whether slavery should exist in the territory

SLAVERY: forced labor of people who are considered property, not free

WILMOT PROVISO: proposed amendment to an army appropriations bill in 1846 which would have prohibited slavery in territories acquired as a result of the Mexican War

Overview

Political conflict over slavery existed in the United States from the very beginning of its national history in the 1770's to the end of slavery after the Civil War. Slavery was the most divisive issue in the history of American politics, and it led to the outbreak of the Civil War in 1861. The politics of slavery usually was not based on disagreements regarding the morality of slavery. Instead, the North and the South typically disagreed about slavery because of the impact it had on the political strength of the two sections and, therefore, the ability of the sections to protect their interests.

In 1776, the Second Continental Congress deleted a mildly antislavery paragraph from the draft version of the Declaration of Independence. In 1787, slavery-related issues nearly caused the breakup of the convention at which the U.S. Constitution was written. The Constitution was saved only by the Compromise of 1787, the first of several cross-sectional compromises which kept peace until 1861. Three-fifths of the slaves were to be counted in determining the apportionment of the House of Representatives, slave owners were allowed to cross state boundaries to recapture their fugitive slaves, and Congress was prevented from interfering with the slave trade for twenty years. Despite these early conflicts, before 1800 Southerners were willing to discuss the gradual abolition of slavery, an institution that seemed to have only a limited economic future in the production of tobacco and rice. After 1800, Southerners became acutely defensive regarding the issue of slavery. The Industrial Revolution gave Southerners a new economic interest to defend as textile factories created a large demand for cotton grown by American slaves.

Several political events from the 1810's to the 1830's caused Southerners to fear that a hostile Northern majority might use the powers of the federal government to injure slavery. Southerners were alarmed by decisions of the Supreme Court under Chief Justice John Marshall that enlarged the powers of the federal government and by the enactment of high tariffs that protected Northern industries at the expense of Southern taxpayers. Above all, the South was alarmed by Northern efforts to restrict the entry of Missouri into the Union as a slave state in 1819-1820. Northerners feared that the admission of Missouri would destroy the even balance between slave and free states in the Senate. For the first time, some Southerners threatened to withdraw from the Union if Missouri was not admitted. The crisis was ended by the Missouri Compromise of 1820. The admission of Missouri as a slave state was counterbalanced by the admission of Maine as a free state. To prevent future crises regarding the admission of new states created out of the Louisiana Purchase, Congress established the Missouri Compromise line. Slavery was prohibited in territories north of the line; slavery was allowed in territories south of the line. Though the immediate crisis was resolved, Southerners soon began to insist that slavery was entirely a "domestic" institution subject to regulation only by state governments. Southern elections became exercises in one-upmanship, in which Southern politicians competed with one another to convince voters that they, rather than their opponents, were the better protectors of slavery.

Until the Civil War, most Northerners conceded that slavery was primarily a local matter to be controlled by Southerners. By the 1830's, however, many Northerners believed that some issues related to slavery could be legitimately regulated by the federal government. Encouraging this trend was the rise of the abolitionist movement during the 1830's. Centering its message on the moral wrong of slave ownership, the abolitionists supported a radical program of immediate emancipation and equal rights for African Americans. This program was never very popular in the North, where racism was nearly as great as it was in the South. Genuine abolitionists numbered only 3 percent of the North's population, and abolitionists were the victims of nearly fifty mob actions in the 1830's-1840's.

Nevertheless, abolitionist agitation did help awaken Northern sectionalism. Southerners tried to censor abolitionist mailings and to suppress the abolitionists' First Amendment right to petition Congress. These Southern actions transformed the meaning of the slavery issue for Northerners: It was no longer simply the unpopular issue of black bondage; it was now also the highly popular issue of white civil rights. Stunned by the willingness of Southerners to trample upon the rights of white Americans to protect the South's slave property, Northerners began to develop the idea of a slave-power conspiracy in which Southerners used their slave-based wealth to control the federal government, contrary to the interests of Northerners.

During the 1830's-1840's, the two major political parties, the Democrats and Whigs, tried to keep the slavery issue out of national politics. The parties were nearly equal in strength and both depended upon cross-sectional support for electoral victory. Both parties, therefore, understood that the sectionally divisive issue of slavery could wreck their electoral coalitions and hand victory to their opponent. By the mid-1840's, however, the parties could no longer keep slavery out of national politics, because slavery became linked to the issue of American territorial expansion. The annexation of Texas in 1845, the Oregon Treaty of 1846, and the Mexican War of 1846-1848 significantly increased the territory of the United States. From the 1840's to 1861, the most significant issue in American politics was the question of whether slavery should be allowed to expand into the territories. Tensions between the North and the South mounted as the sections battled in a series of escalating crises.

The debate regarding slavery increased significantly with the Wilmot Proviso of 1846, a congressional proposal to prohibit slavery in territories acquired as a result of the Mexican War. Though the Wilmot Proviso was never adopted, it gave rise to four positions on slavery that shaped the sectional controversy for years to come. The most extreme Northern position was that slavery should be entirely prohibited in American territories that were not yet states. Many Americans supported a second position, popular sovereignty, which proposed allowing the residents of each territory to decide the fate of slavery in the territory. Some hoped to extend the Missouri Compromise line to the Pacific Ocean; this was a third position. The most extreme Southern position was that no restrictions could be placed on the expansion of slavery into the territories and that the federal government should protect slavery.

California's request for admission to the Union as a free state produced a serious crisis in 1849-1850. Southerners resisted actions by Congress to prohibit slavery in the new state, and Southern militants threatened civil war. The California crisis was resolved by the Compromise of 1850. California was admitted as a free state, the popular sovereignty formula was applied to other new territories obtained during the Mexican War, and Southerners received additional protection for their slave property through the passage of a more effective fugitive slave law.

Although small antislavery parties such as the Liberty Party and the Free Soil Party existed before 1854, most voters retained their allegiance to the Whigs and Democrats while sometimes crossing party lines to defend their sectional interests. As the slavery issue and sectionalism became paramount after 1854, a political realignment occurred in which voters joined new parties based on their sectional interests.

Applications

The Kansas-Nebraska Act of 1854 accelerated the realignment of the 1850's. To win Southern support for new territorial governments in Kansas and Nebraska, Democratic Senator Stephen A. Douglas successfully urged Congress to repeal the Missouri Compromise line, under which slavery had been outlawed in Kansas and

Nebraska. The Kansas-Nebraska Act applied the popular sovereignty formula to these territories, shattering the existing political alignment. The Whig Party, which had been formed when issues besides slavery were important, previously enjoyed the allegiance of both opponents of slavery and Southern slaveholders. Unable to endure continued infighting between its proslavery and antislavery wings, the Whig Party splintered and disappeared from national politics. In addition, many Northern Democrats left their party, alarmed by its pro-Southern drift.

Between 1854 and 1856, Northern Whigs, many Northern Democrats, and members of the antislavery Free Soil Party created the Republican Party, whose central principle was opposition to the expansion of slavery into the territories. The result of the realignment was a highly sectionalized party system, in which the antislavery Republicans dominated the North but had virtually no support in the South. The Democrats drew voters from both sections, but they were strongly oriented toward protecting slavery and Southern interests.

The most significant application of the politics of slavery occurred in the election of 1860. Stephen A. Douglas, the front-runner for the Democratic nomination, criticized the proslavery ruling of the Supreme Court in *Scott v. Sandford* (1857), also known as the *Dred Scott* case. The ruling implied that popular sovereignty could not be used to prohibit slavery in territories before they applied for statehood. Douglas alarmed Southern Democrats by arguing that despite the *Scott* decision, residents of a territory could effectively exclude slavery by failing to enact laws protecting slave property. At the Democratic convention of 1860, Southern Democrats unsuccessfully demanded that the platform endorse a federal slave code to protect slavery in American territories. Southern delegates left the convention and nominated Vice President John C. Breckinridge as their candidate. Delegates from the North subsequently nominated Douglas as their candidate.

The Republican front-runner, Senator William H. Seward, also faced challenges to his nomination because of his position on slavery. Seward created controversy when he stated that if the Constitution did not allow action against slavery, Americans should turn to a higher, moral law to support their actions. Believing the party must support a more moderate position to win the election, the delegates rejected Seward and nominated Abraham Lincoln, a former member of Congress. Lincoln opposed the expansion of slavery into the territories but promised not to interfere with the constitutional right of the Southern states to control slavery within their own boundaries.

A fourth candidate emerged as the nominee of the Constitutional Union Party, a new organization made up mostly of former Southern Whigs. John Bell, a former senator, ran on a platform of preserving the Union and enforcing federal laws. This unionist platform placed Bell at odds with both secessionists, who wanted Southern independence, and Northern antislavery advocates, who favored civil disobedience to the federal fugitive slave law.

Though the election of 1860 featured four candidates, the candidates did not come into direct competition with one another throughout the nation. In the North, the election was a contest between two Northerners, Lincoln and Douglas, both of Illinois.

In the South, the election was a contest between two Southerners, Breckinridge of Kentucky and Bell of Tennessee. So sharply divided had the nation become over sectional issues that in each section two of the candidates were irrelevant to the outcome of the election. The most extreme Northern candidate, Lincoln, received no popular votes in ten slave states. The most extreme Southern candidate, Breckinridge, received fewer than eight thousand votes in ten free states.

Lincoln won the election. Though he won only 39.8 percent of the popular vote, he won an outright majority in the electoral college. This outcome was not the result of the division of Lincoln's opposition among three other candidates. Lincoln won because the Republicans had emerged with a majority of popular votes in the heavily populated states of the Northeast and Midwest. If all the votes against Lincoln had been united behind a single candidate, Lincoln still would have won an outright majority in the electoral college.

Context

The politics of slavery and the rise of a new sectionally based party system prompted the outbreak of the Civil War and, ultimately, the abolition of slavery in the United States. Southerners, reading the results of the election of 1860, believed the American political system had become weighted against Southern interests. The fact that Lincoln could win election with a small plurality of the vote because the Republicans controlled states that had a majority of the electoral vote suggested that the South had become a permanent minority within the United States. Fearing that they could no longer protect slavery against hostile actions by a federal government controlled by Northerners, seven states of the South withdrew from the Union and formed a new country, the Confederate States of America. Lincoln's efforts to enforce federal authority in the Confederate States led to the outbreak of the Civil War in April, 1861, and the subsequent secession of four more slave states.

The politics of slavery continued to affect American government through the Civil War years and beyond. The withdrawal of Southern states from the Union enabled the Republicans to gain control of all three branches of the federal government. Radicalized by the war, Republicans increasingly abandoned their earlier toleration of slavery and began to support complete abolition, a policy strongly opposed by the Democrats. Rarely has any issue so completely divided Congress along party lines as emancipation divided Congress during the Civil War. In 1863, President Lincoln issued the Emancipation Proclamation, declaring that slaves in the rebelling states were free. In 1865, slavery was abolished throughout the United States, including the defeated South, by the Thirteenth Amendment to the Constitution. The Civil War was followed by the period known as Reconstruction (1865-1877), in which Republicans and Democrats argued regarding which rights should be given to the former slaves.

The political debate regarding slavery in the United States was a part of a larger, international movement to abolish slavery in the western hemisphere. Slavery, which had once been a part of every European colony in the western hemisphere, was completely abolished during the nineteenth century.

Bibliography

Anbinder, Tyler. _Nativism and Slavery: The Northern Know-Nothings and the Politics of the 1850's_. New York: Oxford University Press, 1992. Argues that the Know-Nothing Party was a vehicle not only for nativism but also for antislavery sentiment.

Baum, Dale. _The Civil War Party System: The Case of Massachusetts, 1848-1876_. Chapel Hill: University of North Carolina Press, 1984. Stresses the importance of antislavery to the appeal of the Republican Party.

Cooper, William J., Jr. _The South and the Politics of Slavery, 1828-1856_. Baton Rouge: Louisiana State University Press, 1978. Argues that the central issue in Southern politics from the 1820's to the 1850's was slavery. Political battles in the South were based on competition to demonstrate who was the better protector of slavery.

Fehrenbacher, Don E. _The Dred Scott Case, Its Significance in American Law and Politics_. New York: Oxford University Press, 1978. Clarifies the complex legal issues of the _Dred Scott_ case and places the case within the context of the politics of slavery.

Foner, Eric. _Free Soil, Free Labor, Free Men: The Ideology of the Republican Party Before the Civil War_. New York: Oxford University Press, 1970. Argues that Republican Party ideology presented the sectional controversy as a struggle between two antagonistic civilizations, one based on slave labor, the other on free labor.

Freehling, William W. _The Road to Disunion_. New York: Oxford University Press, 1990. Readable study of how Southerners from diverse backgrounds united in political support of slavery.

Gienapp, William E. _The Origins of the Republican Party, 1852-1856_. New York: Oxford University Press, 1987. Good source of statistical tables related to the politics of slavery.

Potter, David M. _The Impending Crisis, 1848-1861_. New York: Harper & Row, 1976. Provides the best overview of the major sectional political controversies that gave rise to the Civil War.

Sewell, Richard H. _Ballots for Freedom: Antislavery Politics in the United States, 1837-1860_. New York: Oxford University Press, 1976. Brief, readable survey of the evolution of antislavery political parties and strategies from the Liberty Party to the Republican Party.

Thornton, J. Mills, III. _Politics and Power in a Slave Society: Alabama, 1800-1860_. Baton Rouge: Louisiana State University Press, 1978. Case study of a single Southern state, arguing that the ideology of Southern Democrats was increasingly given over to defending slavery and laying the foundation for secession.

Harold D. Tallant

Cross-References

African American Politics, p. 28; Civil Rights Protection, p. 304; Human Rights and International Politics, p. 848; Race and Ethnicity, p. 1654.

THE SOCIAL CONTRACT

Field of study: Political philosophy

The social contract is the means by which free and rational people are ruled by others. People promise to obey a ruler or rulers to gain security.

Principal terms

ANARCHISM: view that all forms of government are oppressive and intolerable to free and rational people

AUTONOMOUS: governing one's self, not subject to the rule of others

CIVIL SOCIETY: state of society freely entered by rational people who choose to leave the state of nature and seek stability by establishing a sovereign

FEUDALISM: political and economic system in which nobility hold land and power and others are born to serve

GENERAL WILL: differentiated from particular wills by virtue of being directed at the general good, not anyone's particular good

LIBERALISM: belief that each individual is entitled to as much freedom as does not interfere with the freedom of others; often entails a distrust of organized power and a view of limited government

RATIONALISM: belief that there is a rational principle at work in the universe that is discernible by human reason

SOVEREIGN: supreme ruler of a state

STATE OF NATURE: prehistoric state in which humans exist without society

VEIL OF IGNORANCE: John Rawls' term for the following: people go behind an imaginary veil, stripping themselves of all knowledge of their social position, and then judge what laws would be acceptable to them given the uncertainty of their position

Overview

The basic idea of a social contract is simple. It is based on the idea that people originally lived without society and each person had the right to do anything he or she pleased. There were no moral or legal constraints on people because they had no relations with, or obligations to, others. At some point this "state of nature" was replaced with civil society. In civil society people follow the rules of a sovereign and are subject to both moral and legal constraints. Social contract theory seeks to answer the question of how this move to civil society was made. Further, it seeks to establish that free, autonomous, and rational persons voluntarily choose to form civil society and so they remain free, autonomous and rational even within the constraints of government. Government is, then, not oppressive or intolerable. Rather, living under government is a voluntary choice and rational people should welcome its constraints.

The four basic models of the social contract used in political theory come from the work of Thomas Hobbes (1588-1679), John Locke (1632-1704), Jean-Jacques Rousseau (1712-1778), and John Rawls (1921). While there are hints of something akin to a social contract in the works of Plato, such theory began to gain importance in 1651 with the publication of Hobbes's *Leviathan*. While many did not like the picture of human society drawn by Hobbes his work was nevertheless influential. Locke drew a kinder picture of society in his *Second Treatise of Government*. Rousseau turned the story around, describing the state of nature as peaceful and making the whole notion of a social contract into a necessary evil in his *Social Contract*. While the social contract in one form or another serves as background to, and is an implicit assumption of, much of the contemporary political order it again became a focus of attention in 1971 with the publication of Rawls's *A Theory of Justice*.

Hobbes believed that the only explanation of why free and rational people accept the rule of a sovereign is that they fear one another and seek the security of one common enforcer of law. According to Hobbes, in the state of nature people are equal by virtue of their equal ability to kill one another. This equality creates an atmosphere of competition and a constant threat of being attacked. This threat effectively eliminates any attempt to cultivate society.

People find this state of nature intolerable; they seek security. Reason combined with self-interest leads people to give up the liberty of doing harm to others so that others will do likewise and refrain from harming them. To enforce this mutual pact to refrain from harming one another, Hobbes believes it is necessary that there be an absolute sovereign. This creation of a commonwealth, by covenant, is a transference of authority and power from the people to the sovereign. For Hobbes, to rebel against such a sovereign is to go against one's self-interest and threaten one's self-preservation, for the sovereign keeps society from degenerating back into the state of nature—a war of all against all.

Locke's view of the contract is slightly different. Rather than raw fear and conflict motivating the move to civil society, Locke proposes that people make this move as they begin to accumulate property and so seek protection of their property. Though Locke's state of nature is not the state of war Hobbes describes, it does share the inconvenience of insecurity. As people accumulate property—money—they find it is also necessary to provide a means of protecting it. If each person makes individual judgments concerning what threatens his or her life or property, and then acts on these judgments, the result is a state of chaos where each person is so preoccupied with anticipating threats that he or she becomes a threat to general security.

It is the absence of a common judge that distinguishes the state of nature from civil society. The absence of a common authority causes uncertainty and potential disharmony. Locke believed that people give up some of their freedom and enter a contract to create civil society. They accept a common judge in order to gain the protection of their property and end uncertainty. This agreement, however, entails rights and obligations on both sides. The people surrender certain freedoms and rights to the government, which in turn is responsible for the protection of these freedoms and rights. The sovereign must act as a control to ensure that liberty is both promoted and restrained so that civil society is equivalent to a well-ordered state of nature. The government may not violate one's right of self-preservation. If it does, the people have the right to rebel.

Rousseau differs from both Hobbes and Locke in his ideas about both the state of nature and civil society. Rousseau sees the state of nature as peaceful and desirable. The state of nature is preferable to civil society because one is free in the state of nature and often subject to an arbitrary will in civil society. Rousseau seeks to replace the rule of an arbitrary will—the sovereign—with the rule of the general will—the people.

For Rousseau, freedom of will is the freedom of rational choosing. This freedom is what distinguishes members of civil society from the savage. This does not mean, for Rousseau, that the savage is any less human or exists in a worse condition than members of civil society. In fact, there is much to be envied in this state of innocence. Once possessed of reason, though, there comes a corresponding responsibility to develop it and use it well.

Once forced out of the state of nature, the progress of humanity becomes a conscious, not an arbitrary, experiment in living together—the search for the best possible society. Rousseau believes there are certain necessities which flow from freedom. The fundamental freedom is to choose rationally. This is a natural freedom, but it is and must be, according to Rousseau, socially conditioned and directed.

Through education people will come to realize the arbitrariness of desires. They will come to realize that one must restrict desires in order to be free. Freedom requires one to choose the right balance of abilities, needs, and desires. Excessive desires limit one's potential freedom and happiness. To limit our desires is to be free.

Further, people will come to realize their interdependence and accept certain constraints on their individual wills in the name of freedom. Common needs lead to a common interest and common suffering leads to a bond of affection. This is the true equality of humanity. This is what Rousseau thinks should and will lead people to watch out for humanity. From such awareness should arise affection, and from affection attention to the general well-being—the general will. The individual has a duty to be aware of the general well-being, act in accord with it, and make sure others do so as well. In other words, people freely enter a social contract that limits their freedom.

Rousseau suggests that given the unnatural necessity of living together, and its accompanying dangers, there is only one basic structure with which a rational person can be expected to comply. There is only one basic structure which prevents the possibility of illegitimate and arbitrary wills coming to rule over the general populace. This structure is a form of association that leaves each as free as they were in the state of nature—free to choose for oneself rather than obey the will of one or more others.

In this social association, no one loses the all-important free will because the general will is free from arbitrary partiality. No one is subjected to an arbitrary or illegitimate authority. The individual is free, according to Rousseau, because there is no arbitrary will, no self-interest, no irrational fear or prejudice directing the community. Rousseau thinks that by showing individuals that ultimately there is no difference in vulnerability among people—rationality will then direct such people to form a community that is in the interest of all.

According to Rousseau's conception of the social contract, no one's interest should actively conflict with the interests of others because there is no inequality. No one has the authority to judge for others because all are joined in common. Provided that people have been instilled with the correct sentiments, reason will lead to the formation of the general will and each will be bound only to one's own will.

John Rawls's formulation of the social contract has some similarities with Rousseau's. Rawls also wants rational persons free from prejudice, self-interest, or bias to choose a social order that would be suitable to all. Rawls asks people to go behind a "veil of ignorance," where they know nothing about who they are or their position in society. From such an "original position" he believes justice will emerge because rational persons will agree only to impartial and equal laws when they do not know how they are positioned in society. Rawls' "original position" serves in place of a "state of nature," but there is still the assumption of rational, self-interested agents choosing a form of society that serves the interests of all.

Applications

The idea of a social contract underlies most contemporary democracies. Social contract theory was at work in both the American and French revolutions and serves as the basis for the U.S. Constitution and legal system. The idea of social contract serves as the foundation for constitutional governments in general. A constitution spells out the terms of a contract—in some cases a modifiable contract. It also serves as the foundation for international law and the United Nations. The U.N. charter serves as a contract between nations, delineating the rights and responsibilities of both individual nations and the United Nations.

The idea that free, autonomous, rational people and nations have the right to direct their own affairs is strongly felt in the contemporary political order. In the United States the belief in the social contract is quite evident. Discussion of government obligations, the rights of the people, and citizens' duties represent this deeply rooted theory. There is a belief that the government and the people have their respective duties and rights. People are expected to live up to these rights and there are methods to hold both the government and the people accountable.

In general, elected officials who violate their duties face the possibility of losing their seat in government or being prosecuted for misconduct. Citizens who violate their duties face fines and prosecution. There is a reciprocal relationship between the ruler and the ruled. If one pays taxes one expects the money to be used responsibly. If the government provides for its citizens' education, health, and welfare it expects service when national security requires it. The government expects loyalty from its citizens and punishes traitors. The people expect the government to serve their interests and consider themselves free to rebel if these interests are violated.

There are critics of social contract theory who challenge the idea that a government can demand abstract obligations from its citizens. If people are truly free such service must always be an individual and voluntary choice. People proposing such an argument would claim that the military draft, for example, goes beyond what a free and rational person can be expected to agree to in the abstract and so violates the self-interest of the citizens. Others go further and argue that the idea of free and rational people forming a contract is pure myth and assumes an equality and freedom of choice that clearly does not exist for all. Women and minorities often challenge the idea that the social contract that has been presumed to exist has included their interests.

Context

The story of the social contract emerged to explain how people can be both free individuals and the subjects of a government. As the feudal system broke down, the concept of free individuals making their own choices began to emerge. Anarchy seemed to be the inevitable conclusion. If individuals are equal and free, how can they tolerate being ruled by another? The social contract answers this question by making government the free choice of rational individuals and (with the exception of Hobbes's social contract), it gives people the right to rebel against a government that violates their perceived self-interest.

There was also, at the time of the emergence of social contract theory, an emerging faith in reason. Rationalists assume that there is a rational order to the universe and that human reason can identify the principles at work in the universe. To decide on the proper social order, then, one should consult reason. It was also assumed that all rational persons would agree on what the social order should be because rationalists assume reason is universal and operates in much the same way in all people.

Further, it was believed that reason makes one free because consulting one's own rational capabilities to reach decisions makes one autonomous. In other words, one follows a law not because of any external force, but because one believes the law is just. This is what makes it possible for people to freely bind themselves to the rule of another. This is also why most social contract theorists leave the right of rebellion as an option. As an autonomous individual one must follow only the dictates of reason. If at any point the sovereign violates reason, the contract becomes void.

The simultaneous rise of the individual and faith in reason resulted in a rationalistic, individualistic justification of government. This was a liberating concept at the time, as it gave more room to personal conscience than had ever been imagined before.

Bibliography

Buchanan, James M. *The Limits of Liberty: Between Anarchy and Leviathan*. Chicago: University of Chicago Press, 1975. Discusses the basis of freedom and the paradox of a free peoples' being governed. Considers the possibility of constitutional revolution.

Cobban, Alfred. *Rousseau and the Modern State*. 2d ed. Hamden, Conn.: Archon Books, 1964. Situates Rousseau in the political world of his time and traces the applicability of his thought.

Kymlicka, Will. *Liberalism, Community, and Culture.* Oxford, England: Clarendon Press, 1989. Discusses the relationship between the individual and the community in liberal theory and defends liberalism against communitarian critiques.

Levine, Andrew. *Liberal Democracy: A Critique of Its Theory.* New York: Columbia University Press, 1981. Basic discussion of liberal theory and an examination of its usefulness in politics.

Nielsen, Kai, and Roger A. Shiner, eds. *New Essays on Contract Theory.* Guelph, Ontario: Canadian Association for Publishing in Philosophy, 1977. Essays explaining and critiquing Rawls's theory of social contract.

Okin, Susan Moller. *Women in Western Political Thought.* Princeton, N.J.: Princeton University Press, 1979. Discusses women in political theory. Women are not considered individuals in much of liberal theory. Strong section on Rousseau's view of women.

Pateman, Carole. *The Sexual Contract.* Stanford, Calif.: Stanford University Press, 1988. Argues that the social contract is implicitly and necessarily based on a sexual contract and that in liberal theory women are not seen as individuals capable of entering the contract.

Sandel, Michael J. *Liberalism and the Limits of Justice.* New York: Cambridge University Press, 1982. Situates contract theory in its metaphysical, epistemological, and moral roots. Rawls's work is given special attention.

Smith, Rogers M. *Liberalism and American Constitutional Law.* Cambridge, Mass.: Harvard University Press, 1985. Discusses the aims, applications, and criticisms of liberalism and constitutional law.

Wolff, Robert Paul. *Understanding Rawls: A Reconstruction and Critique of "A Theory of Justice."* Princeton, N.J.: Princeton University Press, 1977. Good introduction to Rawls's theory and a strong critique of its assumptions and applications. Applicable to liberal theory in general.

Erin McKenna

Cross-References

Burke's Political Philosophy, p. 171; Citizenship: Rights and Responsibilities, p. 260; The Constitution of the United States, p. 425; Constitutional Governments, p. 432; Deism, p. 495; Democracy, p. 513; General Will, p. 745; Hobbes's Political Philosophy, p. 836; Individual Versus State Rights, p. 910; International Law, p. 956; Kant's Political Philosophy, p. 1025; Legitimacy, p. 1105; Liberalism, p. 1118; Locke's Political Philosophy, p. 1142; Right of Revolution, p. 1744; Rousseau's Political Philosophy, p. 1756; Spinoza's Political Philosophy, p. 1872; United Nations, p. 2045.

SOCIAL DARWINISM

Field of study: Political philosophy

   Charles Darwin's theory of evolution posited that organisms develop in reaction to changes in their environment. Social Darwinists, led by Herbert Spencer, applied these biological concepts to the development of society. Their theories were used to justify the exploitation of the poor by the rich, and of less developed nations by wealthy, powerful ones.

Principal terms

COLONIALISM: system whereby a country exploits economic and political control over a foreign country for self-serving reasons

ETHNOCENTRISM: notion that one's own culture and way of life are superior to those of others

EVOLUTION: biological theory attributed to Charles Darwin that accounts for the adaptive change of organisms to their natural environment

IMPERIALISM: acquisition of foreign countries as colonies, or the rule of one nation or empire over others

INDUSTRIAL REVOLUTION: economic, social, and scientific changes initiated in England and extended elsewhere, characterized by the replacement of hand tools by power-driven machines

LAISSEZ-FAIRE: doctrine that government should not intervene in the economic affairs of its citizens, except to maintain peace and uphold property rights

MONROE DOCTRINE: 1823 doctrine of President James Monroe warning European governments that the United States would resist any attempts to expand into Central America

NATURAL SELECTION: principle that those organisms that are better adapted to environmental circumstances are more likely to be successful at survival

PLUTOCRACY: government or state in which wealth or the wealthy class exercises its influence for control and has the power to rule

RACISM: belief that human races and their cultures can be ranked on a continuum from superior to inferior

Overview

   Herbert Spencer, a British social philosopher, expressed his early ideas on social evolution in 1857 when he published "Progress: Its Laws and Causes." After the English naturalist Charles Darwin (1809-1882) had published *On the Origin of Species* (1859), Spencer sought to apply Darwin's ideas to human society. With the changing capitalist environment, Spencer's ideas, bolstered by Darwin's scientific justification, perpetuated the conservative status quo supporting an unequal distribution of wealth.

Indeed, it was Spencer and not Darwin who coined the metaphors "struggle for existence," and "survival of the fittest," which Darwin incorporated into his fifth edition of *On the Origin of Species*.

While Darwin's ideas on natural selection were employed to account for biological evolution, natural selection was offered as an antonym to artificial selection. Specifically, Darwin demonstrated to the world that evolution took place, and that its requirements were variation, inheritance, natural selection, and time. Darwin could not have understood the role of genetics on evolution, since his ideas preceded the discovery of genetics by the Austrian monk Gregor Mendel by six years; Darwin believed the environment's role was particularly significant in explaining variation and that biological success was measured by the frequency with which members of a species successfully reproduced. Various environmental forces were thought to influence successful reproduction. For Darwin, the term "struggle" illustrated the subtleties of environmental influence: Animals and plants attempted to survive heat, cold, wind, rain, and competition with other species. While many conservative clergymen took issue with evolution, some social philosophers began to misapply the new evolutionary notions to human social behavior and suggested that human societies changed as a natural and expected consequence of natural laws.

When the groundwork for what became known as Social Darwinism was introduced by Spencer, he did not incorporate Darwin's subtleties. Spencer instead included a host of values and moral judgments in his suggestion that the struggle for existence within society or between societies was a natural condition for cultural evolution. He believed societies were comparable to biological organisms; slowly evolving from simple to complex by means of competition for resources. Spencer argued that such competition was natural, and to be expected, within each society and among societies. Social Darwinists believed those people, institutions, and societies that attained the greatest political and economic power were by definition the most fit, while those that lacked such attributes were by their nature less fit. The idea of Social Darwinism ultimately was used to justify the mistreatment and exploitation of non-Western peoples and those defined as members of the lower class in the West.

Applications

Throughout the late nineteenth century, scientific, social, political, and economic events were interacting to permanently alter the course of history. In the West, more people were better fed and more educated than ever in the past. There was a growing sense of personal economic and political freedom as many monarchies were replaced by constitutional governments emphasizing plutocracy. With new-found political and economic power and pseudoscientific justification, various Western governments initiated steps to adopt or incorporate Social Darwinism philosophy into their domestic or foreign policies.

Not all people benefited equally from Western colonialism and the Industrial Revolution of the late nineteenth and early twentieth centuries. Disparity in access to resources, wealth, and social status was nothing new, but as Western nations were exploiting the people and natural resources of the non-West, a desire to justify such behavior was attempted. The United States and many European governments were experiencing a new sense of nationalism as the Industrial Revolution enhanced their positions and motivated them to expand their political and economic power and influence. At the same time, a small number of successful capitalists and industrialists were seeking plutocratic control in these countries; would-be aristocrats were attempting to fulfill their personal desires for wealth and fame; and the Western clergy saw an opportunity to consummate its mission of spreading the gospel.

By the late nineteenth century, Great Britain produced more coal and iron than the remainder of the world. It also was the home of a successful textile industry that operated more textile spindles and looms than any other nation and employed more people than any other industry. It was with a strong sense of national pride that the British declared their control of colonies around the world, proclaiming that "the sun never sets on the British Empire." Because of England's economic and political success, British ideologists began to express their ethnocentrism by claiming that they were, by nature, the people destined to rule over the inferior races of the world, and that such rule would benefit both the English and those over whom they governed. The works of the popular English author Rudyard Kipling illustrated this idea: In writing of India, he said it was the white man's burden to rule over nonwhites in a mutually beneficial way. Kipling and other Englishmen believed Europeans, especially the British, possessed the knowledge and techniques necessary for advancing the benefits of civilization to non-Westerners.

Psychological factors also promoted Western economic and political expansionism. One such psychological factor was the new nationalism experienced by Germany and Italy, both of which had undergone unification by 1871. Germany was unified by Otto von Bismark following the Franco-Prussian War (1870-1871), while Camillo Benso di Cavour filled a similar role in Italy following the Austro-Italian War (1859-1860). The two new governments were eager to demonstrate their political and economic strengths and, like the British, wanted to be acknowledged for their accomplishments. While few benefits could be suggested for those indigenous peoples ruled by aliens in their own homelands, the rulers benefited from their new-found sources for raw materials and the expanded markets for their manufactured goods. Ruling governments were thus able to feed their growing domestic production and further enhance their political and economic success.

An outspoken advocate of Spencer's ideas in the United States was William Graham Sumner, an American sociologist and economist. As a supporter of laissez-faire economic policy, Sumner argued that people were not born equal, and that millionaires were a product of natural selection working on the body of humankind to discover those who could fulfill the requirements of certain work. A number of U.S. industrialists accepted Social Darwinism, but perhaps none was as outspoken as John D. Rockefeller, the rugged individualist and successful capitalist who founded Standard Oil. Rockefeller is quoted in Hofstadter (1959) as having declared to a Sunday school class that just as an American Beauty rose develops at the expense of several undeveloped buds, "The growth of a large business is merely a survival of the fittest. . . . This is not an evil tendency in business. It is merely the working-out of a law of nature and a law of God." His statements expressed the attitude of many fellow aristocratic tycoons who held plutocratic views. Spencer, Sumner, and other Social Darwinists opposed social and economic planning and any attempts to offer social assistance to the poor. They believed that such a practice would interfere with the natural process of social evolution.

In his book, *Folkways* (1906), Sumner argued that customs and morals were instinctive responses to drives such as fear, sex, or hunger. Thus, Social Darwinists sought scientific justification from nature to promote individual competition, and the exploitation of the poor by the rich classes, or the exploitation of poorer, less well-developed nations by wealthy and politically powerful ones. Because advocates of Social Darwinism supposed that social progress demanded competitive struggle among nations, states, and races when carried to its extreme, it was used to justify western ethnocentrism, racism, and eugenics.

The impact of Social Darwinism on politics in the United States can be demonstrated by the government's growing imperialistic approach. In 1899, a U.S. senator publicly asserted that God had made the English-speaking and Teutonic peoples to rule the primitive peoples of the world.

Such appeals were not uncommon during this period in the United States, because the government was not only attempting to justify its domestic policy of relocating Native Americans from their indigenous lands to reservations, but also had committed itself to an imperialistic foreign policy. The United States adopted the notion of manifest destiny following the Civil War, whereby it claimed it had been ordained by destiny that the United States should reign over much of the Western Hemisphere. By 1867, the United States was becoming a political power in the Pacific Ocean. It had begun occupying the Midway Islands, purchased Alaska from Russia, and was pouring capital into the Hawaiian Islands. In 1881, the United States proclaimed Hawaii to be under its influence. In 1898, five years after it had assisted in overthrowing the Hawaiian queen to establish a republic, the U.S. Congress annexed Hawaii as a territory. Also that year, the United States was arranging to partition the Samoan Islands with Germany. At the end of the Spanish-American War in 1898, the United States had won control of Cuba, Puerto Rico, and Guam from the Spanish. By 1902, the U.S. Army had suppressed an insurrection in the Philippines and made the islands an unorganized U.S. territory.

The newly acquired political and economic power and influence of the United States prompted President Theodore Roosevelt to add his own corollary to the Monroe Doctrine in 1904. The Monroe Doctrine was no longer used as it was originally intended, to prevent European intervention in the Western Hemisphere, but rather to justify the expanded commercial interest of the United States. Thus the United States, like various European governments, was attempting to defend its imperialistic power. To justify its imposed political and economic powers scientifically, the United States adopted Social Darwinian notions into its political system.

Context

For the United States and many European countries, the late nineteenth and early twentieth centuries were a time of progress and prosperity. Life was safer because the danger from interclass struggle was on the wane. People in many European countries were beginning to experience greater political and economic liberty as democratic parliamentary governments were established. Under these governments, the power of monarchs were relinquished to wealthy, successful capitalists. The advantages of applied science in agriculture, industrial production, and health care delivery were broadened to every social level, and the general standard of living was raised.

On the Origin of Species significantly impacted not only science and the ideas concerning the origin and evolution of life on earth, but also ideas on theology and humankind's place in nature. The general populace, various social philosophers, successful capitalists, and others adopted Darwinian theory to bolster long-standing ethnocentric notions. Social Darwinism fueled Western beliefs in their superiority over non-Western peoples and nations. Indeed, the adoption of Social Darwinism encouraged the promulgation of racism.

In retrospect, many would argue that applying Social Darwinian philosophy to the domestic and foreign policies of many Western governments was a mistake that helped to institutionalize racism and bigotry. The ideas of Social Darwinism were carried to their greatest extreme in politics by the fascists in Nazi Germany during World War II. Under Adolf Hitler, the Nazi belief in a master race and the inferiority of Gypsies and Jews led to the genocide of millions who were believed to be less fit. It was in part because of the world's revulsion toward the fascism of World War II that the popularity of Social Darwinism began its decline.

While evolutionary theory has had sweeping effects on the way science views the natural world and humankind's place in it, the notion as applied to developing nations and societies in general has assisted in formulating problems, organizing data, and providing a systematic approach to the study of social change. Unlike its misapplication by Social Darwinists, it is no longer used to account for all social change by means of a few simple principles.

Bibliography

Garbarino, Merwyn S. *Sociocultural Theory in Anthropology: A Short History*. New York: Holt, Rinehart and Winston, 1977. Brief introduction to the history and theories that have affected the discipline of anthropology.

Hofstadter, Richard. *Social Darwinism in American Thought*. Rev. ed. New York: George Braziller, 1959. The single best summary of the impact of Social Darwinian ideas on economic, political, and social philosophy.

Spencer, Herbert. *The Evolution of Society: Selections from Herbert Spencer's Principles of Sociology*. Edited by Robert L. Carneiro. Chicago, Ill.: University of Chicago Press, 1967. Annotates and summarizes Spencer's major ideas on society and social evolution.

_____. "Progress: Its Laws and Causes." *Westminster Review* 67 (1857):

445-485. Spencer's first work outlining his ideas on the notion that later became known as Social Darwinism.

Sumner, William G. *Folkways: A Study of the Sociological Importance of Usages, Manners, Customs, Mores, and Morals.* Boston, Mass.: Ginn, 1940. Sumner's personal beliefs on social and cultural evolution, and the causes and means of its occurrence.

Wallbank, T. Walter, Alastair M. Taylor, and Nels M. Bailkey. *Civilization: Past and Present.* Chicago, Ill.: Scott, Foresman, 1962. Good general introductory history text; specific chapters address the Industrial Revolution, the rise of nationalism, Social Darwinism, and the white man's burden.

Turhon A. Murad

Cross-References

Business and Government, p. 177; Capitalism, p. 197; Caste Systems, p. 203; Colonialism and Anticolonialism, p. 351; Developed and Developing Nations, p. 533; Empires and Empire Building, p. 597; Fascism and Nazism, p. 656; Feudalism, p. 688; Genocide, p. 752; Geopolitics, p. 759; History of Government, p. 829; Imperialism, p. 889; Industrialization, p. 916; Nationalism, p. 1268; Political Ethics, p. 1461; Positivism, p. 1557; Power in Politics, p. 1584; Race and Ethnicity, p. 1654.

SOCIAL DEMOCRACIES

Field of study: Types of government

Social democracies are countries with histories of governmental dominance by social democratic, socialist, or labor parties. These parties seek to produce socialism through democratic procedures, and emphasize economic and political equality and collective democratic control of the economy.

Principal terms
CORPORATISM: process of policy-making involving bargaining by large, organized groups representing business and labor that is formally recognized by, and often includes, the state
KEYNESIAN ECONOMICS: economic theory supporting governmental intervention by spending in excess of tax revenues during recessions, thereby stimulating demand and preserving employment
MARXISM: theory that all human life is based upon the economic system; predicts that capitalism will be replaced by socialism because of the exploitation of labor under capitalism
MIXED ECONOMY: economy based on the combination of free-market capitalism and public ownership and planning
NATIONALIZATION: direct ownership and operation of specific industries or entire industrial sectors by the state
WELFARE STATE: system where basic levels of economic security are guaranteed by the state, usually through the redistribution of wealth

Overview

Social democracy is a form of socialism that seeks to use democratic principles to achieve an egalitarian political and economic order, and to weaken the connection between economic security and people's standards of living and the behavior of market economies. The term "social democracy" is usually applied to the Scandinavian countries, and, to a lesser extent, to certain continental European countries, such as Austria, and such less-developed countries as Jamaica. These countries share a commitment to a particular interpretation of socialist philosophy, and a tradition of democratic governance under social democratic parties.

Social democracies are highly influenced by the philosophy of Karl Marx, but also are influenced by earlier, more democratic forms of socialism that placed greater emphasis on social harmony. While social democrats are strong advocates of the working class, which they perceive as unfairly treated and partially excluded in purely democratic-capitalist systems, they are also concerned with the well-being of society as a whole. Unlike revolutionary Marxists, social democrats couple the evolutionary elements of Marx's theory with a critique of Marx's theory that retains strong links with Marxism. The resulting position has come to be known as revisionism, or, alternatively, democratic socialism. Prominent democratic socialists were simultane-ously theorists and leaders of political movements. Perhaps the greatest example of democratic socialist thought is found in Eduard Bernstein, a theorist and leading figure within the German Social Democratic Party, whose critique of Marx, *Evolutionary Socialism* (1899), asserted that socialism would replace capitalism through an incre-mental process, rather than through revolution. Bernstein suggested that if and when democracy expanded to include participation by the working class, instead of partici-patory rights based on the ownership of property that were the rule in his day, working-class majorities could legislate socialism into existence through their natural interest in socioeconomic reform. As a result, socialism came to accept a democratic political order, and even advocated its expansion. Social democrats used democracy to pursue concrete gains in wages, pensions, working conditions, and ultimately a democratically controlled egalitarian economy.

The emphasis on political democracy, both as an end in itself and as a means to further the cause of economic democracy, gives social democracy a strong connection to democratic philosophy in general. Earlier democratic theorists stressed a close connection between the right to private property and its accumulation, and the right to vote. Thus, economic inequality bred political inequality. The social democrats attacked this position as inherently undemocratic, and in most European countries their movement was instrumental in establishing the right to vote as a right of citizenship, instead of a privilege of the wealthy.

The achievement of this goal, and related economic goals, depended heavily on political and economic organizations designed to maximize the advantages of the working class's numerical superiority, while offsetting their generally poor financial resources. As a result, social democratic movements developed a characteristic set of organizations that have continued, and are often identified with modern democracies in general. The most important of these organizations is the social democratic party, although it often goes by other names, such as the socialist or labor party. Social democratic parties pioneered mass democratic organization. They brought together large numbers of dues-paying members in an effort to use large numbers of small contributions to offset the financial advantages of their political opponents. These parties also provided their members with political and economic education, and provided a key vehicle through which members of the working class could become members of their country's political elite. The various policy programs of social democratic parties have in common a desire to legislate socialism into existence by extending democratic control over economic activity, and redistributing wealth in order to achieve greater economic equality. Trade unions are the second major organizational component of social democratic movements. In an effort to offset the power of businesses over their workers, social democratic movements encourage high rates of unionization, often through legislation. There is a strong tendency for individ-ual unions to coordinate their activities through membership in larger union confed-erations, such as the British Trades Union Congress, (TUC) or the Swedish Landsor-ganization (LO), thus representing workers as a class, rather than as practitioners of a trade. Coordinated action also exists between the unions and the parties, particularly in Northern Europe. Trade unions often receive formal representation within the parties; in some cases a proportion of the unions' membership dues is contributed directly to the parties. Countries where social democratic parties and their trade union counterparts, and consequently the policies they advocate, are dominant parts of political life are termed social democracies; however, most European countries have a strong social democratic presence, and, as a result, display some social democratic tendencies.

Social democratic policies are designed to produce step-by-step increases in economic equality and security, and democratic control of the economy. From their origins in the mid- to late nineteenth century through the 1950's, social democratic parties emphasized the nationalization of industry. Nationalization entails public ownership of industries by the democratic state, thus producing a mixed, rather than a strictly market, economy. Although most countries that have been governed by social democrats continue to have some nationalized industries, this policy has fallen out of favor, in part because of Cold War conflicts between Soviet Communism, which embodies complete nationalization of private property, and the democracies to which social democrats have long been committed. New approaches that were more compatible with capitalist democracy, and had the added advantage of supplementing, rather than hindering, market-driven economic performance, became increasingly important. British Labour Party leader Anthony Crosland, in his book, *The Future of Socialism* (1956), identifies five key themes that have come to define post-World War II social democracy: political liberalism, a commitment to equality, the mixed economy, Keynesian economics, and the welfare state. The emphasis on democratic management of the economy and the maintenance of high levels of employment through the raising and spending of revenues (Keynesian economics), and an explicit commitment to welfare spending within the context of Keynesian economics (the welfare state), have eclipsed nationalization as the central policy approach of social democracies and the public component of the mixed economy. These changes represented an effort to reduce class-based tensions and increase cooperation among the social classes. This is reflected not only in the moderation of their party programs and a further reduction of Marxist elements, but also in a greater tendency for consultation and cooperation between the unions and their business counterparts. For most of the post-World War II era, economic policy-making in the social democracies followed a corporatist model, emphasizing bargains made between unions, business, and government. This type of policy-making gives the working class an important role in the management of the economy, without completely undermining the market or private ownership.

Applications

Sweden exhibits nearly all of the features associated with social democracies, and is perhaps the best-known example of this type of government. As with all social democracies, its social democratic characteristics are the result of successful political movements, rather than a particular type of constitutional order. Swedish social democracy is largely the result of the electoral and governmental success of the Social Democratic Workers' Party (SAP), which was founded in 1889. The first SAP congress in 1891 established a reform-oriented revisionist program, and committed the SAP to cooperation with the Liberal Party in the drive for universal suffrage, which was acquired in 1909. Extremely close connections to the trade union movement were also evident at the outset. Indeed, fifty of the seventy organizations founding the SAP were trade unions. A tight relationship between the party and the unions has continued to exist throughout the history of both types of organizations. In 1978, about 60 percent of all party members were affiliated with the SAP through their union locals. The unions themselves organized into a large, blue-collar confederation, the LO, in 1898, thus exemplifying the tendency toward class-based coordination. This trend continued with the formation of central organizations for salaried employees (TCO) and professionals (SACO), ultimately resulting in a unionization rate of 85.3 percent of the total labor force by 1991.

The SAP first participated in government in 1920, but Sweden's status as a social democracy was principally established by an unbroken chain of SAP-led governments from 1936 to 1976. This period brought the emergence of a corporatist pattern of policy-making. In 1938, the SAP and the LO concluded an agreement regularizing collective bargaining in Sweden that led to economywide bargaining by the central union organizations, their business counterparts, who were also represented by a central organization, the Swedish Employers Association (SAF), and the state. Thus, economic policy-making came to center on class-based, but democratic, organizations, and granted a considerable amount of power to the working class. This tendency is reflected in the composition of royal commissions appointed by Swedish cabinets to tackle issues before legislation is introduced. Although these commissions have been used since the nineteenth century, those dealing with economic issues have increasingly relied upon leading union and business association experts. Representatives of business and labor are also consulted by Swedish ministerial departments through a process known as *remiss*.

Sweden's social democratic policies have become deeply ingrained and have survived nonsocialist governments. Although the SAP was one of the first social democratic parties to embrace Keynesian economics and the welfare state, their policies also have included a significant amount of nationalization and public ownership of industries. In 1980, virtually 100 percent of telecommunications, railways, and natural gas production and distribution were in public hands; 75 percent of steel and shipbuilding and 50 percent of the airlines were also publicly owned and operated. In spite of the extent of public ownership, Swedish social democracy rests primarily on the management of the economy through taxing and spending, the development of an extensive welfare system, and the management of industrial relations through corporatist bargaining.

Sweden's commitment to Keynesian management and welfare requires high personal income tax rates and high levels of government spending to stimulate the economy, preserve employment, and ensure high egalitarian standards of living. In

1991, tax payments equaled 53.5 percent of Sweden's gross domestic product (GDP), almost twice the percentage found in the United States. Thus, over half of the output of the Swedish economy fell under government control. Spending levels have been similarly high, with government spending in 1989 constituting 57.3 percent of Sweden's GDP. By spending such large sums, the government seeks to ensure the security of workers, and by implication, the whole of society. Government spending bolsters economic demand and helps to maintain extraordinarily low levels of unemployment, which averaged only 2.1 percent between 1965 and 1982, compared to 5.7 percent in the United States. Government spending also supports one of the world's most extensive welfare states, whose programs include a universal health care system, extremely generous pensions and unemployment compensation, government-financed maternity care and day care, cash allowances to families with children, and rent subsidies. As a result, Swedish citizens enjoy social and economic security at generally middle-class standards of living.

In spite of its successes, Swedish social democracy has come under significant pressure since the mid-1970's. Though Swedish citizens refuse to give up their extensive benefits, they are increasingly unwilling to finance them through taxation. In addition, the trade unions have made increasingly extensive demands for control over business decision making and for worker ownership of the businesses themselves, resulting in conflict with the SAF, and even with the SAP. These and other difficulties have caused a reconsideration and partial erosion of social democracy in Sweden; however, most of its central elements remain deeply ingrained and are unlikely to be reversed.

Context

The significance of social democracy as a type of government is linked to its status as a third way through the conflict between Marxist communism and democratic capitalism that has existed since the nineteenth century. As a third way, social democracy provides at least a partial remedy to the problems associated with each of the other models. While Marxism certainly provides an exceptional degree of economic equality, it does so at the expense of political freedom and economic efficiency. For many countries, particularly the former Soviet Union and the communist regimes of Eastern Europe, these losses were so great that they ultimately resulted in the collapse of communism. Because of their acceptance of capitalist markets and the democratic political order associated with them, social democrats have been forced to develop forms of socialism that preserve economic efficiency, thus allowing their economies to compete within a capitalist world. Because they accomplish this through democracy rather than dictatorship, they must ensure that the outcomes of their policies satisfy a majority of the citizens that they govern. Thus, social democracies preserve many of the goals of Marxist communism involving equality and collective control of the economy, precisely because of their willingness to compromise with other ideologies and systems. Conversely, social democracies pioneered solutions to the problems of democratic capitalism that have been applied in countries lacking social democratic movements. On the political side, they provided forceful arguments concerning the undemocratic practice of basing the right to vote on the ownership of property. Perhaps more important, they provided workable models of state intervention in the economy that help to preserve economic security and stability and reduce inequality and poverty, conditions that act as a breeding ground for communist revolutions. Thus, social democracy serves to protect capitalism and democracy through the modest application of socialism.

Many were tempted to think that the fall of communism in the Soviet Union and Eastern Europe, combined with efforts in the 1980's and 1990's in many political democracies to reassert the primacy of market economics, marked the end of socialism's era as a dominant political philosophy, but such thoughts may have been premature. Although the significance of social democracy as a third path was clearly linked to a larger struggle between capitalism and communism, this particular type of socialism took on a new significance in the 1990's. Social democracy appeared to be the most popular choice among the newly democratic Eastern European countries, and proved to be resilient in the face of efforts to remove its effects in the established democracies. While changes in Europe in the late 1980's and early 1990's suggested an end to Soviet communism, through social democracy, socialism remained likely to continue as one of the world's important approaches to politics and economics.

Bibliography

Castles, Francis. *The Social Democratic Image of Society: A Study of the Achievements and Origins of Scandinavian Social Democracy in Comparative Perspective.* Boston, Mass.: Routledge & Kegan Paul, 1978. Accessible treatment of the emergence and evolution of Scandinavian social democracy. Its consideration of the conditions leading to social democratic success is particularly good, and its comparative approach provides useful benchmarks for those unfamiliar with social democracies.

Harrington, Michael. *Socialism: Past and Future.* New York: Arcade, 1989. Extremely well-written book contains an excellent discussion of social democracy's place within socialist thought and history in general. A statement of the theoretical and practical adjustments that social democracy must make in the twenty-first century, by one of America's leading socialists.

Milner, Henry. *Sweden: Social Democracy in Practice.* New York: Oxford University Press, 1989. Interesting consideration of life in Sweden from the perspective of a long-term visitor. This book is most notable for its concern with everyday issues, though the author at times seems to lose some of his objectivity.

Padgett, Stephen, and William Paterson. *A History of Social Democracy in Postwar Europe.* New York: Longman, 1991. Excellent history of the social democratic political tradition, which covers key elements of social democracy's evolution, such as the shift away from nationalization, as well as changes in social democracies' bases of support. Also considers social democracy in countries where such parties have governed far less often.

Stephens, John D. *The Transition from Capitalism to Socialism*. London: Macmillan, 1979. Scholarly, but highly readable, examination of the social democratic argument that socialism will occur through evolution rather than revolution. Stephens' analysis considers this interpretation of Marx's theory and the evidence supporting it, and includes an excellent discussion of politics and policy in the social democracies.

W. David Patterson

Cross-References

Capitalism, p. 197; Corporatism, p. 452; Democracy, p. 513; Equality and Egalitarianism, p. 630; Government Types, p. 785; Keynesianism, Monetarism, and Supply-Side Economics p. 1032; Labor Relations, p. 1038; The Left and the Right, p. 1079; National Economies, p. 1248; Political Economy, p. 1455; Political Pragmatism, p. 1519; Social Democratic Parties, p. 1846; Social Services, p. 1858; Socialism, p. 1865; The Welfare State, p. 2135.

SOCIAL DEMOCRATIC PARTIES

Field of study: Politics

Political parties identified as social democratic share a belief that social and economic reform designed to benefit the less privileged should be pursued within a framework of democracy. Social democratic parties have been found principally in Western Europe, Australia, and New Zealand.

Principal terms

COALITION GOVERNMENT: in a parliamentary system, government in which two or more political parties share control because no one political party won a majority of seats in the most recent election

INTEREST GROUPS: organizations that attempt to influence the direction of government policy without themselves seeking to form the government

KEYNESIAN ECONOMICS: theories of John Maynard Keynes that government should intervene in the economy through fiscal policy, lifting an economy out of recession by spending more and controlling inflation by spending less

POLITICAL PARTY: association of people who hold similar views and come together to establish their priorities by gaining control of the machinery of government

WELFARE STATE: form of government in which the state takes on the responsibility of protecting and promoting the basic well-being of its members through legislation that guarantees support for individuals and families

Overview

Debate about what is and what is not social democracy is long and often circuitous. Many would agree that it has the following five tenets: political liberalism, the mixed economy, the welfare state, Keynesian economics, and a belief in equality. For others, however, social democracy simply means democratic socialism, and would include all parties of the non-Communist Left. For others, the operational criterion is membership in the Socialist International.

The Socialist International (SI) was founded in Frankfurt in 1951. Headquartered in London, its members include socialist and social democratic parties from more than sixty countries, as well as a number of "fraternal" and "associated" organizations. From its founding congress, the SI has consistently defined its role as helping the global struggle for a third way between the political totalitarianism of communism on the one hand and the economic inequalities and social injustices of capitalism on the other. The SI has considered socialism and democracy perfectly compatible, and has asserted that neither could be achieved without the other. Although wielding no power, the SI has established itself as a major voice in the international arena. Its opinions matter; its pronouncements have the weight of moral suasion. It is the only international party that enjoys worldwide attention.

Communist and social democratic political parties have a common origin in the socialist political parties of nineteenth century Europe, the most important of which, in size and influence, was the German Social Democratic Party (SPD). These parties hoped to replace capitalism with politicoeconomic systems in which the state would own and control the basic means of production. They were also committed to the construction of egalitarian societies, peace, and international workers' solidarity.

The triumph of Bolshevism in Russia in 1917 led to a split in the socialist movement between those who were prepared to accept Leninist principles and those who insisted on the democratic road to socialism. During the nineteenth century, the terms socialist and social democrat were interchangeable. The label of social democrat was used to distinguish between the minority of democrats who were also socialists and the majority of democrats who were not. After 1917, social democratic parties were perceived as those socialist parties that gave primacy to the maintenance of liberal representative democracy, as opposed to those who gave primacy to the achievement of socialism.

Social democratic parties are also distinguished from Communist parties by contrasting principles of party organization. The social democratic party occupies an intermediate position along a continuum between the loose electoral aggregation typical of the bourgeois party and the centralism of the Leninist party. Bourgeois parties normally have weak organizations and loose membership criteria, while communist parties have strong organizations and an exclusive membership. Social democratic and socialist parties have a less class-specific character, and throughout much of Western Europe they have become people's parties with a broad membership.

Northern European democratic socialist parties often have been happy to call themselves social democratic parties, while parties in southern Europe have been uneasy with the term and have normally preferred to be called socialist parties. Attempts are sometimes made to define social democratic parties in contradistinction to labor parties as those that are friendly to labor but do not have direct trade union affiliation. This distinction is not very helpful, however, because most social democratic parties have had trade unions affiliated to them at some time.

Social democratic parties are committed to the electoral road to power, but have been affected by the numerical decline of the working class in industrial societies. Different parties have responded differently in the struggle for electoral advantage. Some, like the German SPD, have looked for new class allies, the technical intelligentsia. Others, of which the southern European parties are the most obvious examples, have concentrated on projecting charismatic leaders, although they also seek new class allies.

Geographically, socialist and social democratic parties have been concentrated in Western Europe. The notable exceptions are Australia and New Zealand, where the absence of an indigenous capitalist class has been an important contributory factor to the success of the Australian and New Zealand Labour Parties. North America has, in general, proved unfruitful territory, although the New Democratic Party in Canada has had some limited success. In the third world, the most successful parties have been the Chilean Socialist Party, the People's National Party in Jamaica, and Accion Democracies in Venezuela.

Ideologically, social democratic parties exhibit wide variations, although there have been some common developments. For a long period, ideological debate and prescriptions centered on the ownership question. Ideologically the parties are now in a state of disarray.

Many commentators have noted that social democratic parties have been and continue to be in a crisis, which has not been relieved by the collapse of their rival, communism. This crisis of social democratic parties can be seen in several different categories.

The first is its indifferent electoral record. This is most important because parties are electoral machines—elections are their reason for being. The limited support for social democracy in Europe in the early 1990's suggests the inability of social democratic parties to educate the electorate or to satisfy their expectations consistently. It also points to the fragmentation and sophistication of the working class. The new working class is better educated and less dependent upon a party or union for its information and attitudes. Social democratic parties have substantially abandoned a class appeal and have begun to direct themselves to a wide electoral market. Leftist ideology has been largely jettisoned in favor of personality and image politics.

Applications

In the mid-1990's, the German Social Democrats had not won a federal election since 1980; the British Labour Party had not won since 1974. The Swedish Social Democrats, the ruling party for six decades, lost hold of the government between 1976 and 1982 and lost more significantly in 1991. The Norwegian Labour Party assumed the government in 1986 only because the two Progressive Party delegates switched from the ruling Conservative coalition. Throughout the 1980's, Dutch Labour had only been in government as a junior coalition member with the Christian Democrats. Mitterrand's Socialists in France held office at the presidential level throughout the 1980's, but after 1982, as a centrist government. The Spanish Socialists governed from 1982 into the 1990's, presiding over the modernization of Spanish capitalism and integration into the Common Market. The Socialist Party in Italy near the end of the twentieth century had only enjoyed governmental office in junior coalition. The vote for the socialists in Austria has remained consistently in the 45 percent range. In Belgium, it fell from 36 to 28 percent between the 1950's and the 1980's; in Denmark, from 40 to 32 percent; and in Britain, from 46 to 29 percent. In Finland, it has remained at about 25 percent, and in Iceland, at 15 to 19 percent.

In the late twentieth century, capitalism has set the terms of political discourse. Since World War II, social democracy has not seriously represented a transformational project. At its best, in the British Labour government of the late 1940's, it modernized some parts of an aged economic infrastructure and advanced the social life of the British working class.

When excessive inflation and then stagnation developed in the West during the 1970's, the slow improvement in lower-class living standards was halted, debt became chronic, and the solutions once provided by fiscal policy did not work. Conservative ideology virtually destroyed Western socialist options.

Western communism was so badly hobbled by its long subordination to Soviet Communism, that its only reasonable hope for survival was to begin moving toward social democracy. Eurocommunism was the stepping stone. At its most successful in Italy, communist strategy provided reforms in areas such as day care, transportation, schooling, health, and economic growth.

Most of the social democratic parties of Europe in the mid-1990's accepted globalization, the centrality of markets, and private capital as the engine of growth. Social democratic literature continued to emphasize the need to maintain state action to induce employment, protect the victims of the market, and remedy residual and emerging inequities, predatory behavior, and environmental mismanagement.

The evolution of the Swedish Socialist Party (SAP) during the 1980's is perhaps the most dramatic instance of conversion. In September, 1991, SAP lost the election to a coalition of centrist and right-wing parties for the second time in a little more than a decade. This was the result of the attenuation of relations between the SAP and the trade unions, which represented more than 80 percent of the workers. At the time of the election, the SAP was a minority government, unemployment had risen to about 3.2 percent, inflation exceeded 10 percent, the government had introduced an unpopular tax on consumer goods, and general austerity budgeting had been introduced in 1990. Sweden's Social Democrats, who had held an iron grip on political power for 53 of the previous 57 years, finally ran out of steam. A majority of Swedes had grown weary of paying for social democracy at the same time the party's identity and message were becoming less clear. The party's identity crisis was compounded by national soul-searching about the prospect of joining the European Community (EC) and fears of being swamped by laissez-faire capitalism and cheap Danish cheese. The SAP government began negotiations for Sweden to enter the EC, which led to the agreement for merger between the European Free Trade Association and the EC in October, 1991. The SAP had lost its focus on converting capitalism, as had been implied during the 1970's. It was unclear if the interdependence of the party and the trade union movement could be restored.

After the 1970's, capitalism became less focused on production as it underwent restructuring, also known as globalization. Social democratic parties and governments have responded to globalization by seemingly declaring their inability to imagine alternatives. Even if social democratic parties continue to be elected, they are not likely to advance more comprehensive democracy and socially empowering programs in the 1990's. Marxists and other leftist observers have maintained that the entire socialist project must be painfully reconsidered before there will be any renewal.

Capitalism also faces a challenge. With the exception of the British Tories, there are no capitalist parties in Europe large enough to govern securely alone. They must govern in coalitions, which are notoriously problematic, although during the Cold War, such coalitions were reasonably stable. Confronting the unfolding crisis of capitalism will command the efforts of the European Left as a whole. It is as true in the 1990's as it was in the 1890's that socialism develops, not from a blueprint, but from a struggle with capitalism.

Context

A major feature of political history since the mid-nineteenth century has been the establishment and growth of political parties identified with the complex of ideas known as social democratic: the belief that social and economic reform designed to benefit the less privileged should be pursued within a framework of democracy.

The vast majority of social democratic parties were established during the period of the extension of the franchise in the last quarter of the nineteenth century. This early social democracy was confined at the level of national politics to an opposition role before 1914 and was distinctive mainly in its articulation of anticapitalist and internationalist ideas. The outbreak of war in 1914 demonstrated the fragility of its commitment to these ideas, and the claims of patriotism and national solidarity, including solidarity with the reviled capitalists, weighed more heavily than international solidarity with the leaders of the main parties after war broke out. After the collapse of the old order in 1918, social democrats began to experience significant electoral successes in Europe. Unfortunately for these parties, the end of World War I brought about not only the destruction of the autocracies, but led, through the success of the Russian Revolution of 1917, to the establishment in almost all the Western European countries of communist parties committed to the realization of socialist goals by revolutionary means. The threat posed by these parties helped create a situation in which social democratic parties and politicians spent more of their energies in defending democracy, which they identified with existing parliamentary institutions and regimes, than in attempting to bring about the realization of the socialist goals to which they were still largely pledged. After 1919, social democracy generally defined itself in opposition to communism.

By 1945, social democratic parties promised to be the strongest political force in Western Europe. They formed the governing party, or were an important element in coalition governments, throughout much of the area. Their long-term prospects appeared even better. Whereas conservatives and parties of the Right had largely been discredited by the war and occupation, the socialists, through their prominence in the resistance and in Great Britain by their participation in the wartime government, had revived some of the prestige they had lost in the 1930's.

In Scandinavia, the 1950's saw the continuation or establishment of what was to be a lasting period of social democratic rule, but elsewhere in Western Europe the decade was a bleak one for social democracy. In most West European countries, the 1950's were deeply influenced by the twin phenomena of continually expanding prosperity and anti-Communism. Their general impact placed the parties on the defensive. In the

1960's, the fortunes of social democracy revived somewhat.

The impact of the Cold War, allied to the pervasive character of post-war prosperity, moved most socialist and social democratic parties to weaken their commitment to nationalization.

Bibliography

Crosland, Anthony. *The Future of Socialism*. London: Jonathan Cape, 1956. Crosland discusses the five criteria that have constituted the core values of most socialist and social democratic parties from the late 1950's onward: political liberalism, the mixed economy, the welfare state, Keynesian economics, and a belief in equality.

Epstein, Leon D. *Political Parties in Western Democracies*. New York: Praeger, 1967. Comparative study of political parties, including social democratic parties, in the United States, Canada, New Zealand, Australia, Israel, the four Scandinavian nations, Iceland, Britain, Ireland, Switzerland, Austria, France, West Germany, Italy, Belgium, The Netherlands, and Luxembourg.

Paterson, W. E. "Socialist and Social Democratic Parties." In *The Blackwell Encyclopaedia of Political Institutions*, edited by Vernon Bogdanor. New York: Blackwell Reference, 1987. Excellent short history of social democratic parties through the late 1980's.

Paterson, William E., and Alastair H. Thomas, eds. *Social Democratic Parties in Western Europe*. New York: St. Martin's Press, 1977. Excellent introduction to the development and history of social democratic parties through the late 1970's. Includes individual chapters on the social democratic parties in France, Italy, Spain, England, Ireland, Germany, Austria, Denmark, Finland, Norway, Sweden, The Netherlands, and Belgium.

Przeworski, Adam. "Socialism and Social Democracy." In *The Oxford Companion to Politics of the World*, edited by Joel Krieger, et al. New York: Oxford University Press, 1993. A criticism of social democracy placed in the context of the three alternative socialist forms: communitarian, Marxist, and social democratic.

Gregory P. Rabb

Cross-References

THE SOCIAL SECURITY SYSTEM

Field of study: Functions of government

Social Security in the United States includes the basic national social insurance program, Old-Age, Survivors, and Disability Insurance (OASDI), as well as health insurance (Medicare). OASDI is the largest income maintenance program in the country, covering nine out of every ten labor force participants.

Principal terms

ANNUAL MAXIMUM TAXABLE LIMIT: annual dollar amount, above which earnings in employment covered under the OASDI program are neither taxable nor creditable for benefit computation purposes

INSURED STATUS: having sufficient quarters of coverage to meet the eligibility requirements for benefits

QUARTERS OF COVERAGE: coverage needed for insured status, whereby a worker receives one quarter of coverage, up to a total of four, for a specified dollar amount of earnings from employment

TAXABLE WAGE: payment for services rendered in covered employment up to the annual taxable maximum

Overview

The Social Security system in the United States encompasses a broad array of programs, including Old-Age, Survivors, and Disability Insurance (OASDI), Supplemental Security Income (SSI), Medicare, Medicaid, unemployment insurance, workers' compensation, temporary disability insurance, veterans' benefits, Aid to Families with Dependent Children (AFDC), and food stamps. The largest of these programs, OASDI, affects almost all workers in the country.

OASDI is a federal program administered by the Social Security Administration, which was under the Department of Health and Human Services in the early 1990's. OASDI provides monthly benefits to retired and disabled workers and their dependents and to survivors of insured workers. Four basic principles guide the development and implementation of OASDI. First, the program is work-related. The economic security for the worker and his or her family grows out of the person's own work. A worker's entitlement to benefits is based on past employment, and the amount of cash benefits the worker or his or her family receives is related to earnings in covered work. In general, the more that is earned, the greater the protection. Second, there is no means test. Benefits are an earned right, paid regardless of income from other sources. Third, social insurance is contributory. The concept of earned right is reinforced by workers paying earmarked social security taxes, generally through payroll deductions known as FICA taxes. The contributory nature of the program is meant to encourage a responsible attitude toward the program. Knowing that the financing of the present program and any improvement made in it depend on social security taxes that they pay, workers have a personal interest and stake in the soundness of the program. Finally, coverage, with minor exceptions, is universal and compulsory. Spreading the insured risks among the broadest possible group helps to minimize the cost of protection for each participant. In addition, nearly universal coverage is desirable for a social insurance system, because it ensures a base of economic security for virtually everyone in society.

Workers excluded from Social Security coverage fall into five major categories: federal civilian employees hired before January 1, 1984; railroad workers who are covered under the railroad retirement system; certain employees of state and local governments who are covered under other retirement systems; household workers and farmworkers whose earnings do not meet certain minimum requirements; and persons with very low net earnings from self-employment, generally less than $400 per year. Approximately 4.4 million workers were exempt from coverage under Social Security in 1992. Most of these workers were employed in federal, state, or local government.

At the end of 1992, nearly 41.5 million people received benefits from OASDI, which had a total yearly expenditure of approximately $294 billion. Approximately 62 percent of the beneficiaries were retired workers, receiving an average monthly benefit of $653. The next largest category of beneficiaries, widows and widowers (12 percent), received an average monthly benefit of $608. Disabled workers (8.4 percent) had monthly benefits averaging $626, while wives and husbands of retired workers (7.5 percent) had average monthly benefits of just $337. The average monthly benefit of surviving children (4.4 percent) was $432.

OASDI, as well as the hospital insurance programs, are primarily financed through the payroll tax and from income taxes paid on Social Security benefits. Most of the system's income is used directly to meet current benefit obligations. Funds collected in excess of those needed to make benefit payments are credited to the trust funds as reserves, in the form of government securities. These reserves serve as a cushion against temporary shortfalls in revenues or large increases in outlays as a result of economic fluctuations. Reserves also provide interest income to the trust funds. The annual excess of revenues over benefit outlays, commonly called the surplus, is expected to reach almost $90 billion by 1998. Throughout the 1990's, and for the first few decades of the twenty-first century, the favorable demographic pattern of a large post-war generation, born between 1946 and 1964, at their peak earning years, combined with the retirement of the relatively smaller generation born during the Depression of the 1930's, should ensure large trust fund reserves.

In light of the increasing and sizable budget deficits that resulted from government spending throughout most of the 1980's and early 1990's, many critics began to view the Social Security system as a drag on the economy. They argued that Social Security depresses private savings, thereby providing less capital for investment; overpays the elderly; slights younger workers, who could get a better return if they invested privately; and may lead the country to fiscal collapse. Advocates claim that Social Security actually stimulates financial planning for retirement, thereby encouraging savings. They also contend that most payments to those over sixty-five years of age went to households with total annual incomes less than $30,000 in 1990, and thus kept many elderly people's annual incomes from falling below the official poverty line. In addition to these arguments, concern has been expressed about the use of surplus OASDI money, specifically about how the surplus may influence Congress and the administration in making future policy decisions for government as a whole. The surplus can be used to fund other programs, to lower taxes, or to cause government borrowing from financial markets to be lower. The extent to which any of these uses helps or hinders economic growth has been the subject of much debate about the proper role of government in the economy and society.

Applications

A person builds protection under the OASDI program through work in employment covered under Social Security. Taxes on wages and salaries that workers earn, up to a statutory maximum taxable amount each year, are withheld and matched by employers. Self-employed persons pay taxes on their annual earnings up to the same maximum as employees, but at the combined employer-employee rate. Taxes of workers with more than one employer are withheld and matched up to the annual maximum by each employer; if the employee has paid taxes on total wages above the maximum, the excess is refunded through the income tax system. The annual maximum taxable amount in 1993 was $57,600 for OASDI and $135,000 for Medicare or hospital insurance. These maximum amounts are updated automatically each year in proportion to increases in nationwide average wage and salary earnings. The Federal Insurance Contributions Act (FICA) tax rate applicable to each employee and employer in 1993 was 6.2 percent for OASDI (5.6 and 0.6 percent respectively, for OASDI and DI) and 1.45 percent for Medicare. Self-employed persons paid the combined employee-employer rate of 12.4 percent for OASDI and 2.9 for Medicare under the Self-Employment Contributions Act (SECA). All taxes are credited to the Old-Age Survivors Insurance (OASI) and Disability Insurance (DI) Trust Funds. By law, these funds may be used only to meet the cost of monthly benefits when the worker retires, dies, or becomes disabled; lump-sum death payments to survivors; vocational rehabilitation services for disability beneficiaries; and administrative expenses.

To become eligible for one's own benefits and benefits for family members or survivors, a worker must earn a certain number of credits based on work in covered employment or self-employment. These credits are measured in terms of quarters of coverage (QC). In 1993, a QC was acquired for each $590 in annual covered earnings, up to a maximum of four QC for the year based on earnings of $2,360 or more. The amount of earnings required for a QC is adjusted automatically each year in proportion to increases in the average wage level. Eligibility for most types of benefits requires that the worker be fully insured. To be fully insured, a worker must have a number of QC at least equal to the number of full calendar years elapsing between age twenty-one (or the year 1950 if this date is later), and the year in which he or she reaches age sixty-two, becomes disabled, or dies.

If a worker dies before achieving fully insured status, benefits may be paid to his or her children, or to his or her widow(er) caring for such children under sixteen years of age, if the worker was currently insured at the time of death. To be currently insured, the worker must have earned six QC over the period of thirteen calendar quarters ending with the quarter of death. To qualify for disability benefits, a worker must be fully insured and, except where he or she is disabled because of blindness, must also meet a test of substantial recent work activity. Under this test, a worker thirty-one years of age or older must have at least twenty QC during the period of forty calendar quarters ending with the quarter in which the disability began. A worker disabled between twenty-four and thirty years of age must have QC in one-half of the calendar quarters elapsing after he or she reached twenty-one years of age; a worker under twenty-four years of age needs six QC in the period of twelve quarters ending with the quarter of disability's onset.

Context

The Social Security Act of 1935 extended federal responsibility for social welfare. Its programs fell under two basic categories; contributory and noncontributory. The contributory or insurance system included Title II, Old Age and Survivors, the national system financed by taxes on employer and employee plus a subsidy from general revenue; and Title III, Unemployment, a state-based system financed by a tax on employers of eight or more persons. The noncontributory or public assistance systems were of two types: those that gave grants to states for payments to individuals, such as Title I, Old-Age Assistance, Title IV, Aid to Dependent Children, and Title X, Aid to the Blind; and those that gave grants to states for provision of service, such as Title V, Maternal and Child Welfare and Vocational Rehabilitation, and Title VI, Public Health. Since 1935, the Social Security Act has undergone many revisions, but the basic division into contributory versus noncontributory programs remained intact.

Between 1952 and 1971, Congress increased Social Security benefits seven times. In general, these increases equaled price increases, and on occasion, as in 1954, considerably exceeded them. Cumulatively, benefit increases between 1950 and 1971 far exceeded price increases, but lagged behind wage increases. Although the purchasing power of retired workers' benefits improved substantively over time, it lagged behind the overall improvement in the standard of living. Because benefit increases were intermittent and ad hoc, adjusted benefits ordinarily lagged behind price increases.

The Social Security Administration (SSA) used actuarial procedures to facilitate periodic increases in benefits. SSA used the level earnings assumption as the basis for determining benefit increases prior to 1972. This assumption had important political implications. Periodic updating of the program's financial condition ordinarily revealed a surplus, as long as the actuarial assumption was that earnings would not rise. In the U.S. economy of the 1950's and 1960's, this fiscally conservative assumption had liberalizing consequences. On one hand, the level earnings assumption constrained the size of benefit increases. Accounting for higher wages would have projected rising returns from the payroll tax, and these higher anticipated yields could have been used to justify higher benefits. On the other hand, with the level earnings assumption, program growth was made to depend upon economic growth. In times of economic expansion, as in the 1950's and 1960's, benefit increases came to policymakers as actuarial windfalls, which could be distributed without additional taxes. Social Security benefit increases became a means by which politicians gratified constituents and sought their votes.

In 1972, Congress approved a 20 percent benefit increase, and enacted an automatic procedure governing future increases in benefits and the wage base. Benefits rose with prices, and the wage base with earnings, thereby overtly and directly tying the program to the performance of the economy. To the extent that Congress wanted to grant bigger increases than those generated automatically, it would have to raise taxes. In the antitax climate of the late 1970's and throughout the 1980's when the economy grew, the leading issue of social security policy was how to finance a growing deficit. Rapidly rising disability rates, a declining fertility rate, and adverse changes in the economy accounted for the unexpected appearance of a deficit, which threatened to exhaust the trust funds by the early 1980's unless additional revenue was provided. In 1977, Congress responded to the deficit by increasing taxes and revising the benefit formula. In 1981 it began taxing an estimated 91 percent of the earnings of covered workers, far exceeding the 81 percent that had prevailed since the 1950 amendments. Congress also adopted a formula that tied the benefits of retired persons automatically to increases in prices, as had the formula in 1972, but that tied the future benefits promised to currently active workers automatically to increase in wages. In an inflationary period, the 1972 formula overcompensated active workers, because they benefited both from higher wages while working and increased benefits tied to rising prices after retirement. The decoupling of active workers' benefits from retired workers' benefits was seen as essential in stabilizing the replacement rate of beneficiaries, but social security taxation and expenditures as a percentage of gross national product rose, thereby fueling additional changes in the 1980's.

President Ronald Reagan initially proposed major cuts in Social Security, including reductions in benefit payment for early retirement, elimination of the minimum benefit, and a postponement in the annual cost-of-living adjustment. Despite opposition, Reagan appointed a bipartisan National Commission on Social Security Reform in 1981 to examine the entire social insurance system. By January, 1983, the commission recommended retaining the basic structure of the system; that is, it was to remain a compulsory, nonmeans-tested, contributory program, giving low-income workers a better return on their contributions than those higher on the wage scale. To meet fiscal needs, the commission proposed partial taxation of higher-income retirees' benefits, a gradual increase in the retirement age to 67, and increases in the contribution rate. The measures were adopted and the trust fund deficit was not only eliminated, but reversed. The trust funds are projected to peak at about $8 billion by 2025, before declining again substantially by 2040, taking into account the impact of the retirement of the post-World War II generation and the decreased proportion of workers contributing to the system. In the 1990's, however, there were concerns that the fund was too large, placing a heavy tax burden on low-income workers, on the nation's future workers, and on the economy in general.

Bibliography

Axinn, June, and Herman Levin. *Social Welfare: A History of the American Response to Need.* 3d ed. New York: Longman, 1992. Contains original source documents related to the development of social security in the United States through 1990. Detailed introductions to each chapter place the documents in historical context.

Derthick, Martha. *Policymaking for Social Security.* Washington, D.C.: Brookings Institution, 1979. Traces the development of the Social Security system through the advent of the Reagan Administration. Contains a chronology of related legislation and a list of principal executive officials.

Marmor, Theodore R., Jerry L. Mashaw, and Philip L. Harvey. *America's Misunderstood Welfare State: Persistent Myths, Enduring Realities.* New York: Basic Books, 1990. Contains an excellent chapter on Social Security developments and the political debates that surrounded them throughout the 1980's.

Peterson, Peter. *Facing Up: How to Rescue the Economy from Crushing Debt and Restore the American Dream.* New York: Simon & Schuster, 1993. Highlights the contemporary debates about the economic impact on the U.S. economy of funding the Social Security system, and proposes a detailed remedy.

Social Security Bulletin: Annual Statistical Supplement, 1993. Washington, D.C.: U.S. Dept. of Health and Human Services, Social Security Administration, 1993. Contains descriptions and a history of provisions for each of the components of the Social Security system. Narrative summaries, statistical tables related to each of the programs, technical notes, a list of abbreviations, a glossary of program terms, and an index. Some issues of the *Social Security Bulletin* elaborately describe the Social Security system and its components.

Richard K. Caputo

Cross-References

Aging and Politics in the United States, p. 35; Debts and Deficits in the U.S. Federal Budget, p. 489; The Family and Politics in the United States, p. 649; Government Roles, p. 778; Law Enforcement, p. 1059; National Security, p. 1261; Public Policy, p. 1633; Public Utilities, p. 1640; Public Works, p. 1647; Resource Management, p. 1718; Taxation and Appropriation, p. 1941; Urban Policy, p. 2057; Urban Renewal and Housing, p. 2064.

SOCIAL SERVICES

Field of study: Functions of government

Government social services are organized activities, funded by one or more levels of government, provided directly to individuals, households, or designated groups to improve their well-being or social effectiveness. The three main types of social services are remedial, preventive, and developmental.

Principal terms

PRIVATIZATION: full or partial transfer of responsibility for the provision of services from government to private for-profit firms or third-sector organizations

SUBSIDIARITY: principle that the primary duty to respond to human need belongs to the social unit closest to the need, beginning with the family

THIRD SECTOR: organizations that are neither government agencies nor profit-seeking firms, but that serve a public purpose

Overview

In preindustrial societies, families and neighbors cared for and educated each other. Needs were obvious and solutions simple. Most civil and religious traditions emphasized responsibility for kinfolk and compassion toward others in need. Greeks pioneered philanthropy; Romans developed civic foundations and trusts; Jews and early Christians tithed; Buddhists and followers of Islam encouraged charitable practices. Early governments, however, generally did little to address social needs. Doles to the poor, when they occurred, were intended to preserve authority rather than to improve the general quality of life. Other services were sparse and reserved to privileged classes.

Under the influence of expanding trade and industrialization, cities experienced an explosive increase in the concentration of indigent, ignorant, and otherwise needy individuals. Overcrowding, intemperance, disease, and other social ills grew apace, collectively overwhelming traditional methods of providing assistance. In fifteenth century Paris, Europe's largest city, beggars constituted 10 percent of the population. Aside from almsgiving, private hospitals and religious confraternities were the main sources of organized social assistance, caring not only for the sick but also for beggars, prostitutes, poor women, outcast tradesman, invalids, orphans, the blind, and the insane. Government-provided services for the ordinary citizen still were unknown at this time.

In 1597, England became the first nation to require that each parish (county) maintain its poor inhabitants through compulsory assessment. A series of subsequent acts, especially in the nineteenth century, broadened the government's role in providing relief to the poor, elementary education, medical services, and control of workplace abuses.

Benjamin Franklin deplored the British model after he visited London in 1766; he claimed that government assistance encouraged indolence. Although Article 1, section 8 of the United States Constitution authorized Congress to tax for the general welfare, American politicians initially resisted government provision of social services. Instead, an extraordinary range of voluntary organizations arose. Alexis de Tocqueville, a French statesman who visited the United States in 1831-1832, observed that people spontaneously formed organizations, either for mutual benefit or for the good of others less fortunate.

The early laws of the Northwest Territory encoded the principles of voluntary action by requiring the able-bodied to care for the poor, old, blind, lame, and economically incapable. These laws also introduced another important principle, government responsibility for the promotion of general education. The Ordinance of 1785 stipulated that one square mile of each new township should be set aside for support of public schools. At the close of the Revolutionary period, public schooling was uneven and controlled almost entirely by local school boards. This began to change during the mid-1830's, when Horace Mann developed the first effective state board of education in Massachusetts.

The federal government made few forays into social services during the pre-Civil War years. In 1854, Dorothea Dix persuaded Congress to pass legislation creating a federal system of hospitals for the mentally ill, but President Franklin Pierce vetoed the bill on the grounds that it would dry up sources of local assistance. Nevertheless, during the decades immediately preceding the Civil War, many state and local governments ventured into the provision of social services. States established mental asylums, prisons, school boards, and normal schools in which teachers were trained. Municipalities created new types of relief and service organizations to address mounting urban ills. Boston opened the country's first major free library in 1852.

After the Civil War, both the federal government and state governments established new provisions to benefit veterans, especially through health care and pensions. During this same period, public high schools became common. By the end of the nineteenth and the early decades of the twentieth centuries, governments at all levels had assumed a major role as provider of social services, either directly through tax-supported agencies or indirectly through regulation. One study in the 1890's reported that two-thirds of the funds used by private charitable organizations in New York came from government. At the national level, the U.S. Children's Bureau, created in 1912, introduced a broad new federal agenda in matters of health, education, and general public welfare. Concerns about cost helped to defeat President Warren Harding's proposal in 1921 to establish a comprehensive Department of Public Welfare, with separate divisions responsible for education, public health, social services, and veteran's services.

During this same period, the German Weimar Republic (1919-1933) pioneered the modern welfare state, guaranteeing both income payments to the poor and government-provided social services to all citizens, without regard to status or class. The distinctive aspect of the welfare state was its commitment to ensure that its citizens received at least minimum levels of education, health, and nutrition as a political right, rather than as an act of charity restricted to the needy. In the welfare state, tax-supported services usually preempt more traditional family or church responsibility for personal well-being.

The Great Depression of the 1930's created a watershed in government responsibility for social services in the United States. People who previously had never needed assistance suddenly became dependent on government for life's necessities. President Franklin D. Roosevelt's New Deal, which focused on the needs of retirees, widows, and the unemployed, but not children, set a new direction for social policy in the United States. Thereafter, the federal government assumed a mandate to address any social needs that seemed beyond resolution by private enterprise, voluntary action, or local government. The Great Society programs of the 1960's brought this approach to new heights, resulting in a pervasive federal presence in social services. By the early 1990's, only about one-fifth of U.S. federal spending for social programs was targeted primarily to the poor.

At the root of all governmental systems of social service is the question of social rights and state responsibilities. Many scholars have argued that the transition from the Middle Ages to the modern industrial and postindustrial world marked a transition in the meaning of citizenship. Whereas formerly only the wealthy were entitled to full citizenship, including government benefits, in the twentieth century it has been more common for nations to recognize the social right of all citizens to enjoy government-directed or government-provided standards of education, health, and welfare. There seems to be greater international consensus on this point than on the proper mechanisms for delivery of needed social services. One promising sign is that research on these matters is improving in both scope and sophistication.

Applications

In the 1990's, the central governments of Germany, France, and Italy took a relatively strong role in the provision of social services. Germany and Italy delegated more of the direct delivery to local authorities and to third-sector organizations than did France. Germany even collected taxes for churches, which in turn allocated funds to support their service agencies throughout the Federal Republic. In France, the central government retained the lead role in providing health care, education, and other social services, although here, too, there was a trend toward localization of delivery. The Italian government has enjoyed less success than either France or Germany in delivering social services; disorganization and underfunding have hampered efforts to provide a strong network of services.

Switzerland has maintained a dominant government presence in the delivery of basic social services, but it does so through a federal system of cantons and municipalities that are encouraged to create local solutions to their particular needs. The third sector in Switzerland has a relatively small role compared to most other nations in Western Europe.

The social democracies of Scandinavia have exhibited the strongest pattern of government responsibility for social services. Education, health, and other basic services are provided by the state bureaucracy as a right of citizenship, with comparatively little assistance from the for-profit economy or the third sector.

The common law countries of Britain, Canada, and Australia are closer to the United States in their reliance on the for-profit sector and third sector to provide a wide range of social services. As a set, however, these states take a more nationalistic approach to health care and poor relief than does the United States.

The former Communist nations posed a special situation in the 1990's. As they strove to move from a highly centralized form of control to a market economy with democratic government, the provision of social services often was disrupted. Public money was scarce, the voluntary sector usually was undeveloped, private philanthropy was virtually unknown, and vestiges of socialist control hampered reform efforts. Most of these nations appeared to be trying to establish a national model of social services that blended selected features of Western European welfare states with the strong third-sector characteristic of the United States.

Nations in economically less developed regions of the world sometimes have faced insurmountable problems. Political and military instability, lack of capital, poor transportation and communication infrastructures, and a general shortage of trained professionals have made the provision of social services problematic in many nations and regions. Indigenous third-sector organizations usually have relied heavily on international philanthropy for their operating funds, rather than on their own central government.

An unresolved international issue is the provision of essential services to vast refugee populations. Population shifts caused by war, famine, or political repression create centers of need that often exhaust the capacities of affected nations. The international community, under the leadership of the United Nations, responds by monitoring conditions, assessing need, and mobilizing support from every available source. Although such efforts work passably well in dealing with transient crises, they have not proven as effective in eradicating enduring conditions of deprivation. There is no intergovernmental authority to tax sovereign states or intervene with uninvited social services. As a result, millions of people remain without basic services and developmental support.

Context

One unique aspect of political life in the United States is the extraordinary number and variety of governments—federal, state, county, municipal, and special districts. The U.S. Bureau of the Census counted 86,743 governments in 1992, including 3,043 county governments, 19,296 municipal governments, 16,666 townships, and 14,556 school districts. Special taxing districts grew especially rapidly during the previous few decades, numbering 33,131 in 1992. These customarily are single-service taxing bodies associated with fire protection, community development, public health, parks and recreation, libraries, sanitation, and other services deemed worthy of common public funding. Illinois led the way with 6,628 distinct state and local governments.

Despite these many levels of government—or, some experts contend, because of them—the federal government exerts a dominating influence over the delivery of social services. This occurs in part because the federal government finances nearly half of all public service expenditures (down from nearly two-thirds in 1980), and in part because it exercises control through regulation, tax laws, and judicial decisions. Under Republican Party leadership during the 1980's, federal agencies increasingly shifted from direct funding and delivery to indirect financing and delivery. In the early 1990's, the federal government directly administered only about one-sixth of what it spent on services. Federal money is channeled to local governments and nonprofit organizations through three principal mechanisms: federal health, welfare, and education agencies provide funds to state agencies, which delegate them to local service providers pursuant to federal guidelines; some federal agencies provide research and demonstration grants to agencies on a competitive basis; other federal agencies contract directly with service providers or offer portable benefits that eligible individuals can take to their provider of choice. Financial aid for postsecondary education is an example of the third method.

The long-term impacts of each pattern are not clear, although one evident problem that seems to transcend all boundaries is mounting pressure on the budgets of all government units. Health services, in particular, have consumed ever-rising proportions of the public service budget. This problem is not confined to the United States. The welfare states of Western Europe also have come under increasing criticism of late, especially for their bureaucratic overhead and comparatively high rates of taxation.

As service demands continue to expand beyond the resources available to most national and local governments, three principal patterns of response have become evident: retrenchment, privatization, and cost-containment. Retrenchment consists of a reduction in services. Privatization consists of shifting the provision of services from government agencies to private organizations, although in many cases taxes continue to fund part or all of the cost. What results from the first two measures has been called the "hollow state," in which public control of public services is diminished in appearance if not also in fact. Cost-containment consists of efforts to become more efficient in the provision of any given service, such as through increased use of volunteer labor or through computerization of record-keeping.

The principle of subsidiarity undergirds several of these trends. This principle dictates that services should be provided by the most local agent capable of the task. Functions that can be handled by individuals or families should be left to them. Voluntary organizations should take precedence over government agencies, and national government should intervene only when local efforts prove deficient or inefficient. On the other hand, proponents of the classical model of government bureaucracy contend that state taxation and large-scale service agencies provide more complete, professional, and equitable services. In particular, taxation schemes seem to work more equitably the larger the level of social aggregation. The tension between these perspectives remains a continuing source of instability regarding the provision of social services in the developed nations.

Bibliography

Elliott, Doreen, Nazneen S. Mayadas, and Thomas D. Watts, eds. *The World of Social Welfare: Social Welfare and Services in an International Context.* Springfield, Ill.: Charles C. Thomas, 1990. Country-specific analyses of social services and welfare provisions on all continents; helpful chapter bibliographies. Written in nontechnical language.

Gidron, Benjamin, Ralph M. Kramer, and Lester M. Salamon. *Government and the Third Sector: Emerging Relationships in Welfare States.* San Francisco: Jossey-Bass, 1992. Balanced, international analysis of the respective roles of government agencies and nonprofit organizations in providing social services. Chapter bibliographies cite the best of recent literature in English.

Hollingsworth, J. Rogers, and Robert Hanneman. *Centralization and Power in Social Service Delivery Systems: The Cases of England, Wales, and the United States.* Boston: Kluwer Nijhoff, 1984. Slightly dated in details, but useful as a comparative study of international differences in health care and education; focuses especially on the role of centralized decision-making.

Kramer, Ralph M., Hakon Lorentzen, Willem B. Melief, and Sergio Pasquinelli. *Privatization in Four European Countries: Comparative Studies in Government-Third Sector Relationships.* Armonk, N.Y.: M. E. Sharpe, 1993. Detailed examination of relationships between government agencies and third-sector service providers in England, Italy, Norway, and The Netherlands.

Kuhnle, Stein, and Per Selle, eds. *Government and Voluntary Organizations: A Relational Perspective.* Aldershot, England: Avebury, 1992. Ten essays concerning government and third-sector relations in Western and Eastern Europe. Extensive bibliography, not all in English.

Lipsky, Michael. *Street-Level Bureaucracy: Dilemmas of the Individual in Public Services.* New York: Russell Sage Foundation, 1980. Classic treatment of the manner in which individual service professionals, for example, teachers, social workers, and uniformed officers, embody and transform social policy.

MacPherson, Stewart. *Social Policy in the Third World: The Social Dilemmas of Underdevelopment.* Totowa, N.J.: Allanheld, Osmun, 1982. Sweeping overview of the emergence of social policy and social services in economically underdeveloped nations, with special attention to education, health, housing, and social services. Extensive bibliography of early sources.

Olasky, Marvin. *The Tragedy of American Compassion.* Washington, D.C.: Regnery Gateway, 1992. Readable, well-documented history of the shift from private assistance to government service as the primary method of relieving the needs of the underclass in the United States. The author criticizes entitlement programs.

Thompson, Frank J., ed. *Revitalizing State and Local Public Service.* San Francisco: Jossey-Bass, 1993. This publication of the National Commission on State and Local Public Service considers various methods of increasing effectiveness, accountability, and public confidence in government services in the United States.

Thursz, Daniel, and Joseph L. Vigilante, eds. *Meeting Human Needs.* 2 vols. Beverly

Hills, Calif.: Sage, 1975-1976. Still a useful compendium of reports concerning the delivery of social services in twenty-two countries, including nations in Africa, South America, and Asia.

Richard A. Yanikoski

Cross-References

SOCIALISM

Field of study: Political philosophy

Socialist theory advocates that the production and distribution of goods be controlled by government or industrial groups, to replace competition for profit with cooperation and social responsibility, and to distribute income and opportunities more equitably. In practice, socialist systems have ranged from utopian and Christian societies to violent and repressive regimes.

Principal terms

CLASS CONFLICT: Marxian notion that society tends to polarize into two dominant conflicting groups, impoverished workers against wealthy capitalists

COMMUNISM: in theory, a prosperous, noncoercive, conflict-free economy; in practice, a totalitarian system with near-universal government ownership and management of economic activity

DEMAND MANAGEMENT: use of monetary and fiscal policies to influence aggregate demand for goods and services

FULL EMPLOYMENT: situation in which everyone willing and able to work is able to find a job

PROLETARIAT: Marx's term for the working class, exploited under capitalism, expected to bring in socialism through revolution

SAFETY NET: government measures, usually transfer payments, to protect individuals against economic hardship

Overview

The socialist ideology originated in the early nineteenth century as a reaction to the inequalities and injustices of early capitalism and the egalitarian ideology of the French Revolution. In its earliest form, it often involved real or imagined voluntary communities, free from coercion. Under the influence of such socialist thinkers as Robert Owen in England and Charles Fourier in France, several experimental socialist communities were formed in the United States, including New Harmony in Indiana and Brook Farm in Massachusetts. Organized on cooperative principles, they stressed agriculture and handicraft production for material needs, and also emphasized cultural and artistic development, education, and child-raising. Purely secular socialist communities were seldom successful, particularly because they did not provide effective incentives for people to do the mundane tasks of producing food, clothing, and shelter. Where a strong religious bond existed, communities stressing voluntary sharing and mutual help often operated quite successfully. Owen's followers started a highly successful consumers' cooperative movement in Great Britain. These early utopian socialists essentially bypassed existing political institutions.

Socialist theory and political action changed drastically in response to the writings of Karl Marx and Friedrich Engels. In 1848, they published *The Communist Manifesto*, one of the most influential political documents ever written. In this book, they portrayed history as a series of struggles between social classes. In the capitalist world, this struggle pitted workers, the proletariat, against capitalists, the bourgeoisie. The capitalists owned the means of production and exploited the workers, who had nothing to sell but their labor. As capitalism evolved, the working class would become more miserable, but also larger and more disciplined. Ultimately, capitalism would be overthrown by a revolution of the workers.

Marx and Engels believed that the next stage in social evolution would be socialism, with government taking the form of a dictatorship of the proletariat. A major goal would be to abolish private ownership of the means of production, centralizing all instruments of production in the hands of the state, which they thought would end class conflict. Although they avoided detailed blueprints for socialist policy, Marx and Engels did suggest some appropriate measures. Some of these have been adopted in many industrial countries: free public education for all children; centralization of the means of communication, transport, and credit; heavy graduated income tax; expanded state ownership and management of industry. Others were more radical: abolition of private property in land; abolition of inheritance; and "equal liability of all to labor,"—which could be taken to mean forced labor.

Marx and Engels also urged that the state pursue economic growth to increase the total productive forces as rapidly as possible. Increased productivity and greater equality would ultimately enable the state to wither away, and society would evolve from socialism to communism, a stage in which rewards would go to all persons on the basis of their needs and all would contribute on the basis of their abilities.

In Great Britain and France, there was a close link between socialism and labor unions. In the United States, Samuel Gompers kept the American Federation of Labor focused on collective bargaining rather than political programs for nationalization or income redistribution. Another union activist, Eugene V. Debs, formed the Socialist Party of the United States in 1901. In the 1912 presidential campaign, Debs received 6 percent of the vote—the high point for the party. Their platform called for unemployment insurance, socialized medicine, and protection for labor union rights. Subsequently, direct electoral support for overtly socialist or communist political parties declined. Many perceived them as unpatriotic or disloyal, but an important factor in their decline was that the mainstream political parties adopted many of the measures they had proposed, while the market economy brought improved living conditions to most Americans, except in the 1930's.

Between 1870 and 1914, the most extensive political support for democratic socialism occurred in Germany. There the Social Democratic Party verbally supported Marxist ideas, but remained committed to nonviolent methods and to aiding trade union development. Social Democrats played a significant role in the governments of the short-lived Weimar Republic (1919-1933), but were stigmatized as unpatriotic and were swept aside in Adolf Hitler's political triumph in 1933.

The Social Democrats returned to a significant political role following World War II.

They supported the German version of the welfare state, which included government ownership and operation of some major industries, such as the Volkswagen—the "people's car"; substantial power for labor unions; government-controlled medical care; and extensive transfer payments for the elderly, the unemployed, and the poor.

In Great Britain, the Labour Party was officially formed in 1906. Although much of its activity was devoted to protecting union rights, rather than to more general socialist programs, they were responsive to the ideas of Fabian socialists such as Beatrice and Sidney Webb, H. G. Wells, and George Bernard Shaw. The Labour Party won a majority of British electoral support at the end of World War II. The policies it adopted under the leadership of Clement Atlee and Aneurin Bevan were widely perceived as the essence of democratic socialism.

Modern communism came into existence through the Bolshevik Revolution in Russia in 1917. The new government was established by violent revolution, backed chiefly by discontented soldiers, peasants, and urban workers. It called itself the Union of Soviet Socialist Republics, reflecting its adherence to the stages of Marxist thought. Bolshevik leader Vladimir Lenin moved quickly to establish a dictatorship in which the Communist Party enjoyed a monopoly of power, dominating literature, art, education, and the communications media, as well as the political system. After a brief period in which some elements of free-market capitalism were permitted, Lenin's death in 1924 was followed by the state-dominated economic policies of Joseph Stalin. Stalin's death in 1953 led to some easing of extreme statism, but the official end of communism in the Soviet Union and its political break-up did not come until 1991.

After 1980, the trend in many countries was away from socialist policies. Most dramatic was the end of communist rule in the former Soviet Union and in Eastern Europe. In China, although the Communist Party remained in power, agriculture was decollectivized and private market arrangements were permitted, even encouraged, in many sectors. In Great Britain, Europe, and Latin America, many formerly nationalized industries were privatized.

Applications

A central program of traditional socialism was government ownership and operation of industries and economic activities. Marx argued that private ownership of the means of production was the root of exploitation and class conflict. Some key industrial sectors were initially developed by government—railroads in many countries, for example. In the 1930's and 1940's, many European governments developed or took over the electric power, telephone, and telegraph systems. After the Labour Party's electoral triumph in 1945, the British government nationalized coal mining and iron and steel production. Both France and Germany developed sizeable government-owned automobile production in the 1930's and 1940's. Highways had been primarily government enterprises in most countries for centuries, but the British government even nationalized most commercial highway transport, that is, trucks and buses, in the 1940's. The British Broadcasting System (BBC) has been a government monopoly since the 1920's.

Part of the impulse for government ownership and operation of industry came from the notion that workers were unfairly exploited under private ownership, and that a higher degree of self-government by the workers was desirable. This argument was reinforced, in the case of British coal, by a historical record of frequent, bitter, socially harmful strikes.

In communist countries—the Soviet Union, China, and their satellites—government ownership and management extended into most areas of production and distribution. Government takeovers were carried out by forcible confiscation rather than through buying out the former owners, as was done in democratic countries. In the most extreme communist societies, private production and trade were outlawed and severely punished. An important motive of communist domination of industry was to promote rapid economic growth. The governments channeled large amounts of funds into favored heavy industry to promote expansion of production facilities.

Beginning in 1929, Soviet agriculture was collectivized—that is, peasants were forced into large production units that were nominally cooperatives but were in fact government-dominated enterprises. One motive was to tighten the political control over rural residents by the Communist Party. Another was to hold down consumption by the peasants so that more farm output could be transferred to cities to help the rapid industrial build-up. China imitated this pattern in the early 1950's.

In practice, government ownership and management of potentially private production was often unsuccessful. Government enterprises lacked the incentives to be efficient and innovative. Employees of large government sectors became powerful political pressure groups, able to achieve increases in incomes despite slack discipline. Managers of government enterprises were content to incur losses, counting on government subsidies to bail them out. Socialist theory had neglected the potential conflict of interest between workers and consumers: higher wages and easier working conditions for the former meant higher prices and smaller supplies for the latter. In communist countries, state enterprises were notorious for neglecting the needs and desires of their customers.

Agricultural collectivization was particularly disastrous, leading to low productivity and virtual serfdom for rural workers in China and the Soviet Union. Because socialists traditionally regarded middlemen as unproductive, wholesale and retail trade in those countries were often severely neglected. In communist countries, government monopolies in journalism, the entertainment media, and education were used to suppress individual artistic and intellectual creativity or political dissent.

Traditional socialism condemned the unfairness and inequality of income distribution. Democratic socialist governments such as in Britain developed steep graduated taxes on incomes and wealth, while supplementing low incomes either through transfer payments in cash or through free or subsidized food, housing, and medical services. Communist governments suppressed private payment of property incomes and sometimes, especially in China, rigged wages to remove most inequalities. Full employment was another socialist goal. Democratic countries sought this through monetary and fiscal policies; Communist China simply arranged for abundant jobs in government enterprises, without much concern for cost or productivity.

Many socialists, following Marx and Engels, believed socialism could be a powerful force to achieve economic growth. Communist countries pursued growth through successive five-year plans, determining production and distribution patterns for most products. These patterns restrained the amount of resources directed into consumer goods and services, notably housing, in order to direct more into the growth of industry. Democratic socialist countries attempted to promote growth in the 1940's and 1950's by keeping interest rates low to promote capital expenditures. They adhered to the view of John Maynard Keynes that low interest rates and high investment could be achieved by expanding the quantity of money through the banking system. Such policies tended to generate inflation instead, forcing interest rates up.

In democratic socialist countries, a large part of the economy remained in private ownership and management, although many of these sectors were extensively regulated. In Britain, for example, there were comprehensive programs to regulate land use and the location of industries. Agriculture was subsidized, but farmers were instructed on what they could produce and how. Labor conditions were subject to extensive regulations, such as minimum wage requirements, and compulsory bargaining with labor unions.

Many criticisms have been directed at socialist economic programs. Friedrich Hayek argued that a system where government owned and operated most industry would fail to make effective use of information. Government managers would not have incentives to seek efficiency, avoid wasteful activities, and make innovations. In *The Road to Serfdom* (1944), Hayek argued that government domination of the economy would pose serious threats to individual freedom and political democracy. Subsequent experience has validated Hayek's concerns for efficiency and innovation. But democratic socialist countries such as Great Britain did not develop the totalitarian tendencies against which Hayek and novelist George Orwell warned. At the same time, however, the unlimited economic role sometimes undertaken in the Soviet Union and Communist China contributed to oppressive dictatorship.

Context

In actual experience, both socialist and communist systems displayed their own forms of inequality and injustice. Government domination of the economy gave great power to officials and managers of government enterprise, termed "The New Class" by Milovan Djilas. In communist countries, rural residents remained a depressed and disadvantaged group. In democratic socialist countries, tax policies and transfer payments rewarded idle or unproductive people, while burdening more energetic and imaginative scientists, entrepreneurs, and intellectuals. Western European countries have suffered from high unemployment rates since the mid-1980's. Many critics blamed this problem on undue interventions in the labor market—high minimum wages, labor union support, and generous transfer payments.

On the other hand, despite the fears of critics that the mass of poor people would use political power to seize the wealth of the rich, most industrial countries, including the United States, have been dominated by middle-class concerns. The popularity of President Ronald Reagan arose in part from his resistance to further income redistribution through government.

Socialists were usually dedicated to internationalism—opposing war, colonialism, and imperialism—but socialist economic programs usually lacked a workable system for deriving maximum benefit from international trade and finance. Communist regimes had no method for identifying areas of comparative advantage that would be suitable for export development. Democratic socialist regimes in the 1940's and 1950's relied heavily on direct controls of foreign exchange and international capital flows, controls that inhibited trade. Although socialists at times argued that production should be for use rather than profit, economists argued that the market economy tended to produce the things people wanted, and in an efficient way.

The emerging consensus of the 1990's appeared to be toward democratic governments undertaking economic policies that are less comprehensive and ambitious than traditional socialism, but retained a large economic role for government. This role was likely to include a safety net of labor regulations and transfer payments, and demand management policies to avoid substantial inflation or depression, but largely private ownership and operation of business and industry.

Bibliography

Angresano, James. *Comparative Economics.* Englewood Cliffs, N.J.: Prentice-Hall, 1992. College-level text, requires no prior knowledge of economics. Describes the philosophical bases for socialist and communist systems, and the actual structure and functioning of economic and political systems in Nazi Germany, Sweden, France, the Soviet Union, China, and Hungary.

Bornstein, Morris, ed. *Comparative Economic Systems: Models and Cases.* 7th ed. Burr Ridge, Ill.: Irwin, 1994. Diverse collection of essays, many of them retrospectives inspired by decommunization. Particularly relevant is "Economists' Changing Perceptions of Government," by Anne Krueger.

Gregory, Paul, and Robert C. Stuart. *Comparative Economic Systems.* 4th ed. Boston: Houghton Mifflin, 1992. Clearly written college-level text. Surveys theories of socialism, and provides a wealth of detail about many national economies.

Hayek, Friedrich. *The Road to Serfdom.* Chicago: University of Chicago Press, 1976. Warns of ways in which democratic countries seeking expanded economic roles for government risk the loss of political and civil liberty, as well as economic failures.

Kikeri, Sunita, John Nellis, and Mary Shirley. *Privatization: The Lessons of Experience.* Washington, D.C.: World Bank, 1992. Chapter 2 gives a concise review of experience with government-owned enterprises.

Marx, Karl. *Capital, The Communist Manifesto and Other Writings.* Edited by Max Eastman. New York: Modern Library, 1932. There are many editions of Marx, but this one is particularly well arranged; contains the full text of the Communist Manifesto.

Schumpeter, Joseph. *Capitalism, Socialism, and Democracy.* 3d ed. New York: Harper and Row, 1975. Classic scholarly study of the history of socialist ideas and movements, with a pathbreaking analysis of the way democratic governments tend to handle economic policies. Contains a fine assessment of Marx.

Steele, David Ramsay. *From Marx to Mises: Post-Capitalist Society and the Challenge of Economic Calculation.* LaSalle, Ill.: Open Court, 1992. Reviews the debate on whether a socialist economy can achieve economic efficiency. Scholarly but not pedantic.

Paul B. Trescott

Cross-References

Agriculture Management, p. 41; Anarchism in Marxist Thought, p. 72; Chinese Communism, p. 223; Class Conflict, p. 331; Communist Parties, p. 377; Corporatism, p. 452; Entitlements, p. 610; The Left and the Right, p. 1079; Liberation Theology, p. 1124; Marxism-Leninism, p. 1155; National Economies, p. 1248; Revolutionary Governments, p. 1725; Resource Management, p. 1718; Scientific Humanism, p. 1784; Social Democratic Parties, p. 1846; Totalitarianism, p. 1987.

SPINOZA'S POLITICAL PHILOSOPHY

Field of study: Political philosophy

Spinoza's political philosophy specifies political arrangements for supporting individual lives of reason and maximum freedom, and asserts that personal autonomy requires the political community. Spinoza advocated democracy as the most natural form of government.

Principal terms
> DETERMINISM: belief that all events are determined by prior causes
> FREEDOM: for an entity, freedom is existence or action in accordance with its own nature
> NATURAL RIGHTS: capability coextensive with desire and power
> RATIONALISM: philosophical theory in which the criterion of truth is not sense perception but intellect, exemplified in the deductive geometrical method

Overview

Benedict Spinoza (1632-1677) was a rationalist philosopher who was born and lived in The Netherlands. He was educated in orthodox Judaism; however, his independent views led to his excommunication from the synagogue at the age of twenty-four. He chose to live in stringent economic circumstances, supporting himself by grinding and polishing lenses. He refused a professorship at Heidelberg in 1673, because he did not wish to lose his intellectual independence. He died of consumption, a condition worsened by the dust he inhaled while grinding lenses.

Spinoza's political philosophy and thinking are contained in two books. The more fundamental is the *Tractatus Theologico-Politicus*, published anonymously in 1670. The other is the *Tractatus Politicus*, an unfinished work that was published posthumously in 1677. Both works excited substantial notoriety and opposition. For example, the *Tractatus Theologico-Politicus* was denounced by Amsterdam's Reformed Church Council as "forged by the renegade Jew together with the devil in Hell," and it was banned by the civil government four years after its publication.

The main theme of the *Tractatus Theologico-Politicus* is the political desirability of the freedom to philosophize. Some see the book as a plea for religious liberty. Spinoza wanted a state in which there would be freedom for diverse opinions, provided that they did not lead to seditious acts. The book was deliberately written to disguise the radical nature of its contents from the nonserious reader and to lessen opposition. The preface and the first six chapters discuss religion in the Jewish state, and contend that the Bible concerns obedience, not philosophy. Spinoza saw the Old Testament as providing allegories of intellectual truth, and believed that both primitive peoples and unenlightened moderns needed allegories as well as threats and promises to keep them moral and emotionally secure. Biblical interpretation, a crucial political matter in

Spinoza's time, is analyzed in the next seven chapters. This analysis reinforced his conclusion that the Bible was concerned only with moral behavior. The book's last seven chapters discuss the relationship of religion, philosophy, and the state. Theology, for Spinoza, was a matter of morality; philosophy, a matter of truth. Spinoza wanted religion to be put into what he considered to be its proper limited place.

The *Tractatus Politicus* is concerned largely with analyzing systems of government; three-quarters of the book discusses model constitutions. Spinoza believed that constitutional monarchy was the only acceptable form of monarchy. It should include provision for a citizen army, ownership of all fields and houses by the state, and universal admission to the citizen roll, except for certain classes such as criminals, the mentally ill, and menials. The fundamental laws of the state should be regarded as permanent decrees, not to be contravened. Spinoza argued for two types of aristocracy: one centralized, like Venice; the other decentralized, like The Netherlands. The latter he considered to be better, because it would be less susceptible to revolution or outside aggression. The aristocracy he had in mind was a commercial, not a landed, aristocracy. Every aristocrat would be a lifetime member of the ruling council. The council would be checked in part by the existence of a smaller council within the ruling council, consisting of older men known as syndics, to which citizens could appeal directly. There would be equality among the aristocrats, an emphasis on efficiency, and a large number of members of the aristocratic group. Spinoza's section on the democratic model is incomplete.

Spinoza's political philosophy flowed in part from his metaphysics and his ethics, which had similarities to that of the Stoics, a school founded in 308 B.C.E. The metaphysical and ethical system was worked out in rationalist terms, reflected in Spinoza's *Ethics* (1677) in the use of the geometrical method developed by Rene Descartes. Spinoza argues that God, who is identical with nature, is the only substance that exists. God has neither free will, nor any interest in humans. In Spinoza's view, God has an infinite number of attributes, but we know only two of them—thought and extension. These attributes are merely ways of looking at God, one reality conceived in different ways. God is not distinct from the world, but immanent in it. All finite entities, including human beings, are modes of the one substance, God. Spinoza is opposed to any kind of dualism. Just as he opposes the dualism of God and the created world, Spinoza opposes the dualism of mind and body—for him, mind and body are one and the same thing.

To Spinoza, descriptions like "good" and "bad" are misguided, because all acts occur on a deterministic or necessary basis. No event is unnatural, and Spinoza would have rejected such notions as the existence of natural moral law. God, like human nature, is neither good nor bad; bad is a human term to describe what human beings do not desire. Human beings are integral parts of nature. A human is a complex of desire, driven toward self-preservation as a coherent entity. This self-preservation is not merely biological; it also refers to the essential self. A human's essence is the desire to understand. For rational human beings, the goal is the intellectual love of God or, in modern terminology, personal autonomy. To the extent that humans have understanding, they have freedom. Power, for Spinoza, lies in knowledge, and people can aspire to freedom and happiness through knowledge. Freedom lies in acting, that is, being active, in accordance with one's own nature; bondage lies in being passive in accordance with external factors. Freedom is determination from within. Only nature acts with complete freedom; human beings are mostly passive. Spinoza believed that politics should be based on the reality that human beings have, in fact, little understanding. To achieve personal autonomy, individuals need other individuals, and all can benefit from appropriate political arrangements. Individual freedom requires working for the freedom of others; political liberty is in the self-interest of the seeker of personal autonomy.

Individualism was a basic tenet of Spinoza's thinking, but he also believed that humans are social animals. As social animals, they would achieve harmony with others to the extent that they were subject to the rule of reason. With the goal of personal autonomy, it would be in their self-interest to be in a community of rational people. Spinoza wrote of a social contract in order to clarify relations in a political society; he did not suppose the contract to be an historical event. People wish to have a sovereign power; they obey in society, not because of a contract, but because it is in their self-interest to do so. The state is a device for furthering human interests; it is not at all organic. The state's purpose is to provide for secure living and promote freedom. Spinoza was not concerned with identifying the perfect state; rather, he thought in terms of the best state in the particular circumstances for facilitating the common welfare and realizing individual freedom.

Constitutionalism is an arrangement for protecting the governed; Spinoza did not accept the concept of individual rights vis-à-vis the state. The fact that political power is self-limiting offers another protection: it is in the self-interest of the state to support steps that make the ruled more free and more productive. Nations must establish internal mechanisms to foster stability and to facilitate the development of individual autonomy. One can not rely on the wisdom and self-restraint of rulers and ruled; national law is required. Development of a political society must take into account the fact that most people are neither fully rational nor delinquent; they fall between these extremes. They can be governed by opinion, custom, and ignorance, religion, habit, and awe. Spinoza had little confidence in the political understanding of the unenlightened masses. He believed the majority of people were driven by superstition, fear, and opinion. A free person, he thought, should try to avoid their favors.

Applications

Spinoza was the first modern political philosopher to defend democracy. He did not believe that having a democracy is an end in itself, but he encouraged democracy to facilitate the pursuit of rationality and personal autonomy. The democracy Spinoza defended has widely been described as conservative. A society, in his view, would become democratic when its participating citizens agree to live according to reason and rational law; the emphasis is on the rationality of the community, rather than such issues as majority rule. In Spinoza's view, a democracy would occur when there are laws that specify who is eligible to vote, but age and property restrictions could limit the number eligible to vote and hold office. Democracy is distinguished from aristocracy in that democracy does not provide for the ruling council to perpetuate itself by electing new members. Even in a democracy, citizens would hand over their power to the state, which then had unquestioned dominion.

The rationality that is the hallmark of democracy is intended, in Spinoza's view, to facilitate the development of a society in which people can be free from the bondage of their emotions or passions, defined as confused ideas. Human bondage lies in the failure to surmount, through knowledge, the control of these passions. Spinoza did not deny that freedom also could be found under tyranny, but believed that it was less conducive. Democracy, Spinoza argued, is the most consonant with liberty and the most natural. It would be the best form of government because it is most in harmony with human nature, is not experienced as oppressive, and, by providing equality of status, promotes the stability of the state. Democracy, in his view, has more power to achieve its goals than does an aristocracy, although an aristocracy has more power than a monarchy.

Spinoza did not believe that people in nondemocratic regimes should fight to secure democracy; revolution is not acceptable. Its unacceptability is not on moral but only practical grounds: Spinoza discarded such moral obligations. The reason government must be obeyed is that citizens have put themselves in the power of their sovereigns. Because modes of government were based in the psychology of peoples, Spinoza considered effective revolutions to be impossible. His opinion was that England, even though governed by Puritans as a republic during the 1640's, was a monarchy in all but name.

The objective of democratic society, then, is freedom. In this most natural form of government, citizens of a democracy submitted to the control of the government over their actions, but not over their judgment and reason. Spinoza equated natural right and power, and held that one's view of society should be grounded in the laws of nature. The government had the right, because it had the power, to legislate interference with freedom of thought, and the individual would have no recourse to rights if government suppressed freedom of thinking. The best government, however, would not do so; it would promote free thought, and would be concerned only with acts. Not to grant this freedom would imperil society; citizens would have little faith in one another.

Spinoza's writings express a contrast between a fundamentalist and a rationalist political order, and this contrast raises important questions for the modern world to the extent that democracy encounters a resurgence of religious fundamentalism. A characteristic of fundamentalist orders is that, while they may tolerate freedom of thought, it is not as high a priority as executing what is believed to be the divine instruction. Spinoza viewed the intolerance among typical believers of this time as a function of the nature of the fundamentalist political order. Many in the twentieth century see the church as requiring protection against the state; Spinoza would not have shared this attitude. Spinoza's solution to the conflicting demands of church and state was that religion should be under the control of the state. The state should have undivided authority to legislate concerning external behavior, although the individual should be free to believe whatever he chooses. The rationalist order does not seek to unite citizens in a single goal of following purposes that are believed to be divinely revealed. This emphasis on freedom of thought is supported in the plea for tolerance that is the culmination of the *Tractatus Theologico-Politicus*. It is in the chapter entitled, "That in a free state everyone may think what he pleases, and say what he thinks."

Context

Spinoza's political ideas resulted not only from his metaphysics but also from the political situation in The Netherlands in his day. The country was governed by a bourgeois elite of some two thousand people, a commercial class with a republican form of government. It had become an example to those who valued social mobility, free commerce, and free thought. Yet this cosmopolitanism, represented by Spinoza and by the governing elite, was opposed by the monarchist tendencies and Calvinist and other religious intolerance of the masses. Politics was intertwined with religion. Spinoza was a close friend of many in the governing liberal republican elite.

Spinoza's political philosophy has not been of major influence, although it was known to writers such as David Hume, John Locke, and Jean Jacques Rousseau. Spinoza's metaphysics was relatively little known until the eighteenth century. Containing the essence of deism, Spinoza's metaphysics was influential during the Enlightenment. In the twentieth century, it has received less notice than that of his contemporary Thomas Hobbes, with whose views Spinoza's ideas usually are contrasted and compared.

Although Spinoza has been called the last of the medievels, he stands as a formative agent in the creation of the modern outlook. Spinoza lived during a time of transition toward an emphasis on science, the emergence of the secular nation-state, the development of individualism, and the shift away from a united Christendom. Spinoza's metaphysics created a naturalistic ethics and provided a throughgoing basis for the study of science. His writings anticipated elements later found in writers such as Adam Smith and Jeremy Bentham. His political theory addresses questions of significance for twentieth century politics, especially the question of how to reconcile the conflicting demands of individual freedom and social harmony.

Despite Spinoza's achievements in such areas as metaphysics and political philosophy, his major interest was in developing an ethical theory for achieving personal autonomy. An aim of his political thinking was to show how political activity can be structured and understood to provide invaluable benefits for the self and others. For him, the state is a positive and he sees no need for its limitation. His political theory merges individual freedom and the community of human beings.

Bibliography

Blom, Hans W. "The Moral and Political Philosophy of Spinoza." In *The Renaissance and Seventeenth-Century Rationalism*, edited by G. H. R. Parkinson. London: Routledge, 1993. Includes a useful account of the views of other seventeenth century Dutch political thinkers.

Feuer, Lewis Samuel. *Spinoza and the Rise of Liberalism*. Boston, Mass.: Beacon, 1964. Lively description of Spinoza's views.

McShea, Robert J. *The Political Philosophy of Spinoza*. New York: Columbia University Press, 1968. One of the better accounts of Spinoza's political philosophy.

Rosen, Stanley. "Benedict Spinoza." In *History of Political Philosophy*, edited by Leo Strauss and Joseph Cropsey. Chicago, Ill.: University of Chicago Press, 1987. Scholarly, if somewhat obtuse, description of Spinoza's political thought.

Scruton, Roger. *Spinoza*. New York: Oxford University Press, 1986. Succinct, reliable, clear account of the range of Spinoza's philosophy, including his metaphysics and ethics.

Spinoza, Benedictus de. *The Political Works*. Translated by A. G. Wernham. Oxford, England: Clarendon Press, 1958. Includes translations of *Tractatus Theologico-Politicus* and of *Tractatus Politicus*.

Strauss, Leo. *Persecution and the Art of Writing*. Glencoe, Ill.: Free Press, 1952. Contains an excellent analysis of Spinoza's thought, especially the exoteric nature of Spinoza's writing.

David John Farmer

Cross-References

Aristocracy, Oligarchy, and Plutocracy, p. 78; Hobbes's Political Philosophy, p. 836; Individual Versus State Rights, p. 910; Liberalism, p. 1118; Locke's Political Philosophy, p. 1142; Machiavelli's Political Philosophy, p. 1148; Mill's Political Philosophy, p. 1204; Political Philosophy, p. 1505; Republicanism, p. 1706; Right of Revolution, p. 1744; The Social Contract, p. 1827; The State, p. 1878; Stoic Political Philosophy, p. 1904.

THE STATE

Field of study: Political philosophy

As the fundamental building block of the international system, the state is the highest expression of national sovereignty into which peoples and territories are organized and ruled by governments.

Principal terms

EQUALITY: characteristic of sovereign statehood by which each state is treated as a legal equal to other states

INDEPENDENCE: characteristic of sovereign statehood by which states are able to act as autonomous agents without seeking permission from any higher authority

IRREDENTISM: claim by one country to territory lying under the sovereign jurisdiction of a neighboring country, based on the nationality or ethnic ties of the local population to the claimant nation

NATIONALISM: devotion to one's nation and an ideology stressing the unity of a people based on their cultural, linguistic, historical, religious, or ethnic similarity

PEACE OF WESTPHALIA: treaties following the Thirty Years War, which marked the commencement of the modern state system

SELF-DETERMINATION: the right of a people to achieve sovereignty and independence

SEPARATISM: desire of a portion of a country's population to achieve sovereign independence from an existing country, often because of ethnic divisions

SOVEREIGNTY: characteristic of states that accords them the highest legal authority within their own territories and in the conduct of foreign relations

Overview

The idea of the state goes back to antiquity. Wherever individuals, families, tribes, or clans have coalesced to form larger, more self-sufficient, stable, and sedentary communities, governmental institutions were formed to make, enforce, and interpret law and regulate social, political, and economic interaction. States became the means by which private conflicts and feuds could be resolved without resort to vigilante justice. To Aristotle, the polis, which might be defined as a city-state, was the centerpiece of the active human life, and not to live the life of a citizen in common with other citizens was less than human. Political life even established the means to pursue the philosophic life, which Aristotle believed was the best life. The political nature of man, then, gave rise to states.

The city-state, however, was rapidly eclipsed by the Alexandrian and Roman

Empires, at least as the highest expression of human organization. As city-states could be eclipsed, however, so could empires fall, and the decline and fall of the Roman Empire created space once again for feudal estates and city-states. Gradually larger national states emerged from the monarchical courts that had extended their sway over vassal states.

Quarrels between national secular leaders and the church came and went throughout the Middle Ages and into the Renaissance. The emergence of the Reformation, led by such eminent figures as Martin Luther in Germany, John Calvin in Geneva, and King Henry VIII in England, challenged the concept of ultimate church authority. Individual princes and kings, often in league with Protestant religious reformers, defied the Roman Catholic church and its secular authority. In most of these states, the national church became subordinate to the state. In time, these religious disputes became exceptionally violent and intrusive, culminating in the bloody Thirty Years War that wracked Europe in the early part of the seventeenth century. This war was brought to an end by the Peace of Westphalia, which articulated the fundamental principles of a new international order in which the territorial state, usually represented by a prince or monarch, would be the sole and highest source of sovereignty.

Following from the theory of sovereignty that had been articulated by Jean Bodin, the French jurist and philosopher, the Peace of Westphalia demarked the boundaries of states, identified their territories, and gave them exclusive control over the population in those territories. The sovereign ruler would determine the religion of the state as well as its domestic legislation and foreign policy. All of this was to be free from external interference. States, by implication, were to be politically independent and equal. No other authority could dictate to the government of a state what its domestic or foreign policy would be, nor was a state obligated to sign treaties or obey any law that it did not explicitly agree to be bound by. The government of a state could agree voluntarily to abide by customs or treaties, but it could not be forced, as a sovereign entity, to abide by rules made by other states without its consent. When governments chose to limit their behavior by custom or treaty, the expectation was that they would honor such commitments and obligations.

The Westphalian system was, in effect, a European system of states. Implicit in this system was the notion that the original members of the state system were signatories of the Westphalian treaties. To join this elite club of nations, any new state would need to gain the recognition of existing states. This European system became a global one with the colonial expansion of the European states in the seventeenth and eighteenth centuries. The main implications of the Westphalian state system continue to be relevant in twentieth century international affairs.

The contemporary legal definition of the state is rooted in the principles of sovereignty enunciated in the Peace of Westphalia. A state possesses a government that exercises sovereign control, which is recognized by other states, over a territory and a population. States are presumed to be independent, equal, and capable of engaging in international acts such as the sending and receiving of diplomats, the promulgation and ratification of treaties, and the declaration and prosecution of war.

These capacities flow from the concept of the rights of states, which include rights to existence and self-defense, as well as to domestic and external independence and equality. If states are to claim such rights in respect to one another, there are duties and obligations that they must recognize if the international system is to function. First, they must recognize that other states possess similar rights, so each state must respect the sovereignty, territorial integrity, and independence of other states. States must refrain from illegal intervention or fomentation of civil strife in another state's territory, ensure that events on their own territory do not threaten international peace and security, and abide by treaties and agreements to which they have agreed.

The theory of the state and its reality are two different things. The very idea of having many sovereign states contains contradictory elements. Each state, in seeking its own interests, runs into the contrary interests of other states. A world of many sovereigns is potentially a dangerous world where one's sovereignty may only extend as far as the range and superiority of one's artillery. Equally problematic are the ideas of political independence and equality. These are, in a sense, legal fictions, because states have always been politically dependent or interdependent, and great physical and material inequalities have always existed among them. In terms of international law, at least, states are considered independent and equal agents. As such they have a right under international law to self-defense.

Another major problem with the notion of the state is its discontinuity with that of the nation. A nation is a group of people who share common ethnic, cultural, historical, linguistic, and often religious ties, and who view themselves as being distinct from other peoples. Many nations, however, are not self-governing states. Examples include the Kurds of the Middle East, the Basques of Spain, and the South Mollucans and Timorese of Indonesia—all of whom might be called nonstate nations. There are equally many states whose population shares no common sense of nationhood. Examples of this include many of the modern states of Africa, where from a dozen to hundreds of ethnonationalistic affiliations are congregated under the jurisdiction of a single government. In such states, loyalties to the clan or tribe are often much more intense than those to the state or country as a whole. Such discontinuities between the state and the nation are the source of much contemporary international conflict.

State-building, that is, the establishment of governments recognized by other states as sovereign, is far easier than the process of nation-building, which is typically the work of centuries. National sentiments are not easily created overnight. They are the work of common cultural contact, religious similarity, linguistic unity, and shared history. When peoples share these feelings intensely, but do not have a recognized government to further their national ties and aspirations, they are likely to seek them through whatever means possible, including violence. On the other side of the coin, when a state, marked by extreme national and ethnic pluralism seeks to build a new sense of nationhood among such disparate elements, success cannot be expected in the short run. Such groups might in time be assimilated into an eclectic or overarching system of values, as has happened in a diverse country like the United States, but overnight success in generating an enthusiastic new national feeling cannot usually be expected. In multiethnic states, such unity can only be forged over long periods of time, and the experience of several nations in the late twentieth century, such as the former Soviet Union and Yugoslavia, suggests that successes are often more apparent than real.

Applications

Operationally speaking, the state system faces a number of continuing and, in some cases, new challenges. As the highest expressions of political order in international relations, states are both the makers and breakers of international law. They are the policemen and the criminals. They are the aggressors and the peacemakers. The state system, lacking an effective and reliable central enforcement mechanism, has strong tendencies toward anarchy and disorder. There being no higher authority than states, it is up to them to coordinate their affairs through international organizations, law, and diplomacy in order to achieve a more orderly and stable world. On a practical level, these efforts are more coordinative than subordinative in character. Much of the conflict that existed in the international arena in the 1990's was not between existing states, but was conflict within existing states between opposing ethnic communities. Operationally speaking, many states are threatened by the ethnonationalistic and separatist claims of contending groups. Even if nonstate-nations pose a threat to the existence of particular states and complicate international politics, they do not threaten the existence of the state system as such.

In the Middle East, for instance, two prominent nonstate-nations have been active players in high-level disputes. The Palestine Liberation Organization (PLO), which finally achieved recognition from Israel in 1993, long fought for Palestinian rights without the benefit of widespread recognition or effective control over territory. Recognition of its status, and attainment of limited self-rule in the Gaza Strip and Jericho, marked major strides toward peace. Just as nonrecognition of nonstate-nations can give rise to long-term conflicts, so can their recognition be central to the resolution of regional conflict. This, at least, seems to be the lesson of the Middle East dispute. The Kurds residing in Iraq, Iran, Turkey, and Syria represent another nonstate-nation whose predicament was highly visible in the aftermath of the 1991 Persian Gulf War, as hundreds of thousands of Kurds fled from Iraq into Turkey and Iran. Western intervention on their behalf eventually allowed the Kurds to return in relative safety, but the long-term issue of Kurdish sovereignty was not satisfactorily resolved in the view of the Kurds, and thus is likely to remain a source of ongoing tension in the region.

Apart from nonstate-nations, which in the final analysis seek recognition as states, multinational corporations also present challenges to state sovereignty. Such entities possess great wealth that can often overwhelm the economies of small states that need the capital and investment corporations offer. When a state is penetrated by powerful economic forces beyond its control, its independence is compromised and its effective sovereignty threatened. States, however, retain the right to regulate and nationalize foreign investment. Even economically weak states may assert their sovereign legal control over foreign investment and corporate activity. Corporations may adroitly avoid such regulation at times, but ultimately governments establish the terms by which corporations are engaged in their local economy. Corporate entities are unlikely, then, to supplant states as the ultimate political units of organization.

The functioning of the state system, however, remains problematic. States constitute the highest international authorities without effective centralized mechanisms for maintenance of peace and resolution of conflicts. Thus the system is marked by strong tendencies toward anarchy, which can only be resisted by cooperation and coordinated action by the most powerful states. Order, in such a system, does not occur spontaneously, and it is principally the powerful states that must seek to maintain it. The process of coordination involves diplomatic accommodation, the promulgation and observance of international law, and the establishment and activity of international organizations, such as the United Nations. All of these phenomena represent efforts by states to regulate and limit their interactions, facilitate communication, promote cooperation, and resolve potential conflicts. Through these means, governments daily resolve many disputes. Only a small percentage of them reach the stage of dangerous conflict or war. Even when wars occur, they are governed by the international laws of war, and, under the United National Charter, mechanisms exist to marshal international opposition to aggressor states. All of this is contingent on powerful states' willingness to oppose and punish aggression and to maintain global order.

Context

The continued survival of the state system rests on its ability to maximize diplomatic contact, to resolve potential disputes, and to coordinate economic interaction. In the twentieth century, the sovereignty of states was assaulted by a variety of nonstate actors and eroded by growing economic interdependence. Still, states persisted and the state system showed no immediate signs of either disappearing or rapidly transforming into a centralized world government. Many proponents of the latter believe that sovereignty is a fiction, that states are dangerous anachronisms, and that the state system's tendency to anarchy and war must be counteracted by replacing the state with, or transforming it by, a centralized system of global institutions or a world government capable of ensuring peace. The vision of the future, however, rests on the assumption that states will voluntarily revoke their sovereignty, or that they are so weak as to be vulnerable to reorganization. These assumptions are dubious, and the behavior of states and nations suggests that proponents of world government are unlikely to achieve that outcome in the twentieth century.

The resurgence and growth of nationalistic attitudes in the 1990's suggests that the state system will survive for the foreseeable future. Still, states must continue to demonstrate that they are able to promote economic prosperity, resolve disputes, and promote stability. There is ample evidence to suggest that they can do this, but international relations remain an arena of continuing conflicts of interest. Mechanisms of coordination devised to ameliorate disputes cannot eradicate them. What exists in the 1990's is an imperfect, decentralized state system, marked by cooperation and contention. These elements of international relations persist in ways that cast doubt on the possibility of attaining an effective world government in which states cease to exist as sovereign lords of international politics and the mechanisms through which people order their domestic relations.

Bibliography

Akzin, Benjamin. *State and Nation*. London: Hutchinson University Library, 1964. Brief readable introduction to the terminological distinctions, literature, and theory of nations, states, and nationalism. Examines the varieties of nations, single and multiple ethnic states, integrationist and pluralist states, secessionist questions, and the problem of nationalism in developing countries.

Cobban, Alfred. *The Nation State and National Self-determination*. New York: Thomas Y. Crowell, 1969. Classic history and analysis of the rise of nationalism in Europe and the role of the great powers in the affairs of smaller states.

Grotius, Hugo. *The Law of War and Peace*. Translated by F. W. Kelsey. Indianapolis: Bobbs-Merrill, 1925. Classic treatise by a seventeenth century Dutch jurist and philosopher, who is considered the father of international law examines the role of the state and the customary international law that states created to regulate their interrelations and maintain order.

Krasner, Stephen D. *Defending the National Interest: Raw Materials Investments and U.S. Foreign Policy*. Princeton, N.J.: Princeton University Press, 1978. Highly theoretical work asserts a statist approach in studying economic relations of nations. It suggests that corporate and other private interests are substantially shaped by the state, that is, by governments rather than the other way around.

Morgenthau, Hans. *Politics Among Nations: The Struggle for Power and Peace*. 6th ed. Revised by Kenneth W. Thompson. New York: Alfred Knopf, 1985. This classic work on international relations, still a standard in the field, is a treatise on the functions of the nation-state system, the role of states in their interrelations, and a critique of alternative systems of international organization, including world government. Contains a classic treatment on the idea of state sovereignty.

Tucker, Robert. *The Inequality of Nations*. New York: Basic Books, 1977. Examines the discontinuity of power among and between nation-states, making a case for the responsible use of power by those states capable of maintaining global order and stability.

von Glahn, Gerhard. *Law Among Nations: An Introduction to Public International Law*. 6th ed. New York: Macmillan, 1992. This superb treatment of international law contains a very concise description of the rights and duties of states and detailed discussion of both the political and legal interaction of states in the international legal arena.

Robert F. Gorman

Cross-References

Diplomacy and International Negotiation, p. 552; Indigenous Peoples' Governments, p. 903; Intergovernmental Relations, p. 942; International Law, p. 956; International Relations, p. 969; Jurisprudence, p. 1019; The Nation-State, p. 1241; Nationalism, p. 1268; Ochlocracy, p. 1338; Patriotism, p. 1384; Political Pragmatism, p. 1519; Secessionism, p. 1790; Supranational Government Institutions, p. 1922; United Nations, p. 2045; War, p. 2129; World Political Organization, p. 2186.

STATE AND LOCAL GOVERNMENT

Field of study: Local and regional government

Governing the United States is complex; its fifty state governments and more than 80,000 local governments have complex interrelationships with one another to provide many of the basic services to citizens.

Principal terms

DILLON'S RULE: legal precept holding that local governments are "creatures of the state" and exercise only such powers as have been granted to them by the state constitution or legislature

FEDERALISM: form of government in which a central government and subunit governments (states, provinces) have a separate basis of authority described in a written constitution

GENERAL REVENUE SHARING: federal aid to states and cities that does not contain as many restrictions as categorical grant programs do

HOME RULE: provision, partly eroding Dillon's Rule, made in most state constitutions to give a measure of autonomy to various local governments in America

INTERGOVERNMENTAL RELATIONS: interrelationships among the federal, state, and local governments, including such pairings as federal-state, federal-local, state-local, state-state, and local-local

LOCAL GOVERNMENTS: subunits of the states: special districts, counties, and municipalities, which may include cities, towns, villages, and townships

Overview

The United States contains more than 83,000 different governments. These include one national government in Washington, D.C., fifty state governments, more than 3,000 county governments in the various states, more than 19,000 municipalities, and some 16,000 townships. In the United States there are also nearly 15,000 school districts and almost 30,000 special districts of various kinds, making up a very complex pattern of governments.

These different units of government overlap; in some parts of the country a citizen may be within an area served by as many as a dozen different governments. For example, a citizen in the Chicago area is governed by the federal government, the Illinois state government, the Chicago city government, the Cook County government, and an additional dozen or so special districts covering everything from mosquito abatement to parks, zoning, and sewage treatment districts. The existence of so many different governmental units, many of which have a separate taxing authority, leads to a complex situation in which accountability is difficult to determine and the costs of government are frequently high.

All state and local governments are part of the American federal system, but they play different roles. Federalism is the guiding principle behind the relationship between the national government in Washington and each of the fifty state governments. These relationships are described in the U.S. Constitution, in which the powers of Congress are described in Article 1, section 8 of the Constitution. States are protected by the Tenth Amendment, which says: "The powers not delegated to the United States by the Constitution, nor prohibited by it to the States, are reserved to the States respectively, or to the people." After a list of specific powers delegated to the national government (coin money, make roads, post office, and the like) are implied powers: In Article 1, section 8 the last paragraph gives the national government, through the Congress, the power to make laws that are "necessary and proper" to carry into effect the duties given in the list. This slight passage of vague language has led to the great expansion of the federal government, particularly in the twentieth century. Still, the states' many powers are protected by the federalist system.

The same cannot be said for the relationships of local governments to their state governments. These relationships are a unitary, rather than a federal, political system. Under a unitary system, all sovereign power (or critical legal authority) belongs to the state governments, and local governments only have as much power as the state governments grant to them. Within a federal system, state governments have a general police power based on the notion that their reserved powers are quite broad and that state governments can do anything that is not prohibited to them by either the U.S. Constitution or their respective state constitutions. Local governments, however, have only as much power as the states grant to them. This principle exists in a legal precept known as Dillon's Rule, a summary of constitutional law made by John Dillon, a state court judge in the late nineteenth century. Dillon's Rule holds that:

> It is a general and undisputed proposition of law that a municipal corporation possesses and can exercise the following powers, and no others. First, those granted in express words; second, those necessarily or fairly implied in or incident to the powers expressly granted; third, those essential to the accomplishment of the declared objects and purposes of the corporation—not simply convenient, but indispensable. Any fair, reasonable, substantial doubt concerning the existence of power is received by the courts against the corporation, and the power is denied.

Under Dillon's Rule then, all local governments may only exercise as much power as state governments give them. Supreme Court Justice Pierce Butler was even more blunt when he held in *Trenton v. New Jersey* (1923): "In the absence of state constitutional provisions safeguarding it to them, municipalities have no inherent right of self-government which is beyond the legislative control of the state."

These conclusions from early in the twentieth century, however, have been modified by the development of the home rule concept. Local governments may gain some separate autonomy if such authority is granted to them under the state constitution. Home rule provisions give municipalities a broader range of self-governing authority. Generally, the legislature can only deal with such municipalities through general laws that are uniform for all cities in the state. This is significant because many states continue to pass legislation that affects municipalities and counties individually. Home rule normally applies to municipalities—whether cities, towns, or villages—but some home rule provisions are also available for the protection of counties.

The states are the oldest subunits in the American system, with the original thirteen states being older than the national government itself. The second oldest units of government are counties, which were inherited from Britain. Counties exist in all the American states except for certain New England states, such as Connecticut and Rhode Island. In all other states, counties are a territorial or geographical unit performing certain basic, but critical, functions, such as registering the deeds to property, setting a valuation of property for property tax purposes, and providing law enforcement through a sheriff. In those New England states that have no or very weak county structures, these county functions are performed by town governments, which often cover wide geographical areas, much the way counties do in other states.

Counties divide up in a patchwork the entire land area of a state, but municipalities typically do not and large geographical areas lie outside any municipality. State laws governing municipalities are included in a general state chartering act providing for chartered or incorporated municipalities, although the variation is quite great among the states.

Counties tend to be units of the state government and therefore often do not have charters. Virtually all municipalities have some type of constitution-like document called a charter, which is why they may be considered "incorporated." These charters provide whatever legal authority the municipalities have. In some cases, these charters give municipalities a broader range of authority than the counties have, allowing them to pass ordinances—a power often denied to counties.

All counties and municipalities are regarded as general-purpose governments and are given a fairly broad range of authority. In addition to these general-purpose governments, there are a number of single-purpose local governments or districts. Most of these are school districts, reflecting the strong role localities have in the control of primary and secondary education. At one time, there were more than 100,000 school districts in the United States, a number that has fallen to about 15,000 as the result of the school consolidation efforts that began in the 1940's. With the decline in the number of school districts has come a rise of other kinds of single-purpose districts, governing the administration of parks, sewers, water, air pollution, mosquito abatement, industrial development, and zoning. Generally, elected officials who receive little or no pay, but often a limited taxing authority, run these districts. A frequent complaint is that the cost of these districts is too high, but the complexity of these issues leads to a loss of public interest. Many reformers recommend the consolidation of these districts. Once created, however, these districts take on a life of their own. It has proven very difficult to consolidate these or any other single-purpose districts, with the exception of some school districts.

Some states can form voluntary agreements with other states (just as local governments can cooperate with other local governments) to deal with common problems.

Congress has supported these efforts, but it is difficult for such cooperation to take place between separate governments, often jealous protectors of their domains.

Applications

All local governments are creatures of the state unless they are protected by a home rule provision in the state constitution. Without a provision, state legislatures can pass rules affecting a local government as they see fit. State legislatures could, for example, consolidate single-purpose districts at will, but political realities make this difficult. Be they counties, municipalities, or special districts, all local governments resist consolidation. They have their own elected officials, political structures, and constituencies—all of which are reluctant to lose their own identities. Power holders especially are reluctant to give up local autonomy.

San Francisco, California, is unusual in combining city and county governments. Other movements toward consolidation have begun among Minneapolis-St. Paul and Bloomington, Minnesota; Indianapolis and Marion County, Indiana; Nashville and Davidson County, Tennessee; and Miami and Dade County, Florida. This short list of consolidated governments, however, nearly exhausts the total number in the United States. Major cities are typically surrounded by incorporated smaller suburban communities that are reluctant to consolidate with the central city. Political scientists may make theoretical arguments for consolidation, but politicians and citizens resist it, fearing higher taxation and involvement in the social problems of the central cities.

The problems of central cities have grown so large and the problems of consolidation are so great that attempts have been made to sidestep the thorny consolidation issue by seeking federal or state funding to provide additional help for the core cities. One new trait of local government in the last half of the twentieth century has been the development of federal government programs of direct aid to cities. This new federal-local government relationship has complicated intergovernmental relations, even more as the result of new federal funding to the states. In many cases, large portions of state budgets come from the federal government. Much of this funding is passed on to cities that also have the ability to apply for federal funds directly.

Starting in the 1960's, the federal government began to assist state government by providing federal funds directly to the cities. During the 1960's and 1970's, the federal government found it possible to raise more revenue through the income tax than the states could raise through the sales tax or local governments could through their heavy property tax. Given the relative ease of tax collection on the federal level, a concept known as general revenue sharing was introduced to provide funding to the states and then later directly to the cities. This extra federal funding lasted approximately a decade. The federal government soon found its growing deficit made it difficult to come up with funds for state and local governments. During the 1980's, the federal government was so short on cash that its aid to cities and states was reduced. With the decline in federal funding, the states have in some cases attempted to compensate the cities for the loss of federal funds. The states have similarly faced a loss of federal funding, however, and have found it difficult to raise taxes to offset the loss of federal funds and to provide additional aid to cities, towns, and counties.

This situation is complicated by the fact that both federal and state governments pass laws that require local governments to perform certain duties, known as "mandates." When the notion of mandates to local governments was first devised, the higher governmental levels, whether federal or state, would accompany their mandates with offers of financial aid to put the mandates into effect. From the start, there were complaints from the local governments that the mandates were more expensive than the amount of aid provided to fulfill them. As the federal government has found it increasingly difficult to maintain its earlier financial largesse to the states and cities, this extra source of aid has declined. Still, the mandates remain in effect and local governments have found it increasingly difficult to be able to pay for the mandates. All of this is further complicated by the fact that a resistance to increased taxation appears to be increasingly widespread. In California, Massachusetts, and Michigan, taxpayers' revolts have occurred that have led to limitations on the taxing powers of state and local governments. Even outside these states, resistance to new taxes is commonplace, and it has proven difficult for local governments to raise sufficient sums of money to replace that which has been lost by the decline in federal and state funding.

Context

The United States does not have a single government, but rather more than eighty thousand governments of various kinds. While this system of federalism has advantages—it allows for diversity and limits centralized power—it also has a cost in the form of higher governmental expenditures and a loss of accountability as it becomes difficult for voters to know whom to hold accountable.

Federalism does generally allow citizens to take action in their local areas to try to correct problems. The fact that it is possible to organize small local efforts to change the government in some respect is said to generate a kind of individualism that strengthens the country. In any event, the complex system of federal, state, and local governments has existed for more than two hundred years and is likely to continue in the future.

Bibliography

Anton, Thomas. *American Federalism and Public Policy: How the System Works*. New York: Random House, 1989. Argues that federalism influences how public policy is made on the national and state level.

Dye, Thomas R. *American Federalism: Competition Among Governments*. Lexington, Mass.: Lexington Books, 1990. Argues that federalism promotes competition among states and cities for businesses.

Elazar, Daniel J. *American Federalism: A View from the States*. 3d ed. New York: Harper & Row, 1984. Classic for its thesis that America's subcultures may be categorized under such headings as the traditionalistic, individualistic, and moralistic.

Herson, Lawrence, and John Bolland. *The Urban Web: Politics, Policy and Theory*.

Chicago: Nelson-Hall, 1990. Especially well-written summary of conventional arguments about intergovernmental relations.

Nice, David C. *Federalism: The Politics of Intergovernmental Relations*. New York: St. Martin's, 1987. Solid account of basic intergovernmental relations in the United States. Nice accepts intergovernmental complexity as the norm and does not argue for the special value of federalism as Dye and Elazar do.

O'Toole, Lawrence, Jr., ed. *American Intergovernmental Relations: Foundations, Perspectives, and Issues*. 2d ed. Washington, D.C.: CQ Press, 1993. Collection of recent and classic articles on intergovernmental relations.

Ross, Bernard, Myron Levine, and Murray Stedman. *Urban Politics: Power in Metropolitan America*. Itasca, Ill.: F. E. Peacock, 1991. Discusses critical power relationships in America's metropolitan government.

Wright, Deil S. *Understanding Intergovernmental Relations*. 3d ed. Pacific Grove, Calif.: Brooks/Cole, 1988. One of the most detailed classifications of the concepts governing intergovernmental relations in the United States.

Richard L. Wilson

Cross-References

City Government in the United States, p. 266; The Constitution of the United States, p. 425; County Government, p. 458; Courts: State and Local, p. 465; Disaster Relief in the United States, p. 558; Education Management, p. 565; Federal Mandates, p. 662; Fire Protection, p. 700; Grants-in-Aid, p. 791; Intergovernmental Relations, p. 942; Legislative Functions of Government, p. 1098; Local Governments, p. 1136; Rural Community Government, p. 1763; State Government, p. 1891; Urban Governments, p. 2052.

STATE GOVERNMENT

Field of study: Local and regional government

States govern the citizens of legally defined geographical areas within the United States through constitutional frameworks consisting of three branches of government: the legislative, the executive, and the judicial.

Principal terms

BICAMERAL LEGISLATURE: lawmaking body composed of two chambers of elected representatives

JUDICIAL REVIEW: power of courts to declare the actions of government unconstitutional

LINE-ITEM VETO: power of a governor to strike out portions or sections of an appropriation bill

PLURAL EXECUTIVE: structure for multiple popularly elected officials' implementing laws

STATE CONSTITUTION: document describing the general framework of state government

UNICAMERAL LEGISLATURE: lawmaking body composed of one chamber of elected representatives

Overview

The political system of the United States of America consists of one national government and fifty state governments. Citizens of the original thirteen states ratified the U.S. Constitution, creating the national government; it went into effect March 4, 1789. Since then, thirty-seven additional states have been admitted to the union under Article 4, section 3 of the Constitution. Vermont became the fourteenth state when it was admitted in 1791. Alaska and Hawaii were the last two states to be granted admission, both in 1959. Following the precedent established by the original thirteen states, territories seeking statehood are required to have a written constitution. This document must be approved by the individuals residing within the territory in question and then submitted to the national government for approval according to procedures developed by Congress. Constitutions are the fundamental organizational device of state governments.

State constitutions describe the structure, institutions, and processes of state governments. They also delineate powers and responsibilities, and place limits on the use of power, to protect citizens from unreasonable governmental action. No two states have identical constitutions, although a few have borrowed passages from other states in drafting their constitutions. Unlike the U.S. Constitution, which is noted for its simplicity and elegance, state constitutions are notoriously long, detailed, and amended. To understand the governing system of any particular state completely one should consult the constitution and other sources appropriate for that state. State constitutions do share a number of common characteristics, making it possible to outline some general conclusions about the organization of state governments. Among the state constitutions, two important constitutional doctrines stand out: separation of powers, and checks and balances.

All state constitutions adhere to the principle of separation of powers, as does the U.S. Constitution. Separation of powers is a distribution of distinct governmental responsibilities among three branches of government: the legislative, the executive, and the judicial. Each branch serves a unique function, with officials selected by different procedures to ensure political independence. The centerpiece of state government is the legislative branch. State legislatures have the power to determine public policy through the enactment of laws. Fearful of tyrannical rule by a single chief executive, the states generally adopted a governmental model built around a strong elected legislature. This approach is designed to promote the interests of citizens in the lawmaking actions of government.

All states feature a bicameral legislature, with the exception of Nebraska, which has a unicameral legislature. Bicameral legislatures are composed of upper chambers, called senates in virtually all states, and lower chambers, most commonly referred to as houses of representatives, or "houses" for short. Senates, which range between thirty and fifty members, tend to be much smaller than their corresponding lower chambers. A majority of states have houses with more than one hundred members each. Both senators and representatives are elected in legislative districts that are apportioned according to population size. State senators typically serve four-year terms, while a two-year term is the norm for a state's lower chamber. A few states restrict the number of terms a legislator may serve.

Except for Nebraska, the leadership positions in state legislative chambers are divided among political parties, with the majority group controlling the top leadership positions and the committee systems. Leaders are needed to oversee and conduct the daily affairs of a chamber. After a bill is introduced, committees are responsible for recommending or not recommending pending legislation. Committees correspond to the general functional responsibilities of state government, ranging from taxation to education. It is within committees that most legislative work is undertaken. By serving on committee, legislators develop expertise in selected policy areas of state government. For a bill to become a law it usually must survive house and senate committees and then receive the support of a majority of members in both chambers. Most legislative proposals die in committee, though many states have procedures for dislodging bills.

The executive branch has responsibility for ensuring that the will of the legislative branch is carried out. This is done through the enforcement and implementation of state laws. The executive branch is the administrative arm of state government. The structure of the executive branch is a hierarchical chain of command composed of numerous organizations and political leaders. How rigid the chain of command is depends on the state. Sitting at the top is a state's chief executive officer, the governor. Governors are expected to manage and coordinate the daily activities of state government. In most states governors are popularly elected for a four-year term, although some governors have a two-year term. Many states place restrictions on the number of terms a governor may serve consecutively, with the most common being a maximum of two terms.

Below the state governor on the executive chain of command there are two major sets of political leaders. These are distinguishable by their method of selection: those appointed by the governor (subject to legislative confirmation or approval in many instances), and those elected by voters. Appointed officials generally serve at the pleasure of the governor. Elected officials enjoy an independent source of power, voter support, making it more difficult for a governor to exert direct control over their actions. Most states have multiple elected officials, forming a pluralistic executive structure that is less hierarchical.

The number and type of elected and appointed public officials vary considerably from one state to the next. Most but not all states have elected lieutenant governors. The lieutenant governor presides over the state senate in some states and may be empowered to vote in case of a tie. Candidates for lieutenant governor are permitted to run for office independently of the governor in several states and therefore may be a member of a different political party. Below the lieutenant governor are a number of important leadership positions corresponding to the many functional activities of government. These leadership positions represent the major administrative areas of state government, such as transportation, welfare, and health. The agencies that these leaders represent are entrusted to carry out the wishes of the legislative branch under the guidance of the governor.

The third branch of state government is the judiciary. State courts are responsible for the application and interpretation of laws. State courts are usually called upon to apply criminal and civil law, as enacted by the legislative branch and enforced by the executive branch, to regulate behavior and resolve conflicts. In a much smaller number of cases, state courts, especially the highest courts, are asked to interpret laws and evaluate the actions of government officials in terms of constitutional consistency. A state court may find an action to be inconsistent with either the state constitution or U.S. Constitution. This is the power of judicial review.

State court systems follow no singular pattern. Historically, states adopted decentralized and fragmented court systems, establishing numerous lower courts, each having limited legal jurisdiction and covering a small geographical area. The result was an elaborate patchwork of courts, which persists in many states today. In the twentieth century, selected states took steps to reform their court systems by creating more unified and consolidated structures. All states employ a hierarchical court structure with most having a single court, usually called the supreme court, at the top. Below the supreme court there may be intermediate appeals courts, courts of general jurisdiction, and courts of limited jurisdiction. Cases generally flow in the opposite direction, starting in courts with limited jurisdiction and working their way up, on legal appeal, to higher courts. Lower courts are much more likely to engage in the application of law rather than the interpretation of law. In some states, depending on the type of court, judges are popularly elected for fixed terms. In others, judges are appointed for various durations. Yet other states combine the two approaches: Judges are initially appointed and then run for office in retention elections.

A second constitutional doctrine influencing the organization of state government is that of checks and balances. While each branch is empowered to perform a unique function, powers are also granted to each to check or control the activities of the other branches. The legislative branch, for example, determines financial appropriations for the other two branches of government. How an entity is funded can greatly affect its performance. The executive branch exercises discretion in implementing laws and court decisions, possibly altering the original intentions of these decisions. Courts may find the activities of another branch unconstitutional and therefore invalid.

There are other checks and balances in the states, though implementation varies substantially from one state to the next. This includes such powers as legislative confirmation of judges, and executive removal of public officials. Most checks and balances are explicitly identified in state constitutions, while a few are not. The concept of a bicameral legislature, for example, is an implicit check because both chambers must work in tandem to pass legislation.

Veto power is a frequently mentioned example of a check because it offers a state governor direct control over actions of the legislature. In some states, governors can only veto entire bills, much like the president of the United States. In other states, however, the governor may veto portions of bills; this is known as a line-item veto. The governor of North Carolina, on the other hand, has no veto power. Provisions to override vetoes are common. Most states require a large majority vote (either two-thirds or three-fifths) of legislators to override a governor's veto, while others call for a simple majority.

Both doctrines—separation of powers, and checks and balances—establish a governmental system in which power is overlapping and shared. This organizational arrangement is sometimes criticized for being slow and inefficient. Yet it prevents any one branch from completely dominating state government. This basic system, with variations, is reflected in all the states.

Applications

The 1988 New Mexico legislative session was in most respects typical of any state legislative session around that time, although perhaps more combative than usual. A liberal Democratic house feuded with a senate controlled by a conservative coalition of Republicans and maverick Democrats. As stipulated in the state constitution, the session started on the third Tuesday of January. In the waning days of the session a house-senate conference committee hammered out the final details of the general appropriations act of 1988 and returned the bill to the floor of both chambers for a final vote. This bill is the most important piece of legislation each year because it provides annual funding for the operation of state government.

Both chambers approved the compromise bill and, as required under the state constitution, sent it to the governor for approval or veto. Most legislators were feeling a mixture of relief and accomplishment. The constitution had limited the session to a mere thirty days. In odd-numbered years, the session is twice as long. The legislators managed to pass the bill four days before the session ended. This meant the governor only had three days to take action, giving the legislature time to attempt a veto override if necessary. Passing an appropriations act, which is always a source of hard political infighting, in twenty-six days during hard economic times produced a special sense of elation.

Governor Garrey Carruthers carefully examined the appropriations act. The first Republican to occupy New Mexico's governor's mansion in many years, Carruthers was in the second year of a four-year term. A former university professor, he had run a campaign on the themes of administrative control and management. He had promised to bring both to the executive branch. It was not too surprising, therefore, that the governor's office found certain provisions of the legislation disturbing, especially those perceived to be intruding on the management prerogative of the executive branch. On the third day the governor decided to draw the line, literally, and vetoed several provisions he found to be the most restrictive. In New Mexico the governor is entrusted with the power of the line-item veto where spending is concerned and may express disapproval by crossing out portions of the annual spending bill.

The chairpersons of the house and senate finance committees believed the governor had overstepped the boundaries of his power. Instead of seeking to override the vetoes in the legislature, an effort which was not likely to succeed, they petitioned the state supreme court, challenging the constitutionality of certain line-item vetoes of the governor. The legislators argued that while the governor could veto objects of spending (defined as items) his power did not extend to certain words or phrases (called parts). Such vetoes, they maintained, would alter the direct wishes of the legislature.

The state supreme court, composed of five justices, accepted the case for adjudication. In reviewing the case, the court recognized the issues of separation of powers and checks and balances underlying the controversy and also acknowledged its role in resolving disputes between the other two branches of government. Two months later, the court ruled against the legislators in all but one instance, upholding the constitutional power of the governor to veto words or parts if such language placed undue restrictions on the authority of the executive branch. The New Mexico governor was granted one of the broadest possible veto authorities found within the American states.

Context

After the colonies declared their independence from the British in 1776, they sought to organize their own political systems. The result was the formation of thirteen independent states, each constitutionally governed. When representatives gathered in Philadelphia some ten years later and framed a new constitution to govern all the states, they confronted the task of how to address the existing states. The states, as might be expected, did not want to be legislated out of existence. The solution to emerge was the creation of a federal political system that recognizes the authority of both state governments and the national government.

The practice of federalism and the role of states in this partnership have changed over time. Four important periods can be identified. Initially, states and the national government acted independently of each other, exercising power in separate policy areas. During the nineteenth century the balance of power shifted toward the national government, giving rise to a period characterized by the increasing dominance of the national government in domestic affairs. This period gave way to a third stage in the middle part of the twentieth century, as states and the national government worked together to address complex social and economic problems. By the close of the century, however, observers noted a resurgence of the states, as the national government started shifting responsibilities back to states.

As a governmental system, federalism offers certain advantages, particularly when viewed from the point of view of the states. First, it helps to decentralize decision making, as many significant policy decisions are made by state rather than national public officials. States have a far greater impact on their citizens' daily affairs than does the national government. Second, a federal approach promotes policy diversity among the states, as differences in public preferences are reflected in the actions of state governments. Finally, federalism is a mechanism for preventing the concentration of power in a single government. Much like the separation of powers doctrine, federalism distributes power and therefore protects the citizenry against the abuse of governmental authority. The potential for abuse, many believe, is the greatest threat to personal liberty.

Bibliography

Adrian, Charles R., and Michael R. Fine. *State and Local Politics*. Chicago: Nelson-Hall, 1991. Introductory textbook: unlike many, makes a systematic attempt to link state and local concerns within common chapters.

Council of State Governments. *The Book of the States: 1992-93 Edition*. Lexington, Ky.: Council of State Governments, 1992. Authoritative and comprehensive reference guide to the American states. Provides up-to-date information, much of it in tabular format. The Council of State Governments is a valuable source of information about states generally.

Gray, Virginia, Herbert Jacob, and Robert Albritton, eds. *Politics in the American States: A Comparative Analysis*. 5th ed. Glenview, Ill.: Scott, Foresman, 1990. Prominent political scientists summarize recent research on state governments, using a quantitative empirical approach.

State Blue Books. Excellent source of information about individual states, published by each state individually. They include the names, addresses, and phone numbers of appointed and elected officials.

Van Horn, Carl E., ed. *The State of the States*. 2d ed. Washington, D.C.: Congressional Quarterly Press, 1993. Ten essays by leading scholars focusing on major political and institutional challenges facing states.

William A. Taggart

Cross-References

Checks and Balances in U.S. Government, p. 216; The Civil Service in the United States, p. 310; The Constitution of the United States, p. 425; Courts: State and Local, p. 465; Elected Versus Appointed Offices in the United States, p. 572; Executive Functions in U.S. Government, p. 636; Federal Mandates, p. 662; Grants-in-Aid, p. 791; Legislative Functions of Government, p. 1098; State and Local Government, p. 1885; Veto Power, p. 2097.

STATESMANSHIP

Field of study: Political philosophy

The traditional, or classical, view of statesmanship holds that certain unique individuals possess superior knowledge of political matters, along with genuine concern for the common good, rather than their own advantage.

Principal terms
DEMAGOGUE: charismatic leader whose political ambition is based on self-interest
MAGNANIMITY: in the classical tradition, the greatness of soul that contributes to the virtue or character of a true statesman
TELEOLOGY: doctrine that seeks to find explanations for phenomena (such as a statesman's behavior) in the results of the behavior
TRANSACTIONAL LEADERSHIP: leadership of ordinary politicians who tend to see their role as exchanging services for votes or other immediate benefits
TRANSFORMING LEADERSHIP: leadership style that aims at a change, often of a moral kind, among followers

Overview

Traditional, or classical, views of statesmanship are rooted in the political philosophy of the ancient world. The ancient Greeks understood political life to be central to existence. This is exemplified in the centrality of the city (polis) in their political thinking. Implicit in this was the notion that political matters were central to one's identity as a human being and a citizen. The individual who possessed a combination of political skills, good character, and a profound understanding of the political was identified as a statesman (*politikos*). The craft of such individuals was statesmanship.

This is a radically different notion of statesmanship than has been commonly used in modern times. In the 1990's the term "statesmanship" often has been applied to any political action or policy that one happens to like, making it merely another term for political success. In other cases, the concept of statesmanship has been limited to particular skill in the arts of diplomacy. In either case, the skills and knowledge possessed by the modern political leader are seen as no different from those of ordinary politicians. Statesmanship is, however, different in kind—not degree—from ordinary leadership. The distinction between them is not to minimize the skills of successful politicians, but rather to elevate the extraordinary talents of the true statesman.

The traditional concept of statesmanship is best articulated in the works of the Greek philosopher Aristotle. In *Politics*, which was probably assembled near the end of his life in 322 B.C.E., Aristotle outlines his view of political science. In Book Four, Aristotle compares the art of statesmanship with the science of gymnastic. Gymnastic was not a specific sport with set routines but rather the science of what was good for bodies.

The gymnastic trainer must possess knowledge of the ideal body, the standard by which individual bodies are to be judged. He also needs knowledge of the limits of each specific body. Some physical types might be best suited for running and others for throwing. Finally, the trainer must be able to communicate or teach his knowledge of the ideal and the specific to the individual who needs his instruction.

In a similar way, the science of statesmanship requires that the statesman possess knowledge of the ideal government and the best citizen, along with an awareness of the fact that specific regimes require different kinds of advice or training to develop properly toward their ends. The statesman must be able to communicate to individual regimes in such a way as to persuade them to do what they ought to do to improve. The statesman must possess a deep and profound knowledge of the nature of the political, including its theoretical potential as well as its practical difficulties, and be able to communicate or teach this to the citizens that compose the body politic. This traditional view of statesmanship is teleological, or explicitly concerned with the ends or ultimate purpose of political things. The task of the statesman is to use his knowledge to shape the body politic toward these ends.

In twentieth century terms, the traditional view of statesmanship was that it provided transforming leadership: It aimed at a change, literally a "re-forming," of citizens and their politics in accordance with a knowable and objective notion of the common good. In contrast, the contemporary view of statesmanship is that it is merely a successful form of transactional leadership. Transactional leadership aims not at a moral reforming but at adjusting and balancing various conflicting interests in the political community. It lacks a comprehensive vision of ends or of what ought to be. It is concerned with short-term benefits rather than a long-term vision of the common good.

Ordinary politicians who engage in transactional leadership are important to political life. Their skills are important and their motives often good. The statesman not only needs their practical talents, but also must act in accordance with the long-term demands of political justice rather than immediate advantage or short-term popularity.

To illustrate this point, Aristotle argues that there are six fundamentally different kinds of regimes or governments. Three are concerned with the common good (kingship, aristocracy, and polity) and three with the private good of its ruling element (tyranny, oligarchy, and democracy). Ordinary political leaders may have the skills to preserve and stabilize the politics of the latter group of regimes. Genuine statesmen have the vision and skills to reform these imperfect regimes in the direction of the common good. The genuine statesman also must recognize that kingship and aristocracy are considered the ideal in theory, yet would be difficult to achieve in practice. The statesman must be fixated not on the ideal but on the practical. He must understand the limits of what can be achieved in the political world.

Given this teleological understanding of politics and its assumption that genuine political knowledge of these ends is attainable, the traditional understanding of statesmanship implies that the statesman must possess certain characteristics.

First and foremost among these is theoretical knowledge. This is a philosophical understanding of the nature and purpose of individuals and political communities.

Without an objective knowledge of what truly is, there can be no model of the good to inform the actions of the statesman. This theoretical understanding must be coupled with what Aristotle called *phronesis*, or practical knowledge, sometimes called prudence, which enables the statesman to see what is possible in any given circumstance. This can be illustrated by the metaphor of the physician. A physician not only requires theoretical knowledge of medicine, but also must be able to apply this knowledge to individual patients. Not all patients can or should be treated in the same way. Understanding this is a form of practical knowledge that can only be gotten from clinical experience. Likewise, the statesman needs practical political experience and the knowledge that comes with it to improve or reform the body politic.

The statesman also needs practical political skills. Among the most important of these would be the art of persuasion or rhetoric. Statesmen must be able to speak effectively to individuals, groups, and politicians, and use a variety of media and forums. Statesmen must be able to persuade others to do what they know must be done to preserve a regime for the long term or to achieve justice. In the twentieth century, management and organizational skills are also needed for the statesman to be successful. The statesman must be able to work with others to get the job done.

Finally, statesmen must possess good character. They must be motivated not by personal gain or a lust for power but by a real desire to achieve some great good. The traditional name given to this virtue is magnanimity. Magnanimity is a greatness of soul that motivates some to achieve excellence and self-sufficiency in the world. Magnanimous individuals are concerned with fame rather than fortune—not fame in the sense of popularity, but rather a desire to live in history as a doer of great deeds. Founders of nations and their preservers in time of great threatening crises, such as Thomas Jefferson, Abraham Lincoln, and Winston Churchill, are examples of this. Magnanimity does not mean moral perfection, but rather a willingness to exercise political courage.

The traditional view of statesmanship is thus normative and emphasizes the moral dimension of political leadership along with the knowledge, skill, and character that enable great leaders to achieve great things for their nations, and therefore to achieve great recognition.

Applications

While all political actors would like to label themselves statesmen, it is clear from history that not all have the requisite character, knowledge, and skills. It is useful to contrast the traditional statesman with other types of political persons. Without such a comparison, it is impossible to arrive at a comprehensive understanding of political life.

The demagogue is an example of a political leader who has many of the political talents, especially the rhetorical skills, of the statesman, but lacks the abiding concern for the common good essential to statesmanship. The motivation of the demagogue is usually the personal accumulation of power at all costs. The demagogue may use rhetorical appeals to the common good or high purpose, but his political practices and lack of magnanimity betray his nature to classic political analysis. Likewise, the politician motivated by money would fail the test of concern for the common good.

The life of the tyrant reveals him to be motivated by a politics of excluding all but himself from the political sphere. From the classical point of view, this is contrary to human nature. According to the traditional understanding, genuine statesmanship must recognize that its rule is over citizens, not subjects. In Aristotle's viev, man is a political animal by nature. The tyrant denies this by excluding everyone else from participation. From a normative point of view, the tyrant commits the greatest injustice in doing so, and thus cannot be identified with the statesman.

Many ordinary politicians have political skill and are not selfishly motivated. Such persons may have a concern for the common good and even have some of the practical wisdom possessed by the statesman; however, they lack the political courage and theoretical insight into the essence of political matters that are deemed essential to statesmanship. Ordinary politicians may have the potential to become statesmen if challenged by extraordinary crisis or the special demands of founding a new political order. Nevertheless, unless such leaders are tested and found successful, they would not be considered to be statesmen.

The classical concept of statesmanship thus illustrates several key features of political life. First, it shows that not all political action is motivated by selfish group or personal interest. It enables the political scientist to construct normative topologies akin to those of Aristotle. History demonstrates that concern for the common good and the desire to be thought of well by posterity are vital components of understanding political behavior. Second, it asserts that there is an essential difference between the politics of great events like a founding, so one must view such events differently from everyday political life. Third, it raises the possibility that political science must be more than a positivistic, value-free social science if political phenomena are to be completely understood. While the traditional understanding of statesmanship has not been a dominant strain in modern political analysis, such issues remain important.

Context

The classical concept of statesmanship has not been a part of contemporary public discourse for several reasons. First, the modern world has a different conception of the political than did the ancients. The primacy of the political in the Greek polis gave a much higher status to the great leader and to a greater concern for public virtues such as magnanimity as part of statesmanship. Some scholars have argued that the Greek idea that the cosmos was in a constant state of flux led the Greeks to the notion of the great-souled man as an agent of stability. This is analogous to the role the great hero played in the stories and myths of the classical age.

Other scholars have argued that the rise of Christianity contributed to the downfall of the classical idea of the statesman. To early Christians, the universe had a design or purpose, however mysterious it might appear. Denying or defying this divine order was a sin of pride, and was tantamount to undermining the underlying order of being. In this world view, magnanimity was not a virtue to be exalted but a trait to be minimized. This had the effect of undermining the centrality of statesmanship for political life.

The political theorists of the Enlightenment also contributed to this eclipse of classical statesmanship. Thinkers such as Thomas Hobbes and John Locke contributed to redefining the purpose of government away from classical teleological concerns. They stressed instead that government should provide security and economic stability. Therefore, the need for statesmen who would mold public virtue toward a moral vision of the public good began to fade. While Alexander Hamilton, James Madison, and John Jay recognized in the Federalist Papers (1787) the importance of statesmanship during a founding period, they created a constitutional system of checks and balances that would enable ordinary politicians to govern the political affairs of the nation. Great men with the virtue of magnanimity became superfluous, except perhaps in times of great crisis, in the mechanical political arrangements established to govern a large nation of private individuals. The classical polis had no such arrangements or purpose, and therefore was dependent on the statesman to keep the orientation of the community to the common good.

Alexis de Tocqueville, the great French commentator on the United States in the nineteenth century, suggested another reason for the eclipse of statesmanship. In *Democracy in America* (1835) he noted that "the race of American statesmen has strangely shrunk." He attributed this to the dominance of the idea of equality, a concept central to modern democratic regimes. The social conditions of democratic regimes do not provide the nurturing and support necessary for statesmen. As Tocqueville put it, "it is not always ability to choose men of merit which democracy lacks; sometimes it has neither desire nor taste to do so." Potential statesmen are neither understood nor encouraged by people as a spirit of equality comes to dominate political life. The eclipse of statesmanship has been rooted in modern sensibilities that have had a leveling effect on the ambitions of politicians.

Finally, political science as an academic discipline has tended to disregard the concept of statesmanship as a subject of political analysis. Modern political science generally has accepted the idea of the separation of facts and values and has had a strong positivist orientation. It has attempted to define problems empirically. Since the traditional concept of statesmanship involves a normative judgment about the goodness rather than the success of political actors, as well as a notion of a common good, modern political science has tended to discuss leadership styles and roles that can be objectively analyzed without judgment.

Classical statesmanship has not been universally dismissed within the discipline, however. Some political scientists have argued that unless the classical concept of statesmanship is revived and perhaps updated to account for modern political phenomena, a genuine and comprehensive understanding of political reality cannot be reached.

Bibliography

Arnhart, Larry. "Statesmanship as Magnanimity: Classical, Christian & Modern." *Polity* 16 (Winter, 1983): 263-283. Argues that the attitudes and values of the modern world are not conducive to traditional statesmanship. This idea is rooted in the fact that the Christian tradition has tended to equate magnanimity with pride.

Burns, James MacGregor. *Leadership*. New York: Harper and Row, 1978. Monumental study of political leadership that borrows heavily from the classical tradition of the statesman. Burns combines this tradition with modern concepts and cross-cultural analysis.

Eidelberg, Paul. *A Discourse on Statesmanship*. Urbana: University of Illinois Press, 1974. Aims at a synthesis of classical and modern political science. Its key feature is a revival of the classical notion of statesmanship. Persuasively argues that without such a revival, it is difficult to comprehend the nature of politics and U.S. politics in particular.

Frisch, Morton, and Richard Stevens. "Introduction." In *American Political Thought*. Edited by Morton Frisch and Richard Stevens. 2d ed. Itasca, Ill.: F. E. Peacock, 1983. Classic explanation of the traditional idea of statesmanship and its applicability to U.S. tradition.

Graham, George J., and William C. Harvard, Jr. "The Language of the Statesman: Philosophy and Rhetoric in Contemporary Politics." In *Sophia and Praxis*, edited by J. M. Porter. Chatham, N.J.: Chatham House, 1984. The authors explain the importance of rhetoric as a vital ingredient in the practice of statesmanship.

Mansfield, Harvey C. *Statesmanship and Party Government*. Chicago: University of Chicago Press, 1965. Seminal study of Edmund Burke demonstrates how statesmanship was eclipsed with the rise of modern party systems. Demonstrates the philosophical and practical issues that modernity raises for classical political practice.

Nichols, Mary P. *Citizens and Statesmen*. Savage, Md.: Rowman and Littlefield, 1992. Excellent commentary on Aristotle's political science offers a complex and subtle analysis of classical statesmanship. Its final chapter demonstrates the relevance of the classical understanding to modern political theory.

Melvin Kulbicki

Cross-References

Aristotle's Political Philosophy, p. 83; Charismatic Leadership, p. 209; Cult of Personality, p. 477; Demagoguery, p. 507; Dictatorships, p. 546; Leadership, p. 1066; Plato's Political Philosophy, p. 1396; Political Philosophy, p. 1505; Political Science, p. 1532; Self-Interest in Politics, p. 1802.

STOIC POLITICAL PHILOSOPHY

Field of study: Political philosophy

Stoic philosophy arose in the third century B.C.E. in Greece and continued to gain adherents during the time of the Roman Empire. Stoicism seeks to make the personal and the political lives of humans orderly and aimed at following the laws of nature by subjugating self to sense.

Principal terms

ASCETIC: one who renounces comforts and leads a life of austere self-discipline

CYNIC: member of the Greek philosophic school, founded by Antisthenes of Athens, who believed virtue and self-control to be the essential elements of the life of the good individual

LOGIC: in Stoicism, the assertion of the certainty of correct knowledge via the natural criteria available to humans

MACROCOSM: portion of Stoic philosophy dealing with the universe, science, and natural law

MEGARIAN: member of the philosophic school originated by Euclid of Alexandria

MICROCOSM: portion of Stoic philosophy dealing with human politics, ethics, and religion

PHYSICS: portion of Stoic philosophy dealing with metaphysics, religion, anthropology, and psychology

STOA: Stoic philosophy

Overview

People may often view Stoics as phlegmatic and ascetic individuals who allow the richness of life to pass them by. Stoicism, however, is an elegant philosophy of Greek origin whose main objective is a search for how to make the political and personal lives of people orderly, honest, and in keeping with the laws of nature.

Stoicism, as an active and organized sociopolitical movement, began in about 300 B.C.E. and lasted for more than five centuries. During that long time, the Stoics divided into groups. One group was dedicated to the understanding of the macrocosm, which it defined as science and the universe. Another group sought to explore and to understand the microcosm, which it defined as human politics, ethics, and religion. This article is concerned mostly with the latter group of Stoics.

Stoicism is most often chronologically divided into three periods called early Stoa (the third century B.C.E.), middle Stoa (the second and first centuries B.C.E.), and late Stoa (the first and second centuries C.E.). Only a small percentage of the actual writings of the first Stoics exists today. Most extant information about the early Stoa comes from the works of later philosophers and historians such as Sextus Empiricis (third century C.E.), Diogenes Laertes (third century C.E.), and Marcus Tullius Cicero (106-43 B.C.E.). Modern readers are largely dependent upon the analysis and personal opinions of later writers for information about early Stoicism, and there are huge gaps in understanding of the Stoic movement.

Long before Stoicism was codified in the third century B.C.E., the philosopher Heracleitus of Ephesus (c. 540-c. 470 B.C.E.) set down what was later viewed as the Stoic concept of the universe. His belief in subordination of the individual to the laws of nature defined the primary sociopolitical argument of Stoicism and has remained within the movement throughout its existence. It is currently believed that Heracleitus was most influenced by the logical concepts of the Megarians, a philosophic school originated by the great geometrician, Euclid of Alexandria, and by the ethical concepts of the Cynics, who believed that following natural law was far superior to being driven by convention, and sought what they viewed as sensible autonomy for humankind.

Zeno of Citium (c. 340-c. 265 B.C.E.) reportedly codified and formalized the Stoic concepts of Heracleitus into the Stoic school of philosophy. This occurred in lectures given to his adherents in a building called the Stoa Poikile (painted porch). It is from the name of this lecture site that the term "Stoic" is derived. Zeno stressed the great importance of strength of character in all ethical or political actions. This philosophic concept was probably related to the decline—at that time—of Greece as a center of culture and to a growing trend toward internationalism. Two other great Stoics are Cleanthes of Assos (c. 331-c. 232 B.C.E.) and Chrysippus of Soli (c. 280-c. 206 B.C.E.). All three of these philosophers contributed to the formulation of the early Stoa.

The next two centuries saw many changes in Stoic philosophy. The Roman Empire replaced Greece as the seat of power in the Mediterranean. Under the Roman influence, the Stoic philosophy became much more flexible. For example, it began to envision a gradual moral progress toward the ultimate Stoic goal of following the law of nature in political and personal life, rather than insisting on the need for immediate success, as in early Stoa. The major Stoics of that time were Panaetius of Rhodes (c. 180-c. 109 B.C.E.) and Posidonius of Apamea (c. 135-c. 53 B.C.E.). Panaetius, whose ethical principles reportedly shaped the actions of many of the best intellects of the time, is credited with softening the Stoic asceticism enough to enable the involvement of Stoicism in most of the military, social, and political aspects of Roman life. Posidonius' efforts are reputed to have made the Stoic philosophy conceptually much more detailed and more rigorous than it had been before his time. This was the time of the middle Stoa.

The first and second centuries C.E. saw Stoicism both flourish and, supposedly, die. The great Stoic philosophers of this time—the late Stoa—were the Romans Epictetus, Seneca, and Marcus Aurelius. Seneca (5 B.C.E.?-65 C.E.), a statesman, was famous as the author of many tragic plays and as Nero's prime minister. He added to the traditional Stoic submission to natural law the search for tranquillity and the resolution to do one's social duty.

Epictetus (c. 60-c. 110 C.E.) greatly strengthened the Stoic doctrines of love of good, hatred of evil, and obedience to the dictates of one's conscience. He also supported the Stoic trust in the existence of a wise and merciful providence, coupled with the realization that within the tenets of the philosophy, people needed to understand that not all things were within human power. Hence, perfect adherence to Stoic doctrine, according to Epictetus, was not always a viable possibility for its practitioners. Emperor Marcus Aurelius (121-180 C.E.) carried to its logical conclusion the idea that Stoics should strive always to be useful citizens.

It is probably unsurprising that, during its five centuries of development, Stoic political philosophy was very important to Greece and Rome. It was adopted in Greek Rhodes, in many cities of Asia Minor, and in Egypt. Stoicism is generally deemed to have died as an organized philosophy soon after the death of Marcus Aurelius. Others see its "death" as its absorption into early Christianity, with Stoic tenets clearly living in the minds of those seeking to follow natural law and to serve selflessly. Stoic principles also pervade almost all Roman literature from the Christian era on, and much Roman law came from rulers who were either Stoics themselves, or who were influenced by Stoic ministers.

The Stoics—especially Cicero—are seen as being very important to the formulation of the ideas of many great social and political thinkers of modern times. Examples of those reputedly affected by Stoic philosophy are Jean Bodin, Niccolò Machiavelli, and Thomas Hobbes.

Applications

Zeno and his contemporaries reputedly formulated, in the early Stoa, the concept of harmony among the universe, God, and humans. One must say "reputedly" because none of their writings is extant. This political philosophy proposed that the perfect state would comprise the entire world and follow laws that were prescribed by nature. Governance of the world state, it was assumed, would not need courts, judges, or lawyers because being correct, citizens would not be in conflict and all of their actions would be governed by love for one another. In addition, there would be no class distinctions in such a state, and young people would wish to study virtue from an early age.

This ideal state was to be attained by the application of logic, physics, and ethics, which were all inseparable to the Stoics. Their logic argues in favor of the certainty of knowledge, which is to say that the criteria that enable people to distinguish between true and false, or right and wrong, do exist. The criteria include the sensations that leave their imprints on the soul, the comparisons derived from reason, and the inborn ideas, parts of the universal reason, from which the human soul derives. According to Stoicism, careful observation, thorough deliberation, and self-control will ultimately lead to correct action.

Physics, according to the Stoics, includes metaphysics, religion, anthropology, and psychology. The physical essence of humanity, by Stoic precepts, is the soul, which is in turn a fragment of the universal divine force. The soul is thus possessed of reason, which is enhanced by self-control. Stoics built their ethics from the physics, noting that people can be categorized into the good and the bad. Virtue comes through self-control, which is attained by living consistently according to logic and physics. Doing nothing that natural law forbids and practicing self-control lead to intuitive correct choices for one's actions.

These tenets of the early Stoa appear in the political thought of Cicero. For example, he, being a Stoic, viewed natural law as an immutable essence and an embodiment of God. Natural law, according to Cicero, transcends statutory law and customary law, except where they are derived from natural law. Similarly, he denotes justice both as a necessity and as a natural inclination in people. This is a restatement of the ethics of the early Stoa.

Cicero also envisioned four cardinal virtues to be practiced in correct life and politics. These are wisdom, justice, courage, and temperance. These virtues are among earlier Stoic principles. In Cicero's view, the highest form of endeavor is service to the state in an active political life. This concept was accepted by philosophers of the middle Stoa. It probably would have been viewed as unnecessary by Zeno, however, who presumed that the perfect state would naturally arise because all citizens would be virtuous.

Stoicism's absorption into Christianity is viewed as originating with the Apostle Paul (d. c. 64 C.E.). Many sources note similarities between the Pauline epistles and the writings of the Stoic philosophers Seneca and Epictetus. This is not surprising, because Paul was born and grew up in Tarsus, a city with a Stoic tradition. It is also reported that from the third century C.E. on, the Stoa and the Stoics rapidly lost their identity, being absorbed into Christianity. Many of the concepts of Christianity, for example the existence of natural criteria that enable people to distinguish between right and wrong actions, trace their origins to Stoic philosophy.

The English political philosopher Thomas Hobbes, viewed as being a modern Stoic, was influenced most strongly by Cicero. For example, Hobbes stated that peace among people depended upon their recognizing that they gained wealth and security through temperance and respect for the rights of others.

Context

Stoics have, as the core of their actions and interactions with others, the responsibility for the promotion of a personal and political world view based on the order of the physical world, which in turn is begotten by natural law. In the society resulting from such actions, all rational beings are equals and wise; their actions will lend support to other people as a result of enlightened self-interest. This wisdom results from study of Stoic physics and ethics, as well as the careful examination and emulation of others who achieved wisdom previously.

The results expected from appropriate activities may be defined as bravery, justice, intelligence, and self-control (or temperance). Bravery, as interpreted by Cicero and other Stoics, is recognizing what to fear and what is safe. Intelligence is the ability to identify what is good and what is evil in the natural world and how to react to these things. Justice, in turn, is knowing how to give everyone else those rights and the material objects that are due to them and, of course, doing so. Exceptionally important, and perhaps underlying all the other essentials of Stoicism, is the self-control embodied in exercising actions that lead to virtue and to the suppression of all things that cause inappropriate conduct.

Stoicism seems to many to be an excellent approach to living. It remains satisfactory to many and is seen to be as useful now as it was in Greece in the third century B.C.E.. Stoicism thus seems, to many, to be an intellectual attitude that should be strongly sponsored. Those espousing such sponsorship have presumed that Stoicism could serve as a brake on the corruption and passions found in government and life—whether they be of Romans of the first century B.C.E., the moral dilemmas that prompted the writings of Hobbes, or of the moral dislocations of the twentieth century. The great question, as it was in earlier times, is whether the Stoic philosophy can be applied both widely and successfully.

Bibliography

Cicero, Marcus. *Selected Political Speeches of Cicero*. Translated by Michael Grant. Baltimore: Penguin Books, 1969. Seven of Cicero's most important speeches give readers a good view of the man and his politics. It is valuable to those wishing to explore Stoic currents in Ciceronian philosophy.

Mates, Benson. *Stoic Logic*. Berkeley: University of California Press, 1961. Brief, scholarly description of Stoic logic and its development. Excellent bibliography.

Rist, John M. *The Stoics*. Berkeley: University of California Press, 1978. Describes many aspects of Stoicism. Particularly interesting are Stoic logic, the Stoic theory of meaning, necessity and fate, moral responsibility, and moral actions in Stoic ethics.

Stock, St. George. *Stoicism*. Port Washington, N.Y.: Kennikat Press, 1969. Describes the development of Stoicism and deals with the content of Stoic ethics, logic, and physics. With a descriptive chronology of Stoicism.

Wenly, R. M. *Stoicism and Its Influence*. Boston: Marshall Jones, 1924. Contains useful information absent in later texts, especially relating to the development of Stoicism.

Wood, Neal. *Cicero's Social and Political Thought*. Berkeley: University of California Press, 1987. Describes Marcus Tullius Cicero's social and political thought in some detail.

Sanford S. Singer

Cross-References

The City-State, p. 272; Epicurean Political Philosophy, p. 624; Equality and Egalitarianism, p. 630; Hobbes's Political Philosophy, p. 836; John of Salisbury's Political Philosophy, p. 1006; Plato's Political Philosophy, p. 1396; Political Philosophy, p. 1505; Polity, p. 1545; Spinoza's Political Philosophy, p. 1872.

SUCCESSION

Field of study: Political philosophy

Succession is the order under which a person or political party attains governmental power. In monarchies, succession is the accession to the throne of new kings or queens. In democracies, succession is attained through popular elections of presidents and legislative bodies. In dictatorships, succession may be orderly or by force.

Principal terms

COUP D'ÉTAT: illegal, usually violent, change in government

DYNASTY: succession of hereditary rulers with one family line

LEGITIMACY: legal right to govern; hereditary in most monarchies and conferred by constitutions in democratic governments

REGENT: administrator of a kingdom during the minority, incapacity, or absence of the reigning monarch

SHADOW CABINET: in parliamentary democracies, members of the opposition political party holding responsibilities comparable to their counterparts in government

USURPER: one who wrongfully appropriates the authority of the legitimate ruler

Overview

The three most basic types of government are monarchies ruled by kings or emperors who have usually inherited their thrones; democracies governed by elected presidents and legislatures; and dictatorships, in which supreme power is concentrated in rulers whose governments are not subject to election. In each of these types of government, the transfer of power from one ruler or ruling group to another is known as succession. Succession in monarchies is usually governed by precedent, and in democracies by constitutions, but in dictatorships, it is subject to a wide variety of circumstances. Legitimacy, the right to govern, has been a principal factor in both monarchies and democracies, whereas the right to govern in dictatorships is based ultimately on force.

Until 1918, monarchy was the prevailing form of government in the world. For most of that time, monarchies were absolute, with the supreme governing power vested in the ruling king or queen, but beginning in the eighteenth century in Great Britain, a representative body of government, the Parliament, assumed increasingly greater control. Monarchies of the twentieth century are best described as headed by figures who "reign" but do not rule. The United Kingdom, Spain, Saudi Arabia, Japan, and the Scandinavian countries are among the few monarchies still existing at the end of the twentieth century.

Although there have been a few elective monarchies (notably the Papacy and Poland), most have been hereditary, dynasties founded by a ruler who gained or seized the supreme ruling power and was able to pass the kingdom to an heir. Often some sort of divine sanction was applied to the ruling family, as in Japan until 1945, or the ceremonial anointing of French kings with sacred oil until 1830. In most monarchies the heirs to the thrones were the oldest sons, known as "crown princes." Elaborate protocols were established to ensure orderly successions in the event of disruptions to the normal lines. Generally, a crown prince's own sons, then his brothers in order of age, provided the succession. Whether women could inherit thrones differed from one nation to another. It was not the Salic Law of the sixth century that forbade women to inherit land, but assemblies of notables in 1317 and 1322 that excluded women from the throne of France. England, on the other hand, had occasional ruling queens, from Matilda in the Middle Ages to Elizabeth II in the second half of the twentieth century. In virtually all monarchies, illegitimate children were denied the right of succession.

The principle of hereditary succession preserved many kingdoms from power struggle when their reigning monarchs died. On the other hand, the system could not guarantee that a succeeding monarch would be a good one. An excellent example is found in the Old Testament, wherein King Rehoboam informed his subjects "my father chastised you with whips, but I will chastise you with scorpions" in his attempt to exact more labor and taxes. In extreme cases, monarchs could be deposed and even executed, as Edward II and Richard II of England were in the fourteenth century. A regent would be appointed, usually by the senior nobles if not the king himself, in cases where the ruler was a minor, as when Louis XIV of France was succeeded in 1715 by his great-grandson, a boy of five; ailing, as when George III's son assumed power as Prince Regent during his father's bouts of mental illness; or absent, for example, Blanche of Castile while her son Louis IX (Saint Louis) was on crusade.

When dynasties became extinct, there were often savage struggles to establish replacements. Rival claimants to the throne were often members of the same extended royal family. At times there would be a bold usurper—one of the most famous was Boris Godunov of Russia, the regent under whose orders the legal heir to the throne was murdered; he seized power aided by the nobility, who subsequently procured his downfall in 1605.

Political considerations could override traditional legitimacy. When King James II of England was overthrown in 1688, for example, his Protestant daughter Mary (the wife of William III of Holland) was made queen, followed by her younger sister Anne. After Anne's death in 1714, the German Elector of Hanover (the great-grandson of James I) was chosen by Parliament under the Act of Settlement of 1701 as King George I, although the claim of the son of James II and Beatrice of Modena was closer. In this instance, maintaining the Protestant succession to the throne of England superseded claims by birth.

Under democratic forms of government, political succession is usually spelled out in constitutions that provide for regular elections and that ensure orderly changes of government. Such elections confer legitimacy upon incoming governments. In the United States, the election of the Congress is set forth in Article 1, sections 1 through 5, modified by the Seventeenth Amendment for the Senate; and by Article 2 for the president and vice president (who succeeds the president in case of the latter's death or incapacity), modified by the Twelfth, Twentieth, and Twenty-fifth amendments. Elections to the presidency occur every fourth year; to the House of Representatives, every second year; to the Senate, every six years, in staggered terms.

Since the U.S. Constitution went into effect in 1789, there have been only three major challenges to presidential succession. In 1824, when none of the three candidates won a majority of the states, the election was thrown into the House of Representatives, which elected John Quincy Adams president, even though he had won a minority of the popular vote. In 1860, the South refused to acknowledge the election of Abraham Lincoln, and most of its states seceded from the Union, triggering the Civil War. The election of 1876 was marred by charges of election fraud and was settled by compromise: The Republicans gained the presidency, while federal troops were withdrawn from the South. Although the close presidential election of 1960 also contained charges of fraud, the losing candidate, Richard Nixon, refused to challenge the outcome so as not to damage the foreign prestige of the United States.

In parliamentary systems, such as in the United Kingdom, political parties play a greater role than in the United States. To achieve the post of prime minister usually requires working one's way through the party ranks, and a "shadow cabinet" provides for a rapid and orderly transition when there is a change of government.

Applications

Many of the problems of monarchical succession can be shown in the circumstances surrounding the reign of England's King Richard III, who was king from 1483 to 1485. In 1471 King Henry VI died under mysterious circumstances after a battle in which his son, the recognized heir to the throne, was slain. Henry was then succeeded by a cousin, Edward IV. The Duke of Gloucester supported Edward during the revolt of their mutual brother, the Duke of Clarence, in 1478, after which Clarence was executed. On Edward's death in 1483, Gloucester had himself declared protector of Edward's minor sons, Edward V and Richard, whom he placed for safekeeping in the Tower of London, whence they never emerged. Gloucester, although suspected of murdering the princes, became king as Richard III. After Richard's succession, Gloucester's rival, the Duke of Lancaster, who had gone abroad after Edward IV's accession, invaded England. At the battle of Bosworth Field in 1485, Richard was slain, the Plantagenet dynasty was extinguished, and Lancaster became king as Henry VII, the founder of the Tudor dynasty. Nevertheless, there was a remarkable continuity in the king's advisers, except at the highest level, and in the judiciary. Many of the advisers who had served Edward IV continued under both of his successors.

The election in the United States in 1980 provides a modern example of the succession of one party by another in a democratic government. The role of political parties had weakened after World War II, with the wide spread of television, primary elections, and an emphasis on personally charismatic presidential candiates. The incumbent Democratic president, Jimmy Carter, had run in 1976 as an outsider after one term as governor of Georgia. Carter's presidency was marred by battles with

Congress, dramatically increased inflation, and setbacks in foreign affairs, such as the Soviet invasion of Afghanistan and the seizure of the U.S. embassy in Tehran, Iran. The international prestige of the United States was at a postwar low and Carter, although a man of unquestioned integrity and compassion, was increasingly perceived as weak and ineffective. Challenger Ronald Reagan, by contrast, was personally charming and attractive, a former film actor and television host, whose political experience included two terms as governor of California. He had mastered television as a means of communication even better than Franklin Roosevelt—Reagan's model in many respects—had mastered radio. Reagan's message of limited government, reduced taxation, and aggressively countering the Soviet expansion appealed to a majority of U.S. voters, attracting strong middle-class and much working-class support. Not only did Reagan easily defeat Carter, but the Republicans also gained control of the Senate and could attain an ideological majority in the House of Representatives through the defection of conservative Southern Democrats.

Reagan believed in delegating authority and concern for details. A highly professional transition team, comprising representatives from the business community, his California advisers, and members of conservative think tanks, identified government bureaus where cuts could take place and carefully screened all political appointments to ensure that they went to those who were not only competent but also ideologically conservative and loyal to Reagan and his goals. In his dealings with Congress, Reagan concentrated on economic policy. He accelerated the process of deregulation that had begun under Carter, put through a major tax cut, increased defense appropriations, reversed the growth in social programs, and broke a strike by the air traffic controllers. Reagan achieved his goals through excellent liaison work with Congress, his own negotiating skills, and his personal powers of persuasion, whether with individual members of Congress or through televised appeals to the electorate. Reagan did not bring about a deep-seated political realignment comparable to that of Franklin Roosevelt in 1932; however, his legacy persisted through his conservative appointments to the federal judiciary, especially the Supreme Court. Even the sizable federal deficit, Reagan's chief negative contribution, meant that increased social programs could be effected only with substantial broad-based tax increases.

Adolf Hitler's assumption of power in Germany in 1933 is an example of a dictatorship that legally succeeded a democratic government. After the failure of his Munich coup attempt in 1923, Hitler realized that he could achieve power only by political means. His party, the National Socialist German Workers (Nazi) Party, gained increasing support after severe unemployment and economic depression began sweeping through Germany in 1929. Although Hitler and his followers were derided as clowns and thugs, he had a mastery of propaganda techniques and a simplistic message that placed the blame for poor economic conditions on the communists, the Jews, and the victorious nations of World War I. In January, 1933, conservative politicians, thinking they could control Hitler, made him chancellor of a coalition cabinet in which Nazis were the minority. Hitler quickly dissolved the Reichstag (German parliament) and called new elections. In the meantime, he quietly gained control of the police and communications network, especially the state-owned radio. At the end of February, the Reichstag building was burned, probably by Nazis; this served as a pretext to declare a state of emergency that suspended all civil rights, and several opposing politicians, especially communists, were arrested. In the March elections, Hitler obtained a sufficient majority to pass an Enabling Act that effectively made him an absolute dictator.

The Nazis consolidated their power through *gleichschaltung* (literally, "putting into the same gear"), by purging the civil service, abolishing other political parties, dissolving the governments of the various states, and gaining control of the labor movement. Even the arts were subject to *gleichschaltung*, and strict racial and political controls were placed on the professions. In 1934, Hitler laid the foundations of the totalitarian Third Reich and eliminated the remaining sources of potential opposition. He ruthlessly purged his own party, assumed the office of president after Paul Hindenburg's death, and required the armed forces to take an oath of unconditional obedience to him personally. By August, he had gained absolute control with his chief weapon, terror, as the prospect of confinement in concentration camps drove potential opponents to silence or exile.

Context

In the stable democracies of North America and Western Europe, the successions of one government by another are eased by several institutions of long standing. A professional and permanent career civil service ensures that government functions are performed. An independent judiciary, with police that impartially enforce the law and judges that interpret it, provides continuity and stability. The legitimacy of the succession is assured if there is a dependable means for peaceful change of government.

At the other extreme, the government completely breaks down during a succession, often with anarchy and civil war. For example, after the dictatorial president of Rwanda was killed in a plane crash in 1994, warfare broke out not only between the two leading tribes, the Hutu and the Tutsi, but also among factions within the Hutu. More than 10 percent of the population is estimated to have perished, and twice that number fled as refugees to neighboring countries.

Despite the conflicts in some of the successor states to the old Soviet Union or in such developing countries as Somalia or Haiti, there is cause for optimism as the twentieth century comes to a close. In Latin America, countries that have been independent nations since the 1820's have been beset by succession struggles, with elected governments often overthrown by dictators, usually army generals, or coups d'état with rule by military juntas or civilian oligarchies. The last two decades of the twentieth century, however, have seen dictatorships replaced by elective democracies in most of the countries of Central and South America and the Caribbean. The succession system in Mexico has often been cited as a model for the developing world. The reasons for its relative success are interrelated. The Institutional Revolutionary Party (PRI) has been a mass party embracing nearly all sectors of Mexican life. The presidents, chosen usually by their predecessor and PRI party leaders, serve limited terms and are closely involved in choosing their own successors. The fragmented opposition has been better able to elect candidates on a local than national level. Despite corruption and occasional dislocations, the system, on the whole, has held together.

Several challenges resulting from succession in other parts of the world have yet to be solved. Foremost is the question of the successor states to the former Soviet Union that declared their independence in 1991. Because they lack a tradition of democracy and have been beset by severe economic crises, the question arises whether these states will have some kind of dictatorial or collective leadership by oligarchy, will fragment even further, or will form some kind of confederation among themselves. Another crucial event was the relatively peaceful change from a white-run government in South Africa to a multiracial government headed by Nelson Mandela, in which the former white rulers, headed by F. W. de Klerk, continued to play a significant role. The specter of "one man, one vote, once" that typified many newly independent African countries can be exorcised by leadership, restraint, and power-sharing in South Africa. The decisive question will depend on Mandela's successor: He will need to unite previously warring factions, not only white and black, but Xhosa and Zulu as well, and extend prosperity among all peoples without confiscating the property of some. If that person succeeds, he or she can set a model for the rest of the continent to follow.

Bibliography

Burling, Robbins. *The Passage of Power: Studies in Political Succession.* New York: Academic Press, 1974. Excellent comparative studies of succession in African and Indian kingdoms, Latin America, and Manchu China, and a theory and typologies of succession.

Craig, Gordon A. *Germany, 1866-1945.* New York: Oxford University Press, 1978. Solid, readable study of modern Germany, tracing Hitler's ascent to power within a larger context.

Feerick, John. *The Twenty-Fifth Amendment.* 2d ed. New York: Fordham University Press, 1992. Thorough history of the circumstances leading to the adoption and ratification of this amendment. Includes vice presidential successions, presidential inability, and the replacements of both President Nixon and Vice President Agnew with officials selected under this amendment.

Holden, David, and Richard Johns. *The House of Saud.* New York: Holt, Rinehart and Winston, 1981. Fascinating study of the rulers of Saudi Arabia, the leading absolute monarchy of the twentieth century, with its succession problems ably explored against the turbulent background of Middle Eastern history.

Mervin, David. *Ronald Reagan and the American Presidency.* London: Longman, 1990. Comparative account by a British specialist in U.S. politics who compares U.S. and British forms of government and routes to power; especially good treatment of Reagan's first year in office.

Ross, Charles. *Richard III.* Berkeley: University of California Press, 1981. Excellent guide through the complex dynastic web of fifteenth century England. Presents the struggle for succession by Richard III as a north-south conflict with the south, and Henry VII, victorious. Excellent corrective to Shakespeare's biased portrait in his drama *Richard III*, and gives a balanced picture of England's most maligned monarch.

R. M. Longyear

Cross-References

Charismatic Leadership, p. 209; Despotism and Tyranny, p. 527; Elected Versus Appointed Offices in the United States, p. 572; Elections, p. 578; Heads of State, p. 804; Impeachment, p. 882; Insurgencies and Coups d'État, p. 930; Leadership, p. 1066; Legitimacy, p. 1105; Military Governments, p. 1192; Monarchy in History, p. 1221; Nietzsche's Political Philosophy, p. 1300; Political Myths and the Philosophies of Mosca and Pareto, p. 1474; Presidential Elections in the United States, p. 1596; Russian Political History, p. 1770.

SUPERPOWERS AND WORLD POLITICS

Field of study: International government and politics

The term "superpowers" generally refers to the United States and the Soviet Union in the post-World War II era, when they were in direct confrontation for a period exceeding forty years. The Cold War is the term often used to describe this period in world politics.

Principal terms

BIPOLAR WORLD: term referring to two major spheres of influence in the world, especially the Soviet and U.S. blocs

COLD WAR: period from 1946 to 1990, during which the Soviet-U.S. rivalry dominated international relations

CONTAINMENT: U.S. policy adopted in 1947 to limit the expansion of the Soviet sphere of influence

DÉTENTE: period of improved relations between rivals

REALIST THEORY: interpretation of international relations that emphasizes concrete national capabilities and the pursuit of national interest, defined as political power

SUPERPOWERS: states whose power exceeds that of other powers in the military, economic, and political spheres, and who therefore exercise great influence in the world

THIRD WORLD: nations, especially in Africa and Asia, not aligned with the Communist or non-Communist bloc; also, the underdeveloped nations of the world generally

Overview

The concept of a superpower is relatively new in world politics. History books discuss the major or great powers. There is little mention of superpowers, although historically, de facto superpowers have dominated their era. The ancient Roman Empire or Napoleon's France would be called superpowers, if the term were applied to earlier eras. The emergence of the twentieth century superpowers resulted from the convergence of two events: the collapse of the traditional great powers after World War II, and the overwhelming concentration of power in the United States and the Union of Soviet Socialist Republics. Each country had advanced military resources, plus significant economic production, substantial territory and natural resources, scientific capabilities, and a well-trained population. Their political powers in the international sphere were enhanced by their participation in alliances in which they had great influence. As a result, these two superpowers dominated international relations for more than four decades.

Before World War II, the United States and the Soviet Union were major powers, but relatively passive participants in world affairs. The United States avoided participation in the League of Nations and in most international political crises between 1919 and 1939. The Soviet Union, at first ostracized as a renegade power after the Bolshevik Revolution, gained begrudging acceptance by the world of nations in the 1930's, but was not usually consulted on crucial matters. In the years leading up to World War II, Germany, Great Britain, Japan, France, and Italy were perceived as the main players, or great powers, in international relations. Because of the defeat of Germany and Japan, the collapse of Italy, and the weakening of Britain and France during World War II, a vacuum existed in world politics. The United States emerged from the war as the single strongest nation and the Soviet Union, although debilitated by the war, as the second strongest. The United States did not seek superpower status, but was gradually catapulted into the role of leader of the Western world, allied with other Western, but greatly weakened powers. The United States emerged from World War II as the only country possessing nuclear weapons, although other combatants had been on track to acquire nuclear power. Massive reconstruction and the acquisition of nuclear technology gradually propelled the Soviet Union into a superpower in the decades following 1945. The evidence supporting superpower status for the United States reflected virtually all measures of power, political, military, and economic. The evidence for superpower status for the Soviet Union was based principally on its military and nuclear prowess and expanding technological base in selected areas of the economy. The Soviet Union never achieved all-around economic development, a fact overlooked because of its military strength.

After World War II, world politics focused on the bipolar, East-West conflict. Other problems, although not ignored, were subordinated to the agenda and drama of the Cold War. The Soviet Union and the United States, once allied against Nazi Germany in World War II, became rivals in the postwar world. The Soviet Union expanded its sphere of influence in Eastern Europe and Asia in the last days of World War II and in the war's immediate aftermath, in part under the guise of liberating nations from Nazi Germany and in part under the guise of the world communist movement. Beginning in 1947, the United States and its allies thwarted further Soviet efforts to expand its sphere of influence. The United States adopted the policy of containment of the Soviet Union, a policy that influenced U.S. policy toward the Soviet Union and other Marxist socialist countries for the next four decades.

The emerging superpowers faced each other or their proxies in a series of confrontations during the ensuing years. There were electoral rivalries in Western Europe, the Berlin Crisis of 1948, the Korean War (1950-1953), and growing hostility in the United Nations in the early postwar years. The creation of the North Atlantic Treaty Organization (NATO) in 1949 solidified the Western alliance. The entrance of the German Federal Republic (West Germany) into NATO in 1954 was the Soviet justification for formalizing its military arrangements with Eastern Europe to create the Warsaw Pact, which included East Germany.

Initially, the Soviet Union was not considered a real superpower, but after it acquired the atomic and hydrogen bombs, its burgeoning military power seemed more important than the low Soviet standard of living. Joseph Stalin's death in 1953 and his successors' more flexible policies reduced overt tension between the superpowers, but their rivalry persisted. Nikita Khrushchev challenged the West to compete with the Soviet-led socialist camp to prove which side possessed a superior economic system.

Superpower rivalry reached a new stage in international relations in 1957, when the Soviet Union launched Sputnik, the first satellite to circle the globe in space. Achievement after achievement brought the Soviet Union closer to superpower status, although recognition as a full-fledged superpower eluded the Soviets until military investments under Leonid Brezhnev brought them to approximate military parity with the United States. By 1970, both the United States and the Soviet Union were regarded as superpowers, whose preponderance of military and technological power, combined with their large-scale economies, made them formidable forces in international relations.

In the late 1960's and early 1970's, détente existed between the superpowers, a fragile, but notable, improvement in relations that deteriorated by the late 1970's when the policies of the Soviet Union in Africa and Afghanistan, and a resulting anti-Soviet backlash in the United States, led President Jimmy Carter's administration to pull back from détente.

The early 1980's marked the last stage of the Cold War. President Ronald Reagan defeated Jimmy Carter in the presidential election of 1980, in part on the strength of his anti-Soviet and promilitary rhetoric. These sentiments carried over into U.S. foreign policy, and tensions between the two nations were high until 1985 when Mikhail Gorbachev came to power and introduced new thinking into Soviet foreign policy. The Cold War ended in the late 1980's when initiatives by the Gorbachev and Reagan and George Bush administrations slowly but steadily improved relations between the superpowers.

The erosion of Soviet power and collapse of the Soviet Union in 1991 ended the superpower era as it had existed since 1945. The rise of Japan as an economic, but not a military, superpower, the reemergence of strong economies in Western Europe, and the dispersion of power centers also contributed to the end of the superpower era.

Applications

There are numerous examples of the superpowers' interaction or confrontation in international relations over forty years. A major confrontation occurred in Berlin in 1948-1949. After World War II, the four occupying powers (the United States, the United Kingdom, the Soviet Union, and France) divided Germany into four zones. They also divided Berlin, the former capital city, located within the Soviet zone, into four zones. A crisis began when the Soviet Union, as the occupying power of the eastern zone, refused to allow the Western powers highway access to Berlin. For a year, the three Western powers airlifted supplies into the western zones of Berlin, until the Soviet Union reopened the access roads. As a result of the Berlin Crisis, the Western powers consolidated their zones in Berlin and Germany into West Berlin and the Federal Republic of Germany (West Germany) respectively. Shortly thereafter, the Soviet Union authorized the creation of the German Democratic Republic (East Germany). Berlin continued to be a problem in East-West relations, because it was an island of Western influence and an escape route for refugees from East Germany. An effort to end the population drain resulted in construction of the Berlin Wall in 1961, after several minor crises in the late 1950's and early 1960's. Tension between the two Germanies eased after the adoption of West German chancellor Willy Brandt's policy of "ost-politik" (his initiative toward the Eastern bloc) in 1969.

The end of the Berlin Crisis resulted in a shift in the world's attention to Asia. In Asia, the East-West conflict was at the root of both the Korean War, 1950-1953, and the struggle for control of Indochina—Vietnam, Laos, and Cambodia—which continued over several decades.

In the early 1960's, the superpowers focused on Cuba, a country newly declared Communist and allied with the Soviet Union. The Cuban Missile Crisis of 1962 was a direct confrontation between the superpowers. The Soviet Union had placed missiles in Cuba in the early 1960's to counter NATO missiles along the Soviet border in Turkey. In October, 1962, the Kennedy Administration demanded that the Soviet Union turn around the missile-laden ships bound for Cuba. For a few tense days, the world stood on the edge of war. Finally, the superpowers compromised, and war was averted. The United States promised never to invade Cuba, in return for a Soviet promise to remove missiles from Cuba.

The superpowers were also rivals for influence in the Third World. In the late 1940's, the United States began providing foreign aid to a few Third World states. Efforts were expanded in the 1950's during the Eisenhower Administration when Secretary of State John Foster Dulles launched a crusade against communism and furnished aid to Third World countries allied with the United States. Beginning in the mid-1950's, the Soviet Union competed for influence in the Third World, giving aid principally to countries not in military alliances with the United States. Rivalry in the Third World concentrated on regions with strategic or economic significance, most notably the Middle East and Southeast Asia. Competition for the Third World continued, in some form, for three decades, diminishing only during the Gorbachev era.

A rapidly escalating arms race between the superpowers characterized the Cold War in the early 1980's. The arms race had steadily intensified despite the arms reduction talks of the 1970's and the Strategic Arms Limitation Talks (SALT I) agreement concluded in 1972. By the mid-1980's, both countries were spending large sums on defense, weapons development, and procurement. Although costly to both countries, the arms race adversely affected the Soviet economy more profoundly than that of the United States. The post-Brezhnev political leadership, headed by Gorbachev, recognized that the arms race was debilitating the country, which was a major impetus for Gorbachev's new thinking about global interdependence and arms reductions.

Context

There were great powers in the past, and there will be great powers in the future. Few, if any, were called superpowers, although the case can be made that the Roman Empire, the Byzantine Empire, or other dominant powers of their eras were superpowers. The post-World War II period was a special moment, when two military superpowers played dominant roles in world politics.

The era of the superpowers, 1945 to 1990, was a distinctive period in modern international relations, which may not be repeated in the future. Although other issues, such as world peace, the environment, north-south inequities, famine, and civil wars, never totally left the international arena, the agenda of the superpowers eclipsed other issues in international politics, making it hard for people to forget the superpower confrontation. The two superpowers seemed to have reached levels of power no other nation could challenge. After the collapse of communism in Eastern Europe and the breakup of the Soviet Union into fifteen republics, Russia remained a military superpower, but her economic might and political influence were diminished significantly. The United States remains a superpower, although her influence in the world had also diminished by the early 1990's.

The significance of the period 1945 to 1990 was precisely that the agenda of the superpowers superseded other concerns, however urgent or important, and became the dominant issue of world politics. In the post-Cold War era, the focus of international relations has shifted from the East-West conflict to the myriad unsolved problems in the world.

Bibliography

Crockatt, Richard, and Steve Smith, eds. *The Cold War: Past and Present*. Boston: Allen & Unwin, 1987. Traces three major stages of the Cold War from World War II to the 1980's. Examines U.S., British, and Soviet views. This interpretive study is useful for setting the Cold War into an international context.

Ginsburgs, George, Alvin Z. Rubinstein, and Oles M. Smolansky, eds. *Russia and America: From Rivalry to Reconciliation*. Armonk, N.Y.: M. E. Sharpe, 1993. Focuses primarily on relations between the superpowers in the post-Cold War and post-Soviet periods. Explores Russian and U.S. foreign policies and interaction in the rapidly changing world of the 1990's.

Jones, Walter S. *The Logic of International Relations*. 7th ed. New York: Harper Collins, 1991. This fascinating text presents international relations as perceived by the United States, the former Soviet Union, and other major players in international politics.

Kissinger, Henry. *Diplomacy*. New York: Simon & Schuster, 1994. History of diplomacy focusing on the nineteenth and twentieth centuries, written by an important scholar-practitioner of the craft of diplomacy. Although not as objective as critics might wish, presents a good overview of power politics in international relations and interesting case studies of selected events.

Morgenthau, Hans. *Politics Among Nations*. Revised by Kenneth W. Thompson. New York: McGraw-Hill, 1993. This book, issued in numerous editions since 1948, defined the global agenda for generations of U.S. students after World War II. Morgenthau's discussion of the realist perspective in international politics focused attention on national interest and power, rather than on the idealist humanitarian agenda.

Olson, William C., ed. *The Theory and Practice of International Relations.* 9th ed. London: Prentice-Hall International, 1994. Relates theories of international politics, to actual policies and practices. A good source for anyone who wants to learn more about international relations.

Papp, Daniel S. *Contemporary International Relations.* 4th ed. New York: Macmillan, 1994. Examines international relations from the perspective of several different major players, and traces the East-West conflict during the postwar period in the larger context of other major issues and determinants of international politics.

Stoessinger, John. *The Might of Nations.* 10th ed. New York: McGraw-Hill, 1993. Examines the multifaceted dimensions of power in international relations, and presents case studies of major issues and conflicts. Good introductory overview of postwar international relations.

Ulam, Adam. *The Rivals: America and Russia Since World War II.* New York: Viking Press, 1971. Detailed analysis, by a preeminent scholar, of the conflict between the Soviet Union and the United States in the postwar world. Provides insights into U.S. thinking at the height of the Cold War and during the traumatic Vietnam era.

Norma Corigliano Noonan

Cross-References

Alliances, p. 47; Arms Control, p. 95; Chinese Communism, p. 223; Conflict Resolution, p. 397; Diplomacy and International Negotiation, p. 552; Empires and Empire Building, p. 597; Foreign Relations, p. 718; Geopolitics, p. 759; Hegemony, p. 817; Human Rights and International Politics, p. 848; Imperialism, p. 889; International Agreements, p. 949; International Relations, p. 969; Nonaligned Movements, p. 1319; North Atlantic Treaty Organization, p. 1332; Realpolitik, p. 1668; Russian Political History, p. 1770; Treaties, p. 2020; World Political Organization, p. 2186.

SUPRANATIONAL GOVERNMENT INSTITUTIONS

Field of study: International government and politics

Supranational government institutions are organizations of nation-states characterized by possessing some degree of authority over those states. They typically are formed to promote collective security, advance economic interests, or handle regulatory matters.

Principal terms

COLLECTIVE SECURITY: agreement that aggression by one state against another is the same as aggression against all, and should be defeated by the collective action of all

INTEGRATION: process of bringing different nations together into a new political unit

INTERNATIONAL ORGANIZATION: transnational actor or institution whose members are nation-states

NATION-STATE: politically organized territory that recognizes no higher sovereignty, and whose population politically identifies with that entity

SOVEREIGNTY: political independence from any higher authority

Overview

A supranational government institution is an organization created by two or more sovereign states that has authority over its members, making them subordinate units in some way. In its ultimate form, a true supranational government institution can make decisions that are binding on members whether they have approved of the decision or not. It goes beyond being an organization of or between states, and becomes a new political entity that supersedes individual state members. Few international organizations at the end of the twentieth century have achieved this level of political power. Most are transnational institutions, where membership transcends national boundaries in some way, but with no clear authority to enforce their decisions on their members. Therefore, international organizations can be evaluated in terms of the degree of supranational authority they possess, because some international organizations can obligate their members to take certain actions in prescribed areas.

The creation of a supranational government institution is the end of a process, known as international integration, through which authority at the international level comes to replace national authority in some situations. It is a gradual process whereby the nature of relations among more or less sovereign political units changes, and these units slowly accept some kind of new central authority. It therefore involves transferring the right to make some authoritative decisions from the national government to the new international authority. The culmination of this process would be regional and then world or global government.

There is a limited degree of supranational authority in almost all international organizations because of the demands of sovereignty. One of the fundamental principles of the international system since the eighteenth century has been sovereignty, the concept that the rulers of a recognized nation-state have the right to administer their territory as they see fit. This principle was originally established for the purpose of ending religious wars. Monarchs were to determine the religion, Roman Catholic or Protestant, of their nation, and no other nation could impose its religion on that nation. Eventually this principle came to include almost all areas of domestic policy. Supranational institutions by definition violate the principle of sovereignty, because they make decisions that the nation must obey regardless of the interests or ideals of the nation. Not surprisingly, nations have resisted this process.

There are several types of situations in the international system in which cooperation, and in some instances acceptance of supranational authority, offers significant advantages for members. One of the most significant is the promotion of peace and security. Many supranational organizations have developed with a primary, if not exclusive, goal of attempting to prevent regional or international conflict, and restoring peace when violence occurs. The League of Nations, the United Nations, and the Organization of African Unity all have engaged in efforts to provide collective security. The United Nations, for example, has intervened diplomatically to resolve conflicts; has imposed economic and other sanctions on individual states, which all member states are required to follow; and, in some cases, has placed U.N. military forces in areas of conflict as peacekeepers, a buffer between disputants to prevent fighting.

Economic cooperation has been another important source of integration. Since World War II, many national leaders have concluded that economic cooperation, such as lowering tariffs and other barriers to international economic exchange, is crucial for continued economic growth. Initial cooperation in specific nonpolitical areas such as this has often led to broader and higher levels of cooperation, as the effort to become a single economic bloc, or trading unit, has necessitated increasing political cooperation and even subordination of sovereignty by member countries.

Nation-states also have found it advantageous to grant authority to supranational institutions in a number of regulatory areas, such as health, atomic energy, and aviation. In these areas, institutions such as the World Health Organization can make decisions that are binding on the member states. Several supranational organizations are involved in the redistribution of wealth and other resources. The International Monetary Fund (IMF), the World Bank, and the United Nations Children's Fund (UNICEF) collect money from members and distribute it to other nations.

Supranational institutions have been valuable forums for communication. Many organizations facilitate the political interaction of smaller states that might not be able to afford to send ambassadors to every nation. They also provide a valuable opportunity to air grievances in the hope of reaching peaceful resolution of conflicts.

Supranational government institutions can be categorized according to breadth of membership and scope of purpose. Breadth of membership refers to geographic or other limits on potential membership. Organizations are usually divided between those that attempt to be universal, that is, are open to almost every nation in the world, and those that are selective, usually in terms of geography. Scope of purpose concerns how many of the general goals of international organizations the specific organization pursues. Institutions are usually divided between those that are limited in purpose and those that are multipurpose. This creates four different types of supranational institutions.

There are very few examples of universal membership and multipurpose organizations. The two principal ones are the League of Nations (which existed from 1919-1940) and the United Nations. The Organization of American States, the North Atlantic Treaty Organization, and the British Commonwealth are examples of international organizations that are limited in membership but are multipurpose. The World Health Organization is a universal-membership but limited-purpose organization; the Desert Locust Control Organization of East Africa and the International Wool Study Group are examples of limited-purpose, limited-membership organizations.

Despite this great variety in nature and purpose, all supranational organizations share certain basic characteristics. Members of supranational institutions are always nation-states, as opposed to international nongovernmental organizations whose members are individuals. Supranational government institutions are established by treaty or executive agreement, and are voluntary—another manifestation of the principle of sovereignty.

Most supranational government institutions are organized in a similar fashion. They all have a permanent staff, often called a Secretariat, whose personnel are expected to be loyal to the organization, rather than to their state of origin. This is rarely the case, however. This permanent staff is usually responsible for the day-to-day operation of the organization and the implementation of policy decisions.

Almost all supranational government institutions have some kind of plenary representation, a body that includes all members of the organization, the U.N. General Assembly, for example. In theory, this body often is intended to be the most powerful body in the institution, but that is rarely the case. Many supranational organizations also have a second representative body, with a limited membership. These bodies exist because certain states are thought to have a greater stake in the organization's decisions, more responsibility for them, or greater capability to enforce them. The U.N. Security Council, which has fifteen members, five of which are permanent members, is this type of body. This smaller body is considered to be more efficient in decision making than the larger plenary body.

In representative bodies, one of the most important issues is how to allocate votes. The most common method is majoritarian, in which each member has an equal vote, and policy is determined by majority vote. This method, used in the U.N. General Assembly, is a response to both sovereignty and democratic principles. The problem is that small nations such as San Marino, with a population in the thousands, have the same decision-making power in the body as a nation such as China, with a population of almost a billion. Some bodies use weighted voting, where some formula based on population or wealth gives certain members greater voice than others. This is the case in the IMF and the council of ministers of the European Community. A few bodies have negative voting, where one or more nations has a veto, the power to stop action on their vote alone. This is the case for the five permanent members of the U.N. Security Council.

One characteristic that almost all supranational government institutions share is the struggle for financing. Because these organizations are not completely supranational, they do not have the power to force members to support the organization financially. When supranational institutions are not empowered to collect taxes, they must rely on voluntary contributions to fund their activities. Consequently, most supranational government institutions do not have adequate funding for the goals they set.

Applications

The primary struggle for potentially supranational government institutions is addressing the concerns of individual nations and their definitions of their interests. Even the most successful example of international integration and the development of supranational institutions, the European Community (EC), falls far short of the ultimate supranational institution. The EC began as the European Coal and Steel Community in 1952. The Treaty of Rome in 1957 created the European Economic Community and the European Atomic Energy Community; in 1967 all three groups were brought under the single political umbrella of the EC.

The institutional structure of the EC reflects many of the characteristics of supranational government institutions. The European Commission is the administrative arm of the EC. It is headquartered in Brussels, Belgium, and employs thousands of "Eurocrats" who are responsible for technical problem-solving in such areas as trade, agriculture, and finance. The commission itself is made up of seventeen members, two from each of the larger states in the EC (Great Britain, France, Germany, Spain, and Italy) and one from each of the remaining seven. They are appointed to four-year terms by their respective national governments and can be reappointed. A president, who is considered the chief executive officer of the organization, is selected from this group.

The commission's tasks include identifying problems; proposing solutions, sometimes in the form of legislation; implementing policy; representing the EC in international trade negotiations; and managing the EC budget. The EC has an advantage over almost all supranational institutions in that it derives a portion of its revenue from sources that are not controlled by member states, customs or tariffs on goods from outside the community, for example. The commissioners, who function as a cabinet with each commissioner overseeing an area of administrative activity, are supposed to represent the interests of all Europe; because they continue to owe their position to national governments, and because they may have political aspirations in their home country, this is not always the case. Although the commission may be responsible for the day-to-day operation of the EC, it has few, if any, formal, autonomous powers.

The real power in the EC lies with the least supranational institutions, the Council of Ministers and the European Council. The commission formally reports to the

Council of Ministers, which is made up of the foreign ministers of each member state. The structure of this organization reflects the unwillingness of nations to yield sovereignty completely, for while there is a system of weighted voting, most significant decisions are made by consensus, that is, all twelve members must agree. It also reflects the technical, or nonpolitical, focus of the organization in that the foreign ministers often step aside for other ministers, depending on the subject before the council. Together with the European Council, which is made up of the twelve individual national leaders and meets three times a year, the Council of Ministers approves policies and provides direction to the organization. The fact that these two representatives of national interest are the most powerful institutions in the EC is a clear manifestation of the struggle of supranational institutions to overcome the principle of sovereignty.

The European Parliament (EP) is the general representative body of the EC. Unlike almost any other international body in the world, the EP is directly elected by voters in the member states in population-defined districts. The 518 members are watchdogs over the commission, must approve the budget, and can veto some regulations issued by the commission, but have little power to legislate and cannot control the budget item by item. The EP's most significant role is as a debating forum, and a symbol of unity.

Perhaps the most powerful supranational institution in the EC is the European Court of Justice (ECJ). It is made up of thirteen judges, selected by the member states, who adjudicate disputes on matters covered by the Treaty of Rome, the equivalent of the EC's constitution, and on policy passed by the EC. The ECJ's greatest powers are its ability to make decisions that are binding on the member states, and the fact that it has established the right to overrule national laws that conflict with EC law, although it still lacks mechanisms to enforce its decisions completely. Unlike the World Court, the ECJ can hear cases brought by individuals.

It is clear that the European Community has traveled a long way on the path of integration. Greater strides are expected before the end of the twentieth century with the implementation of the Maastrict Treaty of 1991, which calls for a single currency for all members and increased political coordination in foreign and military policy. Nevertheless, it falls far short of the ideal supranational institution. While there are some binding decisions made by EC institutions, these decisions generally still are made by institutions defending national interests, rather than institutions based on the will of the community as a whole.

Context

Although the first modern international governmental organization (IGO), the precursor for supranational organizations, was established in 1815 (the Central Commission for the Navigation of the Rhine), complex supranational organizations are primarily a late phenomenon. Before World War I there were fifty IGOs, and eighty by 1940, when growth in the number of international organizations expanded rapidly. By the 1990's, there were approximately three hundred IGOs, creating a complex network of overlapping national memberships. Over the years, these organizations have grown more complex, more important, and stronger in terms of their ability to make binding decisions.

In addition to the security, economic, and regulatory objectives discussed above, other factors have contributed to the growth in the number and strength of supranational institutions. Perhaps the simplest is the increased amount of international contact, resulting from the communications and transportation revolutions that have made global communication and interaction quicker and easier. The expansion of major transnational problems is another contributory factor. New problems in the international system, such as nuclear proliferation and protection of the environment, affect numerous states and require solutions that are beyond the capacity of a single state to resolve.

Supranational government institutions represent a new, unique innovation in governmental dynamics. Although they share features of national government in terms of organization, they are forced to develop novel twists on these structures in order to address the problems of sovereignty and national interest. Where once one could study international politics by looking exclusively at nation-states, supranational government institutions have become increasingly important actors. In a number of political policy areas, such as economic development, the issues and solutions cannot be completely understood without studying U.N. agencies, the EC, and other regional groups. If organizations such as the United Nations or the European Community become true supranational institutions, the world will witness the birth of a fundamentally new political organization, the first since the development of the modern nation-state.

Bibliography

Archer, Clive. *International Organizations*. Boston, Mass.: Allen & Unwin, 1983. Relatively short but thorough and well-written review of the growth, nature, aims, activities, roles, and functions of international organizations. Bibliography.

Claude, Inis L. *Swords into Plowshares*. 4th ed. New York: Random House, 1984. Discussion of the evolution, present problems, and future prospects for world government. Somewhat theoretically oriented. Includes the U.N. charter.

Haas, Ernst B. *Beyond the Nation-State*. Stanford, Calif.: Stanford University Press, 1964. Somewhat dated, but provides a good analysis of the process of integration, with a case history of the International Labor Organization.

Riggs, Robert E., and Jack C. Plano. *The United Nations*. Chicago, Ill.: Dorsey Press, 1988. Scholarly, but provides a thorough discussion of the history, organization, and purposes of the United Nations. Includes selected readings for each chapter.

Urwin, Derek W. *The Community of Europe*. New York: Longman, 1991. Well-written discussion of the history and early development of the European Community. Includes a thorough bibliographic guide to further reading.

Eduardo Magalhães III

Cross-References

THE SUPREME COURT: ORGANIZATION AND PURPOSE

Field of study: Law and jurisprudence

The Supreme Court is part of the judicial branch of the federal government of the United States. It interprets the provisions of the Constitution of the United States through decisions concerning violations of individual rights and laws passed by the U.S. Congress and state legislatures.

Principal terms

APPELLATE JURISDICTION: authority of a court to review decisions made by another court

CONCURRING OPINION: a justice's agreement with the decision reached by a majority of the justices, but for different reasons

DISSENTING OPINION: justice's disagreement with the majority decision and opinion in a case

JUDICIAL REVIEW: right to review laws and other governmental actions to determine whether they are consistent with the federal or state constitution

OPINION OF THE COURT: decision in a U.S. Supreme Court case and the reasons given for that decision

ORIGINAL JURISDICTION: power of a court to hear the facts of a case and rule on that case

Overview

The Supreme Court of the United States was created in 1787 by Article 3 of the Constitution of the United States. This article gives the basic structure and jurisdictional powers of the judicial branch of the U.S. federal government. It contains only four hundred words. Article 3 says, "The judicial Power of the United States, shall be vested in one supreme Court, and in such inferior Courts as the Congress may from time to time ordain and establish."

The Constitution says little else about the federal court system. It does not specify the number of justices on the Court or their qualifications or duties. It does not specify which other federal courts shall be established. These issues have been decided by laws passed by the Congress of the United States and by tradition.

The Court has two types of jurisdiction, original and appellate. Under its original jurisdiction, the Court is a trial court and hears the facts of a case and then makes a decision. Cases between two or more states, between a state and the federal government, or involving foreign diplomatic personnel may be filed directly with the Supreme Court under its original or trial jurisdiction. Few of the cases that reach the Supreme Court do so under original jurisdiction.

Most cases reach the Court because of its appellate jurisdiction, regarding cases filed in state or federal courts. The Supreme Court in these cases is not a trial court of facts; it will rule only on matters of law. The kinds of cases that may be appealed to the Court are decided by the U.S. Congress. Cases that are appealed to the Court usually involve two types of legal questions. One type of case involves laws passed by the U.S. Congress or by state legislatures. The Court is asked to decide whether these laws violate any provisions of the U.S. Constitution. This power of the Court is called the judicial review power and was assumed by the Court in 1803. The other type of case that may be appealed to the Court involves whether the rights guaranteed to individuals by the U.S. Constitution have been violated by certain types of practices of others. About half of the cases appealed to the Supreme Court come from each of these categories. The Supreme Court itself decides which cases it will review. As many as 5,000 petitions may be received by the Court each year, but only about 150 of these cases are eventually heard by the Court. When a petition for a hearing is received by the Court, at least four justices must agree to hear the case before it will be accepted for review.

There are eight associate justices and one chief justice on the Court. Justices are nominated for positions on the Court by the president of the United States and must be confirmed by a majority of the members of the U.S. Senate. When a vacancy occurs on the Court, the president sends the name of a replacement to the Senate. This nomination is usually referred to the Judiciary Committee of the Senate. Members of that committee question the candidate, at hearings. The Judiciary Committee then sends its recommendation for appointment or rejection of the candidate to the entire Senate, which debates the issue and then votes. If a vacancy occurs in the position of chief justice, the president may nominate a current associate justice to fill that role and also nominate a new associate justice, or the president may nominate someone who is not already on the Court to fill the position. If a vacancy occurs during the last month the Senate is in session or at a time when the Senate is not in session, the president may appoint a replacement without the approval of the Senate. This replacement must later be confirmed by the Senate using the normal procedure for confirmation.

Once appointed to the Court, justices may remain on it for life as long as they maintain "good behavior." What constitutes good behavior is not specified in any written document. Justices may resign at any time, or they may be impeached by the U.S. Senate if they do not maintain good behavior.

Duties of the justices include participating in determining which cases to hear, deciding those cases, and writing and contributing to the opinions of the Court. The chief justice has additional duties of presiding over the hearing of cases and the conferences held to decide cases, chairing the judicial conference of the federal courts, and helping administer the federal court system.

The Court meets beginning on the first Monday of October, working until all of its business is completed, which is usually in late June or early July of the following year. While the Court is in session, it holds cycles of two weeks of hearings and conferences followed by two weeks of recess. During the two weeks of hearings and conferences, open sessions are held on Monday, Tuesday, and Wednesday from 10 A.M. to noon and again from 1 P.M. to 3 P.M. Each case is allotted one hour, and each side in the case usually presents oral arguments to the Court for one-half hour. During this time, the Court may question the attorneys who are presenting the arguments. If the case is an appeal from another court, no facts of the case are reviewed by the Court. Only information concerning the law involved is considered. Closed conferences to discuss these cases are held on Wednesday afternoon to discuss the Monday cases and on Friday to discuss the cases presented on Tuesday and Wednesday. Six justices must be present for any case to be heard and for a decision to be made. It may take weeks or even months to reach a decision in a case. Many of the most important decisions are not handed down until June. The Court usually stops hearing cases in May so that it has time to make decisions and write opinions.

Once a majority of the Court agrees with a decision, one justice is assigned to write the opinion of the Court in that case. The opinion is then given to the other justices to review. Five justices must agree with the opinion that is written before it becomes the opinion of the Court. Some justices may agree with the decision of the Court but not with the reason for the decision given in the opinion. They may write a concurring opinion giving their different justification for agreeing with the decision. Some justices may disagree with the decision of the Court. They may write a dissenting opinion. Decisions are reported in an open session of the Court. Either the full opinion or only a summary of the opinion may be read. During each two weeks of recess, justices work on researching cases, writing opinions, and writing reactions to opinions written by other justices.

Applications

In 1962, the Supreme Court handed down a ruling in the case of *Engel v. Vitale*. A review of this case shows the process by which a case may reach the United States Supreme Court and how the Court upholds the rights of individuals that are guaranteed by the Constitution.

On January 22, 1959, five parents of children in Union Free School District Number 9 in New Hyde Park, New York, filed a lawsuit in a New York state court saying that their children's rights under the First Amendment of the Constitution of the United States had been violated. Their school board had written a prayer and required all teachers and students to recite it at the beginning of each school day. The parents objected to this practice, saying it was an establishment of religion and therefore violated the First Amendment rights of their children; the First Amendment of the U.S. Constitution says that Congress shall not establish any religion or prohibit the free exercise of religion. This amendment applies only to the federal government but had been extended to include the states when the Fourteenth Amendment was passed in 1868.

The state court in New York refused to order the school board to stop this practice. The court did, however, say that the prayer should be voluntary. Any student who did not wish to participate could provide a note from a parent or guardian; such students would be excused from the prayer. The parents disagreed with this ruling and filed an appeal with the New York Court of Appeals, which upheld the state court ruling and allowed the prayer to continue as long as it remained voluntary.

Still dissatisfied with this decision, the parents appealed the case to the Supreme Court of the United States. The Court was asked to rule on whether the practice of voluntary prayer in school conflicted with the constitutional rights of the students involved. In 1962, the Supreme Court reversed the decisions that had been handed down by the other courts. The school board was told to stop the practice of reciting a prayer in school. All justices agreed with this decision except Potter Stewart.

Hugo Black was assigned to write the opinion of the Court. In the opinion, Black wrote that the prayer was a religious activity. Freedom of religion was one reason many people had immigrated to America, and that freedom was guaranteed by the First Amendment. Therefore, the prayer must be discontinued. William O. Douglas wrote a concurring opinion. He wrote that because the teacher in each class is a public employee, the time it takes to say the prayer is being paid for by the government. In addition, few students would probably leave while the prayer was being said. The one dissenting opinion, by Stewart, indicated that this practice of voluntary prayer was not an establishment of a religion and so did not violate the Constitution.

This example illustrates the appellate jurisdiction of the U.S. Supreme Court. The case was filed in a state court. The decision was appealed through the state court system until it reached the United States Supreme Court. Only those cases that fall under the jurisdiction of the Court may be appealed to the Supreme Court. This case involved a possible violation of an individual's Constitutional rights and therefore fell within the Court's appellate jurisdiction. Because the Court receives many appeals, it must choose carefully which cases to hear. The Court has set some criteria for deciding which cases it will hear. Petitions for hearings must address these criteria and show why the Court should hear the case.

This case also shows the various kinds of opinions that may be reached by the Court. Not all justices must agree with the decision reached by the Court, and even those who agree can offer different reasons for agreement.

Because the Court has the power of judicial review, appointments to the Court have political significance. Franklin D. Roosevelt recognized this and attempted to pack the Court with justices sympathetic to his New Deal legislation. His 1937 bill proposing the addition of one position on the Supreme Court for each justice over the age of seventy (up to a total of six) appeared to have congressional support. Various events, including the retirement of one conservative justice that allowed Roosevelt to create a majority liberal Court, convinced the American public that Roosevelt had achieved his goal without the legislation. Support for the bill therefore eroded. This situation is only one example of the political maneuverings surrounding the Court. Political controversy always surrounds presidential appointments of new justices to the Court.

Context

The Supreme Court is a part of the judicial branch of the federal government of the United States. It is the only court specified in the Constitution and is to be supreme over all other courts created by Congress. The Constitution does not spell out the position the Court should take in relation to the other branches of the government. The Judiciary Act of 1789 set up the federal system of courts and granted broad powers to the Supreme Court. The Court was given the power to hear cases brought to it from lower federal courts and from state courts. It was also given the power to direct the actions of federal judges and other federal officials. These powers were ambiguous.

During the time that John Marshall was the chief justice (1801-1835), the Court began to clarify its position within the government. In deciding the case of *Marbury v. Madison* in 1803, the Court assumed the power of judicial review by which it could declare any federal law passed by the Congress to be in conflict with the Constitution and therefore invalid. By doing this, the Court assumed the role of interpreting the Constitution in relation to cases brought before it. Later in Marshall's tenure, the Court also assumed the power to review acts of states and to determine whether they were constitutional. Acts of the executive branch of the federal government could also be reviewed by the Court to determine their constitutionality. This set up a system of checks and balances within the federal government. The legislative and executive branches of the government make laws. The executive branch then executes these laws, and the judicial branch interprets the Constitution in relation to these laws. This assumption of power caused controversy, but eventually these powers of the Court were widely accepted, clarifying the position of the Court in relation to the other two branches of the federal government and balancing power among the three branches.

By assuming these powers, the Court has become an integral part of the American government, with significant effects on society. It has helped resolve many of the most important and controversial issues that have faced the United States. The nature of the issues has changed. Prior to 1865, many of the controversies the Court was asked to settle involved the relationship between the federal government and the various state governments. The Court helped establish the idea that the federal government was supreme. Between 1866 and the 1930's, increased industrialization caused many problems. The Court was called on to determine the appropriate relationship between the government and business and whether government could regulate business. Since 1938, many of the issues considered by the Court have dealt with protection of individual and civil rights.

Bibliography

Anzovin, Steven, and Janet Podell. *The U.S. Constitution and the Supreme Court.* New York: H. W. Wilson, 1988. Series of articles concerning the U.S. Supreme Court and its relationship to the Constitution. Includes the text of the Constitution and gives a good account of how the Constitution developed.

Baum, Lawrence. *The Supreme Court.* 3d ed. Washington, D.C.: Congressional Quarterly Press, 1989. An excellent source of information concerning the Court, including details about how the Court structure has developed through the years. Discusses the Court's personnel and schedule, as well as issues the Court has faced.

Hamilton, Jack A., ed. *The Supreme Court: Guardian or Ruler?* New York: Scholastic

Book Services, 1968. Good source of information about how the power of judicial review was assumed by the Court. Gives specific statements from the Constitution and how those were used to assume the power of judicial review.

James, Leonard F. *The Supreme Court in American Life*. Glenview, Ill.: Scott, Foresman, 1964. Contains information about cases decided by the Supreme Court on various topics such as judicial review, slavery, regulating business, freedom of religion, and separation of church and state. Gives background on these cases and shows the position the Court has adopted on these various topics.

McCloskey, Robert G. *The American Supreme Court*. Chicago: University of Chicago Press, 1960. Examines the Supreme Court during the tenure of John Marshall as chief justice. Shows how the role of the Court in the U.S. government was clarified during this time. Also presents the Court under later chief justices.

Mason, Alpheus T., and William M. Beaney. *The Supreme Court in a Free Society*. Englewood Cliffs, N.J.: Prentice-Hall, 1959. Contains information about the Supreme Court and its development and role in the governmental process.

Rehnquist, William H. *The Supreme Court: How It Was, How It Is*. New York: William Morrow, 1987. Gives a good "insider" account of what it is like to be a part of the Supreme Court. Good information concerning the Court under Chief Justice John Marshall and the role the Court assumed during that time. Also gives good information concerning later Courts.

Brenda Carlyle

Cross-References

The Bill of Rights, p. 134; Civil Rights Protection, p. 304; The Constitution of the United States, p. 425; Constitutional Law in the United States, p. 439; Courts: U.S. Federal, p. 471; Judicial Review, p. 1012; Legal Systems in Anglo-American Governments, p. 1085; The Supreme Court: Role in Government and Law, p. 1935.

THE SUPREME COURT:
ROLE IN GOVERNMENT AND LAW

Field of study: Law and jurisprudence

The U.S. Supreme Court's power has increased notably throughout its history. The Court now has final authority regarding the constitutionality of all laws and governmental actions, with only limited self-imposed restrictions.

Principal terms
> APPELLATE COURT: court of review to determine the validity of the rulings of lower courts
> BILL OF RIGHTS: amendments to the Constitution confirming individual rights
> CONSTITUTION: procedures for and limitations imposed on a politically organized body, such as a nation or state
> CONSTRUCTION: interpreting a statute or a constitution when the meaning of such is ambiguous
> PRECEDENTS: previously decided cases serving as authorities for the disposition of cases
> *STARE DECISIS*: literally, to stand by that which was decided; rule that a prior decision may be overturned only with good cause

Overview

The federal judiciary consists of the U.S. Supreme Court and inferior federal courts such as federal district courts. The U.S. judiciary is appraised as being a branch of government coequal to the executive and legislative branches. Precise lines cannot be drawn between the three branches.

The drafters of the Constitution were uncertain whether to give equal authority to the Court, and its powers were left ambiguous. The Court ultimately granted itself the power to render final interpretation over the constitutionality of all laws and government actions.

When Chief Justice Earl Warren retired from the Court in 1969, he regarded his significant contribution to be his decisions in voting district reapportionment cases. In *Reynolds v. Sims* (1964), the Warren Court imposed a one person, one vote requirement on all the states. Warren postulated that the right to vote freely is the essence of a democratic society. Many of the delegates to the First Constitutional Convention arrived with the intent to protect the national government from the whims and excesses of a popular vote democracy. The Warren Court's decisions thus show a willingness to rule in opposition to original intent, in recognition of a changed political climate.

It took many compromises to bring the nation together; however, Article 1, section 2 of the Constitution reveals one unyielding view, the limitations placed on who may vote. In part, this section states that representatives shall be apportioned according to population, to be determined by adding the number of free persons and three-fifths of all other persons. Restrictions on the voting franchise permeate the Constitution.

The excursion undertaken by the Court to amass sufficient power to change the U.S. voting system was both unassuming and protracted. Early in its history, the Court appeared to be almost powerless. During President George Washington's tenure, the Court was weak and obscure, and its future was uncertain.

Early in its history, the Court experienced a high number of vacancies. For the six positions originally filled by Washington, eight vacancies occurred over a twenty-year period. One detractor for potential justices was the "circuit riding" requirement. Until 1896, justices traveled across the country hearing cases.

Major changes occurred after 1801, when President John Adams appointed John Marshall as the chief justice of the United States. Marshall functioned in this capacity for thirty-four years and is perhaps the most influential justice to serve on the Court. During Marshall's tenure, the Court vested within its jurisdiction an exceptional allotment of power. In *Marbury v. Madison* (1803), the Marshall Court granted itself irrevocable authority when contemplating the constitutionality of legislative acts. Debates still occur concerning the legitimacy of this exercise of control.

When analyzing laws and other forms of government action under the Constitution, the Court follows certain suppositions. These suppositions are rooted in the process of formation of the United States. After the war for independence from England, the states regarded themselves as independent sovereigns. The Articles of Confederation allowed only minimum intrusion into states' internal affairs by the Continental Congress.

Faced with the inability of the confederation to function properly, states had to concede powers to a central government. The delegates at the constitutional conventions, in an effort to fabricate a more concentrated federal government, made many compromises but maintained within the Constitution certain seemingly inescapable limits on the federal government. As a consequence, the Court generally discerns the Constitution as being a limitation on federal power. Without an expressed or implied grant of authority from within the Constitution, the federal government cannot regulate.

The Bill of Rights (the first ten amendments to the Constitution) provides protection from government intrusion upon fundamental individual rights. The government may pass laws that regulate personal freedoms but only after enduring various forms of judicial scrutiny.

When the Court evaluates a case involving constitutional questions, its rationale supporting the decision is as consequential as the ruling itself. These rationales authenticate the Court's credibility within the legal community and to the informed public. There are many approaches to constitutional interpretation. Literalism and "clear meaning" are straightforward methods. When challenging an act of Congress as being unconstitutional, the Court can set the article of the Constitution that is invoked beside the statute and decide whether the latter concurs with the former. With the adaptation method, the justices reason from the Constitution by first identifying principles or values the Constitution contains, then applying them to contemporary circumstances. This idea of structuralism draws its support from several articles within the Constitution. It is the most liberal application and can be found in many decisions. Structuralism is liberal by nature, allowing for interpretation. The original intent method is appraised as being conservative. The original intent method examines the meaning of a particular constitutional provision through the intent of its Framers, taking less account of any changes in circumstances.

In 1803, when *Marbury v. Madison* came before the Court, the final judgment appeared political in nature. The Court was apprehensive about ordering an antagonistic James Madison, as secretary of state, to recognize the appointment of William Marbury as justice of the peace in the District of Columbia. Marbury had been appointed by the prior administration under President John Adams. The Court interpreted an act of Congress that would have discharged Marbury and other federal judges as violating a constitutional provision. Chief Justice John Marshall and the Court declared the law invalid. In doing so, the Court established a precedent for judicial review of laws.

The Constitution positions the jurisdiction of the Court as appellate in most situations. In *Marbury v. Madison*, the Court was petitioned to assume the role of a trial court, hearing the facts of a case rather than deciding only on matters of law.

The U.S. judicial system is forged from English common law, giving the judiciary great latitude in setting precedent. This allows previously decided cases that are authorities to serve as the basis for the disposition of future cases. The many cases referencing *Marbury v. Madison* established that the Court would have the final interpretation of the constitutionality of government action.

Applications

The limitations on the types of cases the Court will hear are few. As a result, power shifts between the branches of government have occurred and continue to transpire.

One self-imposed limitation on the Court is the doctrine of political question. For many years, this kept the Court from involving itself in the fairness of voting practices and district reapportionment schemes. In *Colegrove v. Green* (1946), the issue was one of a peculiarly political nature and therefore was not proper for judicial determination. By 1960, however, a contrary view prevailed in *Gomillion v. Lightfoot*, when racial discrimination in voting practices was ruled to conflict with the Fifteenth Amendment. The Court set aside the political question doctrine so it could decide the case on its merit. Then, in *Reynolds v. Sims* (1964), the Warren Court opened the door further by requiring state legislators to establish a per capita system of representation.

Given the Court's attitude of judicial expansionism and making exceptions to rules, it was only a matter of time before the Court would maneuver from quantity to quality of voter representation. This step was finally taken in 1983 and reaffirmed in 1986.

In *Davis v. Bandemer* (1986), a case alleging gerrymandering, although the Court refused to accept election results as establishing unconstitutional discrimination against a political party, it made a strong assertion to continue to hear issues involving the quality of representation. Simply by agreeing to review these cases, the Court acknowledged that district boundaries, if redrawn, could potentially change election outcomes.

Although the doctrine of political question has substantially eroded over the years, giving the Court greater control, the Court has also interpreted the Constitution as giving greater power to Congress over the states. In 1903, the Court upheld the federal government's potential to prohibit or restrict commerce. The case of *Champion v. Ames* (1903) altered the delineation between interstate and intrastate commerce under Article 1, section 8, clause 3 of the Constitution. The circumstances brought before the Court originated in 1895 with an act of Congress that made it illegal to transport lottery tickets from state to state. C. F. Champion was convicted for sending two lottery tickets from Texas to California. The tickets were transported by commercial vehicle. In 1903, the Court rendered its decision upholding the conviction.

Under the interstate commerce clause, the power to regulate interstate commerce is a concurrent power, shared between the states and the federal government. In *Champion v. Ames*, the use of a commercial vehicle traveling between states was relevant. The Court espoused that that form of transportation entailed interstate commerce and thus allowed federal action. If the federal government has the right to regulate, then any conflicting state statutes will be declared unconstitutional through the invocation of the supremacy clause. Further, the Court viewed the congressional justification for the creation of the act as being rational. It determined that the federal government is the proper authority for protecting U.S. citizens from lotteries.

The Court continues to reform the meaning of interstate commerce, enhancing federal control. A greatly extended application of the interstate commerce clause can be found in *Heart of Atlanta Motel v. United States* (1964). This case implicated the constitutionality of Title II of the Civil Rights Act of 1964. The act strives to eliminate racial discrimination in motels, restaurants, and similar places of public service. It was the Heart of Atlanta Motel's policy to refuse lodging to people of color. The motel had 216 rooms available and was readily accessible by many freeways. It advertised in several states, and 75 percent of its guests were from other states.

The Court upheld the constitutionality of the act as applied to the motel. The decision postulated that the operation of a motel might appear local in nature, but if interstate commerce is involved, the federal government has jurisdiction. As in *Champion v. Ames*, the Court determined that the harm averted by the act was a legitimate national concern. The rationale offered by the Court in *Heart of Atlanta Motel* illustrates the accumulation of many years of precedent setting. The Court asserted that the same interest that led Congress to deal with segregation prompted it to control gambling, criminal enterprises, deceptive practices in the sale of products, fraudulent security transactions, improper branding of drugs, wages and hours, and the protection of small business from injurious price cutting.

The Court's interpretational ability not only affects the legislative branch but also influences the executive branch. In *United States v. Nixon* (1974), a special prosecutor obtained a subpoena directing President Richard M. Nixon to deliver certain tape recordings of conversations held in the White House. Nixon produced some of the material but withheld portions, claiming executive privilege that places confidential documents beyond judicial reach. The Court ruled that the doctrine of separation of powers and the need for confidentiality of high-level communication cannot sustain an absolute, unqualified presidential privilege of immunity. The Court ordered Nixon to produce the missing tapes for an "in camera" inspection. The courts could review the tapes in private, to protect any military, diplomatic, or security secrets they contained. Nixon, by producing all the tapes for inspection, explicitly showed the level of control the judiciary has over the executive branch. In 1803, the Marshall Court avoided the issue of forcing a position contrary to a president's opinion in *Marbury v. Madison*. By 1974, the Court was confident enough to impose a ruling requiring a president to make a choice only the executive branch (the president) could enforce.

Context

In 1936, the Court, in *Ashwander v. Tennessee Valley Authority* (1936), articulated several self-imposed limitations that the court had seemed to follow when analyzing cases. The Court would not hear nonadversary situations or questions before its decision became necessary. It would not formulate broader decisions than a case required and would attempt to dispose of each case on nonconstitutional grounds. The Court would not pass on the validity of a statute without the possible injury to an individual. Whenever possible, statutes were construed to avoid constitutional issues.

Even with such limitations, the interpretation process allows many avenues for rendering decisions without confining the Court. The judicial branch has successfully pushed its boundaries of control on various occasions.

The case of *Dred Scott v. Sandford* (1857) signifies the limits of judicial expansionism. John Sanford (the name was misspelled in court records) was sued by a slave, Dred Scott, who was seeking freedom. The Court, under Chief Justice Roger B. Taney, vetoed a major legislative policy by ruling that Congress could not forbid slavery in the territories. This usurped the ability of Congress to manage an issue that ultimately led to civil war and several constitutional amendments. The Taney Court substituted Marshall's national supremacy with judicial supremacy.

Several external attempts to control judicial expansionism have occurred. The executive branch has ventured to impeach justices and to increase their numbers. Such procedures have proven to be ineffective.

Placing these constraints into perspective, there are only a few practical restraints on the Court's power. They include the moral structure of the appointed justices, societal acceptance, and the number of cases capable of being reviewed annually by the Court.

Bibliography

Cox, Archibald. *The Court and the Constitution*. Boston: Houghton Mifflin, 1987. A well-organized approach to major Court decisions. The author was a solicitor general and the first Watergate special prosecutor. He details how the Court has kept the Constitution an important and creative instrument.

Ezorsky, Gertrude. *Racism and Justice: The Case for Affirmative Action*. Ithaca, N.Y.: Cornell University Press, 1991. Excellent presentation of the historical foundation of affirmative action. Although the author's bias is toward supporting the premise of affirmative action, she makes an attempt to present counterarguments to her position. The major focus is on the benefits derived through affirmative action for people of color.

Gunther, Gerald. *Constitutional Law*. 11th ed. Mineola, N.Y.: Foundation Press, 1985. Well-written textbook that discusses the immense area of constitutional law. It is remarkably detailed and has a tendency to ask more questions than it answers. It provides a superior foundation in beginning constitutional research.

Hilsman, Roger. *To Govern America*. New York: Harper & Row, 1979. Admirable compilation of data describing all features of government including many peripheral aspects, such as philosophy and the future of American democracy.

Mason, Alpheus T., and Donald Stephenson, Jr. *American Constitutional Law: Introductory Essays and Selected Cases*. 10th ed. Englewood Cliffs, N.J.: Prentice-Hall, 1993. Commendable review and analysis of constitutional law that clearly presents intricate and sometimes obscure material.

Sowell, Thomas. *Preferential Policies: An International Perspective*. New York: William Morrow, 1990. This topic is often neglected when analyzing legal issues. The emphasis is on India, Nigeria, Malaysia, South Africa, Sri Lanka, and the United States. For such a diverse approach, the information is well organized.

Tindall, George. *America: A Narrative History*. 2d ed. New York: W. W. Norton, 1988. Constricted narrative that shapes U.S. history into an eventful story. The account presents history in themes such as judicial nationalism.

Brian J. Carroll

Cross-References

The Bill of Rights, p. 134; The Constitution of the United States, p. 425; Constitutional Governments, p. 432; Constitutional Law in the United States, p. 439; Courts: U.S. Federal, p. 471; Federalism in the United States, p. 668; Government Powers, p. 772; Government Roles, p. 778; Individual Versus State Rights, p. 910; Intergovernmental Relations, p. 942; Legal Systems in Anglo-American Governments, p. 1085; Separation of Powers: Presidential Government, p. 1815; The Supreme Court: Organization and Purpose, p. 1929.

TAXATION AND APPROPRIATION

Field of study: Functions of government

Acquiring funds through taxation and appropriating those funds to purposes deemed to be public priorities are fundamental powers of legislative bodies in representative governments. Historically, legislatures have used their "power of the purse" to limit executive absolutism and to provide for the common welfare.

Principal terms

APPROPRIATION: spending or obligation of public funds for authorized purposes

AUTHORIZATION BILL: legislative action that institutes or continues the operation of a program to implement public policies; actual spending may not occur until an appropriations bill provides financing

BUDGET: document that describes a government's plans for spending and specifies taxation and deficit policies for a single fiscal period

IMPOUNDMENT: action (or inaction) by a U.S. federal employee that prevents the expenditure or obligation of funds that Congress has appropriated

LINE-ITEM VETO: power that lets the chief elected official reject a specific item while approving the balance of an appropriations bill

POWER OF THE PURSE: historic nickname for the authority of democratic legislative bodies to control the taxation and appropriations functions of government

SCOREKEEPING: process used by the U.S. Congressional Budget Office to maintain timely tabulations of the impacts of budget actions on overall federal spending, taxes, and debt

taxation: compulsory mechanism used by government to acquire money or other valuable things from people by force of law

Overview

Growth of both government and the importance of economic activities has made taxation and the appropriation of the monies raised through taxation crucial government functions. In representative governments, this "power of the purse" generally has been restricted to elected delegates serving in legislative bodies. In most nations, interest in gaining control over expenditures came later than—and as a by-product of—concern over the appropriate use of taxation by sovereign powers.

In France, there was little effort to secure a popular "budget right" before the Revolution. A decree on June 17, 1789, however, prohibited taxation without common consent. With the notable exceptions of tax impositions by Napoléon and later by his son Louis Napoléon, there have been few infractions of this now fundamental principle of French constitutional practice. For many years, although the French National Assembly required an accounting of funds, they did not try to specify their expenditure. Assembly members apparently feared they would be usurping executive authority by asserting control over expenditures. In 1831, however, the assembly finally established full parliamentary power of the purse in France by adding responsibility for determining the detail of appropriations to their taxation authority.

In Great Britain, the roots of modern "power of the purse" are found in the emergence of representative or popular control over taxation. As early as 1215, England's Magna Carta sought to constrain the monarch's authority to impose taxes. The Glorious Revolution of 1688 and the adoption of the English Bill of Rights established the absolute right of Parliament to consent to the imposition of taxes. Gradually expenditures came to be controlled by Parliament, following early experiences with requiring detailed expenditure reports for the army and navy. When King George III relinquished most of his hereditary revenues in return for an annual grant from Parliament after 1760, the basis was established for today's system of full parliamentary authority over appropriation and taxation.

Despite Parliament's undisputed authority for the revenues of government, there is a strong and centralized executive role in budgeting in Britain. The responsibility for preparing the financial plan or budget rests with the executive, who must propose all spending and defend those requests to the House of Commons. Parliament retains the power to approve, disapprove, or reduce proposed expenditures, while the executive must reconcile expenditures with revenues. Parliament may increase the total expenditure, but for it to do so amounts to a vote of no confidence. Once the budget is approved, the executive controls the administration of programs, with oversight by the Public Accounts Committee of Parliament.

Britain's centralized yet flexible system of taxation and appropriation has had an important influence on developments in other nations, perhaps most notably the United States, in which interest in controlling expenditures also followed concern over appropriate use of taxation authority. Because Great Britain's system of budgeting was not fully developed at the time of the American Revolution, however, there was no defined structure for the Framers of the U.S. Constitution to emulate. The General Welfare Clause of the Constitution (Article 1, section 8) provides Congress with broad power of the purse by granting it the authority "to lay and collect taxes to provide for the common defense and general welfare of the United States." Two other powers granted through the Constitution, the war power and the power to regulate interstate and foreign commerce, extend congressional appropriation authority even further.

The U.S. Constitution requires that all new government undertakings must be approved twice. A program is authorized by Congress through an authorization bill, while its financing is provided separately through an appropriations bill. The two-step process tends to restrain spending, as evidenced by the frequently lower amounts of program finance that are usually approved in appropriations bills.

In the United States, the power balance between Congress and the president has always been delicate. Although it was commonly accepted that Congress has the exclusive power of appropriation, the emphasis prior to the late 1700's was on the Hamiltonian concept of "executive discretion." Under this doctrine, general lump-sum appropriations were first made by Congress, then allocated to more specific purposes by the president. In opposition to Alexander Hamilton, the Jeffersonians began promoting the concept of "legislative restraint," or limitation of executive discretion through the enactment and oversight of specific appropriations.

With the election of Thomas Jefferson as president in 1800 and the demise of the Hamiltonian approach of executive discretion, Congress assumed the dominant role in fiscal matters in the United States. The president was obliged to follow the spending directives of Congress, departing from those only in cases of national emergency. In theory, budget formulation was Congress's role, while the president was relegated to execution without discretion. In practice, presidents have historically found many ways to achieve discretionary powers; periodic efforts by Congress to enforce their specific appropriations often ended in failure.

Passage of the Budget and Accounting Act of 1921 established the basic framework for the modern budget system in the United States. The act made the executive branch responsible for transmitting a national budget to Congress. In addition, the General Accounting Office was established as an arm of Congress, to monitor executive compliance with congressional intent and the limits of appropriations. These changes to the budget system made the U.S. process of national budgeting similar to Great Britain's in structure, though not in terms of the implicit balance of power between the president and the Congress. In the United States, once the Congress receives the president's budget, it has the authority to change any expenditures or revenues. It is not unusual for the final congressional budget to differ markedly from that of the president.

In 1974, Congress' enactment of the Congressional Budget and Impoundment Control Act further strengthened congressional power of the purse and completed the framework for the modern U.S. budget system by establishing the Congressional Budget Office.

The power of the purse granted under the General Welfare Clause appears to give the U.S. Congress unlimited spending power. Whether Congress can raise and spend money for whatever may contribute to the general welfare or only to the extent specified elsewhere in the Constitution (such as through the war powers granted or the commerce clause), however, has long been a source of controversy.

The growth of federal government spending and the state and local spending increases that the federal government has encouraged reveals a permissive interpretation of the constitutional power of the purse. In addition to its own direct expenditures, the national government has used the power of the purse to compel desired activities at the state and local levels of the U.S. federal system. For example, even though the national government cannot directly regulate education or agriculture, through its provision of grants-in-aid, Congress can influence state and local conduct in those policy areas. The power of the purse also has been used to discourage undesirable practices. For example, Congress can stipulate that federal funding will be withheld from a program if any person connected with the program is denied benefits on the basis of race, national origin, or gender.

By the 1970's, the rapid growth of federal programs had produced a large and growing national deficit in the U.S. budget. The United States is not, however, the only nation to see its government spending expand. In fact, relative to national output, its growth in government spending actually lags behind that of other developed nations. From 1900 until 1980, public expenditures in the United States increased from about one-twentieth to one-fourth of the gross national product. Through this same period, public expenditures in Great Britain rose from one-twelfth to nearly one-half of the gross national product, and Germany saw public expenditures rise from about one-seventh to two-fifths of the gross national product.

Despite the fact that the United States devotes less of its national product to governmental activities than do most other developed nations, its huge budget deficit caused many citizens to begin questioning the scope of government activity and its costs. In 1972, President Richard Nixon tried unsuccessfully to force Congress to adopt a $250 billion spending ceiling. His insistence that the U.S. Congress enact a spending ceiling that year and the ensuing battle between the executive and legislative branches of government foreshadowed a continuing spotlight on the appropriate extent of legislative power of the purse.

Applications

During the seven-year period spanning the escalation of U.S. involvement in the Vietnam War and the tumult of the Watergate scandal, battles between President Richard Nixon and Congress over national spending escalated. Eventually, those events precipitated enactment of landmark legislation, the Congressional Budget and Impoundment Control Act of 1974. The events leading up to passage of this act and its content underscore the importance of democratic legislatures' power of the purse.

On October 18, 1972, both the House and Senate approved legislation that raised the limit on public debt, implemented a $250 billion limitation on spending for fiscal year 1973, and at the same time, provided that the ceiling would expire the day after the bill became law. Although this bill was later defeated, its contradictory provisions were evidence of the intense conflict between the president and Congress.

Not to be impeded by the defeat in Congress of his proposal to cap domestic outlays, in early 1973 President Nixon escalated his pressure on Congress. He employed his veto power widely and interpreted his executive impoundment authority broadly. Among his numerous refusals to spend was the impoundment of $6 billion of an $11 billion appropriation for sewage treatment that Congress had passed over his veto in 1972.

The president argued that impoundments were necessary to slow inflation through temporary reductions in federal spending. Congressional Democrats viewed his actions as thinly disguised attempts to reduce domestic spending without congressional approval. Government Operations Committee Chairman Sam Ervin argued that the president's wholesale impoundments were effectively line-item vetoes, which are not permissible under the Constitution. Nearly all members of Congress viewed the president's actions as an affront to their power of the purse.

Congress responded by seeking to limit the president's impoundment authority. The Senate passed a bill designed to compel the president to release impounded appropriations after sixty days unless both chambers ratified the impoundment through a concurrent resolution. The House Rules Committee voted to empower either chamber to override an impoundment. The bill passed eventually, but a presidential veto was certain. When close votes on several Republican amendments to the measure revealed that a division had erupted among the members of Congress, the bill was abandoned.

As Watergate events came to light over the next year, Nixon's presidential power dwindled. At the same time, efforts to reform the budget process and strengthen Congress' role in establishing the national budget gained momentum. Less than one month before his resignation, on July 12, 1974, President Nixon signed the Congressional Budget and Impoundment Control Act into law. This law greatly constrained the president's right to circumvent congressional intent by refusing to spend appropriations. The law distinguished between a temporary impoundment of funds, or what is also called a "deferral" of budget authority, and the more serious type of impoundment, an outright or permanent refusal to spend, called a "rescission" of budget authority.

In cases of both deferrals and rescissions, the law requires the president to send a special message to Congress to report the proposed action. Beyond that point, however, the two types of impoundment requests are handled differently. In the case of deferrals, the act is passive with regard to their use. By not acting to block a deferral, Congress gives de facto approval. If Congress wants to cancel a proposed deferral, it may do so only by enacting a law. The act is more lenient with deferrals because they do provide the executive with an important tool for budget management. Congress ensured that deferrals would be temporary impoundments, however, by requiring them to expire automatically at the end of the fiscal year.

By contrast, the Congressional Budget and Impoundment Control Act took a much stronger stance against rescissions. Under this 1974 act, the president may withhold funds for up to forty-five days while Congress considers a rescission request. If Congress does not act during that prescribed period, however, the funds must be made available immediately for obligation.

Two other components of the Congressional Budget and Impoundment Control Act of 1974 produced significant changes in the way the federal budget is compiled by Congress and in the balance of power between the president and Congress. The first component was the establishment of the Congressional Budget Office. Prior to enactment of this sweeping reform legislation in 1974, budget analysis activities had been concentrated in the executive branch of government. If Congress wanted information about the basis for economic and revenue projections, it had to turn to the president's advisers. The 1974 law established a highly skilled staff to provide Congress with regular economic and budget impact projections, cost estimates, and other data to supplement—and at times contradict—information provided by the president and his staff. Armed with such credible information, Congress became much more able to establish its own budget priorities, separate from the president's agenda.

The Congressional Budget and Impoundment Control Act also required that staff from the newly created Congressional Budget Office institute an activity during budget review called "scorekeeping." Scorekeeping is a procedure whereby staff keep track of appropriation and tax policy decisions being made in a variety of committees of both houses, determine their combined effects on the overall levels of federal spending, revenues, and debt, and report the updated "score" to Congress.

Though scorekeeping may not appear to be a major innovation, its implementation was a critical juncture for federal budgeting. Appropriation and taxation alternatives were previously debated in isolation from each other; scorekeeping caused these interrelated elements of the budget to become linked. Congress became able to know quickly when a proposed spending increase would require additional revenue, or conversely, when a proposed tax reduction would require spending cuts to balance the budget. Equally important, the impact of appropriation and taxation choices on the federal deficit was to be tallied and reported to Congress soon enough for those effects to become part of the budget debate.

Context

At the beginning of the 1980's, in the face of continuing growth of the national debt, President Ronald Reagan argued for two specific changes to the Constitution to compel Congress to contain the nation's fiscal affairs. The first constitutional amendment that Reagan advocated would have mandated a balanced federal budget. Under such a provision, Congress would have been constitutionally prohibited from spending in excess of available revenues. Reagan's second revision would have given the president a line-item veto. With this change, presidents would be able to veto some parts of bills while approving others. This would have ended the practice of requiring presidents to accept or reject entire appropriations bills, which often means refusing to appropriate funds for favored purposes in order to prevent other expenditures.

Of Reagan's two proposals, the balanced budget concept enjoyed the most national support. Supporters of a constitutional amendment argued that only a constitutional provision would force lasting change in federal spending because Congress can change laws at will. By 1984, the legislatures of thirty-two states had called for a constitutional convention to draft a balanced-budget amendment. Congress was responding to the mounting pressure by acting on its own amendments, but it consistently failed to garner enough support. Enactment in 1985, however, of the Balanced Budget and Emergency Deficit Control Act, better known as "Gramm-Rudman-Hollings" (after its sponsors, senators Phil Gramm, Warren Rudman, and Ernest Hollings), came close to requiring Congress to align spending and taxes.

Gramm-Rudman-Hollings established a series of declining deficit targets fashioned to bring the federal budget into balance by 1991. A controversial provision of the law would have required the president to initiate uniform reductions in spending called "sequestrations" if Congress failed to reach specified deficit targets. This provision was voided by a Supreme Court ruling that sequestrations were unconstitutional.

The Gramm-Rudman-Hollings act was acknowledged by many to be too extreme because of its stringent targets and explicit challenges to legislative power of the purse. The focus on deficit reduction has continued in the United States, although by the mid-1990's, Congress had failed to reduce the deficit appreciably.

In Europe resource scarcity has forced a similar careful focus on expenditure restraint. German reunification in particular placed significant strain on finances. As in the United States, efforts to reorder expenditure priorities, particularly with regard to entitlement programs, have proved difficult. In Germany, however, the task became more difficult because a majority of its state governments must agree to reform entitlement programs. During the late 1980's and early 1990's, Spain began revising its budget process following a lengthy period of political and economic change during which expenditure policies could not meet new demands. During the 1970's, efforts to strengthen budget control in Denmark were unsuccessful. Following a transfer of responsibility for welfare programs from the national to the local level in the 1980's, however, a process of budget negotiation between central and local government officials helped to bring local expenditures under control.

Bibliography

Collender, Stanley E. *The Guide to the Federal Budget.* 10th ed. Washington, D.C.: Urban Institute Press, 1991. This publication, which is updated frequently, provides a comprehensive yet easily understood review of the federal budget. For readers interested in deciphering the content of the federal budget and identifying changes in policy, there is no better source.

Leonard, Herman B. *Checks Unbalanced: The Quiet Side of Public Spending.* New York: Basic Books, 1986. Thoughtful look at a number of large public expenditures that occur in the United States without specific legislative action. Areas studied range from public pension systems, social security, and leasing to the private use of proceeds of tax-exempt public bond issues.

Phillips, Kevin. *The Politics of Rich and Poor: Wealth and the American Electorate in the Reagan Aftermath.* New York: HarperCollins, 1991. This well-documented and highly readable volume traces the wealth shift that occurred in the United States during the 1980's as a result of changes in federal tax policies, demographics, and economic trends. Tables and graphs and a detailed appendix present substantial supporting data in an easily accessible format.

United States Advisory Commission on Intergovernmental Relations. *Significant Features of Fiscal Federalism.* Washington, D.C.: Government Printing Office, 1979. This two-volume annual presents extensive data on government expenditures and revenues of state and local governments in the United States, and describes budget processes and tax systems of all fifty states.

Webber, Carolyn, and Aaron Wildavsky. *A History of Taxation and Expenditure in the Western World.* New York: Simon and Schuster, 1986. This comprehensive volume presents a comparative and historical perspective on budgeting in Western nations. One of only a few publications to consider budgeting in a comparative perspective.

Wildavsky, Aaron B. *The New Politics of the Budgetary Process.* 2d ed. New York:

HarperCollins, 1992. There is no better source of information about the internal workings and gamesmanship of the American budgetary process than this updated edition of a now-classic work. This volume is highly readable and quickly acquaints readers with the expectations and strategies of participants in budgeting.

Josephine M. LaPlante

Cross-References

Accountability in U.S. Government, p. 1; Budgets of National Governments, p. 158; Debts and Deficits in the U.S. Federal Budget, p. 489; Federal Mandates, p. 662; Funding of Government, p. 724; Government Powers, p. 772; Government Roles, p. 778; Grants-in-Aid, p. 791; Keynesianism, Monetarism, and Supply-Side Economics, p. 1032; National Economies, p. 1248; Policy Development and Implementation, p. 1414; Political Economy, p. 1455; Voting Behavior in the United States, p. 2109.

TECHNOLOGY AND CITIZEN-GOVERNMENT RELATIONS

Field of study: Politics

The impact of modern technology on politics in the United States resembles the proverbial two-edged sword. One edge gives citizens the power to cut through barriers that hamper their participation in the political process, while the other edge confers on political elites even greater power to manipulate public opinion and behavior.

Principal terms
CYBERSPACE: universe of communications among networked computers
ELECTRONIC MAIL (E-MAIL): messages exchanged through a computer network
INTERNET: worldwide network of local computer networks, allowing all users to share information resources and to communicate directly with each other
VIRTUAL COMMUNITY: special-interest group whose members meet with each other only in cyberspace

Overview

In the summer of 1787, when the Framers of the U.S. Constitution defined the American federal system, the distances spanning the original thirteen states presented a technological challenge. As in ancient Rome, horseback riders and crude signal systems were still the fastest practical means for long-distance land communications, and sailing ships were the fastest means of sea communications. The new federal system provided a means for citizens to participate in running a national government whose officials might convene as much as a thousand miles from their homes. Federalism, which included a system of representation through which officials of state and local governments shared authority with those of the national government, became part of an elaborate system of checks and balances. Representatives, senators, and the president were chosen by different constituencies and for different terms. As a consequence, they were expected to represent different interests.

Although they had their own elected officials, state and local governments were bound by federal law. In practice, however, this obligation was confined mostly to policies of explicit national concern, such as regulating interstate commerce or foreign relations. For nearly all other public matters that affected citizens' everyday lives, the state and local governments maintained jurisdiction. Even the national army consisted largely of musters of state militias. The economy was dominated by family farmers, independent craftsmen, and proprietors of small businesses. Most people lived in rural areas, and they neither required nor expected many services from government.

The federal system reflected the technology of the time. The electoral college met on the same day in separate state capitals, making it difficult, if not impossible, for members to scheme together to elect a tyrant. Because it took time to count, certify, and report the results of the popular election of representatives, and because winter travel was difficult in many areas of the country, a Congress elected in the autumn of even-numbered years did not convene until the following March. While indirect election of senators and the president stemmed partially from the Framers' fears of the excesses of democracy, it also stemmed from the difficulty of citizens gaining firsthand knowledge of the men who aspired to these positions. It thus seemed wiser to have representatives to the state legislatures choose the senators and presidential electors.

In contrast to the slow-paced life of the late eighteenth century, modern industrial societies have motorized vehicles, railroad trains, and airplanes, and engine-driven vessels have replaced sailing ships. Where printed media provided the principal means of mass communication two centuries ago, modern societies have electronic media, including radio, telegraph, telephone, television, motion pictures, audio and video recordings, and computer networks. Where farmers, craftsmen, and small business-men once dominated the economy, great corporations now employ millions of work-ers. Where small independent firms and individual entrepreneurs contracted with one another locally for supplies and services, modern corporations have expanded hori-zontally and vertically to take over competitive enterprises and to absorb sources of supply, distribution, and marketing. Where individual American businesses were once locally owned and managed, the ownership of great firms has separated from their management, and many enterprises have grown roots and branches throughout the entire world. Most workers are now employees of large enterprises or of government, and local economies are far more dependent on global developments.

Local militias of citizen soldiers are no longer a match for massive national armed forces. Technological advances have made it possible for aggressors to strike decisive blows in less time than it would take to mobilize civilian militias for defense. As a consequence, modern nations find it necessary to protect themselves by maintaining substantial armed forces that are in constant states of readiness.

Despite the great differences between the lifestyles of the late eighteenth and late twentieth centuries, formal changes in governmental institutions incorporate only a few of the technological advances. Within the United States, for example, citizens now elect their senators directly and convene new congresses in January. Technology influenced this belated recognition that modern modes of travel and mass communi-cation have brought information about current political events quickly to many previously isolated communities and have permitted safer travel in winter. Neverthe-less, technology has not fundamentally altered governmental institutions. Aside from the size to which government institutions have grown, the Framers would have little trouble recognizing the institutions that the original Constitution created. What technology has drastically changed is the informal patterns of politics. These include the ways that provincial, state, and local governments throughout the world relate to their national governments, how legislative and executive branches of government relate to each other, how citizens monitor governmental activities, and how govern-mental elites attempt to monitor and influence citizens' attitudes and behaviors.

Since the late nineteenth century, the size and scope of the activities of modern industrial firms have become so large that they exert a strong influence on national economies in such diverse areas as employment, marketing, international trade, and environmental quality. In their pursuit of profits, these firms have sometimes acted in manners that seemed unfair, unprincipled, or otherwise not in the public interest. Local and regional governments have often lacked the technical expertise and power to regulate these firms, whose actions often shape the economic welfare of many citizens. To curb their excesses, therefore, the national government has been increasingly called upon to regulate economic activities. This growth in regulatory powers of the national government, however, shifted the balance of power between regional and national governments and also between the legislative and executive branches. Consider again the United States. Based largely on the federal government's jurisdiction over interstate commerce, regulation has spawned an enormous bureaucracy. This bureaucracy—manned largely by unelected civil servants—has become responsible not merely for administering regulations, but often for planning, proposing, and sometimes even promulgating them. Its size and budget dwarf those of state and local bureaucracies, and also the Congress, its staff, and all its ancillary agencies. Moreover, its technical expertise, coupled with the complexities of the problems with which it deals, makes it the dominant decision maker in many areas of public policy. Combined with the huge and technically sophisticated national military establishment, this adds up to a vast proportion of governmental resources devoted to the federal executive branch.

The disparity of resources in itself would not guarantee executive predominance, but the manner of employing them does. Since the onset of the Great Depression of the 1930's, the executive branch has seized most policy-making initiatives. Using its superior bureaucratic resources, the executive has taken over budgetary and legislative planning, and it has supplied information in support of its plans. In many policy areas—particularly national defense—members of Congress lack the technical expertise to generate substantial alternative sources of information that might contradict the executive's presentation or interpretation. Yet the U.S. Congress remains the most powerful legislature in the industrial world. Ironically, the public bureaucracy created to preserve and protect citizens' rights and privileges against the excesses of massive private enterprises at home and the dangers of enemies abroad has undercut the power of the people's elected representatives in the legislature.

One might expect that in a free society the mass media would act as a fourth estate, monitoring government and acting to redress imbalances among its various branches. As the people rarely speak with one voice, however, legislative politics tends to be complicated, messy, and difficult for news reporters to cover. While the politics of the executive branch can also be complicated and messy, much of its give and take occurs behind closed doors. In the end, the chief executive can usually speak for the administration without fear of contradiction from within the executive branch. News reporters often find it convenient to simplify national politics by allowing the chief executives to define political issues, while looking to opposition spokespersons for reactions. Meanwhile, the detailed work of the legislature gets relatively little coverage. The fact that television has become the dominant medium through which people get political news has reinforced this trend. Portraying politics as a struggle between chief executives and opposition leaders on television is easier and visually more satisfying than presenting politics as a complicated struggle involving interactions among legislative committees, bureaucratic agencies, interest groups, and political parties.

To accommodate television, election campaign themes usually focus on personalities and broad symbolic issues. Citizens learn about the candidates' public records or stances regarding public policy through simplistic campaign advertisements. Technology is employed primarily to project positive images of candidates, or, more often, negative images of opponents. U.S. election campaigns have become very expensive as saturation advertising on television has become the norm. Indeed, for most major political contests, candidates conduct capital-intensive campaigns using professional consultants and managers, and emphasizing television, targeted mailing, and other centrally directed communications. Labor-intensive campaigns using local party workers are no longer the norm.

Can legislatures recover the power necessary to overcome the advantages of the executive branch? Can officials of regional governments develop technological expertise to strengthen their ability to act independently of the national government? Can citizens take advantage of new technologies to change their roles from passive recipients of political messages to active participants in public policy formation? Growing public access to computer-based information systems has presented such an opportunity in the 1990's. Computer-based networks allow citizens and their representatives to inquire about information available and to delve as deeply into subjects as they desire. Moreover, such networks also operate as decentralized communication systems. In practical terms this means that citizens possess the power to send informed messages about questions of public policy directly to representatives and others. If the executive's information systems are part of the networks, access to this information can help to level the field, so to speak, upon which the executive-legislative politics is played.

Applications

By the mid-1990's, millions of American citizens were connected with the Internet, a worldwide communications network linking computers. A significant number of these people engage in political discussions. This citizen interaction in "cyberspace" has the potential to affect both the formation of public opinion and the conduct of democratic politics. Offering new ways for citizens to connect with each other, the Internet has fostered what have been called "virtual communities," groups whose members meet only in cyberspace. Many of these communities carry on lively political discussions. The Internet provides a new public space that facilitates democratic participation in politics adapted to advanced societies. Having evolved from a design for a communication, command, and control network that can survive a nuclear attack, the Internet has no center. Communication in cyberspace therefore differs from broadcasting in lacking central clusters of studios from which most information is distributed. Each citizen is thus both a receiver and a broadcaster. In theory at least, public policy can emerge through interaction among participants who share equal powers of communication.

For optimists, political participation in cyberspace approximates an ideal type of democracy that emphasizes mutuality. Not only do citizens share equal power to receive and to broadcast information, they also share equal access to sites that store vast amounts of data. The time and money needed to become informed about any topic drop substantially when citizens can employ simple techniques to locate and retrieve information from remote computers, including information on public policy. Mass democracy becomes feasible. Civic life extends, of course, beyond formal matters of public policy. Citizens can interact with each other on a variety of matters, and such interactions can build a sense of community among those who discover shared interests. This sense of community is reinforced by the formation of special-interest groups, computer mailing lists, and even separate community networks, such as the Cleveland Free-Net or TriState Online in Cincinnati. In some cases virtual communities form distinct conferential networks; other communities operate as cooperative societies in which civic life of the virtual community resembles the mutuality of an old-fashioned barn-raising or a potluck supper.

The civic life of cyberspace may have another advantage over the ordinary interactions of civil society. Because people usually interact with each other in cyberspace only by exchanging texts or documents and do not see each other, the old ethnic and class prejudices they hold tend to become irrelevant. In this regard, the civic life of cyberspace may offer a higher order of democracy than has been achieved elsewhere. Those who consider notions of virtual communities based on mutuality to be overly idealistic may still use cyberspace as an environment that facilitates more traditional civic participation involving organization, mobilization, and bargaining among interest groups. Virtual communities and mailing lists offer two powerful means of communication among group members. They can be used to increase the efficiency and lessen the overall costs of political participation. Positions can be developed; strategies devised; bargains and compromises achieved.

Context

The preponderance of control over modern information technology has resided within the executive branch of government and within established institutional elites, such as private corporations. They have attempted to use this control to ensure that political opinions expressed in the mass media reflect their institutional voices, not those of independent analysts, resource-poor groups, ordinary citizens, or most of their elected representatives. Modern communications technologies, such as those of computer communication provide a means for overcoming this control. By lowering the organizational costs for forming new groups, new political parties, or dissenting factions within established groups or parties, they can revitalize traditional mechanisms of democratic control. If citizens do not take advantage of independent sources from which to access information about matters of public concern, their opinions become even more susceptible to manipulation by the established elites who already control much of the information that is reported in the mass media.

Public opinion, properly conceived, is the collective expression of groups of citizens, not the aggregate expression of individuals who respond to public opinion polls. Such opinion can be articulated by leaders or spokespersons in an orderly fashion, or it can be demonstrated through direct, and sometimes disorderly, actions of groups themselves. Either way, the accumulated opinions of individuals who have developed their ideas in splendid isolation—even those who have used the information bases of the Internet to inform themselves—do not correspond to this conception of public opinion.

At its core, democratic politics involves collective decision making about problems of public concern. Similarly, public opinion involves the collective expression of citizens' considerations about public problems, where those considerations take place within democratic political forums, such as public meetings or sessions of democratically elected legislatures. Political actions by a multiplicity of interest groups, well informed through data acquired via computer networks, may actuate democratic control of modern government.

Bibliography

Abramson, Jeffrey B., Christopher Arterton, and Gary R. Orren. *The Electronic Commonwealth: The Impact of New Media Technologies on Democratic Politics.* New York: Basic Books, 1988. Examination of how various communities have employed modern communication technologies to enhance citizens' political participation.

Barber, Benjamin R. *Strong Democracy: Participatory Politics for a New Age.* Berkeley: University of California Press, 1984. Argument for more active citizen participation in democracies, with suggestions about how to use modern technology to facilitate group participation in community affairs.

Gilster, Paul. *The Internet Navigator.* 2d ed. New York: John Wiley & Sons, 1994. Clear introduction to how to use the Internet computer communications system.

Hamilton, Alexander, James Madison, and John Jay. *The Federalist Papers*, edited by Clinton Rossiter. New York: New American Library, 1961. Contemporary arguments in favor of adopting the Constitution of the United States. They illustrate how the technology of the late eighteenth century influenced the application of political theories.

Margolis, Michael. *Viable Democracy.* New York: St. Martin's Press, 1979. An introductory history of Western democratic thought, with an examination of the difficulties that eighteenth century governmental institutions face in responding to the demands of late twentieth century societies.

Margolis, Michael, and Gary A. Mauser, eds. *Manipulating Public Opinion: Essays on Public Opinion as a Dependent Variable.* Pacific Grove, Calif: Brooks/Cole, 1989. Original essays examining how elites use modern technologies in attempting to control the outcomes of electoral contests, public policy debates, and citizens' acquisition of political values.

Pool, Ithiel de Sola. *Technologies of Freedom*. Cambridge, Mass.: The Belknap Press of Harvard University Press, 1983. History of the development and implementation of communication technologies from the printing press through the networked personal computer and a discussion of the adjustments required to the First Amendment's original concepts of freedom of speech and the press.

Rheingold, Howard. *The Virtual Community*. Reading, Mass.: Addison-Wesley, 1993. Examination of the social consequences of worldwide computer networks, as well as a history of the development of the Internet.

Michael Margolis

Cross-References

Citizenship Rights and Responsibilities, p. 260; Communications Management, p. 370; Federalism in the United States, p. 668; Government Roles, p. 778; The Media and Elections, p. 1161; The Media and the Conduct of Government, p. 1167; Political Campaigning, Planning, and Financing, p. 1427; Political Participation, p. 1479; Political Party Roles, p. 1499; Postal Service, p. 1563; Public Opinion Polling, p. 1627.

TERM LIMITS

Field of study: Politics

Term limits are legal, constitutional, or informal restrictions on the number of consecutive terms or years that an elected official may stay in an office. Supporters of the idea believe that term limits will replace long-serving politicians and restore more competitive elections. Opponents contend that term limits will restrict voters' choices, and that free elections already effectively limit terms.

Principal terms

INITIATIVE: process by which citizens enact their own laws or constitutional amendments by placing them on the ballot to be approved or rejected by popular vote

PROFESSIONAL POLITICIAN: elected official who makes a lengthy or even lifetime career out of public service

RETROACTIVE TERM LIMITS: limits on political service that apply to time a person held office prior to the time the law was enacted

ROTATION: voluntary form of term limits in which elected officials leave public office after brief periods of service

TURNOVER RATE: proportion of officeholders who are replaced by newcomers in an election

TWENTY-SECOND AMENDMENT: 1951 amendment to the U.S. Constitution that limits presidents to two full terms in office

Overview

Beginning in the late 1980's, voters in many parts of the United States began to enact laws that limited the length of time elected officials could stay in office. The extent of popular support for these legal or constitutional restrictions surprised political observers. Nationally, public opinion polls have indicated that as many as 65 to 75 percent of Americans approve of term limits. It is time, say supporters of term limits, that the public's wishes be respected and term limits extended to all elected officeholders in local, state, and federal government.

In the 1990 and 1992 elections, term limits on state legislators, executives, and federal legislators passed in sixteen states. It is unlikely that lawmakers in any state will choose to limit their own terms in office. Therefore, political activists and interest groups in these sixteen states worked to obtain enough signatures on petitions to place initiatives on their ballots for voters to approve or reject. An initiative, a feature of direct democracy at the state and local levels of government, allows citizens to place specific issues such as term limits on the ballot for voters to decide. Only states that have adopted the initiative have passed congressional and state legislative term limits. Twenty-four states have an initiative process; the remaining twenty-six states and the federal government do not.

The first ballot initiative that limited the number of consecutive terms or total years in office for state legislators passed in Oklahoma on September 18, 1990. This ballot measure limited state legislators to a total of twelve years in either house of the state legislature. In November, 1990, California voters approved Proposition 140, an initiative that limited state assembly members to six years of service and state senators and other statewide officials to eight years. These are lifetime limits; and the years served in office need not be consecutive.

Colorado's Amendment 5 was the first in the nation to limit the terms of its members of Congress, as well as state legislative and executive officials. Of the three measures in 1990, Colorado's had the greatest electoral support, with 71 percent voting for it. Colorado limits state lawmakers to eight years: four consecutive two-year terms in the House or two consecutive four-year terms in the Senate. Congressional term limits are set at twelve years: six consecutive two-year terms in the U.S. House of Representatives or two consecutive six-year terms in the Senate. Limitations do not affect present officeholders in Congress until the year 2002. The idea of limiting the terms of delegates to Congress was part of the Articles of Confederation, by which state delegates were limited to a total of three years in a six-year time period. Limiting terms for Congress and the president was debated during the Constitutional Convention in Philadelphia in 1787, but overwhelmingly rejected.

Voters in fourteen more states—Arizona, Arkansas, California, Florida, Michigan, Missouri, Montana, Nebraska, North Dakota, Ohio, Oregon, South Dakota, Washington, and Wyoming—approved term limits on members of Congress in 1992. Twelve states in 1992 had initiatives limiting state legislators' terms in office, and voters in Maine in 1993 passed a term limits initiative. Term limits vary with the different states. For example, Florida limits members of Congress to eight consecutive years, while Michigan limits members of the House to three two-year terms in a twelve-year period and senators to two six-year terms in twenty-four years. Maine and Arizona limit state legislators to four consecutive two-year terms in the House and Senate, while Wyoming limits a state legislator's terms to three consecutive two-year terms in the House in a twelve-year period and three consecutive four-year terms in a twenty-four-year time period in the state Senate.

Present in the debate over term limits is the question of whether the state legislature or voters in a state through an initiative have the constitutional authority to limit the terms of members of Congress. A federal court ruled that Washington State's term limit was an unconstitutional addition to the age, residency, and citizenship qualifications for Congress found in the U.S. Constitution. Thus, limits on congressional service in office may have to be achieved by formally amending the Constitution of the United States. The Arkansas Supreme Court ruled in favor of state legislative term limits but struck down, as an impermissible qualification, ballot access provisions for members of Congress. The U.S. Supreme Court will be called upon to resolve these legal disputes.

Supporters and opponents of term limits have debated the concept's strengths and weaknesses. Supporters believe that term limits would increase turnover in elected office and bring new faces and fresh policy ideas into government. Citizen-legislators, serving fewer years but staying in touch with citizens, would once again dominate the halls of a legislature. The number of women, minorities, and younger people serving as elected officials should increase as limits begin to phase out white, male representatives. Term limits are essential, say their advocates, in order to give talented citizens a chance to serve their communities, and enable presently elected officials to devote more time to governing and making policy and less time to reelection activities.

Opponents of term limits concede that reelection rates among present officeholders are high, but argue that when turnover is measured over a decade or so, it is also high. In the 1988 election in California, 92 percent of state legislators who chose to run again were reelected. On the other hand, between 1979 and 1989, the turnover of members in the legislature averaged 70 percent. Incumbents are reelected, but they also step down from office in large numbers. Critics charge that term limits interfere with voters' basic right to choose whom they wish for public office and for as many times as they wish. Opponents of term limits also argue that replacing legislators frequently will result in transferring political power to the administrators and legislative staff to whom freshman legislators would turn for advice.

Term limits are in place in one-third of the largest cities in the United States, but only in about 11 percent of other local governments. The average limit is eight years, and applies to both mayors and council members. Term limits are more likely to occur in western cities that have the initiative device, and in council-manager cities.

The United States has had almost a half-century of experience with term limits on its chief executive. Presidents were limited to two terms in office by the Twenty-second Amendment to the U.S. Constitution. Furthermore, thirty-six states limit the terms of their governors.

Applications

After vigorous debate, delegates to the Constitutional Convention in Philadelphia in 1787 settled on a four-year term of office for the president. The Framers were silent, however, as to the number of terms that the chief executive could serve in office. George Washington, the first president under the Constitution, was urged to run for a third term, but firmly turned down opportunities to run in 1796 and 1800. His refusals contributed to a tradition of stepping down after two terms.

The issue did not go away, however. Thomas Jefferson, Ulysses S. Grant, and Grover Cleveland each considered running again after serving two terms as president. Each chose not to do so for differing personal and political reasons. These included age, the likelihood of suffering defeat after displeasing powerful supporters and constituencies, splits within their own party as to the wisdom of running for a third time, and the like.

Republican Theodore Roosevelt had served two nearly full terms as president (1901-1909) when he decided to enter the 1912 presidential race as a third-party candidate representing the Bull Moose Party. His candidacy resulted in fracturing the normal Republican Party vote and ensured a win for the Democratic candidate, Woodrow Wilson. It was not until November, 1940, however, that the American electorate rejected a 150-year-old tradition of two-term presidents by electing Franklin D. Roosevelt to a third consecutive term in office. A worsening foreign situation with war looming over the horizon and an improved economy contributed to victory for Roosevelt. A fourth term followed. The accumulation of political power during the Roosevelt Administration over domestic programs and international affairs persuaded congressional Republicans to mount a drive for a constitutional amendment providing for a two-term limit. Democrats generally opposed such a restriction and considered the two-term limit a personal attack on a deceased president and his party, as well as a restraint on the right of a majority of voters to choose their president freely. The vote in both houses of Congress reflected the partisan struggle over the proposed amendment. No Republican in either House or Senate voted against a two-term limit. A minority of Democrats in each chamber joined a united Republican majority to provide the two-thirds vote necessary to pass a constitutional amendment. Ratification by the required three-fourths of the states came in February, 1951. Thus, the Twenty-second Amendment, limiting the number of terms a president can serve in office, was added to the Constitution.

Supporters of President Ronald Reagan in the late 1980's attempted to gain support for a repeal of the Twenty-second Amendment. They argued that the people should be able to reelect a popular president, and that term limits weaken presidential power in the last years of his administration. The movement for repeal collapsed once Reagan indicated he would not seek a third term.

The first successful application of term limits at the state level occurred in Washington in the early 1990's. LIMIT (Legislative Initiative Mandating Incumbent Terms) twice secured enough signatures on petitions to place a term limits initiative on the ballot for Washington State's voters to approve or reject. The Tacoma-based group lost the battle in 1991, but came back to win in 1992. Defeat in 1991 could be traced primarily to the retroactive feature of the term limitation. The initiative (I-553) would have allowed 109 of the 147 state legislators to serve only one additional term before being compelled to leave office. The incumbent governor would have been barred from running for a third term in 1992. More important, U.S. House of Representatives' Speaker Tom Foley, one of the most powerful men in the United States, and all seven of his House colleagues would have their names removed from the ballot after 1994. Most voters were reluctant to discard that experienced leadership and political clout. As the campaign drew to a close, the *Seattle Times* reported that 52 percent of registered voters feared that the state's influence in Congress would decrease if term limits passed with the retroactive clause. Term limits were defeated by 54 percent to 46 percent.

The next year LIMIT introduced a revised initiative (I-573) without the retroactive provision. This proposal allowed sitting state and federal legislators, and the states' elected executives, to run again as if they were freshman politicians. Term limits, furthermore, would not go into effect until not only the Washington initiative passed, but also the voters of nine other states had approved similar limits on their congressional delegations.

Opponents of term limits continued to charge that, once deprived of the state's environmentally protective senior congressional members, citizens would be exposed to future pollution crises. There was also concern that without the political clout of Speaker Foley, California's large congressional delegation would begin the process of increasing electric power rates and diverting Washington State's vast fresh water supply to California's growing population. Issues raised by supporters of term limits included the need for new faces and new ideas; the feeling that professional politicians do not listen to the people; and the perception that elected officials seemed mainly interested in themselves and reelection. Term limits passed by a 52 to 48 margin. A federal district court ruled that Washington State's voter-approved law that restricts terms for members of Congress was unconstitutional, leaving the issue to be resolved by the Supreme Court.

Context

Limits on the number of consecutive terms or total years that one person may serve in the same elected public office can be traced back to practices in ancient Athens and Rome more than two thousand years ago. Rotation in office, a voluntary term limit, was observed also for a brief period of time in the Italian city-states of Venice and Florence during the Renaissance.

Rotation or term limits have been associated with the development of representative democratic government in the United States for more than two hundred years. Colonial Pennsylvania, for example, limited its state legislators to no more than four years of service in elected office, after which compulsory retirement was mandated by law. Seven states limited the number of years that an executive officer could serve in that position. The drafters of the Articles of Confederation in 1781 specified that any delegate selected by the thirteen states to the Congress be dismissed if he had served in office for more than three years in any period of six years.

In 1784, Massachusetts rejected term limits on its governor, and Pennsylvania removed all term-limit provisions from its constitution. The popularity of term limits began to wane when it appeared to political observers that term limits seemed to have reduced the quality of the candidates who stood for office, as competent people were swept out of office and replaced with less qualified persons.

Delegates to the Constitutional Convention in 1787 did not regard term limits as sufficiently important to be included within the new governing rules. The Convention unanimously rejected presidential, judicial, and congressional term limits. Nevertheless, many state political leaders expected that voluntary rotation in office would be the custom and that substantial turnover would occur in the U.S. House of Representatives. Early members of Congress rarely served beyond two terms, and it was not uncommon during the first century of congressional elections for 40 percent or more of the members to be freshman congressmen. Rotation in office was a reality in the first part of the 1800's. President George Washington's decision not to seek a third term set a precedent of voluntary two-term limits in the office of president. State constitutions often limited the terms of their governors, a legacy of the colonial experience.

Things began to change as members of congress, state legislators, governors, and even councilmembers made serving in office more of a full-time job and a career. Since 1950, the percent of officeholders winning reelection has surpassed 70 percent. Term limits would increase membership turnover in those elected offices, bringing an influx of new members and, perhaps, new ideas. Term limits are needed in an institution such as Congress, say their supporters, because the practice of voluntary rotation has long been absent from Congress.

Bibliography

Benjamin, Gerald, and Michael J. Malbin, eds. *Limiting Legislative Terms*. Washington, D.C.: Congressional Quarterly Press, 1992. Best single source for understanding expected consequences of term limits on state legislators, governors, and Congress. Includes a section on turnover and reelection rates of legislators.

DeSantis, Victor S., and Tari Renner. "Term Limits and Turnover Among Local Officials." In *The Municipal Year Book 1994*. Washington, D.C.: International City/County Management Association, 1994. Survey of local governments, which reports term limits for council and mayor.

Richardson, Sula P. *Term Limits for Federal and State Legislators: Recent Proposals in the States (1991-1992)*. Washington, D.C.: The Congressional Research Service, 1992. Includes a selected description of term-limit initiatives passed by voters in the different states. Contains a list of suggested readings on term limits. Term limitation activities are indicated on a state-by-state basis.

Spangler, Earl. *Presidential Tenure and Constitutional Limitation*. Washington, D.C.: University Press of America, 1977. Highly readable historical account of the events leading up to the adoption of the Twenty-second Amendment, limiting the president to two terms in office. Provides a detailed look at the bids by Grant and the two Roosevelts for third terms in office.

Will, George F. *Restoration: Congress, Term Limits and the Recovery of Deliberative Democracy*. New York: Free Press, 1992. Well-written, persuasive essay that term limits can restore Congress to competence and respect, and restore enlightened debate on public interest more often than narrow group interests.

Zeller, Laurie Hirschfeld, and John Calhoon. *Term Limitations for Local Officials: A Citizens' Guide to Constructive Dialogue*. Denver, Colo.: National Civic League Press, 1992. Brief survey of six cities that considered and passed term limitations on its elected officials. Arguments for and against term limits and a useful section on legal and constitutional issues involved are included.

Steve J. Mazurana

Cross-References

Congress, p. 412; The Constitution of the United States, p. 425; Elected Versus Appointed Offices in the United States, p. 572; Elections, p. 578; Leadership, p. 1066; Legislative Body Types, p. 1091; Political Representation in the United States, p. 1525.

TERRORISM

Field of study: International government and politics

Terrorism is the deliberate use of intimidation and physical force by sovereign states and subnational groups for political ends. Although the end of the Cold War in the early 1990's witnessed a temporary decline in international terrorism, several new developments threatened to renew its use as a deadly and significant element of international politics.

Principal terms

COUNTERTERRORISM: methods used to combat terrorism

INSTRUMENTAL APPROACH: notion that terrorism is primarily a means to a political end

NARCOTERRORISM: activities linked to the illegal drug trade

SACRED TERROR: activities believed to be sanctioned by religion

STATE-SPONSORED TERRORISM: use of lethal force internally or externally by governments

TERRORIST NETWORKS: cooperative links among terrorist groups

Overview

Terrorism has deep historical roots. As early as the first century C.E., two Jewish groups, the Zealots and the Sicarii, launched terrorist campaigns to incite a popular insurrection against the Roman occupiers of Judea. In 661 C.E. a radical Muslim group known as the Kharijites routinely assassinated Muslim leaders they found in error. Often associated with a doctrine of anarchy, the Kharijites' motto was "Power belongs only to God." Another early Muslim terrorist group was the "Assassins," who were active during the twelfth and thirteenth centuries. Their Arabic name derived from the hashish they reportedly consumed before assassinating leaders they regarded as corrupt.

Early terrorists groups typically sought to intimidate opponents, revitalize the theological or social order, and force political change. Modern terrorists, like their historical counterparts, are typically motivated by the same three goals. For example, one of the first modern terrorists groups, the Narodnaya Volya (the People's Will) of nineteenth century Russia, promoted a program whose methods included assassination of czarist officials in order to provoke social revolt.

During the 1920's, right-wing terrorism, especially among German Nazis and Italian Fascists, was used to intimidate political enemies and capture publicity. A number of these right-wing groups, particularly in Eastern Europe, were little more than criminal gangs, however. Similarly, the Nicaraguan Contras and groups associated with anticommunist dictatorships in Haiti, Argentina, and Mozambique that relied heavily on right-wing "death squads" through the 1980's were little more than criminal gangs. Apparently guided by the principle that the end justifies the means, policymakers in the West seemed to tolerate terrorism associated with such gangs, regarding it as a lesser evil than the threat of communism.

Similarly, political leaders in the developing world, like policymakers in the West, have supported their own brands of legitimized terrorism. Indeed, guerrilla warfare against colonial rule became the dominant form of terrorism after World War II in the developing world. For example, the Irgun and the Stern Gang used terrorism against British rule in Palestine. Other examples of anticolonial terrorism include Algerian revolutionaries' systematic efforts to assassinate French police officers during the 1950's, and anti-British "Mau Mau" activities in Kenya during the same period. Even the much heralded African National Congress (ANC) of South Africa engaged in bombings and other acts of terrorism in efforts to destroy the system of apartheid, or racial separation.

In 1992 a military takeover of the independent government of Algeria—which had denied Islamists a parliamentary victory that would have given them control of the government—led to a general Islamic revolt in 1992. Algerian Islamicists engaged in aircraft hijackings in Algeria and France and killed Western clerics in Algeria in retaliation for a French commando raid that had killed Islamist hijackers in France. Similar acts of violence and counterviolence on the part of Islamicists against local governments in Israeli-occupied territories and Egypt, for example, illustrate how terrorist violence in the 1990's targeted Western-style secular governments as much as it did the former colonial powers of Europe.

Personal interpretation plays a critical role in assessing modern terrorism. Indeed, one person's "terrorist" is often another's "freedom fighter." For example, during the 1980's the Nicaraguan Contras and the Mujahideen guerrillas of Afghanistan were considered "freedom fighters" by presidents Ronald Reagan and George Bush, while groups employing similar tactics, such as the Palestine Liberation Organization (PLO) and South Africa's ANC were considered terrorists. By contrast, communist and socialist governments of the 1980's promoted the opposite view. For these governments the Contras and Mujahideen guerrillas were terrorists, while the PLO and ANC were freedom fighters.

Few spokespersons for terrorist organizations use the word "terrorism" to describe themselves, although they would agree that "terrorist acts" involve the use or threatened use of deadly force. Spokespersons for such organizations instead tend to emphasize the legitimacy of their terrorist acts in the face of unresolved grievances, and the political goals and values that justify such acts as alternatives of the last resort. Beyond manipulations of the meaning of the term terrorism by governments and politicians alike, accurate definition requires the avoidance of popular images that emphasize the pathological while ignoring the purely political aspects of terrorism. Popular images depict terrorists as deranged killers bent on murder and destruction and as members of the lunatic fringe. Most terrorists, however, do not demonstrate serious psychopathology. In fact, the typical terrorist activist is male, in his early twenties, single, from a middle- or upper-class family, and well educated. Indeed, terrorists are also often university dropouts who join or are recruited into groups while at a university. Similar observations can be made about female members of the organizations that give women leading roles. These include Peru's Shining Path Movement, the PLO, Algeria's FLN of the 1950's, Germany's Red Army Faction of the 1970's, and Sri Lanka's Tamil Tigers of the 1980's. These profiles depart dramatically from the popular image of individual terrorists as the "dregs of society."

Terrorism involves reflective rather than impulsive violence that requires the ability to delay gratification through long and tedious planning states. As a result, a tendency toward violence does not appear to be a dominant aspect of terrorist personalities. Instead, most terrorists are ambivalent over the use of violence and human suffering. For example, one leader of Germany's Red Army Faction was terrified of guns, and the Palestinian terrorist Layla Khalid could deal with the presence of child passengers on a hijacked airliner only by blotting out the possible consequences from her mind.

Because terrorist bargaining is widely viewed as a form of blackmail or extortion, publicity is of critical importance. One consequence of viewing terrorism as a form of blackmail has been that policymakers in the United States have refused to negotiate (at least publicly) with terrorists. The fact that policymakers have also attempted to control press coverage of terrorist acts raises fears among some critics of media censorship.

Many experts believe that individual terrorist groups are unique and therefore must be examined in their own cultural and historical contexts. Nevertheless, modern terrorism has evolved to encompass acts of violence associated with such divergent groups as the national liberation or guerrilla movements in Algeria, Sri Lanka, Rwanda, and many other countries; state-sponsored terrorism associated for example with Libya, Syria, and Cambodia; "sacred terrorism" supported by theocracies such as Iran; and narcoterrorism by organized criminal groups based in Peru, Colombia, the United States, and, to a growing extent, in Russia.

Terrorism is normally associated with groups, rather than isolated individuals. The "Unabomber," who was accused of mailing deadly bombs to American academics and business people in the late 1970's through the 1990's, represents a major exception to this rule. Although terrorists generally seek to influence a particular government's policies, their violence may transcend national boundaries, as in the case of Afghanistan's Mujahideen or Algeria's Islamic Group. During the 1980's, terrorist prevention experts began targeting terrorist networks that linked such groups as the Irish Republican Army's (IRA) Sinn Fein and the PLO; Afghanistan's Mujahideen and Iranian Islamist groups; and the Islamic Group in Egypt and its supporters in the United States.

Beyond the question of whether terrorism is an individual or a group phenomenon, modern terrorism owes much of its character to opportunities and constraints in the international system. Training, financial support, fraudulently produced identification documents, and safe havens are important terrorist instruments that are often provided by sympathetic governments and their intelligence networks. For example, the Nicaraguan Contras and Afghanistan's Mujahideen were supported by the U.S. Central Intelligence Agency (CIA). Lebanon's Hezbollah guerrillas have been linked to Iran. The radical Islamic group, Hamas, a bitter foe of Yasir Arafat's PLO, is rumored to have been supported by Israel. During the 1980's Syria and Libya provided training and safe havens for numerous terrorists, including Abu Nidal, George Habash, and perhaps the best known of all modern terrorists, Ilich Ramirez Sanchez (also known as "Carlos the Jackal").

The Cold War between the United States and the former Soviet Union and their allies had a major impact on modern terrorism. Between 1949 and 1989, the Cold War period generated more arms, training, and logistical support for terrorists than any other period in history. Like conventional warfare, terrorism especially during this period was widely seen as a deadly though significant element of international politics. The end of the Cold War in 1989, however, marked a new chapter in the evolution of international terrorism.

Applications

Changes associated with the post-Cold War international environment have had a major impact on the evolution of modern international terrorism. These changes include a worldwide democratization trend; successful resolutions of longstanding international conflicts; and an increased willingness by combatants to embrace peaceful rather than violent means of resolving conflict. All these changes have diminished the appeal of modern international terrorism. Nevertheless, the termination of most Cold War tensions in 1989 only temporarily dampened the spread of international terrorism, which may well be on the rise again.

The fate of three terrorist movements after 1989 illustrates this point. Shortly after he arrived in Sudan on a false diplomatic passport in August, 1994, Sudanese government officials handed over Ilich Ramirez Sanchez ("Carlos the Jackal") to French intelligence officials. Until his arrest, Sanchez was widely regarded as the world's most wanted terrorist. His most daring action involved the kidnapping of eleven oil ministers attending an OPEC meeting in Vienna in December, 1975, in which three people were killed. At various times his name was linked to guerrilla groups in Japan, Germany, Spain, and Ireland, but he was most closely associated with Arab terrorist groups. Prior to his arrest, Sanchez had been a guest of Syrian president Hafez al-Assad. In earlier years he had been protected by East Germany, Hungary, and Czechoslovakia. Although parts of his reputation may be exaggerated, one French official notes that Sanchez killed fifteen people and wounded two hundred others in France alone. He was sentenced in absentia to life imprisonment by France in 1992 for the murder of two French agents in 1975. After Sanchez had been hunted for two decades, he appeared to have outlived his political usefulness. Syrian and Sudanese leaders may have wanted to improve their relations with the West and to discard their images as proponents of state-sponsored terrorism by having Sanchez arrested in 1994.

On September 13, 1992, Peruvian police captured Abimael Guzman Reynoso, leader and founder of the Shining Path (Sendero Luminoso), a powerful Maoist guerrilla group associated with narcoterrorism in Peru. Sendero's fourteen-year war against the national government was the longest and most violent in Latin America. According to one estimate, it cost 25,000 lives and an estimated $22 billion in property damage. Guzman developed much of his revolutionary thinking as a philosophy professor in the 1960's and 1970's at Peru's Huamanga University. For a time he was revered among revolutionaries as the "fourth sword" of revolution after Marx, Lenin, and Mao by waging a violent campaign on behalf of Peru's impoverished and politically oppressed Indians. The movement witnessed a sharp decline in its 5,000 fighters following the capture of Guzman and his subsequent denunciation of armed struggle, and many of the group's fighters surrendered to Peruvian authorities while Guzman himself began serving a life sentence for treason. At its peak, the Shining Path financed its operations from the cocaine trade that it continued to control and protect. Guzman's capture is partly attributable to U.S. and Peruvian efforts to destroy drug trafficking between the two countries.

Context

While changes in the international system may have dampened its rapid rise, terrorism nevertheless remains a serious threat to international peace and security. Grievances associated with terrorism often display such deep historical roots that it is unrealistic to expect that changes in the international system alone will eliminate the problem altogether. While the overall incidence of international terrorist activities apparently diminished after 1989, some aspects of the problem have actually worsened. For example, in spite of the fact that the PLO and other Arab states attempted to forge peaceful relations with the state of Israel, other groups—such as Hamas and Hezbollah—intensified their opposition to Israel. The bombing of a building housing Jewish organizations in Buenos Aires, Argentina, in July, 1994, is believed by some to be linked to Hezbollah, and its primary supporter, Iran. Serious political challenges by Islamists in Algeria, Egypt, and Tunisia further illustrate the persistence of the problem.

The February, 1993, bombing of the World Trade Center in New York City raised the threat of a new and potentially more deadly development of terrorist violence on American soil that was realized with the bombing of a federal building in Oklahoma City, Oklahoma, in 1995. Great Britain, France, Spain, Italy, and Germany all witnessed even greater numbers of terrorist incidents than the United States. Yet it would be a mistake to conclude that Islamicists represent the only threat. The emergence of organized crime in the former Soviet Union and attempts to sell stolen nuclear material abroad have become a source of growing concern. Also, new hostilities involving nuclear powers such as North Korea, China, Pakistan, and India threaten the return of competition between nuclear powers and the possible spread of low-intensity conflict (including terrorism) by sponsoring states. Thus, while the post-Cold War era witnessed a temporary decline in terrorism, terrorism may once again increase as conflict rather than cooperation becomes the dominant characteristic of relationships between communities.

Bibliography

Esposito, John L. *The Islamic Threat: Myth or Reality?* New York: Oxford University

Press, 1992. Comprehensive treatment of what to some is a major source of modern international terrorism.

Gurr, Ted Robert. *Minorities at Risk: A Global View of Ethnopolitical Conflicts.* Washington, D.C.: United States Institute of Peace Press, 1993. Documented survey of the increase in ethnic conflicts in the post-Cold War era.

Hanle, Donald J. *Terrorism: The Newest Face of Warfare.* Washington: Pergamon-Brassey's, 1989. Examination of the significance of terrorism in the broader context of world conflict.

Long, David E. *The Anatomy of Terrorism.* New York: Free Press, 1990. Long offers a useful examination of terrorism's broad features.

Mernissi, Fatima. *Islam and Democracy: Fear of the Modern World.* Reading, Mass.: Addison-Wesley, 1992. Useful information on premodern Muslim terrorist groups.

Poland, James M. *Understanding Terrorism: Groups, Strategies, and Responses.* Englewood Cliffs, N.J.: Prentice Hall, 1988. Analysis of the basic characteristics of terrorism.

Ra'anan, Uri, et al., eds. *Hydra of Carnage: The International Linkages of Terrorism and Other Low-Intensity Operations.* Lexington, Mass.: Lexington Books, 1986. Sociological analysis of worldwide terrorist networks.

Reich, Walter, ed. *Origins of Terrorism: Psychologies, Ideologies, Theologies, States of Minds.* New York: Cambridge University Press, 1990. Excellent discussion of the origins of modern terrorism.

Schlagheck, Donna M. *International Terrorism: An Introduction to the Concepts and Actors.* Lexington, Mass.: Lexington Books, 1988. Useful study of the most essential concepts and actors associated with terrorism.

Tarazona-Sevillano, Gabriela, with John B. Reuter. *Sendero Luminoso and the Threat of Narcoterrorism.* New York: Praeger, 1990. Detailed study of an important form of terrorism based in Peru that directly affects the United States.

Samory Rashid

Cross-References

Conflict Resolution, p. 397; Disaster Relief in the United States, p. 558; Fascism and Nazism, p. 656; Force, p. 712; Insurgencies and Coups d'État, p. 930; International Relations, p. 969; Islam and Government, p. 994; Legitimacy, p. 1105; National Liberation Movements, p. 1255; Political Violence, p. 1539; Radicalism, p. 1661.

THEOCRACY

Field of study: Religion and government

In theocratic governments human agents claim to derive their authority to rule directly from God or the gods. Such a government is legitimate so long as it faithfully enforces the divine will. Historically these divine lieutenants have been either semi-divine kings, priests, or other religious functionaries.

Principal terms

CHARISMATIC THEOCRACY: rule by spiritually dynamic leaders who mediate or represent a divine will

DIVINE RIGHT: theocratic claim that a monarch rules by the grace of God, which has been bestowed as an absolute right

ESCHATOLOGICAL THEOCRACY: spiritual form of theocracy that hopes for the future establishment of God's direct rule over humankind

HIEROCRACY: rule by priests acting as intermediaries for God or the gods

ROYAL THEOCRACY: monarchy in which the ruler is regarded as a sacred person, or one who rules as a representative of divine will

THEONOMY: system of government in which divine revelation is adopted into law

Overview

Generally speaking any political system that claims to be governed by gods can be called theocratic. This means that the divine rules both the invisible private soul and the visible political order. In theocratic states it is hard, if not impossible, to distinguish between the civil and religious parts of the government.

The term theocracy was coined by the ancient Jewish historian Josephus Flavius, who used the word to describe the theocratic idea which organized and directed the Hebrew people in Old Testament times. He coined it from two Greek words, *theos* (god) and *kratia* (rule), on the model of aristocracy or democracy, to denote rule through divine lieutenants. The divine lieutenants in ancient Israel included patriarchs, priests, judges, kings, and prophets. These religious functionaries were not viewed as individuals who ruled in the general name of the divine, but as human organs through whom God ruled—just as a legislature may be described as the organ that expresses the will of the people.

Charismatic theocracy was the first of the three major forms theocracy took in ancient Israel. At Mount Sinai the Hebrews entered into a covenant with their God. Loyalty to the terms of the covenant was expected from the people who had been chosen to be a "holy nation." When the Hebrews accepted the covenant they became a theocratic aggregation of neighboring states united in reverence and service. The charismatic theocracy was decentralized, lacking a permanent political and military organization. In times of trouble the Spirit of the Lord was thought to come upon an individual, who, through the divine gift of charisma, could perform military feats of deliverance. These charismatic leaders were called judges.

Moses exemplifies the prophetic and charismatic type of leader who functioned as an instrument of divine rule. His successor, Joshua, was not a priest either, but a charismatic military leader. This type of religious functionary was to last until the prophet Samuel instituted the monarchy at the end of the period of the Judges, a two-hundred-year era described in the Old Testament books of Joshua and Judges during which leaders were believed to be temporarily endowed with the Spirit of God and were given power to lead.

The period of royal theocracy saw the first Hebrew monarchy established. The First Book of Samuel describes how the people demanded a king to meet the military threat posed by the Philistines. Samuel anointed Saul to be king by divine command, despite his opposition to the popular mood. The Deuteronomic historian saw the monarchy as a rejection of God's kingship rather than Samuel's leadership. The kings of ancient Israel, especially in the southern Kingdom, were considered to be the anointed servants of God, earthly representatives of his theocratic authority. These kings were viewed as divine agents, royal sons by divine adoption. Even their thrones were viewed as the Throne of the Lord. They held permanent office, but kept the theocratic functions of leadership in war and judgment in peace from the premonarchy period. They were to be pious students of the commandments of the Lord. To King David was given a sacred promise of an eternal theocracy through his dynasty.

The monarchical period also saw faithless disobedience of divine policies by the kings and the people, so the prophets spoke truth to power as religio-ethical agents of the theocratic ideal. Discouraged with kings who failed to live up to the theocratic ideals, the prophets began to prophesy of a coming ideal king who would be perfectly obedient to the Covenant. This anointed king, Messiah, would institute the kingdom of God. The Babylonian Exile began after the destruction of both the northern and southern kingdoms of Israel. Exile should have ended their existence as a people. Instead aspirations for a return to the land and for a renewal of the theocracy developed under prophetic preaching. The conquest of the Babylonian Empire by the Persians ended the exile. Under the leadership of Nehemiah and Ezra, returnees rebuilt Jerusalem and its temple. Hopes arose that the theocratic monarchy would be restored. Instead a hierocracy (rule by priests) developed.

The period of hierocratic theocracy saw two major developments. First, in the synagogues a spiritual theonomy developed centered on the Torah, or divinely revealed scriptures. The religious law was to control all aspects of community life. The period also saw the development of eschatological theocratic hopes. Eschatology theocracy hopes for a future time when the earth will be ruled directly by God without any mediation whatsoever. It has two forms—messianic and apocalyptic. The latter is often spiritual in character, but can have immediate political applications. Apocalyptic theocrats often see an active role for human efforts to help in bringing in the reign of

God. All the apocalyptic literature of the intertestament period and New Testament times was theocratic. Where patient waiting for the coming of the kingdom wears thin, attempts to bring in the kingdom by human efforts can develop. During New Testament times groups such as the Zealots believed that the way for the apocalyptic theocracy might be prepared by violence. The Zealot attempt to purge the Holy Land started a fatal war with Rome. It ended the original history of the Israelite/Jewish theocracy and evoked the literary work of Josephus. The last battle in this attempt to create an apocalyptic theocracy was at Masada.

Spiritual rather than political Messianic theocrats wait for the advent of the kingdom of God, which will be the rule of God on earth as it is in Heaven. This form of eschatological theocracy is common to most Christians, as well as to some other groups.

Judaism of the postexilic period had set out to be a pure theocracy. When the monarchy was not restored, the priests, left to rule alone, eventually stagnated. The corruption of the priests during New Testament times led to separatism by many groups such as the Essenes at Qumran. It also invoked new directions for theocratic hopes. In the New Testament itself Jesus preached a spiritual theocracy to begin with the coming of the kingdom of God. The advent of the new age when God will rule directly is a core belief of the New Testament.

Applications

Early Christian theocratic impulses were spiritual and not applied to politics. In the early medieval period Christian theocratic societies, shaping every aspect of life, arose in both the Roman West and the Byzantine East. These were a new blend of theocratic ideas. Both societies were viewed as the body of Christ on earth with the temporal power in charge of earthly things and the spiritual power in charge of the soul. In the West the Holy Roman Empire was theocratic in nature because it was held that God ruled through both the Holy Roman Emperor and also through the pope. In the Byzantine East the theocratic beliefs were similar to the Roman West. Byzantine emperors came to unite both spiritual and temporal powers in a theocratic system called Caesaropapism. After Constantinople fell to the Islamic Turks in 1453, the Orthodox Christian rulers of Russia developed the theocratic claim that they were the new caesars (czars), ruling from the Third Rome.

Medieval and Renaissance theocratic examples included the Papal States in which religious interests dominated civil authority, the time of Girolamo Savonarola in Florence, pastor Ulrich Zwingli's Christian congregation of the elect, and early life among the brotherhood in the Moravian church. The City of Muenster affair involved a radical Anabaptist attempt to repristinate the theocracy of ancient Israel. Their chiliastic theocracy was destroyed by military action.

The Swiss city of Geneva during John Calvin's ministry is generally viewed as a theonomic theocracy. Calvin held no civil offices, but the influence of his preaching led to the enactment of many laws organizing Geneva into a place where the Gospel ruled all areas of life. This was done through the lay officers (elders) of the church who were also the holders of civil offices. The first key to understanding Calvin's theonomic theocracy lies in the religio-political revolution that occurred in Geneva about six months prior to his arrival in 1536. After expelling the Roman Catholic bishop, the leaders of the reform movement gathered with all the people, including the city officials, on the banks of the Rhone River. There in a public ceremony they swore to "live according to the Gospel forever." Calvin's task in Geneva was to enable the Genevans to keep their promise. Late in life Calvin believed that his efforts to reform Genevan life in accordance with the Bible were only partially successful. In contrast, the Scottish reformer John Knox declared that Calvin had indeed made Geneva into a theocracy, city of divine light.

The second key to Calvinist theocratic ideas lies in the strong emphasis put upon the whole Bible, including the Old Testament by the Reformed tradition. All spheres of life should be theonomically ruled is the basic principle. The terms "nomocracy" or "bibliocracy" to describe the rule of the Word of God through the scriptures have been suggested for the theonomy found in Geneva. The Calvinistic Pilgrims and Puritans in New England also established a theonomic theocracy, a "Holy Common-wealth" of the Bible ruled by the saints. The Puritan clergy did not hold civil offices. Through their preaching they sought to organize every aspect of life according to their understanding of the teachings of the Bible.

Millennial theocratic impulses, similar to those motivating the Puritans, also shaped the Quakers. Eventually a "Holy Experiment," a society governed according to God's will, was conducted in Pennsylvania and other places.

In Europe kings developed royal theocratic claims to legitimize their rule. For example, King James I claimed he was a divine monarch with his authority resting upon divine right. Robert Filmer, the author of *Patriarchia* (1680), justified divine right by arguing that kings ruled by the grace of God. This meant kings had been given a grant of divine authority to rule on behalf of God and were answerable only to God.

In the ancient world royal theocracies based on divine beings existed among the Egyptians, Babylonians, Assyrians, the Hellenistic kingdoms, and elsewhere. Stories about goddesses giving birth to kings, or nursing them in infancy, thereby creating a living human-deity were well known. Claiming to be semidivine enabled royalty to act as intermediaries between men and the gods. Royal theocracies have also been found in Africa, Europe, and Asia.

Other royal theocracies include the Incas in pre-Columbian Peru, who ruled as living sun gods. Across the Pacific, the emperors of Japan, professing to be divine descendants of the sun goddess, Amaterasu, ruled. In 1945 the Japanese emperor's theocratic claims were suppressed. In China the establishment of a republic ended the divine mandate of the emperor.

Before the Chinese Communist takeover in 1950, Tibet traditionally had a theocratic government. The Buddhism practiced there is called Lamaism. Monks (lamas) be-longing to several sects accounted for 20 percent or more of the population. The Dali (High) Lama was the supreme political and spiritual ruler, while the Pachen Lama was the chief spiritual authority. Each Grand Lama was chosen after the death of his predecessor as a new reincarnation of Buddha and viewed as a divine ruler living on earth. Other Buddhist kingdoms have also been theocratic.

Theocracy also occurs in Islamic societies, which believe that the will of God (as revealed in the Koran) is the seat of authority. From its beginning Islam has been a religious community with no sharp distinction between faith and civil power. Nevertheless, two different traditions—one definitely theocratic and another that would develop a secular tradition of separation of mosque and state—developed. Theonomic theocracy in Islam lies in Islamic law, which is called the Shariʿah. The legal order created by the Shariʿah developed from the Koran, and the traditions associated with Muhammad. Therefore, the rule of Shariʿah is rule by a legal code which implements a divine revelation. The practical implication is that Shariʿah in Islamic countries directs every aspect of life and makes the state theonomic theocracies. In Saudi Arabia the Koran is the constitution, and the Shariʿah is the only legal code.

There is a major difference between the egalitarian theocratic practice in Sunni Muslim countries and the hierarchical theocratic practice in Shiite Muslim countries. In Sunni countries, such as Saudi Arabia, the religious teachers are not a formal clergy, and all the faithful have a right to question and interpret the Koran as members of the theocratic community. In the Islamic Republic of Iran the Shiite clergy have great influence. They are organized more hierarchically, with mullahs, ayatollahs, and an imam—who is accepted as the infallible authoritative interpreter of the Koran. The Shiite clergy serve in the Iranian government and have a virtual veto over it. Many modern Islamic fundamentalist (or revivalist) movements seek to re-create the theocratic society of Islam as it was in the days of Muhammad.

Context

From the beginning of recorded history until the Enlightenment, theocratic ideas shaped most governments. Theocracies declined in number during the twentieth century, but the secularist Cold War struggle renewed theocratic impulses. The threat of atomic destruction combined with other forces to inspire movements seeking new forms of theocratic government.

There is a rich history of Christian eschatological movements in the West. Those pursuing the millennium have included Seekers, Quakers, Fifth Monarchists, and others. All were seeking a millennial age when Christ would rule on earth. Some theocracies, such as that of the early Mormons in Salt Lake City, Utah, have been successful; others, such as the People's Temple of Jonestown, Guyana, have failed catastrophically.

Israel, the original home of monotheistic theocracy, began in 1947 as a secular state, but there are forces pressing for a restoration of the Temple in Israel and a return to the theocratic ideal. Jerusalem without theocratic pressures is difficult to imagine. Chinese rule in Tibet has a checkered history. If Chinese Communism were to change to a capitalist society, it is possible that the Dali Lama would return to Tibet and restore it to a traditional theocracy.

Bibliography

Barclay, William. *The King and the Kingdom.* Grand Rapids, Mich.: Baker Book House, 1980. Contains a readable history of the theory and practice of theocratic kingship in ancient Israel and presents a clear discussion of the many aspects of the eschatological type of theocracy.

Dekmejian, R. Hrair. *Islam in Revolution: Fundamentalism in the Arab World.* Syracuse, N.Y.: Syracuse University Press, 1985. Detailed description of Islamic fundamentalist theocratic ideas and how they apply in Islamic states.

Figgis, John Neville. *The Divine Right of Kings.* New York: Harper & Row, 1965. Classic source on discussions of divine right theory. Quite readable and informative.

Frankfort, Henri. *Kingship and the Gods: A Study of Ancient Near Eastern Religion as the Integration of Society and Nature.* Chicago: University of Chicago Press, 1978. Useful book with which to begin any study of kingship as divine monarchy.

Gaer, Joseph, and Ben Siegel. *The Puritan Heritage: America's Roots in the Bible.* New York: New American Library, 1964. Written by two rabbis, the book is an easy-to-read treatment of the Old Testament theocratic influence on American government and society from the Puritans to modern times.

Monter, E. William. *Calvin's Geneva.* New York: John Wiley & Sons, 1967. Describes the Genevan revolution and Calvin's role in developing Geneva into a holy city ruled by the Word of God.

Sanders, Thomas G. *Protestant Concepts of Church and State.* Garden City, N.Y.: Doubleday, 1965. Rich source for discussions of theocratic ideas and movements among Protestants attempting to develop a political order under God.

A. J. L. Waskey, Jr.

Cross-References

Buddhism and Government, p. 152; Charismatic Leadership, p. 209; Church and Government in History, p. 230; Church and State Relations in the United States, p. 236; Church Government, p. 241; Confucianism and Government, p. 405; Dante's Political Philosophy, p. 483; Islam and Government, p. 994; Monarchy in History, p. 1221; Religion and Politics, p. 1685; Utopianism, p. 2084; The Vatican, p. 2091; Zionism, p. 2192.

THOMAS AQUINAS' POLITICAL PHILOSOPHY

Field of study: Political philosophy

Medieval philosopher and theologian Thomas Aquinas integrated the thought of Aristotle into Western culture. Aquinas' theory of natural law, concept of the limited authority of government, and emphasis on the responsibility of government to promote the common good have continued to influence political thought and action.

Principal terms
> COMMON GOOD: commitment to the well-being of all of a society's members, not simply that of a select group
>
> ENCYCLICALS: papal letters issued to provide theological and moral reflection and guidance on church doctrine and social concerns
>
> ETERNAL LAW: principles known only to God, by which creation is ordered and the moral realm structured
>
> HUMAN LAW: laws developed by persons to regulate the interaction of people in particular societies
>
> LAISSEZ-FAIRE: political ideology that supports only minimal government activity and allows maximum freedom to persons and corporations, regardless of the social effects of their actions
>
> NATURAL LAW: universal principles that structure creation and the moral order, which can be known to all persons through the use of reason

Overview

Thomas Aquinas (1225-1274 C.E.) was born to a noble family in the Kingdom of Naples. By the age of eleven, he was studying at the University of Naples, and by his late teens had chosen a religious vocation with the Dominican brotherhood, against the strong objection of his family. In 1245, he went to Cologne to study with Albertus Magnus (Albert the Great), where he studied Arabian and ancient Greek philosophy, as well as theology. Until this time, the Roman Catholic church and Western culture had operated on a worldview developed by Augustine (354-430 C.E.) that combined Christian and Platonic thought. By the thirteenth century, Western scholars were discovering the philosophy of Aristotle through contact with Arab philosophers, particularly the works of Avicenna (980-1037 C.E.) and Averroës (1126-1198 C.E.). The Church, however, had condemned Aristotle's thought and discouraged its study. Deeply impressed with what he discovered, Aquinas devoted much of his scholarly work to demonstrating the consistency of Aristotle's philosophy with Christian faith. To facilitate his work, he commissioned new translations directly from the original Greek and discovered that some texts attributed to Aristotle were actually the works of other philosophers. Aquinas thus made Aristotle and similar philosophers more directly available to Western scholars.

His nearly one hundred works established a basis for the Christian-Aristotelian synthesis that dominated medieval thought and became the foundation for Roman Catholic theology, ethics, and political philosophy into the twentieth century. Although his work was initially banned by the Church, in 1323 he was proclaimed a scholar saint by Pope John XXII. Pope Leo XIII's encyclical, *Aeterni Patris* (1879), mandated that priests and theologians make Aquinas the basis for theological reflection.

Aquinas' political philosophy was highly influenced by Aristotle, but was also informed by Christian tradition and the medieval milieu. As such, it is a remarkable blend of radical and conservative elements that at times seems very modern and at other times quite antiquated. The central body of his political thought is found in the *Summa Theologica*, Part II; *De regimine principum* (On Kingship); *In Libros Politicorum Exposito* (Exposition of Aristotle's Politics); *In Decem Libros Ethicorum Exposito* (Exposition of Aristotle's Ethics); and *De Regimine Judaeorum, ad Ducissam Brabantiae, in Opuscula Philosophica* (Letter to the Duchess of Brabant on Governing Jews).

Aquinas viewed government as a natural outgrowth of humanity's social nature and so proclaimed it both necessary and good. Humans are dependent upon one another for meeting individual and collective material and psychological needs. Social interaction, however, requires some form of government in order to avoid anarchy. Aquinas believed that government had the positive functions of assuring adequate material goods for the populace, maintaining civil peace and order, and encouraging moral development. In the negative sense, its functions were to restrain human egoism and sinfulness and their harmful effects on the community, and to protect the community from foreign aggression.

Drawing directly on Aristotle, Aquinas identified six possible forms of government, three good and three bad. The good forms are law-abiding democracy, aristocracy, and monarchy. The harmful forms are parallels: demagogic, irresponsible democracy; oligarchy; and tyranny. Of the three, tyranny is the worst. According to Aquinas, government is regarded as good or evil depending on its commitment to the common good. All the harmful forms serve the good of only a portion of the political community. Aquinas preferred having a single governmental authority, which he believed was more efficient. Recognizing human egoism, however, he supported the notion that the governing authority should be elected in some manner by the general populace. Aquinas was influenced by his medieval culture in his continued support for monarchy, but at the same time laid the groundwork for modern democratic theory. Although his ideal form of government was constitutional monarchy, his thought allowed for the historical evolution of governmental forms. Central to his thought was the importance of the character of those in authority. Government functions best when it is headed by those who are both wise and morally committed to the common good.

Aquinas also adopted from Aristotle the principle of a social hierarchy based on the recognition that persons have varying talents, intellectual abilities, and moral character. In this view, society works best for the common good when the greater rule over the lesser as the head rules over the body and God over humanity. This hierarchy must be based on concern for the good of all, and ensure that all members of the hierarchy have both rights and responsibilities. No superior may morally use a subordinate simply for the advantage of the superior; the superior must exercise authority with the well-being of the subordinate as a primary concern. Consequently, Aquinas regarded slavery as immoral, for it has no regard for the well-being of the slave. Here, Aquinas drew on the Christian tradition, departing from Aristotle, by arguing that the social hierarchy is only functional, but essentially one must recognize a fundamental human equality. In the eyes of God, all persons have equal worth and the freedom of moral agency, so all persons must be treated with dignity and respect.

Belief in the dignity of all persons and the moral obligation of government to provide for the common good informed Aquinas' understanding of political economy. He supported private property, not as natural to persons who once held all in common, but as a historical development that contributed to peace and social order. Private property is good to the extent that persons care more fully for what is theirs than for what is held in common; it divides community responsibility into clearly defined spheres; and it more readily assures that persons have control over the resources needed for their material well-being. Nevertheless, the use of private property is limited by the common good. Aquinas asserted that the wealthy are obligated to provide the poor with necessary resources. This principle is so strong that the poor who are unable to meet their needs by other means may legitimately steal from the wealthy without committing a sin. Here Aquinas drew on a long-standing Christian teaching that the wealthy are guilty of hoarding that which God intended for the welfare of all people. Consequently, government is enjoined to take an active role in meeting the material needs of all its citizens.

The core of Aquinas' political theory, however, was his understanding of law. Expanding upon Aristotle, Aquinas postulates a creation ordered by God according to both physical and moral laws. This original law, the principles of creation known only to God, he labels eternal law. Through the use of reason, humans can discover the principles that order the natural and moral worlds. These discoverable principles are called natural law. Aquinas thus recognized a set of universal moral principles accessible to all persons regardless of religious tradition or absence of religious faith. These laws are to be used to order private lives and to provide the general principles for governmental law. Natural law, however, provides only general moral principles. Practical reason must be used to develop laws for specific human communities and circumstances. Murder, for example, is clearly prohibited by natural law, but practical reason is needed to define murder—for example, are killing in self-defense or carrying out capital punishment murder?—and to determine appropriate penalties for violation of the law, such as setting a different penalty for accidental murder than for premeditated murder. Rulers are required to create and refine the actual body of law, which Aquinas called human law, that governs a particular community. Such law, unlike the natural law, varies from society to society and with changing social circumstances. Ideally, however, it should be based upon the principles of natural law.

Applications

Aquinas provided a number of foundational concepts for modern political theory and aspiration. Rejecting traditional notions of the unlimited authority of government and the divine right of monarchs, he placed strict limits on the authority of government and rulers. First, government is responsible to higher ends and higher laws. It must serve the common good and be in conformance with the natural law. When the laws of the state violate these higher ends, the laws are not legitimate. In fact, Aquinas argued that such laws are actually acts of violence that can be legitimately resisted, a principle adopted by Martin Luther King, Jr., and contemporary advocates of civil disobedience. Aquinas argued that even a law that conforms to the natural law is unjust and may be resisted if it unfairly distributes the burdens and costs of its enforcement. Natural law even limits government authority in international relations, where war is permitted only when in conformance with the principles of just war. Second, Aquinas advocated further limiting government's power and making it more accountable through elections. The concept that the dignity and equality of persons requires that all have a voice in choosing their rulers has become a centerpiece of modern political theory. As a final check on the power of rulers, Aquinas supported the use of revolution as a last resort, as long as it did not create a climate of violence and anarchy worse than the tyranny it sought to replace.

Aquinas' theory of natural law has been pivotal for modern political discourse. The contemporary notion of universal human rights is grounded in a concept of natural law that assumes universal moral principles and entitlements. Aquinas admitted that these rights might be met under a variety of governmental and economic forms, while insisting that all governments are required to protect and promote these basic rights. This concept provides the basis for modern pluralistic societies. Since natural law is accessible to all through human reason, persons of varying religious and philosophical beliefs may live together peacefully in a common society governed by these universally accepted moral principles. Here Aquinas' views are in opposition to religious fundamentalist movements that would establish governments on sectarian religious beliefs and principles. Finally, this principle of natural law provides the basis for the World Court, and the emerging vision of a global community of diverse states bound together by the rule of a common law and a concern for the common good of all the peoples of the earth that transcends limited commitments to national self-interest.

Aquinas' emphasis on the use of human reason, invoking Aristotle, contributed to the emergence of political science as a discipline and to the modern use of analysis and reason in conducting human affairs. He has provided a foundation for the modern liberal conception of the state, which emphasizes its positive, active role in solving social problems and seeking the common good. There is a clear rejection of political conservatism and laissez-faire ideology that would limit the activity of government and leave the development of human society to the chance interaction of individual and corporate actors.

Context

The work of Aquinas reoriented both medieval government and the Church. It shifted the emphasis from the other-worldly perspective of the prevailing Augustinian worldview to a new concern for human affairs. Proclaiming that human reason and Christian faith were complementary, his work encouraged both church and government to work to embody God's law and justice in this world. This new outlook shaped the Counter-Reformation of the Roman Catholic church, which attempted to eliminate corruption in church and state and provide a new, positive worldview to counteract the growing power of the Protestant Reformation and its associated political territories.

In eighteenth century Europe and the United States, the concepts of natural law and human rights, the equality and dignity of persons, and the limited authority of government played formative roles in the establishment and eventual success of democratic movements. These concepts were passed from Aquinas to John Locke through the work of Richard Hooker. The influence of these ideas is evident in the language and spirit of both the American Declaration of Independence and the U.S. Constitution. The conception of a universal human law accessible to reason is central to the vision that led to the creation of the United Nations and its predecessor, the League of Nations. Natural law theory also is the foundation for the United Nations' various covenants on human rights.

Since Leo XIII's encyclical, *Rerum Novarum* (1891), the work of Aquinas has served as the basis of papal encyclicals on social and political issues. For more than one hundred years, the encyclicals have stressed the moral requirement of persons and governments to foster a peaceful and just social and world order. This tradition has included strong statements that have influenced international debate on such issues as disarmament (*Pacem in Terris*, 1963, by John XXIII) and the moral obligation of wealthy nations to aid in the development of poorer nations (*Populorum Progressio*, 1967, by Paul VI). These encyclicals were also influential in the development of liberation theology and the corresponding political movements in developing countries. These commitments have continued in the encyclicals of John Paul II, whose *Laborem Exercens* (1981) places a moral requirement on all national economies to provide fulfilling, adequately paid jobs for all their peoples. In 1991, John Paul II issued *Centesimus Annus*, commemorating the hundredth anniversary of Leo's *Rerum Novarum* and restating the Church's ongoing commitment to human rights, economic justice, and world peace.

As modern technologies and the global economy continue to link the world's political communities ever more closely together, the search for common values and laws to provide the basis for nonviolent means of conflict resolution is likely to continue. Many problems, including terrorism, economic instability, resource scarcity, and environmental pollution, could be addressed more effectively by cooperative global solutions. Thus the principles articulated by Aquinas continue to be relevant to political theory.

Bibliography

Copleston, Frederick. *A History of Philosophy, Volume 2: Medieval Philosophy, Part II: Albert the Great to Duns Scotus.* Garden City, N.Y.: Image Books, 1962. Overview of medieval thought by a foremost scholar in the field and an expert on Aquinas. Locates Aquinas in relationship to his predecessors, especially Aristotle and Augustine, and highlights his continuing significance.

National Conference of Catholic Bishops. *Economic Justice for All: Pastoral Letter on Catholic Social Teaching and the U.S. Economy.* Washington, D.C.: United States Catholic Conference, 1986. This document is intended to provide moral guidance on the economic responsibilities of individuals, corporations, and the government of the United States. Provides a specific example of the implications of many aspects of Aquinas' political theory when applied in the context of contemporary American society.

Porter, Jean. *The Recovery of Virtue: The Relevance of Aquinas for Christian Ethics.* Louisville, Ky.: Westminster/John Knox Press, 1990. Excellent treatment of the continued use, relevance, and renewed influence of Aquinas in ethical thought and theory. It also treats the application of his ethical theory to contemporary politics, economics, and political philosophy.

Sibley, Mulford Q. *Political Ideas and Ideologies: A History of Political Thought.* New York: Harper & Row, 1970. One of the best histories of political thought by an eminent scholar. Chapters eleven to fifteen locate and explain the political theory of Aquinas, focusing on aspects of his thought that have remained influential.

Thomas Aquinas. *An Aquinas Reader.* Edited by Mary T. Clark. Garden City, N.Y.: Image Books, 1972. Comprehensive selection of Aquinas' most influential works arranged by topic, with a helpful introduction to each section. Includes major sections on ethics, law, and politics, including portions of his commentaries on Aristotle.

_____. *The Pocket Aquinas: Selections from the Writings of St. Thomas.* Edited by Vernon J. Bourke. New York: Washington Square Press, 1960. Accessible anthology of selections from Aquinas' most important works arranged by topic. Includes his core writings on ethics, law, and politics.

Walsh, Michael, and Brian Davies, eds. *Proclaiming Justice and Peace: Papal Documents from Rerum Novarum Through Centesimus Annus.* Mystic, Conn.: Twenty-Third Publications, 1991. Collection of one hundred years of papal teachings as they pertain to issues of political and social justice. The influence and evolution of thought based on Aquinas is evident throughout. These teachings provide a record of concrete applications of Aquinas' ethical and political theory to particular social problems and a changing historical context.

Charles Louis Kammer III

Cross-References

Aristotle's Political Philosophy, p. 83; Augustine's Political Philosophy, p. 121;

TOCQUEVILLE'S POLITICAL PHILOSOPHY

Field of study: Political philosophy

Tocqueville believed the drive to equality of opportunity and conditions among all economic and political classes was the dominant trend throughout the world. His classic work, Democracy in America, *describes, explains, and draws lessons from the United States, which had implemented the democratic experiment more fully than any other country.*

Principal terms

ARISTOCRACY: government by a hereditary privileged ruling class or nobility

BICAMERAL LEGISLATURE: legislature with two separate and distinct lawmaking bodies

CAPITALISM: economic system that allows private property and open competition between businesses in a free market

CONSTITUTION: fundamental laws and principles that underlie all other laws in a political unit, often limiting the powers of government

DEMOCRACY: government of, for, and by the people of a political unit, usually through electing representatives

EQUALITY: concept that every individual has the same rights, privileges, and status before the law

FEUDALISM: medieval organization of society in which everyone belonged to a fixed strata in a hierarchical chain, from peasant up to lord and king

INDIVIDUALISM: concept that each person's interests should take precedence over interests of the state or group, and that people should be free to pursue economic initiative and a personal philosophy

LIBERALISM: in Tocqueville's time, support for a democratic and republican government

SEPARATION OF POWERS: division of power among the executive, legislative, and judicial branches of government

Overview

Alexis de Tocqueville (1805-1859), a Frenchman of aristocratic origin, wrote his classic book on the U.S. political system, *De la démocratie en Amérique* (*Democracy in America*), in two volumes published in 1835 and 1840. He stated his intention clearly in the introduction, where he said that for seven hundred years the rising tide in human affairs was the movement to equality, a term often synonymous with democracy in his writing. Nowhere was this in such an advanced stage as in the United States, where men had thrown aside the feudal past to pursue self-determination in their economic and political lives. He wrote his book as a means to study this great experiment in human organization, so that European nations could modify their institutions to incorporate the inevitable.

The two volumes of Tocqueville's work on America differ in their emphasis and tone. The first describes in detail the institutions that Americans employed to administer and oversee their country. The second volume tends more to sociological analysis and broad speculations. Both focused on the Northern states, particularly those in New England, as purer examples of the new democracy, because Tocqueville saw vestiges of aristocracy in the Southern landowners and in the slavery still prevalent there. Tocqueville identified several fundamental characteristics of democracy in the United States. One was the decentralization of power from the federal level to the state and down to the township, which he recognized as the basic unit of democratic government. Another was the election of officials, necessary to ensure accountability and to fight corruption. He saw the separation of powers as an ingenious device to counter the control of any single branch of government. He marveled at the power of the judiciary, both in grand juries, which gave a voice to the people, and in the Supreme Court, which provided important decisions on constitutional issues.

An aristocrat in a liberal age, Tocqueville saw good and bad in the U.S. system. He admired the freedom of the press, which he believed was vital to preserve and forward the march of democracy, although he abhorred its vituperative and partisan qualities. He regarded free association as almost of equal importance, and remarked on the use of small groups to advocate, protest, and wield power. While contrasting democratic laws with those of an aristocracy, he concluded that those of a democracy were more just, even though probably less well thought out. The ultimate moral justification for democracy was that it provided the greatest happiness to the greatest number.

Nevertheless, he saw many disadvantages in the U.S. system, among them his often-repeated observation on the low quality of people in public life. Although he recognized that Americans made good businesspeople and disliked overspending in government, he thought that in a democracy it would be difficult to make fiscal decisions requiring self-sacrifice by the electorate. More damningly, he thought the U.S. presidency would be weak in time of war, and that foreign policy in general would be ill-considered because of the short-term passions of people in groups.

He concluded that the most serious danger in democracy was the possibility of a tyranny of the majority, although he did not think the United States he explored had fallen into that trap yet. With that famous phrase, he pinpointed a situation where nonconformist individuals and groups would be oppressed by a majority holding common beliefs, opinions, and loyalties. As evidence, he cited the lack of real independence of mind and the general conformity of behavior in the United States. Even though the press was free, in fact it expressed this freedom within unconscious limits set by the national consciousness.

Regarding the future course of American life, he emphasized that the mores or manners and behavior of the people were ultimately more important than any institution or law. Tocqueville thought religion was the main influence on people's mores and behavior, and an essential component for maintaining order and coherence in any democratic society. Religion supplies fundamental beliefs, over and above the tribal arguments of politics: It creates a framework within which society may progress. He also thought women were more important in shaping the mores of society than men.

He ended the first volume with his famous prediction that one day Russia, representing the tradition of servitude, and the United States, representing liberty, would rival each other as the two global superpowers in the world.

The first volume of Tocqueville's book was mainly descriptive, the second prescriptive and speculative. In it, he explored the social relationships, opinions, and behavior found in democracies, in a word, the mores to which he gave so much weight in volume one. Volume two returned to subjects already touched on in volume one and sifted through their deeper philosophical implications. He asserted that the basic separation of religion and state must continue. He believed that Americans questioned the usefulness of everything skeptically, including religion, so if religions confined themselves to matters of the spirit and steered away from secular topics and associations, their authority would be less challenged. He was adamant that to lose faith could only end in misery for the individual and would result in placing one's hope in a despot.

Honor and nobility were important to Tocqueville, but democracy attaches little direct importance to these aristocratic virtues. Additionally, Tocqueville predicted that art in a democracy would be energetic but vulgar, tending to the lowest common denominator of public taste.

One of his most important insights regarded the costs of individualism. In democracy, feudal relationships are gone; individuals stand by themselves and see themselves as separate from the mass. This brings a proud independence, but can also bring isolation, selfishness, and loneliness, which in turn can lead to despotism in a divide-and-conquer scenario. Tocqueville's advice to prevent this dreaded outcome of democracy was to do everything to ensure true liberty. Frequent elections and local self-government were institutional means to achieve this by promoting liberty, not as a passive satisfying of desires, but as an active involvement fostering belief in the political structure.

Tocqueville was ambiguous about equality, which he thought tended to make society a bland stew of separate individuals who eventually would become more conformist. He placed liberty as the foremost political virtue to be defended before all others. By thinking of freedom as interdependence and as self-mastery, by achieving it through mores rather than laws, and by using it to overcome narrow self-interest, a democratic society could defend itself against the negative tendencies of equality, notably jealousy.

Tocqueville emphasized that the United States was a special case of democracy, principally because of the vastness and availability of the wilderness, and because no democratic revolution had occurred there that would have created antidemocratic feeling. Americans had achieved decentralized government and respect for private property by luck. Europe could achieve it by political art and, through studying the United States, avoid the pitfalls of democracy.

Applications

Tocqueville's genius lay in his ability to see all sides of issues. For this reason, many different political persuasions have claimed him as their own. Conservatives admire his warnings on the tyranny of the majority and on centralization. Liberals quote him on freedom and individualism. Tocqueville's emphasis on mores and the general will of the population as the most important influences of politics makes his philosophy open-ended, because of the difficulty of pinning down such factors as human behavior, ideals, and customs.

Conservative analyst and television commentator George Will has said that Tocqueville's basic question was whether a nation founded on self-interest can survive. Tocqueville thought it could because many small self-interests cancel each other out and, more important, because Americans actively engage in formulating their own laws they recognize their value and respect their application. Will sees the many lobbyists and interest groups in Washington, D.C., subverting this process. He also agrees that American democracy finds it difficult to refrain from increasing public spending even while demanding low taxation by government. He wonders if Americans live in the bland welfare state predicted by Tocqueville, where instant self-gratification is the only impetus. He points to the permanent electioneering mentality of political life, also condemned by Tocqueville, in which short political cycles overwhelm longer policy cycles.

One of Tocqueville's prescriptions for a healthy democracy was a strong religious element in society. In the U.S. Constitution's First Amendment, the clause guaranteeing freedom of religious worship, precedes the clauses on a free press and the right to assemble. Many major political issues in the United States in the late twentieth century, such as the Fundamentalist Christian influence on mainstream lawmaking, the debate concerning the legitimacy of abortion, conflicts over the teaching of Darwinian evolution in schools, and challenges to the ban on public funding of religious-based education, all point to the continuing relevance of religion in American democracy. Religion also influences American life in a less obvious way—through the Protestant work ethic brought to America with the Puritans. Tocqueville, like Karl Marx and Max Weber, linked this with capitalism, possibly the most important "ism" to affect mores in the United States. George Kateb sees capitalism as systematizing acquisition and thinks the work ethic advocates it as a duty. In this way, the United States can be seen as a Protestant culture.

Tocqueville has long sections in his book on the influences of race and women on American culture. He saw these issues as peculiar to the United States, rather than part of the democratic situation, and the importance he gave them was prescient and accurate. Although some contemporary thinkers believe that Tocqueville was too pessimistic about the possibilities of racial harmony, many others disagree.

Tocqueville expected the status of women would rise to an equal level with men's through democracy. He observed a difference between the lives of unmarried and married women in the United States in the 1830's: The former were educated and remarkably free, while the latter's lives were strictly circumscribed by the roles of mother and homemaker. He thought that the United States defined the roles of the sexes clearly, with women enjoying a high status in the home. He attributed the prosperity and increasing power of Americans to the superiority of their women over those in Europe.

Tocqueville's concept of individualism has grown immensely in importance since he used it in his book to describe this new social ideology he found in the United States. Ralph Waldo Emerson, Henry David Thoreau, Herman Melville, and Nathaniel Hawthorne were among the nineteenth century writers who took it as an important theme in their work, implicitly or explicitly. After the 1950's, individualism took on the negative connotation long warned of by Tocqueville—selfishness and isolation on an individual level, apathy and low participation in public life on the political level.

Context

Democracy in America was a huge commercial and critical success on publication, particularly the first volume. It was one of the best-sellers of the nineteenth century and exerted great influence on Western philosophers. Tocqueville wrote it for the instruction of his fellow Frenchmen, but the English-speaking countries took it even more to heart. The first volume was used as a standard textbook on U.S. political institutions during the 1800's, but the second volume was read more in the 1900's. The book belongs to the great tradition of writings on political systems, such as Plato's *The Republic* (about 400 B.C.E.) and Charles Hobbes's *Leviathan* (1651). Both those works were based on fictional political entities, whereas *Democracy in America* is rooted in fact and describes very accurately the United States Tocqueville visited from 1831 to 1832. He was one of the first European visitors to write favorably on the United States, and the first person to analyze democracy in depth.

Tocqueville read widely and owed much to the great political philosophers, particularly Montesquieu and Jean-Jacques Rousseau. Through studying Montesquieu, he honed his methodology and deductive style. From Rousseau he got the concept of the general will, which Rousseau called the civic religion: what the people really want and think, whether they are aware of it or not. In his interpretation of democracy, Tocqueville can be said to have rewritten Montesquieu by extending Rousseau's interpretation of human nature and incorporating the general will into the schema.

Tocqueville's ideas on freedom and self-interest strongly echo both Montesquieu and Rousseau, as well as the classical political tradition of Greece and Rome, in advocating that the state should strive for the highest good, not the satisfaction of individual desires. He thought freedom involved self-sacrifice of some kind to elevate humanity and the nation to glory, often through military exploits.

Tocqueville's speculations and concerns were very much those of his turbulent times. His great-grandfather was sent to the guillotine during the French Revolution of 1789; Tocqueville himself witnessed the departure of the French king in 1830, and held political office during the 1848 uprising. Born to wealth and position, he recognized the inevitability of democracy and the morality of equality, and sought to impress these on his readers. His keen insight enabled him to see the embryonic dangers of the new politics, and he wanted to reconcile the new equality with order and high virtue.

Bibliography

Boesche, Roger. *The Strange Liberalism of Alexis de Tocqueville*. Ithaca, N.Y.: Cornell University Press, 1987. Places Tocqueville in historical context, showing that his concerns were also those of his time.

Brogan, Hugh. *Tocqueville*. London: Fontana, 1973. Lucid, concise exposition and critique of Tocqueville's major writings.

Koritansky, John C. *Alexis de Tocqueville and the New Science of Politics: An Interpretation of Democracy in America*. Durham, N.C.: Carolina Academic Press, 1986. An attempt to link Tocqueville with the broader tradition of political philosophy, particularly with Rousseau.

Reeves, Richard. *American Journey: Traveling with Tocqueville in Search of Democracy in America*. New York: Simon and Schuster, 1982. Interesting, if flat, comparison of the United States of Tocqueville and the United States circa 1980.

Tocqueville, Alexis de. *Journey to America*. Edited by J. P. Mayer. London: Faber and Faber, 1959. Excerpts from the notebooks Tocqueville kept while touring in the United States. His description of life in the wilds is fascinating.

Philip Magnier

Cross-References

TOTALITARIANISM

Field of study: Types of government

Totalitarianism developed as a political doctrine in the first half of the twentieth century. It is characterized by the dictatorial rule of a single political party and its leader in the pursuit of a political ideal. Totalitarian governments require that individual citizens be completely subservient to the state.

Principal terms
> AUTHORITARIANISM: rule characterized by monopoly of power by a government that lacks the desire to control all facets of its citizens' lives
> GENOCIDE: organized mass extermination of a group of people; one of the extreme methods totalitarian regimes may adopt in pursuit of their goals
> IDEOLOGY: set of stringent beliefs held by political leaders as to what the economic, political, and social organization of a society should be
> LIBERALISM: the opposite of totalitarianism; a set of political tenets that puts the individual before the state
> NAZISM: ideology of racial supremacy used by the National Socialist German Workers' Party and its leader, Adolf Hitler, to justify totalitarian rule in Germany
> UTOPIA: ideal social and economic state

Overview

The principal characteristic that defines totalitarian political systems is the role that ideology plays within them. Totalitarian leaders have a vision of what the ideal society looks like and they want to see that ideal realized in their countries. An attempt is made to mobilize all the human and natural resources a society has to offer in an effort to realize the chosen ideal. While different ideologies (communism, fascism, Nazism) offer different visions of utopia, totalitarianism can be adopted as the means to achieve any given ideal. Since the introduction of totalitarian methods in the 1920's and 1930's, not a single political, social, or economic utopia has been successfully created in the world. A number of leaders and their countries have made attempts, however, with disastrous results.

In totalitarian political systems, a single political party and its leader rule. The rule is dictatorial in nature and highly centralized. The leader of a totalitarian government normally is typically charismatic and frequently claims some form of prophetic capability based on a superior understanding of the ideology being used to legitimize the regime.

A totalitarian government tries to control absolutely everything and everybody in the country it rules. It wants total power, thus the term "totalitarian" is used to describe it. In a totalitarian society, schools and their curricula, the mass media, the economy, trade unions, and all other forms of social, political, and economic organization are run and controlled by the state. Literature and art serve as tools the state uses to glorify itself. Religion and houses of worship, if not prohibited, are subordinated to the state. The leader, ruling party, and preferred ideology of the country only are allowed to be worshipped in a totalitarian society. Frequently, the totalitarian leader is even promoted as a mystical and omnipotent figure on a par with a deity.

Under totalitarian rule, the interests of individuals are subordinated to those of the state. Individuals are supposed to serve the government in its attempt to create the ideal society. Individual rights and liberties are at the discretion of the state to the extent that the government has the power to determine what career an individual will pursue, who will marry whom, and the number of children, if any, a couple may have. The logic behind such government control is that it cannot allow individuals the freedom to make their own decisions because such decisions might hamper the pursuit of ideological goals. The government's collective goals are considered much more important than the desires and happiness of any individual citizen.

Totalitarian governments recognize that not all of their citizens will willingly submit to the state, nor will all of them accept the leading ideology. Therefore, they view it necessary either to change the minds of dissenters or to eliminate them from the society. The means totalitarian governments use to change minds or eliminate people are propaganda and terror.

Propaganda techniques deny a diversity of opinion and political debate. The state-controlled mass media and educational system report to the public that everything the leader, party, and government does is right and in accordance with the official ideology. Propaganda encouraging citizens to work harder in pursuit of ideological goals is omnipresent in any number of forms, including billboards, posters, banners, loudspeakers, and even theatrical productions. Totalitarian governments believe that the attitudes and beliefs of citizens can be changed and molded to fit the needs of the state.

Totalitarian systems have powerful and pervasive secret police forces. These forces have the responsibility of engendering fear and discouraging dissent in the society. They do so through arbitrary arrest and confinement to prisons, forced labor camps, and psychiatric hospitals. Those who are viewed as expendable, as enemies, or as a hindrance to progress are routinely executed or starved to death. The terror created in totalitarian societies has led sons and daughters to turn their parents over to the secret police. The orphans have later been publicized as heroes by their government.

Totalitarian regimes tend to have relationships with foreign countries that are based on suspicion, hostility, and aggression. The principal reason for this is that totalitarian leaders believe they have found the ideal form of social, political, and economic organization not only for their own country but also for the world. Countries that have political systems based on competing ideologies are viewed by a totalitarian government in much the same way as citizens who oppose its rule at home are: The foreign country must either change its ways or face elimination.

Applications

Perhaps the best example of totalitarian rule in the twentieth century is the regime of Adolf Hitler and the National Socialist German Workers' (Nazi) Party, which ruled Germany from 1933 until 1945. Hitler was born in Austria on April 20, 1889. At the age of twenty-three, he moved to Germany. He fought with some minor distinction as a corporal in the German army during World War I. Embittered by the German defeat in the war, he became active in politics by becoming the leader of the Nazi Party in 1920. In 1923, Hitler and his party attempted to take over the government of the German city of Munich but were unsuccessful. Hitler was arrested and imprisoned for one year. During this time, he wrote *Mein Kampf*, expressing his rage against those he believed responsible for Germany's defeat in the war and outlining his plans for the future.

In January, 1933, despite the fact that the Nazi Party did not hold a majority of the seats in the Reichstag, the German parliament, Otto von Hindenburg, the German president, appointed Hitler chancellor. A month later, a mentally disturbed Dutch communist set fire to the Reichstag building. The Nazis claimed that the fire proved the existence of a communist threat to the German state. Under the constitution, Hitler claimed special emergency powers, suspended the civil liberties of citizens, and sought to arrest any communists or purported communists. Hitler never revoked the special emergency powers he claimed in early 1933 throughout his tenure as the ruler of Germany.

In March, 1933, elections to the Reichstag took place. Despite Nazi attempts to manipulate the voting, the party did not receive a majority. Nevertheless, through tactics of fear and intimidation, Hitler was able to convince the newly elected members of the Reichstag to pass an enabling act granting him the right to rule by decree. By the middle of July, 1933, all German political parties except the Nazi Party had been disbanded and outlawed. By the close of 1933 all vestiges of legal political opposition to Nazi rule had been eliminated.

In 1934, after having eliminated all challenges to his rule outside the Nazi Party, Hitler looked within the party for any potential rivals or challengers to his position as party leader. From June 30 to July 2, 1934, a period known in German history as "The Night of the Long Knives," Hitler ordered the purge and execution of between five hundred and one thousand members of the Nazi Party. Following these events and the death of President Hindenburg in August, 1934, Hitler consolidated his position as leader of his party, government, and country and was thereafter able to exercise absolute power in Germany.

The political ideology of Nazism was one of racial superiority and intolerance of those races perceived to be inferior. The chosen, according to Nazism, were those of Aryan descent, namely Germans, whose bloodlines and genetic composition, the Nazis believed, made them smarter and stronger than members of other races. Nazism envisioned world domination by Germans because of their presumed superiority. The ideology called for some races that are viewed to be inferior, such as the Slavs, to be placed in bondage and servitude in support of German rule. It also called for the extermination of races viewed to be the most inferior, namely the Jews, Gypsies, and people of color.

The ideal society envisioned by Nazism would be a hierarchical one ruled by genetically pure Germans that would span the globe and be devoid of supposedly inferior races. At the top of this society would be the ruler, who would be viewed as a supreme being and would exercise absolute political power. Following the ruler in order of importance would be his closest advisers, military officers, enlisted men, male German civilians, German women, and, finally, non-Germans who were targeted for slavery instead of extermination.

The Nazis' use of propaganda and terror can be traced back to a moment shortly after they assumed power in Germany. Hitler, who preferred to be known as the Führer (leader), with the assistance of his propaganda minister, Joseph Goebbels, made sure that his regime's power and purpose were known throughout Germany, Europe, and the world. The Nazi swastika, salute, and uniform became internationally recognized symbols of the 1930's and 1940's.

The Nazi elite guard, the SS, under the command of Heinrich Himmler, was the principal force charged with instituting terror in German society. It was also the group responsible for carrying out the Nazi regime's plan for extermination of the Jews and other races viewed to be inferior. The SS (*Schutzstaffel*) was assisted in some of its endeavors by the Gestapo, the secret police.

The open discrimination and targeting of Jewish people by the Nazi regime commenced in 1933. In that year, Jews were excluded from service in the German civil service and state-sponsored boycotts of Jewish shops and businesses began. In 1935, the Nuremberg Laws took away the citizenship of German Jews and prohibited marriage and conjugal relations between Jews and non-Jews. In November, 1938, "The Night of Broken Glass" (*Kristallnacht*) took place, during which thousands of Jewish stores and synagogues were destroyed. In 1941, the Nazi regime approved plans for conducting genocide against the Jews. This plan, called the "final solution," proposed the liquidation of Jews as a race. By the collapse of the Nazi regime in 1945, more than six million Jews had been killed in death camps located across central and eastern Europe.

Hitler's foreign policy was aggressive and opportunistic. The goals of Nazi foreign policy were the repudiation of the terms of the Treaty of Versailles, which had concluded World War I; the consolidation of all ethnic Germans and the lands on which they lived within the German state; and the continual territorial expansion of Germany so that Germans could have the "living space" (*Lebensraum*) that the Nazis said they deserved.

Nazi efforts to achieve their foreign policy goals began with their occupation of the Rhineland in 1936, an act that was specifically prohibited by the Treaty of Versailles. Unchallenged by any of the signatories to the treaty, Hitler violated it again with the annexation of Austria (*Anschluss*) in 1938. In late 1938, at the Munich Conference, Hitler received approval from the French and the British to annex the Sudetenland, the highly industrial sector of independent Czechoslovakia where many ethnic Germans lived. By the spring of 1939, the Nazis had occupied what was left of Czechoslovakia and were making demands on Poland.

On September 1, 1939, after entering into a neutrality pact with the Soviet Union, Nazi Germany invaded Poland, an act that finally prompted a declaration of war by the British and the French and marked the beginning of World War II in Europe. By June, 1941, Nazi Germany had occupation forces in Poland, Denmark, Norway, Belgium, The Netherlands, France, Yugoslavia, and Greece, and was undertaking massive aerial bombardments of the United Kingdom. In that same month, Hitler ignored the neutrality pact that his regime had signed with the Soviet Union, and the Nazis launched an invasion of that country.

Following the retreat of German forces from the battle of Stalingrad in the Soviet Union in 1942, the Nazi war effort went into decline. In June, 1944, the democracies allied against Hitler, led by the United States, successfully commenced operations to liberate France and the European continent. On April 30, 1945, faced with encirclement by enemy forces, Hitler committed suicide. The war he and his regime had started, having cost an estimated fifty-five million lives, came to an end on May 8, 1945.

Context

Totalitarianism, authoritarianism, and constitutional democracy have been the three leading doctrines upon which political systems have been based in the twentieth century. Constitutional democracies are representative of the principles of classic liberalism. The ideology of classic liberalism and constitutional democracy is the antithesis of totalitarianism. Classic liberalism argues that individual citizens have certain inherent rights, including the right to life, the right to personal liberty, the right to own property, and the right to pursue happiness. Classic liberalism does not allow that governments may violate these natural rights. If they do, classic liberalism calls for the revolt by the people against the governments, their overthrow, and their replacement by governments that will honor the rights of their citizens.

A constitutional democracy allows for the equal protection under the law of all of its citizens and for the participation of individual citizens in government. In constitutional democracies, the media are free and independent of government control, political leaders are responsive to public opinion, government officials are not allowed to stand above the law, and free elections with broad suffrage are held periodically.

Authoritarianism has the distinction of being the most prevalent form of political organization in human history. As do totalitarian regimes, authoritarian regimes typically have dictatorial, highly centralized rule by a single leader or small group of leaders and do not allow for political dissent. The point that totalitarianism is an extreme form of authoritarianism has been made by numerous political commentators.

While totalitarianism and authoritarianism are more closely related to each other than either ideology is to constitutional democracy, there are still important distinctions between the two. Unlike totalitarian regimes, authoritarian regimes are not intent on the achievement of a utopia. Attempts to mobilize the masses in pursuit of collective goals are not made. With the exception of political activity and participation, the citizens of authoritarian societies enjoy some degree of freedom to make individual choices in religion, the arts, education, and personal lifestyle, more than their counterparts in totalitarian systems do. The establishment and maintenance of a monopoly of political power is enough to satisfy an authoritarian leader.

Bibliography

Arendt, Hannah. *The Origins of Totalitarianism*. 2d ed. Winchester, Mass.: Allen & Unwin, 1958. The classic that describes the characteristics of anti-Semitism, imperialism, and totalitarianism. The section on totalitarianism has long been recognized as a standard in scholarship.

Chamberlin, William Henry. *The World's Iron Age*. New York: Macmillan, 1941. Account of the political, economic, and intellectual forces underlying the rise of totalitarian rule in a number of countries, including Nazi Germany and the Soviet Union.

Dallin, Alexander, and George W. Breslauer. *Political Terror in Communist Systems*. Stanford, Calif.: Stanford University Press, 1970. Major contribution to the literature comparing communist political systems. Provides a general conceptual framework to explain how and why terror has been used by different communist countries.

Friedrich, Carl J., and Zbigniew K. Brzezinski. *Totalitarian Dictatorship and Autocracy*. 2d rev. ed. Cambridge, Mass.: Harvard University Press, 1965. Arguably the single best work on totalitarianism and totalitarian governments ever published. Offers a general model of totalitarian dictatorship and the type of society that it produces.

Hitler, Adolf. *Mein Kampf*. Boston: Houghton Mifflin, 1962. Infamous tome that blames communists, capitalists, and Jews for the defeat of Germany in World War I.

Orwell, George. *1984: A Novel*. New York: Harcourt Brace Jovanovich, 1949. Describes the totalitarian system that may be possible through advances in technology. Has contributed greatly to popular understanding of totalitarianism.

Samuel E. Watson III

Cross-References

Autocracy and Absolutism, p. 127; Charismatic Leadership, p. 209; Chinese Communism, p. 223; Dictatorships, p. 546; Existentialism, p. 642; Fascism and Nazism, p. 656; General Will, p. 745; Genocide, p. 752; Human Rights and International Politics, p. 848; The Left and the Right, p. 1079; Marxism-Leninism, p. 1155; Military Governments, p. 1192; One-Party Systems, p. 1350; Pluralism, p. 1402; Police States, p. 1408; Political Crimes, p. 1448; Propaganda, p. 1615; Revolutionary Governments, p. 1725; Russian Political History, p. 1770; Utopianism, p. 2084.

TOWN MEETINGS

Field of study: Local and regional government

The classic mode of small-town government in New England, town meetings are the modern version of the ancient Greek participatory democracy in which all citizens had the right to participate in discussion and vote on issues. They survive in modern times in some small New England communities.

Principal terms

ANNUAL TOWN MEETING: basic town meeting that votes on financial issues before the town

BOARD OF SELECTMEN: three, five, seven, or nine persons elected to provide continuous authority in a town and prepare the warrant for the town meeting

BYLAWS: local ordinances passed by town meeting and having the force of law

CONSTABLE: local official whose task it is to publicize the calling of a town meeting and to preserve order during the meeting

FREEMEN: town proprietors to whom participation in the earliest town meetings was restricted

GENERAL COURT: the legislative body of the colony, then of the province; this term is still used for the legislature of Massachusetts

OPEN TOWN MEETING: town meeting in which all citizens can participate

REPRESENTATIVE TOWN MEETING: body elected by the citizenry to deliberate and vote on town issues; used in towns where population growth has made open town meetings impractical

SPECIAL TOWN MEETING: town meetings other than the annual town meeting, called by selectmen to deal with nonfinancial issues

WARRANT: agenda of every town meeting, prepared by the board of selectmen

Overview

The town meeting was the form of local government devised by the earliest European settlers in New England. It was a response to the need for some form of local decision making in the initial settlements. Because the earliest settlers were all of equal importance, they decided to provide for local government by meetings of all inhabitants at regular intervals. One of the earliest written documents in the colonies was the Mayflower Compact, signed by all the Pilgrims agreeing to work together to determine local issues that affected them all.

Even more important in marking the beginnings of town meeting as a form of local government were the decisions of the General Court of the Massachusetts Bay Colony, chartered by King Charles I of England. The charter gave the freemen who constituted the original General Court the right to make decisions about local government in the settlements established in the Massachusetts Bay. In 1641, in a document called the Body of Liberties, the General Court detailed local government. It provided for the annual election of selectmen and other local officials by the freemen of the town gathered together in town meeting, and specified their duties; it outlined the methods to be used by town meeting in passing bylaws or local ordinances; and it required each town to elect representatives to the General Court.

In 1684, King Charles II suppressed the charter of the Massachusetts Bay Colony. In 1692, the new government in England created in its place a province to be governed by a governor appointed in England and a council appointed by the governor; however, a representative legislative body called the General Court, its members elected by town meeting in each town, was retained. This General Court reauthorized local self-government in essentially the same fashion as it had existed in the Massachusetts Bay Colony. The act of 1692 made it clear, however, that the authority of the town meeting and other local officials to govern the individual towns was delegated to them by the General Court.

The legislation of 1692 contained many more specifics about local government. It required annual town meetings in each town. It called for the regular election, by town meeting, of a board of three, five, seven, or nine selectmen who, meeting regularly, would provide continuity of administration in the town. It also called for the annual election, by town meeting, of numerous other local officials to deal with the growth in population of the towns since their early settlement. Assessors, overseers of the poor, constables, and a number of other officials were to be elected each year. It also required that any bylaws passed by town meeting would become valid only after the approval of the court of quarter sessions, a judicial body appointed by the governor of the province. Although there was theoretically a property qualification for participation in town meeting, in practice every established resident could vote.

In 1715, the General Court added new requirements to the proceedings of town meetings. It required that, as the first order of business at annual town meetings, voters should elect moderators to serve as presiding officers over the town meetings. The moderators had to recognize voters before they might speak, and had the right to fine unruly persons. Items not on the agenda of the meetings, called the warrant and prepared by the selectmen, could not be discussed. If ten citizens wanted to discuss a subject that the selectmen had not placed on the warrant, they could petition for its inclusion and the selectmen were required to include it.

Town meetings as a form of local government flourished during the eighteenth century. Indeed, they were the active participation by the citizenry in local politics that laid the groundwork for the American Revolution. The town meetings provided forums in which colonists could air their grievances against the attempts of the British government to tighten control over the colonies, and to extract more from them in taxation. The British government attempted to prevent this local opposition by forbidding any town meetings not authorized by the royal governors of the provinces. The citizens ignored this prohibition and met anyway.

The Massachusetts state constitution of 1780 was created by a constitutional convention composed of representatives elected by the town meeting of every town. After being drafted, the proposed constitution was sent back to the towns for approval. It was modified in accordance with the criticisms expressed by the various town meetings before going into effect. This constitution is still in effect, although it has been amended frequently.

The General Court established in the Massachusetts constitution of 1780 reauthorized local government through town meetings in 1786. The entire state was divided up into towns, which were made corporate entities that could sue and be sued. Town meetings were required to be held in March or April, later extended to May. Town meetings were required to elect moderators to preside, and to elect local officials, beginning with the selectmen and including a host of others. Until 1857, town meetings also had the task of electing the representatives to the General Court. The rules regarding the manner of passing bylaws and their form were spelled out. If a vote at a town meeting were in doubt, a formal poll was held, often by written ballot. The agenda or warrant was to be prepared by the selectmen of the preceding year, but ten or more citizens could by petition secure the addition of topics not included by the selectmen. Most of the provisions of this law still apply, although in many towns local officials are elected on a separate occasion in a local election, rather than by town meeting.

Town meetings as a system of local government were first developed in Massachusetts, as the first permanent European settlements in New England were located there. Both Connecticut and Rhode Island were settled by individuals who, for varied reasons, could not fit into culturally monolithic Massachusetts towns. They received separate charters from the crown in the 1660's, but these provided for the same conditions of self-government as prevailed in Massachusetts. Maine was part of Massachusetts until 1820, when, following petition by the residents, the Massachusetts legislature agreed to allow it to separate. On separation, Maine retained the traditional system of local self-government through town meetings. New Hampshire became a royal province in 1679, but copied the governing structure of neighboring Massachusetts. Vermont became a separate entity during the American Revolution, but likewise adopted the prevailing form of local government.

While the system of local self-government through town meetings worked very well during the colonial era, when the European settlements were overwhelmingly agricultural and communities tended to be like-minded, developments in the nineteenth century made the system unworkable in many places. The enormous growth of population, including many people of different ethnic backgrounds, particularly in the industrial cities that developed, required adaptation of the system to meet the new realities. Boston was the first to recognize that large population centers could not be governed in the old way. After petitioning the legislature, Boston was reauthorized as a city in 1822.

Communities that became cities abandoned town meetings as their legislatures and adopted various forms of the mayor-council system of government, in which the voters elect representatives to councils. This system, used throughout the rest of the United States, has not been overwhelmingly popular in New England, so that many communities, although their size would justify it, have chosen not to become cities; none has chosen to do so in Massachusetts since 1923.

An alternative to becoming a city for local government purposes that developed during the twentieth century was the representative town meeting. The representative town meeting, like the city council, is composed of individuals elected by the voters; they have the authority to vote on any issues on the town warrant, though individual voters continue to have the right to speak. Representative town meetings, in contrast to town councils, tend to be large bodies; the most common number in Massachusetts is 240, the same as the number of legislators in the lower house of the General Court.

Prior to the 1950's, communities in New England that wanted to change their local government from the traditional town meeting form had to apply to the state legislature for a special act applying only to their particular town. All such acts required subsequent approval by the local voters. In order to reduce the burden on the legislatures—there are more than one thousand communities in the New England states, each with its own local government—all the New England state legislatures enacted "home rule" statutes during the latter half of the twentieth century. Rhode Island was the first to do so in 1951. Connecticut followed in 1957, Massachusetts in 1966, and Maine in 1969. New Hampshire made provision for limited local alteration of governing charters in 1963, and Vermont has done the same. Under "home rule," communities may elect charter commissions with the mission of proposing an alternative charter. This must then go before the voters in a referendum, and many reform charters have been turned down by the voters. In matters of local government, New Englanders have remained conservative; this conservatism has kept town meetings in place as the legislature in most of the smaller communities of the region.

Applications

Town meetings are the annual gatherings of the citizenry of the towns of New England to vote on their governments for the forthcoming year. Before they can be held, constables post the warrant in several public places to notify voters. The most important decision that a town meeting must make is over the budget submitted in the warrant, or agenda, by the selectmen, who are continuous government of the town between town meetings.

In order to facilitate decision making in town meetings, many towns have appointed special committees to evaluate and report on the issues to be voted on in the meetings. Almost universally there is a finance committee, whose role is to go over the budget proposed by the selectmen. Members of the finance committee are appointed by the moderator, since the committee is intended to serve the town meeting. A good finance committee will have gone over the proposed budget item by item, and unless there is a special interest in the community affected by a budget proposal, town meetings generally vote in accordance with the recommendations of the finance committee.

Some communities separate their budgets into an operating budget and a capital budget, and vote the items separately. Where there is only a rudimentary local government, budgets are often voted in one up-or-down vote. Where there is active citizen interest in the budget, town meetings may vote the operating budget item by item, and the capital budget is nearly always voted that way.

The rules of procedure followed by the moderator generally conform to one of the standardized codes of parliamentary procedure. Each town meeting, however, has the authority to adopt its own rules of procedure through bylaws of the town passed by town meeting. The moderator, by state law, has the authority to decide who shall be recognized, and to call the vote. The most successful moderators are those who, often by the infusion of a dash of humor, can keep debate on an issue from becoming too heated. Many town meetings have individuals who are traditionally known to "move the question," that is, propose that an immediate vote be taken on the issue. If the majority vote "yes" on a motion to move the question (which must be voted on immediately), debate ends and voting begins. Having such individuals present at a session of town meeting can help move the proceedings along.

In towns of more than one thousand inhabitants, the agenda for the meeting, called the warrant, tends to be lengthy. By law, the warrant must be prepared by the selectmen; however, if ten voters petition to have a subject included on the warrant, the selectmen must include that subject, whether they wish to or not. Since the selectmen can arrange the order of the warrant, individual petitions tend to be grouped at the end; by this time some voters will have left, and unless there is a strong constituency pushing the petition issue, it may not have a sufficient number of supporters present to pass.

Traditionally, town meeting was held on a Saturday, and often continued all day, with lunch served by a local women's group. In Vermont, there must be a vote on whether to permit the sale of alcoholic beverages in town. In larger towns, where the warrant tends to be lengthy, town meetings are scheduled in the evening on weekdays, and may continue over a number of evenings. In representative town meetings, extending the meeting over a number of sessions runs the risk that a quorum will not be present. Since all participants in town meetings are volunteers, lengthy town meetings can deter citizens with heavy personal schedules from participating.

Besides financial issues, another controversial topic for town meetings is apt to be zoning. Zoning is imposed by local bylaw, and since it can have significant financial implications for individual citizens, controlling how they may use their property, is apt to be debated hotly. Zoning bylaws generally require a two-thirds vote, as do bonding proposals; where a two-thirds vote is required, the vote must actually be counted unless it is unanimous. The town clerk must record the actual vote. All bylaws passed by town meeting in Massachusetts must be approved by the attorney general before they can go into effect.

The budget must be voted in the annual town meeting, but nonfinancial items can be dealt with in special town meetings, called by the selectmen during the rest of the year when needed. In some communities, nonfinancial issues are put off until a special town meeting, in order not to make the annual town meeting too long. Nonfinancial issues can range from the adoption of a townwide zoning code to the details of which street lights to turn off to save money on the electric bill. There are frequent petition requests to change the zoning classification of a particular parcel.

Context

Town meeting is the classic example of participatory democracy. As such, it has certain great advantages. It gives the citizenry an opportunity to express their opinions on a proposed governmental measure before it goes into effect. To the extent that all effective government depends to some degree on acceptance by the governed, it reduces the amount of direct enforcement that is needed. It was originally adopted because no other enforcement mechanism, except the force of public opinion, was available in the colonial towns.

The passage of time has also revealed some of the weaknesses of the town meeting form of local government. The complexity of some of the issues that must be dealt with by local officials, interconnected as they often are with state and federal systems, makes it difficult for the ordinary voter to understand what is at stake. Because participation is voluntary, it tends to be low, although in the case of representative town meetings, those who put themselves up for election generally have a greater measure of commitment to the process. Where open town meeting still prevails, it is sometimes difficult to find a hall large enough to accommodate all voters. Too often, local issues are decided for personal reasons, rather than sound public policy.

Because participation is voluntary, town meetings can be dominated by committed special-interest groups. Because the constitutions guarantee every citizen the right to participate, groups such as municipal employees, who will be voting on the budgets of their agencies, often play a disproportionate role in the decision making.

In the late twentieth century, there has been a renewed emphasis on participatory democracy. National politicians have found a publicity advantage in holding "town meetings" on major policy issues, and although such meetings usually involved a carefully selected membership, they gave the impression that the ordinary citizen had a voice in government. Despite major, worldwide commitment to democracy as a form of government, making it work has never been easy. Where appropriate, in small, relatively homogeneous communities, town meeting has been one of democracy's most successful mechanisms.

Bibliography

Gere, Edwin A. *Modernizing Local Government in Massachusetts*. Lanham, Md.: University Press of America, 1984. Excellent source for information on town meetings in Massachusetts, including some information on town meeting practices in other New England states. Extensive historical material. Descriptions of the governmental form adopted by communities that have given up the town meeting.

Gould, John. *New England Town Meeting: Safeguard of Democracy*. Brattleboro, Vt.: Stephen Daye Press, 1940. Account of a typical town meeting in small-town New England, with many photographs. Although not a serious analytical study, it captures the flavor of a town meeting.

Johnson, Richard B. *Town Meeting Time: A Handbook of Parliamentary Law*. 2d ed. Malabar, Fla.: R. E. Krieger, 1984. Originally prepared by the moderator of the Swampscott, Massachusetts, town meeting, and since revised by a committee of the Massachusetts Moderators Association, this is a comprehensive guide to the proceedings of town meetings.

Nuquist, Andrew E., and Edith W. Nuquist. *Vermont State Government and Administration*. Burlington: University of Vermont Government Research Center, 1966. Although this book deals primarily with state government in Vermont, it contains a chapter on local government.

Palmer, Kenneth T., G. Thomas Taylor, and Marcus A. LiBrizzi. *Maine Politics and Government*. Lincoln: University of Nebraska Press, 1992. Deals fundamentally with state government but has a chapter on local government. Maine is a largely rural and small-town state, where town meeting is a frequently used form of government.

University of Connecticut Institute of Public Service. *The Connecticut Town Meeting*. Storrs: University of Connecticut, 1964. Manual for town meetings in Connecticut, devoted primarily to detailing the procedures.

Zimmerman, Joseph F. *The Massachusetts Town Meeting: A Tenacious Institution*. Albany: Graduate School of Public Affairs, State University of New York, 1967. In many respects the classic study of the town meeting, with a brief history of its development and a description of the changes in state law that have affected town meetings.

Nancy M. Gordon

Cross-References

Accountability in U.S. Government, p. 1; Citizenship Rights and Responsibilities, p. 260; City Government in the United States, p. 266; The City-State, p. 272; Civic Education, p. 278; Funding of Government, p. 724; Initiatives and Referendums, p. 923; Legislative Body Types, p. 1091; Local Governments, p. 1136; Rural Community Government, p. 1763; State and Local Government, p. 1885; Taxation and Appropriation, p. 1941; Urban Governments, p. 2052; Voting in History, p. 2116.

TRADE WITH FOREIGN NATIONS

Field of study: Functions of government

Foreign trade is the economic activity of buying and selling goods and services between countries or among several countries. Since no single country is entirely self-sufficient and there is growing interdependence among the world's nations, the flow of foreign trade is of concern to governments.

Principal terms

COMPARATIVE ADVANTAGE: economic theory that if countries produce what they can efficiently, and purchase from others what they do not produce efficiently, real output, income, and consumption will increase

EXPORTS: products and services that a nation sells to other countries

FREE TRADE: trade in which goods and services can be exchanged without tariff or nontariff barriers

GATT (GENERAL AGREEMENT ON TARIFFS AND TRADE): forum of more than one hundred member countries based in Geneva that undertakes negotiations for more liberal international trade

IMPORTS: products and services that a nation buys from other nations

MARKET CONCENTRATION: situation in which a nation relies on certain countries from which to buy products and services, or to which to sell their products and services

PRODUCT CONCENTRATION: situation in which a nation has only one or two products to sell in the international market; for developing countries, this is often a single agricultural product

PROTECTIONISM: policy of raising tariff and nontariff barriers on products coming from other countries in order to shield domestic industries from competition

TARIFFS: tax on the value of a commodity being imported into a country

Overview

Enterprises within nations produce products and services for consumers in order to satisfy various needs. Once domestic consumption is satisfied, surplus production can be channeled to the international market. Nations will buy and sell goods and services from one another if they find it advantageous. The concept of comparative advantage is that a country will produce a product if it has the factor endowments (resources, labor, capital) to produce that item at a low cost. If it is more efficient for a nation to buy a product from another country than to produce it domestically at a higher cost, nations will engage in trade. As the world's economies have become more interdependent, foreign trade has become the subject of increasing political debates.

Exportation is the selling of goods and services to other countries to obtain needed foreign exchange. This is especially important for developing countries, which rely on foreign exchange to purchase investment products that will spur their economic development. The amount of foreign exchange obtained from exports depends on the nature of the product; the quantity and the price at which the product can be sold in the international market; and the nature of the competition in that specific product from other producers and sellers. The sole producer of a commodity that is needed by many nations will obtain more foreign exchange than the seller whose primary product has many producers and competitors in the international market.

Developing countries historically have relied on one or two agricultural products for export. Sometimes several developing countries compete against one another for the sale of the same items, as in the case of Latin American and African countries selling coffee. Reliance upon a few products for income from trade is called product concentration.

Many developing countries tend to sell to the same buyers, leading to severe competition among them in selling to developed countries; this is the case in the sale of clothing and footwear to the United States. Reliance upon selling the same product to one or a few countries is called market concentration.

Reliance upon a few products and a few markets does not seem to be beneficial to developing-country trade. There is, therefore, a growing trend for countries to try to diversify their products and markets. Product diversification implies going into further manufacturing of primary agricultural products, for example, turning fresh bananas into banana chips, or looking for entirely new products in which to specialize. Market diversification means looking for nontraditional markets in which to sell products. For example, if a country relies on the United States to buy its products, selling to the European Community countries or to the Pacific Basin countries would mean market diversification.

Because of the ability to obtain foreign exchange for development through exports, governments of some developing countries have launched incentives to promote exports through various export promotion schemes, such as tax exemptions, favorable treatment of exports, and investment incentives.

Importation, on the other hand, is the buying of goods and services from other countries, either because a nation cannot produce the product itself, it cannot produce enough of the product and therefore must supplement its needs by purchasing from others, or it is cheaper to buy the product from another country than to produce it domestically at a higher cost to consumers. To import requires that a nation have enough foreign currency to pay for its purchases.

An importing nation can also be dependent on one supplier for the product, so that market concentration exists. As the United States, Japan, and other developed countries learned from their dependence on oil from the Middle Eastern countries, diversification of sources of supply for a product is preferable to overdependence on certain markets.

Because excessive imports can drain a nation of foreign exchange and breed dependency on a volatile international market, some developing countries in the

1960's launched unsuccessful efforts at import substitution. Import substitution, however, can set back efforts at economic development if comparative advantage and the efficiency of producing versus importing are not taken into account. The developing countries did not benefit from import substitution when they invested in national car, steel, and airline manufacturing industries that were expensive to initiate and did not provide them with the profits to keep them afloat. These efforts made products more expensive, which ultimately hurt their consumers who had to pay more for these items produced at home.

When receipts from exports are greater than what is being spent on imports, a nation's national accounts will show a trade surplus. When the expenditures on imports are greater than the receipts from exports, then a nation will exhibit a trade deficit. Although it is commonly thought that a trade surplus is preferable to a trade deficit, a trade deficit that is born out of purchases of investment items that are to be channeled to further production is not necessarily detrimental to continued economic expansion.

After World War II, the international community established the goal of liberalizing trade among nations. Trade liberalization is the reduction or removal of tariff and nontariff barriers that hinder or prohibit the free flow or movement of goods among nations. The most common types of trade barriers are tariffs, quotas, and exchange controls. Tariffs are taxes imposed on products entering one country from another. The purpose of a tariff is to decrease either the volume or the value of the product coming in, or to discourage entirely the entry of such products. For example, a country that wanted to discourage the entry of foreign-made cars could impose a 100 percent tariff on the value of those cars, thus doubling their price for the buyer. This could discourage buyers from purchasing foreign cars and encourage them to purchase domestic cars. Without the tariff, the foreign car could have been a cheaper, more efficient alternative, but the consumer is prompted to buy a seemingly cheaper domestic car as a result of the tariff, although it may be a less efficiently made product.

Nontariff barriers are all other types of prohibitions that discourage the entry of goods into a certain market. Nontariff barriers can be quotas, which are restrictions or limitations on the quantity or value of products coming into one's country. Another form of nontariff barriers are exchange controls, which are restrictions on the value of foreign exchange that importers can obtain in order to bring in products from other countries, for example, limiting travelers to take less than $1,000 worth of foreign exchange to other countries. Nontariff barriers can also take the form of health regulations or sanitation requirements that are meant to make it harder for a product to enter a country. For example, in the 1970's, the Japanese banned Philippine mangoes until fumigation requirements were fulfilled.

Tariff and nontariff barriers are established to protect domestic industries that may be affected by the entry of competitive products. "Protectionism" is the term used for the policies adopted by a government to discourage the entry of products that are similar to those of existing industries in that country that may be adversely affected by the competition. Protectionist policies often are used in order to protect so-called infant industries, new industries that are part of an import substitution scheme.

Protectionist policies often result in subsidies to the infant industry. The length of time that an industry can remain an infant is controversial, since protectionism can take on a permanent nature. This defeats its original purpose of helping a fledgling industry to become efficient and competitive in the international market.

In 1947, the General Agreement on Tariffs and Trade (GATT) was signed by twenty-three countries with the main goal of bringing about a freer environment for international trade whereby tariff and nontariff barriers eventually would be eliminated. Member nations have engaged in numerous multilateral trade negotiations in order to dismantle these barriers.

Most favored nation (MFN) treatment is a provision in a commercial transaction or treaty between two or more countries that guarantees that all partners will automatically extend to one another any tariff reductions that they might offer to a nontreaty country. All GATT members have agreed to extend MFN treatment to each other's exports. The granting of MFN status has been used frequently to further the foreign policy objective of gaining a nation's goodwill. At the same time, the denial or threat of removal of MFN has been used to express criticism of a nation's policy. In the 1970's and 1980's, the extension of MFN to the People's Republic of China was part of the U.S. policy to improve relations with China, while in the 1990's, the threat of removal of the status served to express U.S. criticism of China's human rights policy.

Because worldwide free trade has been difficult to achieve, some theorists have suggested that the road to international free trade will be paved by regional integration schemes. This five-stage theory of economic integration starts with a free trade area, evolves into a customs union, to a common market, to economic union, and then full economic integration within a region. In a free trade area, member countries abolish tariffs and nontariff barriers against each other, but each country retains its own barriers against nonmember countries. A customs union is an agreement among countries to abolish tariffs among the members of the union, while adopting a uniform tariff against other nations outside of that union. In a common market, not only trade restrictions, but also restrictions of factor movements such as capital and labor, are abolished. The harmonization of national economic policies, such as the Common Agricultural Policy (CAP) of the European Economic Community, differentiates economic union from a common market. Total economic integration, which was the direction in which the European Community was headed in the early 1990's, entails the unification of the member countries' monetary, fiscal, and social policies, which also requires the setting up of a supranational authority whose decisions can be binding upon the member countries. The efforts of the European Community and the North American Free Trade Agreement are examples of the practical application of this theory.

Applications

Efforts at trade liberalization have been undertaken simultaneously on global, regional, and bilateral levels. In 1994, members of GATT concluded trade negotiations under the Uruguay Round. This agreement was considered the most far-reaching global trade agreement in history. Tariffs on manufactured goods would be cut by 50 to 100 percent. Rules to govern trade and investment in telecommunications, professional services, and financial services, as well as the protection of intellectual property rights, were formulated. A World Trade Organization was created to ensure that those who are entitled receive the benefits under the agreement. The conclusion of the Uruguay Round of negotiations under GATT was considered a victory for encouraging further trade liberalization on a worldwide level.

On a regional level, the North American Free Trade Agreement (NAFTA) was an effort at seeking more open trade practices among the United States, Canada, and Mexico. Trilateral negotiations culminated in the signing of the agreement by U.S. president George Bush, Mexican president Carlos Salinas de Gortari, and Canadian prime minister Brian Mulroney on October 7, 1992, in San Antonio, Texas. This heralded what was considered to be the largest, richest, and most productive market in the world, because it allowed for a freer flow of goods, services, and investments among the three member countries. It went into effect on January 1, 1994, after ratification by the governments of the three countries. The creation of a free trade area meant that most tariff and nontariff barriers among the three countries would be eliminated in five to ten years and would be eliminated totally in fifteen years.

Individual country policies can be used to influence free trade on a bilateral level. Such is the case of U.S. trade policy with China, which allows for the renewal of most favored nation (MFN) status on an annual basis. From 1988 through 1994, the president of the United States exercised his authority to grant most favored nation status to China, despite protests regarding China's human rights record in treating political prisoners; unfair trade practices of using prison labor to create products for export; selling nuclear weapons to Pakistan and Syria; and cooperating with Iran and Algeria to develop nuclear technology. The United States found itself in a dilemma, because the policy of withdrawing MFN status had to be weighed against the importance of China's size and power in the Pacific region. As a permanent member of the United Nations Security Council, China has veto power that the United States did not want exercised against its interests. Restricting U.S. imports of Chinese goods by revoking MFN would have affected American investors and consumers alike. Attempts at revoking MFN status would have invited retaliation against U.S. exports, especially of food and agricultural products, which would have adversely affected exporters shut out of China's potential billion-person market.

Context

The international community has worked for a more liberal trading environment since the conclusion of World War II. In a world that is always becoming more interdependent, the choices that countries make with regard to free trade are intertwined with domestic issues such as food, the environment, and investments. There are those who have called for isolationism and protectionism in the face of growing domestic problems. Equally strong have been the voices for continued attempts at trade liberalization and internationalism.

Governments are perennially concerned about the direction of their trade because it is always a major component of their gross national product, the value of goods and services produced within the economy in a given year. Particular attention thus must be paid to the balance of trade, the difference between the value of goods that a nation exports and what a nation imports during a given period, because of the implications to foreign exchange and resources for development that a country can amass as a result of its ability to trade.

Bibliography

Balassa, Bela, ed. *European Economic Integration*. New York: American Elsevier, 1975. Analyzes the direction in which the process of European integration is evolving.

_____. *The Theory of Economic Integration*. Homewood, Ill.: Richard D. Irwin, 1961. Clearly explains the stages of reaching full economic integration.

Blake, David H., and Robert S. Walters. *The Politics of Global Economic Relations*. 4th ed. Englewood Cliffs, N.J.: Prentice-Hall, 1992. Focuses on the various issues involved in international economic relations; puts the issue of the trade dilemma into a more global perspective.

Dudley, William. *Trade: Opposing Viewpoints*. San Diego, Calif.: Greenhaven Press, 1991. Series of articles that take opposing sides of issues relating to trade, discussing the various factors that are involved in trade policy-making.

Rourke, John T. *International Politics on the World Stage*. 3d ed. Guilford, Conn.: Dushkin, 1991. Good discussion of the various aspects of international politics. Contains a section with an accurate description of the North American Free Trade Area.

Trade: U.S. Policy Since 1945. Washington, D.C.: Congressional Quarterly, 1984. Focuses on the various trade policy issues facing the United States in the 1980's, and traces the development of U.S. trade policy since the end of World War II.

Cecilia G. Manrique

Cross-References

TRANSPORTATION MANAGEMENT IN THE UNITED STATES

Field of study: Functions of government

Regulation of national transportation is an extensive, complex, and historical function of government. The nature of transportation makes it one of the most significant contributors to the nation's economy and social environment.

Principal terms

CARRIER: private company or person that provides a transportation service, such as an airline or shipping line

DEPARTMENT OF TRANSPORTATION (DOT): department of the federal executive branch of government that administers national transportation regulations through more than thirty bureaus and agencies, including the Federal Aviation Administration, Federal Highway Administration, Federal Railroad Administration, and others

DEREGULATION: removal of government restrictions and controls

INTERSTATE COMMERCE: carrying of goods or services across state lines

INTRASTATE COMMERCE: commerce carried entirely within a single state's borders

PASSENGER-MILE: moving of one person one mile; in the aggregate, passenger-mileage is the total distance that individual passengers have traveled

TON-MILE: moving of one ton of freight one mile

TRANSPORTATION: carriage, movement, or conveyance of passengers or goods

Overview

As in virtually all modern nations, the primary modes of transportation within the United States include railroads, highways, water, oil pipeline, and air transport. Each method of transportation is unique, with both private and public funding, specific infrastructure, and thus unique governmental jurisdiction and economic regulations. Transportation is vital to the nation as a whole, which depends upon it for economic, social, recreational, educational, cultural, political, and other purposes. Transportation services are continually challenged and beset by financial, operating, technological, political, and other problems. These challenges are an unending concern and high priority for governmental units at the local, state, and national levels.

Railroads have played a particularly significant role in the development and creation of transportation systems in the United States. As early as 1830, they were established in the eastern states, including New York, Pennsylvania, and New England. As the nation expanded west, the railroads played a key role. In 1869 the first transcontinental railroad service was opened by the Union Pacific and Central Pacific railroads. By 1916, a quarter of a million miles of railroad tracks crisscrossed the United States. Although initial railroad development was bitterly opposed by water canal and turnpike interests, government generally aided the railroads by granting them the power of eminent domain, allowing them to incorporate privately without state legislation, and by providing various types of financial aid from local, state, and federal governments. Although railroad mileage has declined since the early 1900's, it still totaled 184,000 miles in 1979. The volume of freight and passenger traffic has also declined from the early 1920's as a result of intense competition from other developing transportation services. In 1980 there were approximately 330 line-haul railroads in the United States. Of these, only forty Class I railroads (those with operating revenues in excess of $50 million) accounted for 98 percent of the freight traffic carried by the industry, 94 percent of the mileage, and 92 percent of the industry employees. Several of the major existing railroads include the Southern Pacific, Burlington Northern, Chessie-Seaboard Coast Line, Union Pacific, Santa Fe, Norfolk and Western, Southern, Missouri Pacific, and the Illinois Central Gulf.

Highway freight transportation has also played a significant role in the development and creation of transportation systems in the United States. Although the railroad industry had earlier beginnings and thus greater market hold, the highway freight industry has experienced phenomenal growth and expansion. In 1916, the number of registered trucks in the United States totaled approximately 250,000, most of them small vehicles engaged in local delivery service. The growth of intercity truck transportation was aided by technological improvements such as the pneumatic tire, expanding intercity use of automobiles (which increased public demand for better roadways), and better service capabilities than the railroad could offer. The number of non-government-owned trucks registered in the country grew from approximately 4.6 million in 1940 to more than 34 million in 1980 and the total intercity ton-mileage carried grew from 62 billion to more than 600 billion in 1979. In 1980 there were approximately 17,000 interstate for-hire trucking companies regulated by the Interstate Commerce Commission (ICC). The motor trucking industry makes use of an extensive road and street system in the United States. As of 1980 there were over 3.9 million miles of developed roads and streets, including the national system of interstate and defense highways.

Water transportation served an important role for colonial America, making use of the ocean and navigable rivers. Since the nation's founding, water transportation has expanded to include ocean coasts (coastal) and between coasts (intercoastal), the Great Lakes, rivers, canals, and between the mainland United States and offshore states and possessions such as Hawaii and Puerto Rico. Robert Fulton's invention of the steamboat in 1807 greatly expanded the growth of water transportation on the Mississippi and Ohio rivers. By 1880, however, the steamboats had all but given way to competition from the railroads. During the early nineteenth century, canals were built as state government enterprises throughout the country, including New York, Virginia, Maryland, Massachusetts, Pennsylvania, Ohio, Michigan, Indiana, and Illinois. Like the steamboat, however, canal transportation became a victim of railroad competition. After both World War I and World War II, the federal government provided funding for various programs to improve inland waterway systems and initiated a tow-boat-barge system for commodity shipping. By 1980, river transportation was again an important part of the nation's intercity freight transportation system, with emphasis on transporting bulk commodities. By 1980, excluding seacoasts and the Great Lakes, the country had approximately 25,500 miles of navigable waterways, with almost 16,000 miles having depths of nine feet or more.

The first oil pipeline transportation system was built in 1865, providing a two-inch crude oil pipeline from an oil field in Titusville, Pennsylvania, to a railroad terminal approximately six miles away. By 1900, there were some 6,800 miles of interstate crude oil pipelines in the country. Total pipeline mileage in the United States nearly tripled between 1915 and 1931, amounting to more than 115,000 miles in 1931. Because of increased demand for oil products during World War II, the federal government financed two major oil pipeline projects. One project provided a twenty-four-inch crude oil line from Longview, Texas, to the New York-Philadelphia area. Another project built a twenty-inch line connecting the Gulf Coast refining area with the New York area. Since 1950, the demand for petroleum products has accelerated and the development of new oil fields in North Dakota, Montana, Utah, Arizona, Colorado, Alaska, and off-shore areas has greatly expanded the need for oil pipeline transportation. By 1977, there were over 67,000 miles of crude-oil gathering lines, 77,000 miles of crude oil trunk lines, and 81,000 miles of product lines in the United States. In 1980, pipelines transported 575 billion ton-miles of crude oil and its products (gasoline, natural gas, and aviation jet fuel). Also in 1980 there were 125 interstate for-hire oil pipeline companies regulated by the Federal Energy Regulatory Commission (FERC).

Although the airplane was functional in the early 1900's, it did not begin to impact the transportation industry until after World War II. The Kelly Act, passed in 1925, provided that the U.S. Post Office Department would contract private air carriers to carry mail and also provide limited facilities for the transportation of passengers. Not until after the war, however, was aircraft technology greatly accelerated. In the 1950's, the advanced piston engine aircraft was developed; in the late 1950's and early 1960's the first pure jet passenger planes were developed; and in 1969 the first wide-bodied or jumbo jets were introduced. Meanwhile, airlines gradually dominated the for-hire intercity transportation of passengers. Air freight service also began to expand, but to a lesser degree. In 1939, for-hire air transportation carried 800 million passenger-miles, or only 2.3 percent of all for-hire intercity passenger miles carried. By 1980, for-hire air transportation carried 202 billion passenger-miles, or 82.7 percent of all for-hire intercity passenger miles carried. Although air freight continued to expand, air carriers still handled only two-tenths of one percent of all intercity freight ton-mileage in 1980. Also in 1980 there were more than 208,000 general aviation aircraft and over 2,500 airline aircraft flying from approximately 620 airports in the United States with scheduled airline service.

Applications

Transportation is one of the nation's most important industries. In 1988 it accounted for nearly 18 percent of the gross national product. By its very nature, transportation is a highly developed infrastructure industry, along with the communications and energy related industries. Because of the "public utility" aspects of transportation, the industry has had a long history of governmental regulation. Ironically, transportation was both the first industry to be regulated by the federal and state governments and—a century later—the first to be deregulated.

In the late nineteenth century, unfair price discrimination and destructive competition in the railroad industry led Congress to establish the nation's first independent regulatory agency, the Interstate Commerce Commission (ICC) in 1887. Interstate oil pipelines (crude oil and product lines) came under regulatory control in 1906 under the original Interstate Commerce Act (ICA). In 1977, Congress created a new federal Department of Energy and responsibility for economic regulation of oil pipelines was transferred to the Federal Energy Regulatory Commission (FERC). Highway transportation came under economic regulation with passage of the Motor Carrier Act of 1935, also part of the original ICA. The airline industry fell under government regulation with creation of the Civil Aeronautics Board (CAB) in 1938. Water transportation (intercoastal and U.S. inland waterways) came under economic regulation with passage of the Water Carrier Act of 1940.

These various transportation regulatory agencies were charged with the responsibilities to control entry and exit of competing firms, establish rate and fare structures, review and approve routes, mandate levels of service, provide guidelines for accounting and financial matters, determine and grant federal subsidies, and regulate industry abandonments and mergers.

Over a ninety-year period, the transportation industry has been besieged with tremendous fluctuations of economic stability and business financial losses and increasing public complaints of degraded service. During the 1970's and 1980's, regulatory failure became the catalyst for a movement toward governmental deregulation. Various forms of interstate deregulation resulted from legislation passed by Congress in the mid-1970's and early 1980's. It was argued that pricing and entry restrictions gave consumers excessive service and insufficient pricing competition, inflated operating costs, and denied the various industries adequate profits.

Specific examples of transportation industry deregulation included the Airline Deregulation Act of 1978, which provided for a transition to deregulated entry and rates for the airline industry and the elimination of the CAB in 1985, with its remaining responsibilities transferred to the U.S. Department of Transportation (DOT). The Railroad Revitalization and Regulatory Reform Act of 1976 provided for relaxation of the regulation of railroad rates and a change in the regulation of railroad abandonments and mergers. The Staggers Rail Act of 1980 provided for additional reform of railroad regulation, with emphasis on a reduction of railroad rate structures. The federal Motor Carrier Act of 1980 amended the ICA and significantly changed specific areas of economic regulation of motor trucking. The act provided greater freedom of entry and price making for the trucking industry while at the same time retaining an extensive regulatory structure.

In addition to federal regulation for the transportation industry, each state has a regulatory agency with responsibility for economic regulation of transportation. Their names vary, but examples include public service commissions, public utilities commissions, railroad commissions, commerce commissions, and transportation commissions. The degree of jurisdiction over the carriers regulated also varies widely from state to state. The commerce clause of the U.S. Constitution delegates the regulation of commerce between the states to the federal government. Regulation of intrastate commerce is left to the states themselves. States and local entities also maintain agencies or departments for the purpose of operating and collecting revenues for transportation related needs. Examples include airport authorities, port authorities, mass transit authorities, ferry authorities, highway departments, and revenue collection departments—which regulate fuel taxes, toll authorities, vehicle licensing, and trucking permits.

Context

The federal government has been actively involved with national transportation policy since the late 1800's. The Interstate Commerce Act of 1887 was an initial effort to dictate economic regulation on transportation carriers caused primarily by unfair price discrimination and destructive competition in the railroad industry. Eventually, federal legislation proved restrictive and somewhat punitive in nature, and it tended to promote pattern-setting influences that could negate future planning for changing circumstances and conditions. National transportation policy has followed fragmented, special-interest, crisis-reaction orientations. The nature of governmentally imposed economic regulation has resulted in both negative and positive effects on carriers as well as users.

Carriers have discovered the extreme restrictiveness of regulation. Economic regulation reduces the freedom of any regulated carrier to add or subtract services, to change prices, and to make other changes that unregulated industries do regularly. Another problem evolves from the nature of delays in decision making. Because of methodical bureaucratic process and approval delays, it is difficult for regulated carriers to react quickly to changes in the competitive marketplace. Regulated carriers often find their operational expenses are higher than they should be. Excessive expenses are incurred as a result of delays in decision making and inefficiencies forced on the carriers by regulation, such as those created by route, point, and commodity restrictions. Users are often subjected to inflexibility in transportation services. A related drawback for users is a reduction in transportation alternatives as regulation tends to reduce the number of carriers and available services between any two points.

Positive effects of economic regulation for both carriers and users include an avoidance of destructive competition. Service is maintained at acceptable levels and turnover is reduced in the transportation industry. Economic regulation has also produced a stable environment for carrier operations and user dependence on availability and pricing. In addition, economic regulation has eliminated unfair and discriminatory treatment of users in the form of unjust discrimination in prices and service and exorbitant prices.

Bibliography

Altschiller, Donald, ed. *Transportation in America*. New York: H. W. Wilson, 1982. Reprints of articles, excerpts from books, and addresses on transportation issues and trends within the United States. Topics include problems and prognostications in transportation, the railroad industry, mass transit issues, and issues concerning transportation of the handicapped. An excellent book for a quick review of pertinent transportation issues.

Dempsey, Paul, and Andrew Goetz. *Airline Deregulation and Laissez-Faire Mythology*. Westport, Conn.: Quorum Books, 1992. Traces the history of the airline industry and details how the Civil Aeronautics Board regulated the industry for four decades. Discusses the impact of the Airline Deregulation Act of 1978 and concludes that neither economic nor equity goals have been advanced by deregulation, supporting this theory with examples of industry bankruptcies, increased costs, and degraded services.

Dunn, James A. *Miles to Go: European and American Transportation Policies*. Cambridge, Mass.: MIT Press, 1981. Does an excellent job in discussing problems, policies, and paradigms in transportation policy. Dunn compares and contrasts European and American transportation policies relating to railroads, mass transit, highways, and automobiles.

Harper, Donald V. *Transportation in America: Users, Carriers, Government*. 2d ed. Englewood Cliffs, N.J.: Prentice-Hall, 1982. Excellent overview of the principles of economic regulation in the transportation industry, discussing the impact of economic regulation in terms of the users, the carriers, and the government. Covers the railroad, highway, waterway, oil pipeline, and airline industries.

Mertins, Herman. *National Transportation Policy in Transition*. Lexington, Mass.: Lexington Books, 1972. Good recap of national transportation policy formulation and rationalization; discusses the history of transportation legislation, the role and significance of the Department of Transportation, and the impact that technology has on transportation policy and regulation.

Miller, James C., III, ed. *Perspectives on Federal Transportation Policy*. Washington, D.C.: American Enterprise Institute for Public Policy Research, 1975. Informative and interesting collection of papers presented on surface-transportation regulation, air-transportation regulation, problems of public policy reform, and evaluations of federal transportation programs.

John L. Farbo

Cross-References

Business and Government, p. 177; Commerce Regulation, p. 357; Energy Management, p. 604; Environmental Protection, p. 617; Funding of Government, p. 724; Government Agencies, p. 765; Industrialization, p. 916; Land Management in the United States, p. 1045; Public Utilities, p. 1640; Public Works, p. 1647; Regulatory Agencies in the United States, p. 1678; Research, Development, and Planning, p. 1711; State and Local Government, p. 1885.

TREASURY SYSTEMS

Field of study: Functions of government

For millennia, money has facilitated the exchange of goods and services, serving as a standard of value and a means of storing wealth. Modern governments have increasingly used their treasury systems to manipulate the money supply in order to stabilize and develop national economies.

Principal terms

CENTRAL BANK: government entity that functions as a "bankers' bank" and acts to influence the money supply and interest rates as part of monetary policy

CURRENCY: bills and coins that are acceptable in exchange for goods and as a settlement of debt

DEMAND DEPOSIT: check drawn on a bank, a demand that payment be made from the assets in the account

FEDERAL RESERVE: central bank of the United States, created in 1913 to act as the lender (to banks) of last resort and as the nation's monetary authority

FRACTIONAL RESERVE REQUIREMENT: banks are required to hold only a portion of deposits in reserve against depositor demand and may lend out the remainder

LEGAL TENDER: money that must be accepted in payment of debt

MONETARY POLICY: the way that the monetary authority influences the money supply and interest rates

PANIC: sharp contraction in the economy, often accompanied by bank failure and a constricting money supply

SPECIE: coins minted from precious metals that have value as a commodity as well as a set value in exchange

TREASURY: the nation's fiscal agent, collecting taxes, making expenditures, and borrowing, as necessary, to finance the spending deficit

Overview

The earliest method of exchanging goods and services was barter. In barter, goods or services are exchanged directly for each other. A major hindrance to a barter economy is the mutual coincidence of wants necessary for a transaction to occur. For example, farmer A, a pig producer, and farmer B, a wheat producer, must want each other's goods, and at the same time, for a transaction to occur. To circumvent the barriers to commerce that barter presents trading commodities were advanced as crude measures of value (for example, beans, shells, metals, and tobacco). These trading commodities could then be exchanged in measured rates for goods and services. Large variances in size and quality of trading commodities, however, made exchange a slow process.

Efforts to standardize trading commodities increased the level of commerce but revealed new flaws in the exchange system. Commodity monies such as rings or metals, precious or nonprecious, were subject to large variations in supply, as mines were opened or closed. Thus, the value of early money was given to enormous fluctuations. As a result, at the community level, efforts were made to control the currency (that is, whatever presently constituted a means of exchange).

Trading communities came to stamp metals with their own particular seal and to forbid the circulation of other coinages. This intervention of trading communities, that stated in law what was currently (hence the word "currency") acceptable in exchange, constitutes the beginning of money.

Money is an elastic concept, however, since what is acceptable in exchange for goods and services changes with economic conditions. Only governmentally designated money must be accepted in resolution of debt. While the acceptability of various forms of money may change, the characteristics of an acceptable money do not. An effective money functions as a medium of exchange, a store of value, and a standard of value and debt. Acting as a medium, money encourages exchange while removing the encumbrances of barter. Since money gained in a transaction is held by the seller, that money must be able to retain its value until the seller makes a purchase decision. Finally, a reliable money serves as a yardstick for comparing values and for allowing long-term debt contracts.

In the United States, the evolution of the money system and of the respective roles of the Treasury and central bank is an ongoing process. In colonial times and after, corn, tallow, wheat, skins, pork, fish, and brandy circulated as commodity monies. In 1789, for example, the salary of the governor of Tennessee was stated as 1,000 deer skins. Additionally, the currencies of Spain, England, France, and most European trading partners circulated in the United States as well. The scarcity of foreign specie and the absence of minting facilities in the colonies, however, prolonged the use of commodity monies and encouraged the circulation of promissory notes, colonial bills of credit, and private monies as media of exchange.

One of the most onerous tasks facing the Founders of the United States was establishing a standardized, efficient currency. With the ratification of the Constitution, Alexander Hamilton, the first secretary of the Treasury, launched a campaign for a national bank that would increase the quantity of paper currency in circulation while acting as the nation's bank and source of loans. Patterned after the Bank of England, which had been successfully operating as Britain's central bank for one hundred years, the First Bank of the United States functioned both as a commercial bank and as the Treasury's bank. The First Bank was privately owned, the largest bank in the new nation, a lender of specie to smaller banks, and the depository for federal tax receipts. The bank monitored the quality of the money supply by presenting notes drawn on other banks for payment in specie.

The congressional charter for the First Bank was not renewed in 1811. Opponents had successfully attacked it as unconstitutional, controlled by foreign investors, and a money monopoly.

Difficulties in financing the War of 1812 and other monetary problems inspired the establishment of the Second Bank of the United States in 1816. Under the presidency of Nicholas Biddle, the Second Bank prospered, extending the central banking functions instituted by its predecessor and tightening control over the national money supply. The election of President Andrew Jackson in 1828, however, provided Biddle and the bank with a formidable opponent. In his premier address to Congress, Jackson questioned the constitutionality of the Second Bank. Thus he fired the first shot in what was to become the Bank War. After a furious battle in the press and on the floor of Congress, Jackson delivered the deathblow to the bank by transferring federal deposits to state banks. In 1836, the charter of the Second Bank of the United States was allowed to lapse.

Between 1836 and 1914, there was no entity performing the functions of a national, central bank in the United States. In the aftermath of the Second Bank fiasco, advocates of a "hard money" policy urged a complete separation of banking and the federal treasury. Arguing that the federal government should receive only specie in payment of debt, opponents of hard money legislated a "divorce" between the Treasury and the banks in 1846. Thereafter, monies paid to the government in hard currency would be stored in the Washington treasury, or in Treasury-owned buildings.

The negative economic consequences of sequestering government surpluses in treasury vaults soon became apparent. For seventy-five years, a succession of secretaries of the Treasury found means to circumvent the law. For example, one way to recycle government revenues was for the Treasury to buy government bonds on the open market, effectively returning monies to the bank system. The independence of the Treasury from the bank system existed in law but not in fact.

After the concept of central banking was allowed to lapse, an era of free banking commenced. Under free banking, anyone or any group of people could begin a bank provided that they complied with state regulations—which varied considerably. Needless to say, many banks were founded with the sole, and soon-realized, intent of bilking depositors out of their hard-earned savings. Despite this, the bank industry flourished during the period before the Civil War. Economically developed states required heavy specie reserves against issued bank notes, but only a few required reserves against deposit liabilities. The number of state banks grew from 330 in 1830 to more than 1,500 by 1860.

Although the overall bank industry grew and prospered during the antebellum period, the issuance and acceptability of paper currency had become a serious problem. By 1860, with 1,500 banks issuing six or more denominations of notes each, 10,000 different bank notes circulated in the economy. Whereas some notes were as good as the specie backing them, others issued by less scrupulous banks were either unacceptable or acceptable only at a huge discount. Counterfeiting was rampant. Periodicals that itemized notes in circulation and approximated their discounted value in exchange became a necessity for merchants.

In 1863, the federal government ended its hands-off policy toward the bank industry and intervened with the passage of the National Bank Act of 1863 and subsequent amendments. The purposes of the bill were twofold: to control the proliferation of currency; and to help finance the Civil War. Under the enactment, national banks were to be chartered by the newly formed office of comptroller of the currency. Capital requirements for the new banks varied by population served, while the purchase of war bonds in an amount at least equal to one-third of a bank's capitalization was required. In return, the nationally chartered banks received a new issue of legal tender, national bank notes equaling 90 percent of the face value of the new bonds. A tax of 10 percent was imposed on the state bank notes, with the intent of driving them from circulation. Initially, the 10 percent tax caused the number of state-chartered banks to dwindle. Demand deposits soon replaced bank notes as the primary medium of exchange, however, and the number of state-chartered banks rebounded to more than 9,000 by 1900, while the entire banking system included more than 13,000 banks.

After the Civil War, while state bank notes ceased to circulate, national bank notes, U.S. bank notes, specie, and specie representatives all functioned as money. Different currencies resulted in different price systems and a clamor for more uniform currency. In 1900, the Currency Act formally placed the United States on a pure gold standard. Henceforth, currency would be priced in gold, redeemable in gold, and trade deficits settled on the basis of gold. It appeared that America's money woes had ended, but this was not the case.

Applications

The word "panic" might be defined as hysteria in the face of crisis. In U.S. history, financial panics swept the economy in 1819, 1837, 1857, 1860, 1873, and 1907. Generally speaking, in a panic, depositors ran to banks to withdraw their deposits, banks suspended specie and cash payments, banks failed, and the economy contracted. The triggering mechanism for a panic might be a cyclical downturn, a drop in stock markets, or banks restricting depositor demands for cash. The Panic of 1907 was typical. From 1907 to 1908, net national product fell by more than 10 percent. A silver lining for the last panic was its role as catalyst in the creation of the Federal Reserve System.

Actually, one person, J. Pierpont Morgan, was responsible for quelling the Panic of 1907. By marshaling loans from and to financial institutions, Morgan was able to provide sufficient liquidity to resolve the crisis. His status as the premier financier and banker of his era enabled Morgan to act as a one-man central bank. The emergency, and Morgan's rescue of the economy, again convinced politicians that some form of a central bank was needed.

In 1908, Congress passed a partial measure toward creating a central bank in the Aldrich-Vreeland Act, which focused on the necessity of the bank system's being able to provide depositors with large quantities of cash on demand. Under the present system, a depositor run would quickly deplete reserves, leading to the calling in of loans (typically to brokerage houses), the dumping of stocks to generate capital, and a plunge in the stock market. This sad scenario had played out too many times. Therefore, the Aldrich-Vreeland Act allowed banks to form national currency associations which could, in an emergency, issue cash backed by commercial paper and bonds. At the conclusion of the money crisis, the emergency paper would be retired.

An important provision of Aldrich-Vreeland was the creation of the National Monetary Commission, which provided the basis for the Federal Reserve Act. The commission studied the monetary system in order to identify its deficiencies and suggest plans for reform. The results of the study were somewhat ambiguous, suggesting a weak form of a central bank that would operate only in emergencies. Nevertheless, the commission report brought the issue into sharp focus and energized Congress to improve upon its suggestions.

In 1913, President Woodrow Wilson signed the Federal Reserve Act into law. The bill was a compromise between congressmen who favored greater centralization of power in Washington and those who favored a retention of power at the state and regional level. As a result, a Federal Reserve System (Fed) was established with twelve separate bank districts, each headed by a Federal Reserve bank, and a seven-member Federal Reserve Board of Governors in Washington. The new Federal Reserve was created to serve two basic purposes: to provide a currency that was responsive to the demands of commerce and depositors, and to act as a bankers' bank—a lender of last resort. Unfortunately, the Federal Reserve would selectively renege on both mandates in the years to come.

The new banking system was technically owned by its members; all members were to buy stock in, and receive nominal dividends from, the new entity. All national banks were required to join, while membership was optional for state-chartered banks. All members were required to maintain reserves at the district Federal Reserve Bank. Although 100 percent of its shares were held by member banks, the Federal Reserve was created to be independent of outside influence. The past interferences of the Treasury in money matters and previous tinkering of Congress were instrumental in the decision for Fed independence. Furthermore, the Treasury needed help from a central bank. The isolation of Treasury activities from the bank industry after 1836 resulted in a system of increasingly outdated procedures with respect to taxing, spending, borrowing, and foreign exchange transactions. An official, independent institution of high stature was needed to guide the increasingly complex monetary system of a rapidly growing economy.

Context

The Federal Reserve System of today bears slight resemblance to its predecessor of 1913. Over time, the Fed's responsibilities as the nation's central bank grew, as has its role as monetary authority. The failure of the Federal Reserve to act decisively in the early years of the Great Depression worsened the economic landslide and prompted new reforms.

The increased awareness of monetary significance in stabilization policy is reflected in the Bank acts of 1933 and 1935. The Glass-Steagall Act of 1933 regulated interest rates but, most important, created the Federal Deposit Insurance Corporation, which insured depositor accounts and effectively eliminated disastrous runs on banks. The Bank Act of 1935 vested more powers in the Federal Reserve Board of Governors and added to the kit of Fed stabilization tools. Whereas in 1913, the Fed essentially relied on changes in the discount rate (rate charged on Fed loans to members) as the instrument of credit and money control, effective instruments of Fed policy grew to include changes in bank reserve requirements and open market purchases of government securities on a daily basis to affect the money supply.

Furthermore, the money supply itself has become more complex since the early 1900's. New monies have evolved from innovations in the financial industry, and the distinctions between different categories of money has softened, blurred by a common denominator of greater liquidity in nearly all components of the money supply.

Monetary policy has become the stabilization instrument of choice, with fiscal policy being a recourse only during recession. Through manipulating reserves, the Federal Reserve seeks to hit money supply and interest rate targets. By fine-tuning the economy through appropriate day-to-day monetary policy, the Fed hopes to lower the amplitude of business cycles and reduce the need for more drastic policy prescriptions.

As the economy has become more global in nature, economic phenomena elsewhere may negatively impact the United States, requiring a monetary policy response. Through the Federal Reserve Bank of New York, official reserve transactions are conducted with other central banks. Finally, the Fed will occasionally decide to intervene in foreign exchange markets to buy or sell dollars or other currencies in support of domestic or foreign economic policy.

Bibliography

Degen, Robert A. *The American Monetary System*. Lexington, Mass.: Lexington Books, 1987. Provides clear insights into the U.S. monetary system since the turn of the century.

Del Mar, Alexander. *History of Monetary Systems*. New York: Augustus M. Kelley, 1969. A trove of minutiae about ancient money systems, first published in 1895.

Hughes, Jonathan. *American Economic History*. 2d ed. Glenview, Ill.: Scott, Foresman, 1987. Readable text, largely free of graphs and math but with many informative tables.

Marshall, Alfred. *Money Credit and Commerce*. New York: Augustus M. Kelley, 1960. No one explains as well the microeconomics of the functions of money and why people hold money. A classic work, first published in 1929.

Timberlake, Richard H., Jr. *Money, Banking, and Central Banking*. New York: Harper & Row, 1965. Lucid delineation of the roles of banks, the central bank, and Treasury.

Walton, Gary, and Hugh Rockoff. *History of the American Economy*. 6th ed. San Diego: Harcourt Brace Jovanovich, 1990. Excellent overview of the American economy, explaining the economic rationale behind historical events.

John A. Sondey

Cross-References

Budgets of National Governments, p. 158; Bureaucracy, p. 164; Business and Government, p. 177; Debts and Deficits in the U.S. Federal Budget, p. 489; Funding of Government, p. 724; Government Agencies, p. 765; Keynesianism, Monetarism, and Supply-Side Economics, p. 1032; National Economies, p. 1248; Public Policy, p. 1633.

TREATIES

Field of study: International government and politics

A major source of international law, treaties are adopted by states to formulate rules that they agree to follow in their mutual interrelations. Treaties are adopted to promote peace, stimulate commerce, and facilitate communication, cooperation, and collaboration on issues of common interest.

Principal terms

EXECUTIVE AGREEMENT: in the United States, an agreement carrying the full legal force of a treaty, which the executive branch can effect with or without prior or subsequent authorization

NEGOTIATION: process by which nations reach agreement on the terms of a treaty

PACTA SUNT SERVANDA: international customary doctrine by which states recognize their duty to observe treaties to which they are parties

RATIFICATION: formal action by the executive branch of a country indicating its willingness to be bound by the terms of a treaty

REBUS SIC STANTIBUS: legal doctrine that asserts that treaties lose legally binding force when the circumstances surrounding their promulgation have changed fundamentally or been altered radically

RESERVATIONS: qualifications made by states upon ratifying treaties indicating special interpretations of, or assertions not to be bound by, particular provisions

Overview

Treaties have been used since ancient times to resolve disputes and regulate the activities of different societies. Twentieth century governments have used them with increasing frequency to do much the same thing. Treaties constitute one of the major sources of international law, that is, one of the means by which governments establish mutually binding, obligatory rules in their interrelations. States may choose to limit their sovereignty and their behavior toward one another by ratifying treaties. Because states are sovereign, no state can be forced to ratify a treaty against its will, nor can any one group of states create a treaty obligation for third parties who have not agreed to a treaty's provisions. Thus, treaties serve as a source of international law only among those countries who are party to them. In cases where membership in the treaty is universal or nearly universal, such a treaty may create new customary norms of law that might in time have a universal obligatory character. The vast majority of treaties that exist between states, however, are bilateral in nature or involve smaller numbers of states in a region. Such treaties create law only for those states party to the treaties.

Apart from treaties, customary law is the other major source of international law, and for centuries, the bulk of universal international law was customary in origin. In recent times, however, with the emergence of multilateral lawmaking treaties, treaties have become the more prominent means of creating international law. Treaties often are more explicit than custom, and can often be negotiated and brought into force in shorter periods of time. As the rapid pace of technological change affects international relations, states increasingly rely on treaties as a means of developing new legal norms or revising old ones to regulate their affairs more effectively.

A distinction is often made between a Treaty with a capital "T," which is a formal agreement that takes a specific format, and treaties more generally, which vary in the degree of formality and in their actual format. A Treaty is an agreement among nations that is formally divided into five parts, the preamble, a main body with articles, final clauses, testimonial, and signatures. Many agreements not called Treaties, such as covenants, charters, constitutions, conventions, and pacts, also follow this format. The formality of such agreements suggests the importance attached to them by governments; however, all kinds of treaties, whatever their format or formality, bind the parties who ratify them. Thus, protocols, memoranda of understanding, exchanges of letters, annexes, and other types of treaties, although less formal, and perhaps not submitted to the formal domestic processes of ratification, still bind the parties who agree to them. On the other hand, declarations and resolutions usually do not create binding obligations, and agreements called by these names are often explicitly characterized as nonbinding in their effects. Such agreements serve as general statements of aspiration or as recommendations that states are encouraged to follow. Ultimately, however, the name given to a treaty is not so important as the intention of the states that are party to the treaty to create obligations and bring them into effect.

In this connection, the U.S. government distinguishes between treaties that require the advice and consent of Congress, and executive agreements, which usually deal with more routine matters, that the executive branch can enter into on the basis of its constitutional authority to conduct foreign relations. Most executive agreements, however, are given prior or subsequent authorization from Congress, especially since performance of obligations under executive agreements usually requires money, which Congress alone can authorize under the Constitution. The U.S. Senate does not actually ratify treaties; rather it advises and consents to the ratification of treaties by the president. Ultimately, ratification is an executive, not a legislative, act. Once executive agreements are effected, they cannot be revoked simply because a new government comes into power. Like all treaties, executive agreements create international obligations that governments are expected to observe.

A question that all legal systems must ultimately address is how to create mechanisms to ensure continuity while responding to pressures for change. Since a legal system is intended to affect the behavior of its constituent elements, there needs to be stability and predictability with regard to legal duties and obligations. Nevertheless, legal systems need a capacity to respond to change and to adapt to new and different pressures. Concerning the role of treaties in international law, two major principles are widely recognized as enabling stability and adaptability. The *pacta sunt servanda* principle, which is a time-honored customary principle of international law, stipulates that good faith must be kept in treaties, that states must observe their treaty obligations. On the other hand, when the original reasons for or circumstances surrounding the promulgation of a treaty have fundamentally changed, there need to be mechanisms to revoke outmoded treaties and treaty provisions. The *rebus sic stantibus* principle, or doctrine of fundamentally changed circumstances, is sometimes invoked by states who seek relief from burdensome and outdated treaty regulations. Other mechanisms for change are often integral parts of treaties. Treaties can be renegotiated, amended, or even terminated by terms specified within the treaty itself. Usually treaties contain clauses that allow for adaptation and even withdrawal. At other times, the legal force of treaties is lost through simple disuse, or supersession by subsequent agreements.

The power to make treaties rests with sovereign states and with subsidiary groups, such as international organizations, to which states have given a treaty-making capacity. Procedurally, treaties are first negotiated. Once governments have achieved consensus on the terms of a treaty, they usually sign it, which implies that they will take steps to pursue its final ratification. In the days of monarchs, the signature of a king or queen was tantamount to ratification, but with the rise of parliamentary democracy, treaties began normally to pass through certain domestic procedures prior to formal ratification by the executive branch of a government. Thus, treaties are not considered binding on initial signature, but only after ratification has been formally announced. In the case of bilateral treaties, once the executive branch of each government has formally ratified an agreement, it comes into force. In the case of multilateral treaties, ratification by a certain number of signatory states may be required before the treaty formally enters into force. Treaties remain in force unless terminated by the terms of the agreement itself; by virtue of egregious violations of the treaty that provoke retaliation; and, especially in the case of military, political, or commercial agreements, on the commencement of war between the parties. In other cases, such as extradition agreements, war may only suspend the enforcement of treaty obligations; the obligations resume with the conflict's termination. Still other kinds of treaties continue to be enforced even between belligerents in wartime. Examples include the Geneva Red Cross Conventions and other agreements that explicitly regulate state behavior during war, as well as boundary agreements and certain multilateral lawmaking treaties to which both belligerents and neutral states are party.

Applications

Treaties serve a variety of functions in international relations and address a vast array of subjects. They regulate air traffic, maritime activities, extradition, diplomatic and consular affairs, commercial relations and trade, migration, dispute resolution, and communications. They deal with the economic, political, military, social, legal, humanitarian, and cultural affairs of nations. Some treaties are multilateral in nature, governing relations among many states, while others are strictly bilateral in character. Three treaties, two multilateral and one bilateral, will be examined to see how they operate and the functions they perform.

One important multilateral treaty is the Vienna Convention of the Law of Treaties

(1969). This treaty, ratified by more than a hundred nations, served several important functions. In one sense, it codified existing customary principles of state practice in regard to treaties, collecting and clarifying existing rules in a coherent way. For example, it codified the major principles that states have recognized regarding the interpretation of treaties, and it reemphasized the *pacta sunt servanda* doctrine. The treaty also established new principles of treaty law to regulate the treaty process. For example, it adopted new principles for handling reservations to multilateral agreements, and included controversial provisions regarding the application of the *rebus sic stantibus* principle. Some states, such as the United States, although recognizing the continuing validity of the codification elements of this treaty, have refused to ratify it because of its innovations.

A multilateral treaty that is even broader in scope is the Law of the Sea Treaty. This treaty was painstakingly negotiated over a ten-year period, culminating in its signing in 1982. It codified many elements of the customary law of the sea, and established new legal principles, procedures, and institutions. It established the principle of a twelve-mile territorial sea in which coastal states could claim absolute jurisdiction, with an additional economic zone extending out from the territorial sea to a point two hundred miles from shore, in which coastal states exercised rights over seabed resources, fishing, pollution control, and scientific research. Coastal states could also claim exclusive jurisdiction over the continental shelf out to two hundred miles. Beyond this point, states agreed that resources found in the high seas, or on the deep seabed beyond the limits of national jurisdiction, could not be claimed by individual states for their exclusive use. The treaty protected the right of innocent passage through international straits; developed new rules for the measuring and delimitation of archipelagos; and solidified principles for the measuring of baselines from which territorial waters are measured and for the delimitation of claims to the continental shelf, where shared by more than one state. It reemphasized the right of landlocked states to have access to seaports and established legal machinery to resolve jurisdictional disputes.

The most controversial provisions of the treaty dealt with deep seabed mining, where the traditional notion of the freedom of the seas conflicted with the new doctrine of the common heritage of humankind, on which the deep seabed mining provisions rested. At issue was whether states possessing the technology to mine for deep seabed nodules could do so, or whether they would be regulated by an International Seabed Authority that would allocate mining sites and ensure that technology for mining was transferred either to those states lacking it or to an international enterprise that would engage in such mining on behalf of the international community as a whole. After the treaty was signed in 1982, the United States and many other Western nations refused to ratify it, and developed their own dispute resolution mechanisms with a view to pursuing individual mining operations. As of 1994, the treaty had not yet attained the sixty ratifications necessary to come into force, but renegotiation of several controversial provisions had opened the way for a promise of eventual U.S. support.

The process of extradition provides an example of the operation of bilateral treaties.

Bilateral extradition treaties grow out of the desire of governments not to allow criminals to escape punishment for their crimes by fleeing across international boundaries. No right of extradition can be claimed in international law, outside of the terms of specific bilateral extradition treaties. These treaties normally establish what offenses are extraditable in nature and set up a process, usually including an extradition hearing, by which the two governments in question agree to reciprocal extradition of fugitives. Political offenses are usually exempted from extradition, while most criminal offenses punishable under the laws of the two governments entering into the extradition agreement are included.

Context

Treaties have long been a means by which countries peacefully adjust their interrelations. Records from ancient times suggest that treaties were negotiated to cement alliances, determine borders, protect holy places, preserve peace, promote commercial relations, or end wars. Little has changed since ancient times; states continue to use treaties for these and many other purposes in the twentieth century. There are, however, many more treaties and many apply on a global scale. Since the formation of the League of Nations, efforts have been promoted to register treaties so that the frequency of secret agreements would be minimized. Treaties that remain unregistered with the United Nations cannot be cited by any state before any U.N. body as justification for its actions.

States have found over the years that treaties are an indispensable means of regulating their routine affairs. New technologies that emerge, such as telegraph, telephone, radio, or airplane flight, require regulation across international boundaries if peoples in different countries are effectively and safely to enjoy their benefits. Air flight safety needs to be regulated, traffic lanes identified, rules of navigation observed. Electronic communications can be jammed or interfered with unless countries cooperate to ensure effective and shared access to the airwaves. Likewise, when deep seabed mining techniques are developed, rules will need to be established to avoid potential conflicts over mining claims at sea. Rules that establish accepted routines help to facilitate and harmonize interstate relations and avoid conflict. Because states enjoy reciprocal benefits from such treaty regulation, they have greatly expanded the use of treaties in the twentieth century.

When governments realize that ad hoc bilateral diplomacy is no longer effective in meeting the routine needs of their international relations, they often create international organizations to look after such questions. The Universal Postal Union, the International Telecommunications Union, the World Health Organization, and the International Maritime Consultative Organization are examples of where routine matters affecting the economic and commercial intercourse of nations were placed under the supervision of international organizations. All these organizations were formed by treaties, which established the authorities and mandates of the organization, created the institutional machinery and budget processes, and provided them with the capacity to function.

Treaties comprise an essential element of modern international relations, providing states a quick and reliable mechanism to order their affairs. They can be used to regulate the most mundane as well as the most crucial questions in international affairs, from trade to collective security, and from extradition to human rights. They appear to be a permanent feature of the international political landscape.

Bibliography

Akehurst, Michael. *A Modern Introduction to International Law*. 4th ed. London: Allen & Unwin, 1982. Contains a useful chapter on treaties that analyzes the Vienna Convention on Treaties; chapters on treaties as a source of international law; and the Law of the Sea Treaty, which was in draft form at the time.

Bowett, D. W. *The Law of International Institutions*. New York: Praeger, 1963. Although dated, is a thorough analysis of international organizations in their legal setting and of the treaties that authorized the creation of important global and regional organizations.

Brierly, James. *The Law of Nations*. Oxford, England: Oxford University Press, 1956. Still a valuable and insightful treatment of the fundamental principles of international law, this book examines the origins of international law, its chief sources including treaties, questions of jurisdiction, and mechanisms for regulating the use of force.

Brownlie, Ian. *Basic Documents in International Law*. 2d ed. Oxford, England: Clarendon Press, 1972. This useful anthology of treaties contains verbatim versions of the United Nations Charter, the Vienna Convention on Diplomatic Relations, numerous human rights declarations and treaties, and the Vienna Convention on Treaties, and includes helpful suggestions for further reading concerning each document.

McNair, Lord. *The Law of Treaties*. Oxford, England: Clarendon Press, 1961. One of the most extensive and authoritative analyses of international treaties and treaty law, this book meticulously examines the conclusion and termination of treaties; treaty classification; the scope, operation, interpretation, and application of treaties; breach of treaties; and the effects of war on treaties. It incorporates diplomatic correspondence and documents to illustrate cases.

Rosenne, Shabtai. *The Law of Treaties: A Guide to the Legislative History of the Vienna Convention*. Dobbs Ferry, N.Y.: Oceana, 1971. This highly technical book follows the drafting and negotiation of the Vienna Convention on the Law of Treaties. Lengthy introduction contains valuable insights into the codification process. Gives an article-by-article comparison of the draft text of the treaty and the final text in its English, French, and Spanish versions, which illustrates how the negotiation process changed the original draft.

von Glahn, Gerhard. *Law Among Nations: An Introduction to Public International Law*. 6th ed. New York: Macmillan, 1992. Comprehensive treatment of international law containing a superb chapter on the functions and legal effects of treaties. The entire volume discusses treaty aspects of the spectrum of international legal activity, including territorial jurisdiction issues, extradition, the Law of the Sea, war, recognition, the jurisdiction over persons, and diplomatic activity.

Robert F. Gorman

Cross-References

TRIBAL GOVERNMENT

Field of study: Types of government

A tribal government is a socially cohesive political system that encompasses closely related kin groups. Usually smaller than a nation, a tribe occupies a common territory, and its members generally share a common language, culture, descent, and sense of mutual identity.

Principal terms

BAND: social unit of perhaps twenty people who wander the countryside collecting food and resources; membership is based on kinship and marriage

BIG MAN: informal leader who creates his reputation through entrepreneurship and generosity

CHIEFDOM: small-scale political unit whose members are related by kinship, marriage, and descent, with political organization being temporary and regional

DESCENT GROUP: permanent social unit whose members claim a common ancestry along either the paternal or maternal line.

SEGMENTARY LINEAGE ORGANIZATION (SLO): system of political organization based on descent, usually patrilineal, whose multiple descent segments form at different genealogical levels and have different functions

TRIBE: horticultural or pastoral group in which social and political rankings are based largely on prestige, kinship, marriage, and seniority with the governmental functions being incorporated in nongovernmental institutions such as religion or kinship

Overview

In order better to understand group behavior, anthropologist Elman Service proposed a typology of four levels of social and political organization: band, tribe, chiefdom, and state. By definition, each category is an ideal type positioned on a continuum. At one end are bands, which subsist by wandering to hunt and gather. Bands do not cultivate crops, raise animals, or have concepts of land ownership (however, they may have concepts of individual bands possessing rights to particular areas during particular periods). Bands are also egalitarian, with no one person having prestige or authority over others. Bands are usually small groups with about twenty members (and never more than several hundred). Most members do the same kinds of work, with the men hunting, making tools, and telling stories; and the women gathering food and handling domestic chores, such as cooking. In the absence of formal governmental structures, decisions are made by consensus.

At the other end of Service's political continuum are state societies, which have economies based on agriculture and industry. States have class systems and permanent centralized governments with authority over everyone within their territorial jurisdictions.

The second ideal type in Service's classification scheme is the tribe. Unlike a chiefdom—Service's third type, which has a permanent political structure, practices intensive agriculture, and grants some members preferential treatment or authority over others—a tribe unites bands of pastoralists and horticulturalists. Tribal horticulturalists tend to move; as their land loses its fertility, they move to fresh land, allowing the spent earth to remain fallow for several years so that its fertility will be replenished.

Although the numbers of people living in bands, tribes, and chiefdoms has dropped dramatically since the nineteenth century, tribes are still found on all continents and major island groupings in a wide variety of habitats. Tribal societies vary greatly. Their economies can be agricultural, pastoral, or a mixture. Demarcations are not always clear. For example, the Bushmen of Southern Africa's Kalahari have traditionally been foragers and hunters; now they tend flocks of animals. Yet their group size and social behavior resembles the band. In fact, it is sometimes difficult to determine, for example, whether a community practices intensive agriculture or if it even has an agriculturally based economy. A community may be in transition from one form of organization to another and not fit perfectly into a classification scheme. Indeed, few communities fit perfectly into one of Service's ideal types.

Just as an organism's central nervous system regulates bodily functions, a government regulates and controls a society. Tribal societies, however, generally lack specialized governments that regulate society and provide direction. Other tribal institutions perform the functions that regulate and maintain order. These institutions are classified according to descent, decision-making processes, conflict resolution, and pan organizations.

Tribal membership is based on descent, that is, membership is at least theoretically based on common ancestry—descent from the same person. Descent groups, or lineages, are permanent and the basic units of tribal society. They may originate as minor lineages; minor lineages can combine to form major lineages; and major lineages can unite to become clans (groups that claim common ancestry but cannot actually trace it). All groups are equal, but each has a recognized leader. The leader is a "big man" or consensus builder, who leads by determining group opinion and acting on what the consensus indicates. The big man has no coercive power—he only leads by example or persuasion.

Some tribal villages have councils and headmen, but, again, council decisions are by consensus and the headmen are followers of public opinion, not its determinants. Nevertheless, a village council can help bring about united action among the various descent groups within its residential unit.

Pan organizations include villages and panvillage or pantribal groupings. They may be secret societies, age sets, warrior groups, or other groupings based on criteria other than descent or residence. As an example of a pan institution, the "big man" is usually a male who gains influence through his own initiative. He differs from village headmen in that his influence extends beyond his own village. He may gain his position by working hard and using wealth to obtain a following. He may have outstanding skills, such as hunting or leading in time of war, and he generally has charisma. The position is not formal and is not passed on hereditarily. In theory, it is a position anyone can achieve, and all tribes have a big man.

Different means of conflict resolution keep tribes from dividing. The potential for conflict and fission is always present because tribal members regard themselves as equal and are reluctant to submit to authority. Since there is no central enforcing institution, no one feels subordinate to another.

An important organizing aspect related to descent groups is the solidarity of a segmentary lineage organization (SLO). The SLO is based on the principle that close descent-group relationships foster greater mutual support. This provides a feeling of identity and regulates disputes. When fights break out, people take sides according to their descent. At the same time, however, an important person who shares an ancestor common to both disputing parties will generally mediate the conflict. For both him and other members of the wider lineage, there is too much to lose to allow their unit to be divided by disputes.

Other means of conflict resolution include marriage and rituals. Marriages unite families, rituals provide ways of resolving conflicts without threatening the unity or safety of the tribe and its members. One ritualized conflict resolution occurs when contesting parties settle their differences by competing in contests or games. Alternatively, shamans, or other persons recognized as having special supernatural powers, often determine causes and offer solutions to social conflicts.

Private property is not as important in tribal societies as it is in state societies. Tribal members have possessions, but maximizing wealth is not highly valued. Thus, a major source of conflict, wealth, rarely provokes theft, envy, or disputes over ownership.

Applications

A classic study of a tribal community is E. E. Evans-Pritchard's *The Nuer* (1940). The Nuer are a pastoral people of Sudan who also practice horticulture. During the rainy season, they live in villages on high ground and cultivate crops. After the rainy season, they burn their villages and move to camps near streams. They do not recognize permanent rights in land, but cattle are owned by individuals. Some families are richer in cattle than others, but this does not cause a variation in living standards. Large herds, however, lend prestige to the families that own them.

The Nuer contrast sharply with a band such as the !Kung Bushmen of Southern Africa, who wander or forage but do not have herds. For a tribe such as the Nuer, the minimal economic unit is the family, which is either a small nuclear family or an extended family comprising a patriarch, his sons, and their families. During the wet season in the village, families tend to be isolated. During the dry season, however, associated families combine into camps to herd their cattle, and their social life becomes communal. In either case, however, members remain kindred, and all Nuer consider themselves to be related.

This also contrasts with a band such as the !Kung, whose smaller-scale society consists of three levels: immediate family members (husband, wife, and children); related family groups that tend to travel together; and consanguinal (relationship by descent) and affinal (relationship by marriage) relatives. In bands like those of the Bushmen, it is not necessary actually to trace descent, merely claiming relationship is enough.

Matrilineal relationships are important to the Nuer, but the most significant relatives are in the patrilineal descent line. Such is the case in most societies, be they bands, chiefdoms, or states. To the Nuer, kinsmen should maintain peace among themselves and defend one another; the closer the relationship, the more necessary it is that peace prevail. Thus, lineages play a strong political role in that membership means participation in decision making, sharing territorial rights, and having common rights and obligations. Because lineages often have members in more than one village, they help link villages and bring unity to groups that are residentially dispersed. Related lineages form clans, and the combination of clans form Nuer tribes. Marriage is also a means of establishing cross-lineage ties while maintaining tribal unity. To the Nuer, marriage is a union of families. They have elaborate rules governing marriage; the strictures maintain clan exogamy but tribal endogamy.

As among most tribes, Nuer villages contain several lineages and residents have strong affinities to their villages. They share economic and social activities. They are egalitarian and do not accept authority of others unless it is within the family or age-set. There is no specialized governmental structure or institution, no regularized authority, and no laws or lawgivers. Influential men have a degree of authority based on their individual ability to command respect, and usually come from a dominant clan, but neither influence nor wealth are inherited.

For the Nuer, the position most resembling a political office is the leopard-skin chief—a man entitled to wear a leopard-skin wrap. His main function is to perform ritual duties and mediate feuds. For example, murder can bring retaliation and the beginning of a feud. Although there is no governmental institution to stop feuds, the Nuer prevent them from developing. When a Nuer kills a person, he might seek sanctuary with the leopard-skin chief, who goes to the murderer's family to persuade them to pay a specified number of cattle to the victim's family. He then visits the victim's family to persuade them to accept the payment in lieu of revenge. As a mediator, he has no authority to force payment or acceptance of it. In other kinds of disputes, Nuer prophets, shamans, or healers have political influence and they also unite the group for battle.

In units known as bands—such as those of the !Kung—political functions rest in kinship or religious institutions, as they do among the Nuer, but on a smaller scale. By contrast, chiefdoms have more formal political institutions, such as chiefs and advisory councils.

Context

Until the late nineteenth century, political philosophers viewed politics as a product of civilizations, and they regarded bands and tribes as lower stages, characterized by anarchy. It was Sir Henry Maine in *Ancient Law* (1861) who challenged the notion that anarchy prevailed in band and tribal societies. Maine postulated that "primitive" (a term that later fell out of usage because of its pejorative connotations) societies were organized along kinship lines, were patriarchal, and were ordered by sacred prescriptions. He viewed the evolutionary process toward secularization and organization based on territory. Lewis Henry Morgan, in *Ancient Society* (1877), built on Maine's insights to show that kinship is primary in sociopolitical structures at precivilization levels.

By the early twentieth century, evolutionary theories of social organization were being challenged. Scholars in England and France formulated new theories based on the functionalist thinking of Émile Durkheim. Functionalism sought to identify social laws. Following the model of the biological sciences, it emphasized the structure, or arrangement of parts, and function, how parts contribute to the survival of the society. Assuming that the parts tend to move toward an equilibrium, functionalism denied the importance of history in its analysis. In the United States, Franz Boas went further, arguing that anthropology is a humanity, not a science, and thus should only describe historical developments, not seek to find social laws.

In 1940 the classic work *African Political Systems*, edited by Meyer Fortes and E. E. Evans-Pritchard, categorized two types of societies in Africa: primitive states (with centralized authority and judicial systems) and stateless societies (those without central institutional authority). This book marked the beginning of the field of modern political anthropology. Its articles demonstrated the central role of kinship in the integration and decision-making process even in so-called stateless societies.

In the 1950's, the structural-functional assumption of societies being in or moving toward equilibrium was repudiated by Edmund Leach's *Political Systems of Highland Burma* (1954), which showed that there was actually constant tension between the various systems and subsystems. Max Gluckman, in *African Political Systems, Custom and Conflict in Africa* (1956) and *Order and Rebellion in Tribal Africa* (1960), argued that equilibrium is neither static nor stable, but grows out of a dialectical process where conflicts in one set are absorbed by another. He also showed that crosscutting loyalties tend to unite societies. The works of Leach and Gluckman shifted the focus of research from structure and function to process and conflict.

During this time in the United States, the influence of Leslie White and Julian Steward led to a new school whose emphasis was on change on a panoramic scale within an ecological and materialist context. In the meantime, Victor Turner, in *Schism and Continuity in an African Society* (1957), built on the work of Gluckman and employed the "social drama" methodology of focusing on an individual through a series of episodes where individual and communal norms and values were manipulated. Thus, the orientation changed from structure to process theory with a stronger emphasis on particular situations.

Bibliography

Bodley, John H. "Small Scale Culture: The World Before the State." In *Cultural Anthropology: Tribes, States, and the Global System*. Mountain View, Calif.: Mayfield, 1994. Useful summary of the knowledge about band and tribal societies.

_____. *Victims of Progress*. 3d ed. Mountain View, Calif.: Mayfield, 1990. Excellent analysis of the impact that state and industrial societies have had on tribal communities.

Evans-Pritchard, E. E. *The Nuer: A Description of the Modes of Livelihood and Political Institutions of a Nilotic People*. Oxford, England: Clarendon Press, 1940. Classic ethnography of a tribal people.

Fortes, Meyer, and E. E. Evans-Pritchard, eds. *African Political Systems*. Oxford, England: Oxford University Press, 1940. A foundation work on political anthropology, this set of articles provides a comparative study of political systems of small-scale societies in Africa.

Kottak, Conrad Phillip. "Bands and Tribes." In *Cultural Anthropology*. New York: McGraw-Hill, 1994. Good summary of current knowledge regarding band and tribal societies.

Lewellen, Ted C. "The Development of Political Anthropology." In *Political Anthropology: An Introduction*. 2d ed. Westport, Conn.: Bergin & Garvey, 1992. Good summary of the development of theoretical issues relating to tribal government.

Sahlins, Marshall D. *Tribesmen*. Englewood Cliffs, N.J.: Prentice-Hall, 1968. Classic description of tribal society, with case studies.

Service, Elman R. *Primitive Social Organization: An Evolutionary Perspective*. New York: Random House, 1962. Delineation of four types or levels of sociopolitical organization.

_____. *Profiles in Ethnology*. 3d ed. New York: Harper & Row, 1978. A collection of summaries of ethnographies illustrating Service's classification of sociopolitical organization.

Thomas, E. M. *The Harmless People*. New York: Vintage, 1959. Well-written classic account of the !Kung Bushmen.

Arthur W. Helweg

Cross-References

Africa: Politics and Governments, p. 21; American Indian Governments, p. 59; Asia: Politics and Governments, p. 108; Charismatic Leadership, p. 209; Cult of Personality, p. 477; Government Types, p. 785; Indigenous Peoples' Governments, p. 903; Nomadic Peoples' Governments, p. 1306; Pacific Islander Governments, p. 1362; Political Economy, p. 1455; Social Darwinism, p. 1833; The State, p. 1878.

TWO-PARTY SYSTEMS

Field of study: Politics

Two-party systems provide voters within democratic systems the simplest possible electoral choices. They also increase the likelihood that a party that wins an election will have a majority in government.

Principal terms

MAJORITY PARTY: party that has a majority of the seats within the legislature

MINORITY PARTY: party or parties that have fewer seats in the legislature than the majority party

PARTY IN THE ELECTORATE: group of voters who can generally be expected to support a party's candidates

PARTY IN THE GOVERNMENT: elected officials who openly identify themselves as party members and provide the leadership for the party

PARTY IN THE ORGANIZATION: people who hold official office within the party organization

PARTY LEADER: the most powerful party official within the legislature

PARTY WHIPS: group of high-ranking party officials who keep track of party members' voting behavior, to help implement party strategy

Overview

Two-party systems are the most easily understood among the many party systems in existence. Party systems are generally broken down into three types: multiparty systems, two-party systems, and single-party systems. Two-party systems give the voter a simple choice between the party in power and the party out of power. Once elections are over and the elected officials assume office, a two-party system produces the party in power (majority party) and the opposition party (minority party). As in all other party systems, it is the role of political parties in a two-party system to win elections and then to organize government in a manner consistent with the principles the party espoused during the campaign.

The party that does not receive a majority of the seats in the legislature becomes the opposition party. The opposition or minority party assumes the role of critiquing the majority party and offering alternative policies to those advanced by the majority.

Two-party systems are rarely purely two-party systems. Third-party movements are not uncommon in any two-party system, and large interest groups can divide a party. Even the most secure two-party systems are not static systems. In the United States, for example, the two political parties that make up its two-party system have changed over the years. The two parties that make up the American party system have been, over the years, the Federalists and the Republicans, Democrats and Whigs, and the Republicans and Democrats. During transitional periods of the American party system there have always been a number of partisan groups hoping they would emerge as one of the two major parties.

Even during periods of relative party stability, there have been third-party movements that have challenged one or both of the major parties. A classic example of such a third-party challenge occurred in the early twentieth century when the Progressive Party challenged the two major parties in America. The two major parties were able to withstand this challenge by incorporating progressive policies into their own party platforms. A number of third-party movements have ended with one or both of the major parties' incorporating key third-party policy proposals into their own party platform.

A hallmark of two-party systems has been the willingness of the major parties to accommodate popular policy proposal. It is their openness to new initiatives and their ability to recruit new leadership that keeps major parties strong. The Labour Party of Great Britain and the Whig Party of America are two examples of major parties that lost their dominant position when a third-party challenger proved more willing and able to adjust to changing political times.

The most enduring two-party systems are found in Great Britain and the United States. In both countries the political parties evolved independently of their constitutional systems. Political parties usually begin as informal associations of people who share a common set of concerns or principles. The informality or spontaneity of party origins sometimes makes early party history difficult to establish. There are numerous political coalitions forged among legislators and candidates for public office. Some of these are quite transient and have no lasting impact beyond a single issue; other coalitions may be reestablished over a series of similar issues and, in time, become a fairly permanent group that has a high degree of cohesion over a wide range of policy issues. In the latter case, the group of politicians may even attempt to spell out some clear set of political principles that will guide their future political behavior. It is at this point that they may legitimately be considered an organized political party.

Two-party systems tend to develop in countries that have single-member electoral districts that utilize a winner-takes-all selection process. Election laws could very well be the most important variable in determining the kind of party system that develops in any given political system.

Other variables that can influence party structure are the constitutional biases of the system. For example, countries that do not encourage freedom of speech find it easier to develop and maintain one-party systems than countries that permit freedom of speech. Similarly, countries that utilize proportional representation are far more likely to have a multiparty system than countries that do not.

It has been argued that two-party systems tend to be an Anglo-Saxon phenomenon. While this is not strictly true, the two most enduring two-party systems are found in the United States and Great Britain. These two-party systems also demonstrate how parties are shaped by the constitutional system within which they function. The presidential system in the United States has produced and sustained a very decentralized party system. Separation of powers, which is the defining characteristic of a presidential system, seems to work against a strongly unified party system. In contrast, the parliamentary system in Great Britain clearly encourages a centralized party system. The principle of parliamentary sovereignty makes it easy for parliamentary parties to maintain control at the top levels of their organization.

As different as these two systems are, they provide the most stable and enduring two-party systems the world has witnessed. This fact has led some political observers to conclude that two-party systems require a fairly sophisticated electorate and a stable political environment. Two-party systems are, no doubt, enhanced by a political system that recognizes the importance of coalition building and political compromise. Narrowly defined, ideological parties have not enjoyed much political success in two-party systems. Both presidential and parliamentary systems have witnessed their greatest political unrest when there was not a dominant majority party at the helms of their governments.

Applications

The responsibilities of the majority party are quite different in a parliamentary democracy than they are in a presidential democracy. Within both systems the starting point for their activities is organizing and winning elections. If a political party cannot win elections, it has little need to worry about other party functions.

Once a political party has been organized, it must come up with a slate of candidates for public office. How parties go about selecting their candidates for office is one of the defining characteristics of a party system. In centralized party systems, the party in the organization plays a major role in determining party candidates. The party in the organization may do this through selection committees, party caucuses, or some form of party convention, but whatever the method, there is a specific group assigned the responsibility for selecting and recruiting candidates for public office. The ideal candidate is one who can present and defend the party's policies and win the general election.

In decentralized party systems, the method of selection is usually turned over to the party in the electorate. This may be done through a caucus system or a series of conventions, but the process begins at the grassroots level and places greater control over the process in the hands of the party in the electorate. Increasingly, the most common way for the party in the electorate to select party candidates is through primary elections. Primary elections appeal to people because they appear to be the process most open to the voting public.

There has been considerable debate among politicians and academics over which of these two methods produces a stronger party system. The centralized system for selecting candidates makes it easier for political parties to pressure their elected officials to support the stated party policies. The decentralized system for selecting candidates provides voters with greater control over candidates and, therefore, increases the likelihood that the candidates will have grassroots appeal.

Throughout much of the twentieth century, the American party system has been actively discussing the merits of switching to a more centralized party structure. Many party scholars have actively proposed reforming the American party system to make it more centralized, but efforts have not had much impact on the politicians and the general voting public. In fact, many of the reforms of the last half of the twentieth century have actually weakened the party structure.

The way that two-party systems go about the task of organizing the government after elections varies considerably between parliamentary systems and presidential systems as well. The first task of the majority party within a parliamentary system is creating the cabinet that will make up the executive branch of government. Since the executive cabinet is made up of members of parliament, the cabinet usually consists of the leading party figures in parliament. With control over both the executive and the legislative branches of government, the majority party has an easy time setting the legislative agenda.

In a presidential system it is possible for voters to make one party the majority in the legislature and then to give another party control over the executive branch of government. When this occurs there are often considerable tensions between the executive and legislative branches of government. Presidential systems that utilize a bicameral legislature might even have periods when there is a different party in the majority within the two legislative chambers. This kind of divided majority occurred in the United States after the 1980 election. The Democratic Party had a majority in the House of Representatives, the Republican Party had a majority in the Senate, and the Republicans also captured the executive branch. In the 1986 election the Democratic Party gained a majority in the Senate and maintained its majority in the House of Representatives. With the variety of options available within a presidential system, it is sometimes difficult to determine who is the majority party.

The combination of a parliamentary system and a centralized party structure makes it very easy for voters to know which party is in control of government and what policies that party is trying to advance. As a result of this fact, it is relatively easy for voters to decide whether they like what the majority party is doing. Democratic systems that combine a presidential system and a decentralized party system are the most difficult for determining party policies and party successes.

Both forms of two-party systems can point to considerable success in supporting and helping maintain democratic institutions. Both types of two-party systems can also point to success in recruiting candidates for governmental offices, advocating political policies, critiquing existing public policies, and providing important political symbols for voters.

Context

The first practical two-party system to be developed and sustained is arguably the American two-party system. Like most party systems the American system developed in stages. The first truly national party structure in the United States was organized in the House of Representatives in the early 1790's. Congressman James Madison organized House members to block the economic proposals of Alexander Hamilton, the United States' first Secretary of the Treasury. While Madison's efforts met with only limited success, the party structure he created became a lasting part of the American political scene.

The congressional party system was so strong that, by 1800, congressional caucuses were utilized by the parties to nominate candidates for the presidency. These congressional caucuses (also called King Caucuses) controlled the presidential nominating process until the 1820's. By 1832 a number of political parties had organized national presidential nominating conventions to select their presidential candidate. It was at this point that national parties in America developed as something more than merely congressional parties.

A formal grassroots party system was clearly in place in Great Britain by the twentieth century. Two-party systems are more the norm than the exception in some other countries as well, Canada and Israel for example. Two-party systems will probably become more common in the world. Organizations such as the United Nations are taking a more active part in monitoring elections throughout the world. The United Nations does not have a bias in favor of two-party systems; however, the more stable various democracies become, the greater the likelihood that many nations will develop two-party systems.

Economic development has a role in the development of two-party systems as well. It is no accident that the most stable two-party systems exist within countries that have a relatively large and politically important middle class. Anything that advances the general tranquillity of democratic political systems, such as an emergent middle class, also increases the likelihood of developing their two-party systems.

Bibliography

Charles, Joseph. *The Origins of the American Party System: Three Essays*. New York: Harper & Row, 1961. Historical account of the events that helped shape the development of the American two-party system.

Duverger, Maurice. *Political Parties: Their Organization and Activity in the Modern State*. New York: John Wiley & Sons, 1954. Still the best comparative work on political parties available.

Mansfield, Harvey, Jr. *Statesmanship and Party Government: A Study of Burke and Bolingbroke*. Chicago: University of Chicago Press, 1965. The best theoretical work on the origins of the British two-party system.

Ranney, Austin. *The Doctrine of Responsible Party Government: Its Origins and Present State*. Westport, Conn.: Greenwood Press, 1982. Concise statement on the strengths and weaknesses of changing from a decentralized to a centralized party system.

Weatherman, Donald. *Endangered Guardians: Party Reform Within a Constitutional System*. Totowa, N.J.: Rowman & Littlefield, 1994. Examines the origins of the American party system and assesses a number of reform efforts in the light of the party founder's intentions.

Donald V. Weatherman

Cross-References

The British Parliamentary System, p. 146; The Democratic Party, p. 520; The Electoral College, p. 584; Multiparty Systems, p. 1235; One-Party Systems, p. 1350; Political Campaigning, Planning, and Financing, p. 1427; Political Machines and Bosses, p. 1468; Political Parties, p. 1485; Political Party Conventions, p. 1492; Political Platforms, p. 1512; The Republican Party, p. 1699.

UNDERDEVELOPED NATIONS

Field of study: International government and politics

Underdeveloped and undeveloped nation-states comprise more than a third of the total membership of the United Nations today. They can be found in Central and Latin America, Asia, Eastern Europe, and Africa. Although home to more than half the world's population, they have little influence over international politics and their presence is felt only when famine, disease, war, or environmental disaster requires a response from the international community.

Principal terms

AUSTERITY MEASURE: World Bank/IMF policy aimed at lessening the debt burden of underdeveloped economies by tightening controls on government spending

COLONIZATION: process whereby a colonizing country administers the colonized country for its own economic benefit

GROSS NATIONAL PRODUCT (GNP): monetary value of all goods and services produced by a nation during a defined period (usually a year)

Overview

"Underdeveloped" and "undeveloped" have become common terms for the nation-states that used to be called the "Third World"—in contrast to "First World" countries such as the United States and Western European nations, and "Second World" countries, such as the Soviet Union and its Communist allies. Unlike "Third World," which is ideological in origin, underdeveloped and undeveloped have political and economic implications. Politically, the terms refer to countries that tend to have few effective political institutions (such as legislatures or strong judiciaries) that are deemed necessary for governing a state. In the vast majority of these states, long periods of colonial rule led to the creation of economic and political mechanisms designed to control and effectively extract raw materials and other products from the colonized territories. The weakness of political institutions in the modern nation-states can be traced to the lack of correspondence between the governing institutions operated by the colonizing powers and the people, living within the colonial boundaries. The result in many cases has been civil war and conflict, which only serve to weaken political institutions even further. For example, underdeveloped countries such as India, Indonesia, Nigeria, and Sri Lanka have experienced separatist movements and ethnic conflicts. In many instances conflicts, within states have led to an increase in the power of the military, which often has been called on to restore order. Underdeveloped nation-states therefore tend to have relatively powerful militaries; in many cases they have experienced prolonged periods of military rule, as in Nigeria and Indonesia. The period of the Cold War further exacerbated this tendency toward military government in some of these countries because both the United States and the former Soviet Union supported and actively assisted military regimes perceived to be friendly to their ideological causes.

Development is commonly used as an index of economic progress. For the concept of development to be useful in making comparisons between countries, it must be capable of measurement. The three most popular measurement indexes are gross national product (GNP); the Physical Quality of Life Index (PQLI), which measures a composite of three components (infant mortality, life expectancy at age one, and literacy); and the Index of Social Progress (ISP), which consists of forty-four social, economic, physical, and political components.

All three methods have been criticized. The use of purely economic indices such as GNP has been criticized because they measure only such activities as those to which monetary values can be attached. They thus fail to account for noneconomic social phenomena that are important to human welfare and social well-being, which are themselves important aspects of development. The PQLI method is also seen as deficient since two of its three indicators (infant mortality and life expectancy) measure only the adequacy of national health services, while the third (adult literacy) assesses the adequacy of educational services. At the same time, PQLI makes no attempt to refer to areas of social development such as the status of women and children. The ISP method, which is the most complex, has been criticized for being too cumbersome in its methodology.

Both the PQLI and the ISP indices rank countries in the Indian subcontinent and those in sub-Saharan Africa as the least developed countries of the world. These are the countries that have large populations and huge disparities in wealth and that are most dependent on the industrial powers for export of goods and import of technologies. World Bank classifications based on per capita GNP identify most of these countries in the category of low-income economies with individual incomes of $270 and less. Slightly higher in the rankings are countries such as Brazil, China, Indonesia, Malaysia, Nigeria, and Vietnam—underdeveloped countries that possess natural resources which have not been adequately exploited for improving the living standards of their people. Rankings of these countries vary depending on which measure is being used. Individual countries whose characteristics defy accurate measurement are occasionally left out altogether—for example, the ISP method does not evaluate China.

The measurement of development is a difficult and contentious process because it is difficult to get a consensus on what the concept even means in international politics. The concept presupposes a commitment to change, materialism, progress, science, and technology—all of which are Western values, and hence are extremely problematic when applied in the non-Western world. The undeveloped by these criteria are the nations that have made the least progress toward these values, while the underdeveloped nations are those that have begun the process but still have far to go.

Measuring the status of countries on a development index serves the purpose of identifying the areas of strength and weakness for the developing nations of the world, while also providing information to the international community regarding the need for external assistance. For decades, development programs in the underdeveloped and undeveloped countries focused on infusion of Western money and technology in the hope that this would propel these nations down the road of industrialization, self-sufficiency, and material prosperity. This approach to development has come in for much criticism from those in the West who are involved in the actual administration of development programs, and from grassroots activists in the developing world who have witnessed firsthand the problems posed by such methods of development.

Nonprofit agencies engaged in development such as Oxfam America, have identified several problems in traditional attitudes toward development in the underdeveloped countries. These agencies argue that there are structural problems, externally and internally, that make current goals of Western-style development nearly impossible for some countries. External structural problems include the inequitable relationships between the industrialized world and the nations of the underdeveloped world that lead the latter to produce goods that find most favor among Western consumers in the former—products such as fruits, vegetables, canned fish and meats, cotton, and minerals. The problem that this poses for development lies in the fact that land that might otherwise be used to produce food for domestic consumption is used to produce crops that generate foreign exchange. The profitability of such crops leads to higher prices for land and higher costs for irrigation equipment, fertilizers, and pesticides—all of which makes farming ever more expensive for subsistence farmers, who end up being displaced by commercial farmers. The result is increased landlessness and greater urban poverty and hunger as farmers join the exodus to cities in search of work. The problems are exacerbated by government policies that foster commercial farming as a way of repaying some of the debt that they owe to Western lending agencies, such as the World Bank. Often this debt was incurred in order to get the very technology and equipment that was supposed to lead to development. The role of the World Bank and the International Monetary Fund in forcing these austerity measures on these governments has also come in for criticism.

External problems are further complicated by internal structural problems caused by the disparities in wealth within many of the underdeveloped countries of the world. The result is that elites control access to most resources in these countries including much of the Western aid that is remitted for development purposes. Attempts by the poor and the underprivileged to resist exploitation and immiseration are often met with hostility and repression. Development agencies also cite the fact that traditional attitudes toward women in many of these countries contribute to low levels of literacy and a subordinate status for women that undermine attempts to generate development.

Grassroots activists in the underdeveloped countries have also voiced their concerns. They point to the damage that is underway in their societies as Western "scientific" modes of production and distribution undermine traditional ways of farming and agriculture. Recent studies done by groups and individuals from these regions have shown that the emphasis on "scientific" farming often results in the replacement of hardy indigenous seeds, plants, and trees with hybrid varieties that are ill-suited to local climates, less resistant to local pests, and more demanding of chemical fertilizers and water—all resources that are in short supply. At the same time, the focus on technology and agricultural expertise has resulted in the virtual displacement of women from this sector of the economy in many underdeveloped societies, contributing to a decline in their social status, with a corresponding increase in negative social practices such as female infanticide. In the view of many, conflict, violence, and environmental degradation are inevitable, given current models of development.

Applications

Underdeveloped nations have attempted to mobilize politically against perceived global inequities. In the 1960's and 1970's some consensus was reached regarding a set of demands called the New International Economic Order (NIEO), which aimed at stabilizing commodity prices on the international markets, opening up Western markets for export, and increasing commitments for resource transfers from the developed nations, as well as debt relief. The response from the developed industrial economies was not encouraging, and, in the 1970's and 1980's, the nations of the underdeveloped world became even more dependent on multinational corporations to bring in investment capital and other development resources. Private lending agencies also stepped in to fill the gap created by declining multilateral lending. Nonprofit agencies and grassroots activists point out that this trend only made matters worse. Large multinational corporations and private lenders joined forces to make development a profitable enterprise. These efforts have not been uniformly successful, however. This becomes clear in the case of rice, which is the staple food for Asia. In India alone over the last half century more than 30,000 different varieties of rice were grown. In 1950, India set up the Central Rice Research Institute (CRRI) to study rice production based on indigenous knowledge and varieties. In the 1960's the CRRI's goals ran into conflict with those of the newly created International Rice Research Institute (IRRI), which was set up in 1959 as part of the "Green Revolution" in India that was funded by the Rockefeller and Ford foundations. The IRRI focused on the cultivation of hybrid varieties, the so-called high-yielding varieties, which began to erode the genetic diversity of rice in the country. The director of CRRI was removed under international pressure after he refused to hand over his collection of rice germ plasm to IRRI and he challenged the rapid introduction of high-yielding varieties.

During the 1990's, CRRI scientists pointed out that most of the high-yielding rice crops are highly susceptible to pests, resulting in crop losses of 30 to 100 percent. At the same time, the centralized production and transfer of high-yield rice seed has led to virus diseases that did not exist in India before 1962. The natural resistance built on diversity has been destroyed by the uniformity imposed by scientific farming, making Indian rice production more vulnerable to pests and disease and driving the Indian people closer to food shortages and more debt.

In the 1980's and 1990's as these countries became better integrated into the world market economy, awareness also grew about the problems posed by environmental damage. As developed countries passed environmental regulations restricting production and sale of various products determined to be harmful to the environment in their countries, more and more manufacturers of these products relocated to the underdeveloped states, where such environmental regulations were absent or laxly enforced. The consequences of badly enforced environmental regulations and the profit-oriented policies of international manufacturers can be seen in disasters such as the explosion of toxic gas at the Union Carbide plant in Bhopal, India that killed at least 3,000 people and injured thousands more. The pollution of the air and groundwater systems in many countries, as well as the increased incidence of toxic-waste dumping in these powerless states, is a matter of concern for all people because it has global ramifications. For example, the pollution of water and land in underdeveloped countries results in the import of contaminated produce into developed countries, which are major markets for such products.

Context

More than half of the world's population live in countries that are categorized as underdeveloped or undeveloped. As these countries become integrated into the world economy, urban poverty, violence, crime, and environmental degradation have become serious problems for their governments. At the same time, a small but growing middle class in these countries has become aware of the extravagant consumption patterns of the industrialized world, and they seek these same privileges for themselves. The desire for Western technology and consumer durables leads to further indebtedness and exploitation of the poor and weak in these countries. Economically this spells disaster, while politically the potential for civil unrest and revolution increases.

The consequences are already visible in higher levels of immigration and the growing tide of refugees from rural to urban areas in the undeveloped world and from these regions to the industrialized West. Attempts to change direction in these countries must focus on a greater understanding of the meaning of development. The current definition focusing on the Western experience may have to be rejected in favor of one that takes into account human welfare and social well-being and stresses simplicity, discipline, and respect for the environment—values that have strong roots in the cultural experience of the underdeveloped world.

Bibliography

Clark, Robert P. *Power and Policy in the Third World*. New York: Macmillan, 1991. Useful survey of the complexity of developing societies and the socioeconomic and cultural context of underdevelopment.

Kothari, Rajni. *Towards a Just World Order*. New York: Institute for World Order, 1980. Articulates the objections of the underdeveloped and undeveloped nations to the "free-market" world order.

Mathews, Jessica Tuchman, ed. *Preserving the Global Environment: The Challenge of Shared Leadership*. New York: W. W. Norton, 1991. Collection of essays examining the possibility of global cooperation in the area of the environment.

Rau, Bill. *From Feast to Famine: Official Cures and Grassroots Remedies to Africa's Food Crisis.* London: Zed Books, 1991. Examination of the causes of modern Africa's food crisis, with close attention to impact of European colonialism and postindependent policies, as well as African responses to the crisis.

Shiva, Vandana. *Women, Ecology and Development.* New York: Zed Publishers, 1993. Examines the impact of Western development models in India and the connections between environmental degradation and the status of women in the subcontinent.

Ward, Barbara. *The Lopsided World.* New York: W. W. Norton, 1968. Provides an introduction to the role played by colonization in deindustrializing the Third World.

Sudha Ratan

Cross-References

Africa: Politics and Governments, p. 21; Developed and Developing Nations, p. 533; Immigration and Emigration, p. 868; Imperialism, p. 889; International Monetary Fund, p. 963; International Relations, p. 969; Mexico: Politics and Government, p. 1179; Nonaligned Movements, p. 1319; Self-Determination, p. 1796; The World Bank, p. 2153; World Government and Environmental Protection, p. 2167.

UNITED NATIONS

Field of study: International government and politics

The United Nations is a collective security organization established in 1945 to maintain peace and promote human rights and economic development. All sovereign states are eligible to join, and more than 180 nations participate in its activities.

Principal terms

COLLECTIVE SECURITY: system in which nations agree to defend one another against attack; an attack against one is considered an attack against all

GENERAL ASSEMBLY: central organ of the United Nations, responsible for discussing questions of international concern and making recommendations for action

SECRETARIAT: branch of the United Nations made up of the secretary general and a staff of more than twenty-five thousand advisers and specialists

SECURITY COUNCIL: branch of the United Nations responsible for keeping the peace and dealing with emergencies; includes five permanent members and ten states elected for two-year terms

VETO POWER: power to prevent passage of resolutions by the Security Council, requiring only one "no" vote by a permanent member

Overview

The United Nations is an international peacekeeping agency with more than 180 member nations. Organized in 1945, it continued the work of the League of Nations (1920-1939), the first attempt by the world to keep peace through collective security. Designers of the United Nations, chiefly President Franklin D. Roosevelt and his advisers in the state department, tried to correct the deficiencies in the League of Nations structure that had made that earlier body incapable of action during world crises. Under the league, covenant members decided for themselves whether they would comply with the league's recommendations. This proved inefficient and led to inaction by many states, so the United Nations mandates compliance. The league did not have an army of its own, but the United Nations can acquire a military force under its control, as witnessed in the Korean War and the Persian Gulf War. The league acted only after a unanimous vote of its general assembly, while the United Nations requires a simple majority. Roosevelt resolved another major problem that weakened the league by committing the United States to membership in the new international organization after winning support for his idea in the U.S. Senate. The Senate had rejected league membership in 1920, a move that severely limited the organization's power.

The U.N. Charter, signed by fifty states on June 26, 1945, expressed the organization's purposes. Article 1 gave the United Nations the responsibility for maintaining the peace and security of the world. It was charged with working to create friendly relations among the world's peoples, while promoting respect for equal rights and self-determination. Member states pledged to cooperate in solving the world's economic, social, cultural, and humanitarian problems. Article 2 outlined the United Nations' major principles: All members recognized the equality of other states, promised to fulfill their obligations under the charter, pledged to settle disputes with other states peacefully, and agreed not to intervene in the domestic affairs of other nations. Under the principle of sovereignty, internal problems, whether famine, revolution, or mass killing, remained strictly in the hands of the nation involved.

The United Nations welcomed all peace-loving nations as members, if they would accept the principles and obligations of the charter. States could be expelled for violating the charter, but only by a two-thirds vote of other members. In 1974, the assembly banned the Republic of South Africa from attending meetings because of its racial policies. Twenty years later, after democratic elections in that nation, the new majority-rule black government regained the South African seat.

The United Nations' principal branches include the General Assembly, the Security Council, the Economic and Social Council (ECOSOC), the Trusteeship Council, the International Court of Justice, and the Secretariat. English and French are the official working languages, although documents and speeches are also translated into Chinese, Russian, and Spanish.

In the General Assembly, all member nations have one vote, regardless of their size or population. In the General Assembly, which meets once a year beginning on the third Tuesday of September, members discuss, debate, and make recommendations. They can also initiate studies that promote economic, social, and educational progress and that lead to the expansion of human rights. The assembly elects a president and vice president each year.

Most important U.N. decisions, especially those involving war and peace, must be made by the Security Council. The council has fifteen members, five permanent and ten elected by the General Assembly for two-year terms. The permanent members, the United States, Russia (formerly the Soviet Union), Great Britain, France, and China, have veto power over Security Council resolutions. All five must approve a question or the recommendation fails. During discussions of United Nations structure in 1944 and 1945, each of these states, the key powers involved in winning World War II, insisted on having a veto to protect their sovereignty. The United States and the Soviet Union, especially, wanted to have power to block any action that had a negative impact on their interests. One "no" thus can cancel out fourteen "yes" votes, but without the veto power, the United Nations would not have come into existence.

The Security Council investigates disputes and recommends methods of resolving the situation. Any U.N. member can ask the council for a meeting concerning a problem. The council can vote for enforcement measures, such as economic sanctions or armed action against an aggressor. The charter commits all members to make troops available to maintain peace, if the council decides force is necessary. Security Council decisions require nine affirmative votes, including the votes of the five permanent members, although a party may abstain from voting on questions in which it is involved. The council meets continuously and is led by a president. The presidency is determined by alphabetical order (in English) of the council members and changes monthly.

The Economic and Social Council has fifty-four members, with eighteen states elected every year by the General Assembly for three-year terms. ECOSOC issues studies and reports on economic, cultural, and health matters, and promotes respect for human rights. Its most important work is done by the Statistical Commission, the Commission for Social Development, the Commission on Human Rights, the Commission on the Status of Women, and the Commission on Narcotic Drugs. In 1971, ECOSOC opened a Disaster Relief Office in its Geneva, Switzerland, headquarters.

The Trusteeship Council supervises territories under the International Trusteeship System created by the League of Nations. This council has promoted self-determination and self-government in these protectorates. In 1945, eleven territories came under council control; in 1990, only the Trust Territory of the Pacific Islands (also called Micronesia), which is administered by the United States, remained, the others having achieved independence.

The International Court of Justice in The Hague, The Netherlands, continues the work begun by the League of Nations. The court has fifteen judges elected by the General Assembly for nine-year terms. Court jurisdiction includes any cases submitted to it by any nations and all cases involving the U.N. Charter. Participants may declare that they will accept court decisions in advance; if they do not, its decisions are not enforced. All questions are decided by a majority vote of judges present. If there is no judge of one of the nations involved in the case on the bench, that nation can choose a judge from its homeland to participate in that particular decision.

The Secretariat consists of the secretary general, appointed by the General Assembly after recommendation by the Security Council, and a staff of more than twenty-five thousand people working out of United Nations headquarters in New York City and in regional offices around the world. Trygvie Lie of Norway was the first secretary general, from 1946 until his resignation in 1952, followed by Dag Hammarskjold, who died in a plane crash on a mission to the Congo in 1963. The General Assembly then chose U Thant of Burma (1963-1971), Kurt Waldheim of Austria (1972-1981), Javier Perez de Cuellar of Peru (1982-1991), and Boutros Boutros-Ghali of Egypt (1991-   ). The secretary general is the chief administrator of the United Nations and can call upon the Security Council to discuss any matters threatening peace and security.

Many independent, intergovernmental agencies report to the Economic and Social Council, including the International Atomic Energy Agency, established in 1956 to ensure nonmilitary uses of atomic energy; the International Labor Organization, created in 1946 to set standards of wages and safety for workers and employers around the world; and the Food and Agriculture Organization (FAO), founded in 1945 to raise levels of nutrition and to eliminate world hunger. The United Nations Educational, Scientific, and Cultural Organization (UNESCO) was begun in 1946 and has continued to expand its work toward eliminating illiteracy and pressing for human rights. The World Health Organization came into being in 1948, with the goal of attaining the highest level of health for all peoples of the world. By 1990, it had immunized millions of children in every region of the world against diphtheria, measles, polio, tetanus, tuberculosis, and whooping cough. The International Bank for Reconstruction and Development (World Bank) lends money for agricultural and rural development, energy programs, health care, family planning, and roads and railways. Another independent department, the General Agreement on Tariffs and Trade (GATT), established in 1948, writes rules for world trade and has brought together more than ninety nations to discuss lowering tariffs.

Two other key international agencies—the United Nations International Children's Emergency Fund (UNICEF), created after World War II to feed starving children in Europe, Asia, and Africa, and the United Nations High Commissioner for Refugees (UNHCR), established in 1950 to feed, clothe, and shelter millions of homeless people around the world—have brought hope and subsistence to millions of abused and desperate citizens. The commissions and organizations reporting to the United Nations have reduced suffering and helped promote economic development and peace throughout the world.

The United Nations performs its duties with a small budget, less than $4 billion in 1992, which is far smaller than the budgets of many U.S. cities. The money comes from assessments imposed by the General Assembly. Each member contributes according to its ability to pay. The poorest states pay 0.01 percent of the U.N. budget, and the richest, the United States, pays 25 percent.

Applications

Since 1945, the United Nations has worked to keep the peace, to promote democracy and free elections, and to fight hunger and poverty around the world. From 1950 to 1953, U.N. forces fought their first successful war and demonstrated that collective security could work to stop aggression, if the nations of the world asserted the will to act. Sixteen nations sent troops to South Korea to help repel an invasion from North Korea. The Security Council obtained unanimous consent for military force only because the delegate from the Soviet Union had walked out several weeks earlier to protest the General Assembly's refusal to seat the new Communist government of China. Fighting continued on the Korean peninsula for three years with thousands of casualties, but the action made the point that nations could cooperate to defend a free nation from attack.

In 1960, the United Nations acted to solve a major crisis in the Republic of the Congo (later known as Zaïre). A bloody civil war broke out in the capital city of Leopoldville shortly after Belgium removed its troops and granted its former colony independence. Secretary General Dag Hammarskjold requested that a multilateral force be sent to restore order, and the Security Council gave its approval. The force eventually reached twenty-three thousand men, who fought the rebels trying to break up the new nation. The United Nations chief himself died in a plane crash while on his way to peace talks. The operation successfully maintained the unity of the Congo, however, and the United Nations force withdrew in 1964.

Other successful United Nations military action took place in Cyprus in 1964 and 1974, and during the Persian Gulf War of 1991. In Cyprus, the United Nations Peacekeeping Force has continued to maintain a contingent of more than two thousand to supervise a cease-fire between Greek and Turkish factions and to work toward a negotiated settlement of this long dispute. In the Gulf War, U.N. forces successfully defended the independence of the tiny state of Kuwait and defeated the army of Iraq's dictator Saddam Hussein. From 1973 to 1989, a seven thousand-man United Nations Emergency Force patrolled the border between Egypt and Israel. In Lebanon, a United Nations Interim Force lost 164 men and suffered 233 casualties in the 1980's while attempting to preserve peace. The United Nations Military Observer Group in India and Pakistan kept a small force along those nations' borders to protect a cease-fire established after a 1971 war. These few examples illustrate the extent and diversity of U.N. peacekeeping operations. Costs for these operations came from voluntary contributions from member states, although contributions rarely covered the expenses and the United Nations went heavily into debt.

The International Court of Justice's work includes cases concerning boundary disputes and interpretation of treaties. In 1953, for example, the court declared that disputed islands in the North Sea belonged to England rather than France, and in 1986 decided the boundaries between Mali and Burkina Faso. In a key 1971 opinion, the court advised South Africa that it could no longer claim territory in Namibia, formerly Southwest Africa, and that it had to remove its military forces. In 1980, the United States won its case against Iran when the court ordered the latter's government to release all U.S. hostages being held and pay reparations for damages to the embassy. These are only a few of the eighty cases heard by the court since 1946, but illustrate the type of decisions made by the justices.

Among the most important tasks of the United Nations has been the establishment of emergency and disaster relief programs. In 1971, the General Assembly created the Office of United Nations Disaster Relief Coordinator in Geneva, Switzerland. This office has supplied emergency food and relief to millions of people in Africa, India, and Southeast Asia. Since the 1960's, the nations of central and eastern Africa have been hard hit by drought and famine. The United Nations Sudano-Sahelian Office has brought relief to Ethiopia, Somalia, the Sudan, and a dozen other impoverished nations since its creation in 1973. In 1986, the General Assembly committed the nations of the world to the Programme of Action for African Economic Recovery and Development. Under this plan, African nations themselves would raise billions of dollars to promote food production, build infrastructure, and develop human resources. The United Nations High Commissioner for Refugees has provided assistance for the four million refugees living in camps in the famine-ridden region of Africa. The high commissioner has also worked in Indochina, especially Kampuchea (formerly Cambodia), to feed thousands of people suffering from the disruptions of war and famine.

Context

The United Nations succeeded the League of Nations as the world's international security organization in 1945. The league collapsed in 1939 after the outbreak of World War II. On June 12, 1941, an Inter-Allied Declaration signed by Great Britain, France, and other European states declared that the allies would fight together to defeat aggression and to promote "economic and social security." Two months later, the United States joined these allies in issuing the Atlantic Charter, calling for the final destruction of the Nazis and a world free from fear and want. The charter also pledged self-determination and democratic elections in all nations freed from Nazism. On January 1, 1942, speaking for the first time as the United Nations, the twenty-six states fighting Germany, Japan, and Italy called for complete victory over the enemy and the abandonment of the use of force in the future. In 1944, delegates to the Dumbarton Oaks Conference in Washington, D.C., agreed to the structure and format of the United Nations. Representatives from the Soviet Union and the United States also gave their approval to a plan giving the five permanent members veto power over important Security Council resolutions. Franklin D. Roosevelt and the Russian dictator Joseph Stalin accepted these ideas at the Yalta Conference in February, 1945. Nations fighting against Germany and Japan as of March 1 were to be invited to San Francisco to prepare the final charter.

On April 25, 1945, delegates from fifty nations came together and drew up the 111-article Charter of the United Nations. They voted unanimously to adopt the document on June 25, and it came into force on October 24, when twenty-six of the signatories ratified the final agreement. After an opening meeting in London in January, 1946, the United Nations accepted an offer from John D. Rockefeller, Jr., to locate on land donated by him in New York City. Crews completed construction of the headquarters building on eighteen acres between 42nd and 48th streets, and the United Nations General Assembly, Security Council, and Secretariat have resided there since. Although the United Nations has little permanent financing and great economic problems, it remains the only international agency with the potential power to deal with problems of war, poverty, and human repression.

Bibliography

Hammarskjold, Dag. *The International Civil Servant in Law and in Fact*. Oxford, England: Clarendon Press, 1961. The still-useful ideas of one of the most effective, hard-working, and influential leaders of the United Nations.

Rovine, Arthur W. *The First Fifty Years: The Secretary-General in World Politics, 1920-1970*. Leyden, Netherlands: Sijthoff, 1970. Series of biographies of the leaders of the League of Nations and the United Nations. Well-written and detailed descriptions of their lives and contributions to world peace.

Russell, Ruth B. *The United Nations and United States Security Policy*. Washington, D.C.: Brookings Institution, 1968. Still outstanding study of United States responses to United Nations actions. Good description of the early conferences and the development of international policy during World War II.

United Nations. Department of Public Information. *Everyone's United Nations*. 10th ed. New York: United Nations, 1986. Useful survey of the history, structure, and activities of the United Nations. Detailed descriptions of yearly expenditures and actions.

Yearbook of the United Nations. New York: United Nations Publications. Issued annually. Best resource for finding resolutions, actions, and programs initiated by the United Nations.

Leslie V. Tischauser

Cross-References

Ambassadors and Embassies, p. 53; Conflict Resolution, p. 397; Diplomacy and International Negotiation, p. 552; Food Politics, p. 706; Human Rights and International Politics, p. 848; International Law, p. 956; Peace, p. 1390; Superpowers and World Politics, p. 1916; Supranational Government Institutions, p. 1922; The World Bank, p. 2153; The World Court, p. 2161; World Government and Environmental Protection, p. 2167; World Government Movements, p. 2174; The World Health Organization, p. 2180; World Political Organization, p. 2186.

URBAN GOVERNMENTS

Field of study: Comparative government

Comparative urban government is the study of urban institutions, politics, and policy among various nations or across jurisdictions within a single nation. Comparing urban institutions, common social or economic problems, governmental processes, or policy alternatives enables urban governments to learn from one another's successes and mistakes.

Principal terms

CENTRAL-LOCAL GOVERNMENT RELATIONS: pattern of relations between the national government and local governments, such as transfers of money and delegations of authority

MEGACITIES: the world's largest cities, often defined as those having populations greater than seven million

METROPOLITANIZATION: development of a complex urban environment with suburbs and satellite cities arrayed around one or more central cities

SUBURBANIZATION: process in which urban population migrates to less developed areas on the fringes, and usually outside of the taxing jurisdiction, of a central or major satellite city

URBAN DESIGN: population distribution, communication and transportation networks, economic and social activity, and cultural life of an urban area

URBAN REGIME: governing coalition in an urban area, based upon the joint resources and cooperation of city officials and influential private actors

URBANIZATION: process in which rural population migrates to towns and cities, frequently creating problems of traffic congestion, high levels of unemployment, housing shortages, and crime

Overview

To the extent that political, social, and economic problems may have common roots that can help explain their origins, predict their courses, and offer possible solutions, the study of governance in urban communities in other regions, states, or nations can provide information on what does and does not work in addressing those problems. Institutions, policies, administrative techniques, technologies, and other actions that are successful in one urban area may also succeed in another. At minimum, urban governments can avoid the mistakes made by other governments in similar circumstances.

The initial task in examining urban governments is to define the terms. Historically, comparative urban government has focused on particular cities and drawn comparisons based on common sets of characteristics. Urban government, however, can describe the governing structures of relatively small villages and towns, as well as cities with millions of inhabitants. Urban government may also refer to a collective or regional coordination body, including one or more general-purpose governments in central cities and suburban communities, and a variety of intergovernmental bodies and special districts. Increasingly, however, such large governmental structures are referred to as metropolitan rather than urban, although both terms may be applicable.

The initial large-scale issues of comparative urban study were differences in such phenomena as crime rates, unemployment, building regulations, public housing, government corruption, violence, innovative government programs, citizen satisfaction with urban services, and other variables on which data could be found for more than a few urban governments. The objective was to identify patterns in urban development and human behavior that would help explain and predict differences among urban areas. Such macro-level studies have become less common in the 1990's. Comparisons of urban policies and programs in two to four nations, usually drawn from among the major industrialized states, the developing states, or a geographic region, are more practical. Studies of narrower policy issues, such as citizen empowerment, or programs, such as economic development, also may focus on urban governance in several nations.

The use of the term "urban" may also be related to the particular urban design characteristic of a nation or locale. Issues of urban governance are very much dependent upon the design of cities. Older cities were most often founded on major waterways. Locations on seacoasts, rivers, or major lakes were chosen because of access to water transportation or, perhaps more important, because proximity to water was related to the fertility of the land. As populations expanded, the waterways and other geographic features, such as mountains, pushed development in particular directions. In older industrial cities, populations generally were concentrated close to factories and transportation facilities. Workers lived within walking distance of the factories until the advent of mass transit systems; the owners and wealthier merchants lived farther away, but still within a short commute. The neighborhoods that developed reflected the economic classes of their residents.

Mass transit fundamentally altered the process of urbanization, and expanded access to private automobiles encouraged middle-class migration to suburban communities. To some extent, this has been the pattern in major cities around the world, although the automobile has had a much greater impact upon urban areas in the United States, and American life in general. Outside the United States, more limited private capital, limited availability of high-priced foreign or domestic automobiles, high gasoline costs, less support among governments for road-building, and lifestyles less centered upon the mobility that automobiles provide have created different patterns. Reliance on public mass transit systems in Europe, for example, has helped to preserve central city business districts, although that has begun to change as the number of automobiles increases and housing patterns change.

Differences in government policy also provide contrasts in urban governance. Many city governments in the United Kingdom, for example, own and operate a large proportion of the available housing. National and local policies have supported the acquisition of substandard housing, particularly during the 1960's, and the expenditure of government funds either to replace or renovate the substandard housing. Lacking private funds for such social programs, and faced with a quickly deteriorating housing stock, government action was initiated. By contrast, urban governments in other nations have had little involvement in the provision of housing. In developing nations, large urban centers are surrounded by shantytowns created as thousands of rural, and sometimes foreign, populations move to the city seeking work. Urban governments in the United States and other developed nations increasingly have focused on the need to encourage private investment in housing, including using public funds to leverage private investment.

One of the first focuses of comparative urban analysis was the structures of government. Contrasting the relationships between central or national governments and urban governments drew attention to the processes of urbanization and the growing influence of urban populations in national politics. National financial and political support to urban governments was considered an indicator of the relative influence of urban governments and citizenry in national politics, and the perceived importance of urban areas as the cultural and economic centers of the nation. Structural or institutional studies focused on such factors as the professionalization of urban government officials, interest group participation in urban politics, the roles of community-based organizations, public-private cooperation, and government regulation of such activities as land use and building. As interest in administrative reform increased, institutional studies became more common.

Increasing attention has also been given to the special problems of the world's megacities. According to 1990 population estimates, these included Tokyo-Yokohama, Japan, with a population of more than twenty-seven million; Mexico City; São Paolo, Brazil; Seoul, South Korea; New York City; Osaka-Kobe-Kyoto, Japan; Bombay and Calcutta, India; Buenos Aires, Argentina; Rio de Janeiro, Brazil; Moscow; Los Angeles; Manila, the Philippines; Cairo, Egypt; Jakarta, Indonesia; London; Teheran, Iran; Paris; Delhi, India; Karachi, Pakistan; Lagos, Nigeria; and Essen, Germany. Another half-dozen cities are projected to become megacities by the end of the twentieth century. Problems of traffic congestion, substandard housing, inadequate municipal services, health care, transportation, and many other issues in these cities are on scales that do not compare with the problems of smaller cities. The sharing of information among urban governments is increasing, and the study of their problems is a compelling research issue.

Applications

Many analysts have suggested that global economic changes are forcing local officials to develop new relationships with the private sector and other governments. These analyses have focused on the centralization of economic decision making in most nations during the 1980's, and the assumption that urban governments were ill-equipped to deal with global change and too small geographically to address the kinds of issues that were arising. The problems created as national governments in the United States and other countries withdrew support, particularly fiscal support, from local governments and declined to address local problems have also been studied. In the United States, for example, the Reagan Administration (1981-1989) sharply cut intergovernmental transfers of money that city and county governments had used to address local problems, and the states tended to centralize authority over programs. As a consequence, local officials, particularly large-city officials, found themselves with growing social and economic problems and declining resources.

The new localism suggests that many communities have become creative in responding to local issues. In the United States and Great Britain, for example, local governments have created public-private enterprises to take advantage of the flexibility of private administration and to leverage the public and private financial resources that such quasi-governmental organizations offer. The proliferation of quasi-governmental bodies has caused some difficulties in terms of accountability, because it is more difficult to monitor their decisions and to assure that the public interest is being furthered.

The new localism also complicates national politics and international relations. Many urban governments now have offices in their national capitals to lobby executive and legislative offices, and in foreign capitals to promote local economic development. In the absence of effective regional and national support, local officials and their supporters have become creative in furthering local interests.

In political terms, the new local activism reflects major restructuring of the relationships among government officials, economic elites, and social interests. At issue is whether the restructuring means that urban governments are encouraging greater public participation or empowering a small segment of the citizenry at the expense of the rest. It is clear, however, that the dominant elites have been changing in response to new economic and social challenges. These changes and their effects may be discernible through comparative study of the many urban governments in which they are happening.

Context

The comparative study of urban government developed from the study of nations and, as such, has tended to focus on institutions and the broad social and economic context in which the institutions operate. The study has focused increasingly on the similarities and differences among urban areas in particular geographic regions, or at particular levels of economic development. The interest in comparative studies of all kinds and of urban governments in particular is likely related to both increasing international economic interdependence and fundamental changes in the political, economic, and social structures in the former states of the Soviet Union, in Eastern Europe, and in Africa. As proponents of the new localism might suggest, increasing pressure for urban governments to act creatively may also be feeding the interest in cross-national studies.

Bibliography

Chandler, J. A., ed. *Local Government in Liberal Democracies: An Introductory Survey*. London: Routledge, 1993. Focuses on the structures and processes of local government in nation studies that cover local governments in England and Wales, Ireland, France, Italy, Germany, Sweden, the United States, and Canada.

Fried, Robert C., and Francine F. Rabinovitz. *Comparative Urban Politics: A Performance Approach*. Englewood Cliffs, N.J.: Prentice-Hall, 1980. Focuses on the methods of measuring urban performance, theories that may explain the relationships between political variables and citizen perceptions of government performance, and how to improve urban performance.

Goetz, Edward G., and Susan E. Clarke, eds. *The New Localism: Comparative Urban Politics in a Global Era*. Newbury Park, Calif.: Sage Publications, 1993. Analyses of the growing roles of local, largely urban, governments in Great Britain, Poland, Hungary, Nigeria, Kenya, and the Caribbean Basin, as central governments struggle to address local problems.

Gottdiener, M., and C. G. Pickvance, eds. *Urban Life in Transition*. Newbury Park, Calif.: Sage Publications, 1991. Discusses issues of economic development, immigration, ethnic diversity, gender, crime, poverty, privatization, public-private cooperation, and urban regimes in the United States, Great Britain, and other nations.

Heady, Ferrel. *Public Administration: A Comparative Perspective*. 4th ed. New York: Marcel Dekker, 1991. Classic work on comparative public administration. Outlines the development of comparative study of public organization and introduces the new focus on the study of reform among national and local governments.

Jacobs, Brian D. *Fractured Cities: Capitalism, Community, and Empowerment in Britain and America*. London: Routledge, 1992. Examines the development of community-based organizations seeking to overcome economic and social conflicts, forge cooperative relationships with corporate and municipal leaders, and strengthen local control over economic development.

Keating, Michael. *Comparative Urban Politics: Power and the City in the United States, Canada, Britain, and France*. Aldershot, Hants, U.K.: Edward Elgar, 1991. Discusses the abilities of urban governments to meet the challenges of social and economic change, and the roles of business and other elites and social interests in urban politics.

William L. Waugh, Jr.

Cross-References

URBAN POLICY

Field of study: Functions of government

The concerns of local governments that constitute the realm of urban policy include taxation and tax revenues, urban blight, transportation systems, pollution, and unemployment. The trend toward suburbanization forced cities to pay increasing attention to such concerns.

Principal terms

CITY: political entity or subdivision that has been established to provide a general local government for a specific population concentrated in a defined area

INFRASTRUCTURE: the underlying foundation or basic framework of a system or organization

METROPOLITAN AREA: any county containing a central city or contiguous cities of fifty thousand or more people

MUNICIPALITY: an association of inhabitants of a limited area legally incorporated or duly authorized for local governmental purposes

SUBURB: outlying part of a city or town, or a smaller community adjacent to or within commuting distance of a city

SUBURBANITE: one who lives in a suburb

Overview

Urban policy concerns governmental actions or decisions affecting the growth and operation of cities and urban areas. It is among the most widely discussed issues in American life. One reason for this is that the United States has urbanized at an accelerating pace. By 1920, more than half of the U.S. population lived in urban areas. Urban growth was later marked by a flow of white, middle- and upper-income people to the suburbs and a flow of poor rural dwellers into the central cities.

Throughout American history, cities have been conceived more in economic than in cultural, social, or political terms. The purpose of American cities was to make money; they came into being as centers of trade and commerce. Throughout the nineteenth century, the movement west across the continent placed towns at the leading edge of territorial expansion. National economic growth was promoted through movement into unsettled land, and exploitation of that land and resources was made possible by the continuous expansion of cities, towns, and villages. Villages and towns were the first to arrive, and farmers settled the land between cities. Each city was its own capitalist system, held together by the independent actions of individuals in search of fortune. The primary goal of government was to maximize the opportunities for individual economic advancement.

The pattern of American urban development has been different from that of any other country. The great cities of Europe and Asia evolved as places of commerce, as did American cities, but they also served as centers of religious, military, cultural, and political power. Before the modern nation-state, there was the city-state. The city has been viewed throughout history as the seat of civilization and commerce.

Modern Rome has been continuously occupied since 1500 B.C.E. By the sixth century B.C.E., the city had established political control over the central Roman province and was beginning to assert authority over much of the Italian peninsula. In the next few centuries, it became the political and administrative center of a large empire. Even as the empire weakened and dissolved, the city continued to exert enormous cultural and religious influence around the globe as the seat of the Roman Catholic church.

Another example is Paris, the capital of France. It sits in the center of the huge basin of the Seine River. For more than two thousand years it has been a center of trade and commerce. It also became a center of religion, culture, and political power. It was designated a capital in Roman times; since then, no city in France has challenged its preeminence.

Urban development in the United States took a different course. Despite its status as a global center of finance and corporate power, New York does not approach the cities of ancient times in terms of importance to various aspects of society. New York began as a Dutch colonial settlement in 1609. In 1625, it became a city called New Amsterdam. By the time of the American Revolution, New York was the largest city in the United States, but it never exerted political or administrative authority on behalf of the central government. It was never the center of religious authority, mainly because the United States was a nation that had specifically divorced religion from state power. In 1790, Congress designated Washington, D.C., as the new nation's capital, making it one of the few cities in the world to be planned solely as a capital.

In the United States, cities were practical. They were places of economic opportunity, lacking in long cultural, social, and political history. Cities in the United States have been regarded with distrust and as threats to, rather than as seats of, civilization. There is a habit of equating cities with corrupt political power as well as with a breakdown of social morals.

The combination of antiurban attitudes and the tradition of privatism has had the effect of limiting the public powers of cities. City governments are far more restricted in the United States than in most other nations. As creatures of the states, however, American cities have grown as public corporations with considerable power and responsibilities. One of the main reasons for the expansion of public power of cities was the desire of urban residents to expand the local private economy. Entrepreneurs in cities recognized that the way to keep and expand their wealth was to promote the city as a whole.

The key to economic growth was internal improvements, such as canals and railroad connections. Municipalities were conduits that could help finance transportation links that could give one city an advantage over another. After the 1850's, cities bought railroad stocks, made loan guarantees to railroad companies, and gave away land in an effort to be linked by rail. American cities still use their powers and resources to promote local economic prosperity. They offer tax abatements and hand out subsidies to encourage the construction of malls, they run tourism bureaus, they restore historical buildings, and they intensify crime control.

A second important reason that public powers and responsibilities of cities have grown is that any time large numbers of people converge in a relatively small area, problems arise that cannot be solved without collective efforts. The tradition of privatism tended to make people believe that they need not be concerned about how their actions might affect others. As cities grew in the nineteenth century, however, the consequences of unrestrained private activity became impossible to ignore. People saw rising crime rates, poor housing, unemployment, and problems in provision of education and transportation. They believed that they were powerless to correct or to escape these problems.

Municipal governments assumed increasingly complex responsibilities, such as supplying water, disposing of waste, fighting fire and crime, and building and maintaining bridges and streets. The expansion of the public sector was fueled by recurring crises that threatened not only the health and welfare of urban residents but also local economic vitality. Riots, fires, outbreaks of contagious disease, and other maladies could easily force people to move. Municipal institutions were used to address such problems because only the government could claim the legitimacy to act on behalf of all the citizens. States had delegated powers to cities through state constitutions.

After the Civil War, industrial cities began to expand their responsibilities, not only in response to the problems threatening the health, safety, and welfare of urbanites but also because conditions that, in the past, had seemed tolerable and inevitable, such as muddy streets, polluted water, and open sewers, had come to be regarded an unacceptable. Municipal governments provided a range of new and expanded services administered by full-time employees. They built parks, adopted building codes, and paved streets. They wrote health and sanitation codes. They granted franchises and licenses for telephone service, gas and electric service, and public transportation. Much of the infrastructure and many of the responsibilities of American cities date to this period of city building.

Today, cities provide a wide variety of services. For example, they build and maintain a public infrastructure of roads, bridges, sewer lines, sewage treatment plants, water mains, parks, zoos, hospitals, and schools. They provide fire and police protection. They collect garbage, and run public health services. Through city zoning ordinances, they influence the location of homes, factories, office buildings, restaurants, and parking lots. Through local building codes, they regulate plumbing, wiring, building materials, height of structures, and architectural styles. These public activities and more are essential to the safety and well-being of city dwellers. Without them, life in most cities would become intolerable.

Applications

Urban policy looks at relationships among urban environments, political systems, and policy outputs. Population movement from central cities, for example, is a common feature of urban development that urban policy addresses. With the introduction of new flexibility in transportation and communication through the automobile and the telephone, the fate of central cities in the United States was dramatically altered. Prior to World War II, city transportation centers were the dominating factors of surrounding territories. This dominating influence decreased after the advent of the automobile.

Although they were valuable nexus points in the transportation network, cities began to lose appeal. Cars and trucks began to pollute the cities. Many people found cities to be dirty and congested. City apartments that once were convenient when people depended on street cars and subways lost their appeal as distance to work became less of an issue. Suburbs became more attractive with affordable, spacious homes, clean neighborhoods, and less crime and pollution. As a result, taxpayers moved out of the central cities and into the suburbs.

This left the economies of central cities either stagnant or in decline. Cities lost their socioeconomic dominance and political influence. For example, central cities could no longer regularly annex surrounding territory in order to expand their tax bases.

As suburbs grew, they become economically prosperous, leading to demands for political independence from central cities and from one another. Metropolitan areas were split into cities and suburbs. Sometimes only haphazard arrangements linked them together to help combat common metropolitan problems. Special interests often focused on problems particular to one suburb. This prevented the central cities from directing the development of the metropolitan community as a whole.

This fragmentation causes problems for public policies that require coordinated planning throughout the metropolitan area. General planning is necessary to build a transportation system that links residential suburbs to industries and jobs in central cities. Furthermore, geographic fragmentation perpetuates inequalities in urban areas. For example, housing opportunities for low-income groups can be restricted if there is no agency with the metropolitan-wide authority necessary to build public housing. Local communities typically exhibit the "not in my backyard" syndrome and oppose low-income housing for fear that it would foster a host of problems, including increased crime, pollution, traffic congestion, unemployment, and a general deterioration of the area. The result is that either such housing is concentrated solely in the central cities (which already suffer from a decreased tax base and too few job opportunities) or the housing projects are not built at all.

Fragmentation also causes financial disadvantages. The increased numbers of people moving outside city limits and outside city tax collectors' reaches causes the per capita cost of government for the central cities to increase. Suburbanites who do not pay city taxes continue to contribute to the cities' traffic and parking problems, use city streets and parks, and frequently receive city services without charge. This places an inequitable burden on metropolitan taxpayers. Cities experience a serious loss of revenue from state spending that is apportioned on the basis of population. A large portion of their daytime population cannot be counted because the suburbanites work in the cities and live in the suburbs. Thus, the central cities' local tax burden per capita is considerably greater than that of the suburbs.

Inequality also comes from those residing in blighted areas of the central cities, which pose the most costly problems of public health risks, crime control, fire protection, and slum clearance. Such areas often contribute little in taxes because residents have low incomes, property values are low, and businesses generate little taxable revenue.

In metropolitan areas where suburban communities are separately incorporated, there exists an unequal distribution of government services. Low-value property is generally excluded from the boundaries of suburbs as those lines are being drawn, resulting in underprivileged pockets of the metropolitan area being left to their own inadequate resources. Metropolitan dispersion tends to result in an unhealthy difference in the quality of governmental services within a given metropolitan area.

Fragmentation has widened the social distance that exists between the central cities and the suburbs. Central cities are melting pots of ethnic minorities, while the residents of suburbs tend to be predominantly white. Central cities have a looser concept of family, with more single mothers as heads of households, while suburbs tend to have more traditional nuclear families. City dwellers typically are less educated and more likely to be unemployed than suburbanites. City residents normally rent, whereas suburbanites tend to own their homes. Incomes of city residents tend to be lower. These contrasting general characteristics result in a conflict of political and policy orientations, with central cities favoring social programs to meet their needs and suburban areas opposing high-cost social changes and programs. The political consequences of these differences are significant when proposals for unified action by central cities and suburbs are made to achieve order in the entire metropolitan area.

Context

The study of urban policy can make an important contribution to the understanding of relations in American cities as well as relations in foreign cities. By examining how specific urban policies are made and the consequences of these policies for different groups living in a metropolitan area, one can see whether government responds to the needs and aspirations of unorganized and less affluent groups in society, or whether it listens primarily to the demands of rich and powerful special-interest groups.

Urban policy can be understood as a complex interaction among the institutions, actors, and resources of both the public and the private spheres. Modern urban life would hardly be possible without governments, which are vested with the capacity to represent the collective needs of citizens. Governments both manage the processes of democratic decision making and provide essential services. City governments, however, are particularly dependent upon marketplace institutions if they are to advance the general welfare of urban dwellers. An inexhaustible variety of private institutions, such as defense contractors, large corporations, banks, insurance companies, retailers, and real estate companies, make critical decisions that determine the well-being of urban communities. They provide jobs and housing, influence land-use patterns, affect air and water pollution, and determine a plethora of other matters of importance to urban dwellers. Urban policy attempts to organize these private decisions so that the urban area as a whole benefits.

Governments must implement policies that promote local economic growth and, at the same time, must maintain popular support for their actions. In turn, private actors know that their own well-being is related to the urban community's quality of life, which depends on governmental services and policies. This interdependence is often expressed as tension between the two spheres rather than cooperation. Urban policy attempts to manage that tension for the overall benefit of the city.

Bibliography

David, Stephen M., and Paul E. Peterson. *Urban Politics and Public Policy: The City in Crisis.* 2d ed. New York: Praeger, 1976. The relationship between the New York processes of urban politics and the substance of urban public policy is the focus of this book.

Erber, Ernest, ed. *Urban Planning in Transition.* New York: Grossman, 1970. Discusses the urban crisis and the need to confront urban problems through social planning. Also describes the roles of professional planners and the tools necessary for planning.

Grant, Daniel R., and Lloyd B. Omdahl. *State and Local Government in America.* 6th ed. Madison, Wis.: W. C. B. Brown & Benchmark, 1993. Combines research in state and local government with historical perspectives. Gives special attention to such urban problems as drugs, crime, homelessness, and environmental exploitation.

Harrigan, John. *Politics and Policy in States and Communities.* 5th ed. New York: HarperCollins College Publishers, 1994. Themes include rejuvenation of state and local governments, the role of those governments in political economies, and the influence of political ideology in state and community politics.

Kohler, Heinz. *Economics and Urban Problems.* Lexington, Mass.: D. C. Heath, 1973. Discusses a framework within which urban economic problems occur as well as offering basic facts about fundamental economic urban problems. Develops the principle of rational behavior and shows how a market economy might coordinate the actions of a large number of independent decision makers in view of a city's evolution.

Mahood, H. R., and Edward L. Angus, eds. *Urban Politics and Problems: A Reader.* New York: Scribner, 1969. This compilation of readings provides an analysis of some of the critical issues of urbanization confronting American political institutions.

Porter, Paul, and David Sweet. *Rebuilding America's Cities.* New Brunswick, N.J.: Center for Urban Policy Research, 1984. Discusses successful recovery efforts that revitalized cities and talks about how cities function to enrich the lives of residents.

Susan M. Taylor

Cross-References

City Government in the United States, p. 266; County Government, p. 458; The Family and Politics in the United States, p. 649; Government Roles, p. 778; Industrialization, p. 916; Land Management in the United States, p. 1045; Local Governments, p. 1136; Public Policy, p. 1633; Rural Community Government, p. 1763; State and Local Government, p. 1885; Town Meetings, p. 1993; Urban Governments, p. 2052; Urban Renewal and Housing, p. 2064.

URBAN RENEWAL AND HOUSING

Field of study: Functions of government

Government has undertaken programs related to housing and urban renewal to assist citizens in obtaining adequate shelter and to direct development toward land uses that contribute to the livability of urban areas. Programs have ranged from slum clearance to attempts to eliminate homelessness.

Principal terms

BLIGHT: condition of an area that has deteriorated to the degree that it is unsafe, unsanitary, and no longer serves the needs of its inhabitants

CONSERVATION: prevention of the deterioration of buildings or neighborhoods to avoid their removal and the displacement of their inhabitants

DISPLACEMENT: relocation of previous, usually low-income, residents that results when urban renewal or rehabilitation causes the loss of previously affordable housing

EMINENT DOMAIN: power implied by the Constitution, allowing the government to acquire land by purchase or condemnation when it is determined to be in the national interest

GENTRIFICATION: effect of renewal or rehabilitation making previously dilapidated areas more attractive to those of higher income, often displacing the original occupants

HUD: acronym for the federal Housing and Urban Development department

REHABILITATION: improvements made to a structure or an area, bringing it to standards considered appropriate by the government

RENEWAL: activities undertaken to change or replace dilapidated or outmoded buildings and facilities in response to economic and social pressures

Overview

Housing and urban renewal were concerns of the United States government long before they were formally recognized functions of government. During the twentieth century, federal involvement in these activities changed according to the altering social, political, and economic conditions in the country. The philosophies of the various presidential administrations also caused changes in the level of government involvement in these activities. Some presidents have placed great importance on direct involvement by the federal government, while others have advocated decentralization, which gives more control to the localities in which the programs are carried out. Governmental programs in housing and urban renewal have been diverse, ranging from slum clearance during the Great Depression, to mortgage lending programs, to assisting local governments to lure upscale department stores to inner cities in the late twentieth century.

The original goal of urban renewal programs was to improve the social and economic conditions of the urban setting so that the middle- and upper-class populations would return from the suburbs to which they had fled, partly in response to the deterioration of the inner city. Their return, it was hoped, would result in an increase in property taxes collected and a reversal of the decline and decay of the central city.

Between 1892 and 1908, studies were conducted to examine slum conditions, which resulted in recommendations that unsanitary housing be condemned and that the government purchase and improve substandard housing. None of these studies resulted in federal intervention in the cities' situations. During this period, urban problems such as overcrowding, deterioration of housing, and racial strife were thought to be best dealt with by state and local authorities, not by the federal government.

The primary government objectives during the Depression of the 1930's were to provide employment and stimulate economic recovery. During this period, the federal government attempted to eliminate slums by acquiring buildings through powers of eminent domain. Slums that were cleared in this manner often were replaced with towering concrete housing projects such as are found in New York City and Chicago. Conflict arose, however, when the government attempted to use eminent domain to eliminate slums in Louisville, Kentucky. In 1935, a legal challenge was made opposing the government's authority to do this. It was determined that providing housing to a relatively few people could not be considered to be in the national interest and did not justify the government's actions. After this decision, the government began to grant funds to localities to carry out the same purposes.

During the Depression era, the federal government also became involved in home ownership programs when presidents Herbert Hoover and Franklin D. Roosevelt initiated mortgage lending systems to help people buy homes. These programs had a dual purpose: to rescue the banks that had survived the Depression, but which held loans on mortgages that people were unable to repay under the original terms; and to stimulate the construction industry and provide jobs. The Federal Home Loan Bank Act of 1932 began a system to enable people to purchase homes on credit when there was a reasonable expectation that the loans could be repaid. The Federal Housing Administration (FHA), created in 1934, insured the loans, and enabled people to buy houses on credit by making a down payment that was small relative to the cost of the home. Construction of these homes was financed by loans to builders, who were required to pay only 15 percent of the costs if they satisfied the FHA requirements that they correctly judge the housing market and the value of the home, and that they build according to certain codes.

Following World War II, the Veterans Administration (VA) began approving mortgage loans to returning servicemen, with low down payments and twenty-five-year repayment terms. During this period, decent, affordable housing in the nation's cities was in short supply. VA loans enabled people to buy new homes in the suburbs for monthly payments often lower than their rent would have been for the substandard housing then available in the cities. This resulted in the rapid and sustained exodus of people from the cities to the suburbs, where land was plentiful and inexpensive. As people left the inner cities to live in the suburbs, their tax dollars went with them, and the deterioration of the cities accelerated.

The Housing Act of 1949 was intended to eliminate residential blight, and established a federal program for central city redevelopment. Part of this legislation was captioned "Slum Clearance and Community Development and Redevelopment." The act's purpose was to provide a decent home and a suitable living environment for every U.S. family. It focused primarily on physically deteriorated areas, which were eligible for federal funds to be used for clearance and redevelopment. After the local government applied to the federal authority and was granted approval, it could acquire, through purchase or condemnation, property in the area to be renewed. Thus, residential areas that met the standards for deterioration could be cleared and redeveloped for commercial, industrial, or any other use. Under this program, the federal government provided grants of up to two-thirds of the project's costs. The act required that any federally funded urban redevelopment program follow a general plan for the entire community, which was the first time a community plan had been required. Critics claimed that middle-income housing construction was favored, and that the residents of these cleared areas—people of lower-middle and lower income—were displaced without help in relocating. Those who were displaced generally could not relocate in the growing suburban areas, because the housing there was expensive and often governed by discriminatory policies that excluded them for racial, ethnic, or other reasons.

The Housing Act of 1954 changed the focus of governmental programs from redevelopment to urban renewal, and aimed to clear the slums, prevent the development of new slums, and conserve housing that had not yet deteriorated. Congress specifically required that urban renewal projects be part of a workable program for community improvement. Each city seeking funding from the federal government needed to provide a comprehensive plan for community development; an analysis of the neighborhoods in the community used to identify the blighted areas; administrative resources to carry out a community program; evidence that the entire community had been informed and had been given a chance to contribute to the planning and administration of the program; enough housing to accommodate people displaced by urban renewal; and enough money to fund the community's share of the costs. Although the legislation emphasized involvement of citizens in the development process, local governments often sidestepped the issue by creating special advisory boards to approve the plans, without giving the people on the boards any meaningful opportunity for input.

Government urban renewal entered the area of business renewal in 1959 and allowed for 20 percent of federal monies to be allocated for nonresidential purposes. Business renewal was intended to preserve the healthy commercial and business districts of the central city and encourage further development there.

As federal involvement in housing programs and urban renewal increased, it became necessary to coordinate the many programs related to these concerns more efficiently. In 1965, President Lyndon B. Johnson signed legislation creating the Department of Housing and Urban Development (HUD). Giving these activities cabinet-level status acknowledged their growing importance.

Applications

Many programs that the government undertook from the 1960's through the 1980's had far-reaching goals and enduring effects. The Model Cities program, Community Development Block Grants, and rent assistance programs are typical of HUD's efforts.

The Demonstration Cities and Metropolitan Development Act of 1966—known as the Model Cities program—was an experimental program in cities with seriously deteriorated areas. In addition to the physical problems that previous programs had addressed, this program also targeted the social and economic needs of low-income people who lived in the cities. The legislation included broad requirements that stated that a program would receive assistance only if it was of significant magnitude to make a great impact on the physical and social problems in the city. The program was intended to eliminate blight and decay in entire sections of the city or neighborhood, requiring plans that would contribute to the sound development of the entire city and make progress in reducing social and educational disadvantages. Rather than the limited planning required by previous programs, Model Cities required comprehensive planning and widespread citizen participation that considered physical, social, and economic planning for the entire model area. HUD provided funding for an entire year's planning to occur before the program began.

Although the Model Cities program fell short of its goals and was considered by many to have spread the economic resources of the government too thin to have any major, lasting effect on the problems it was intended to help solve, it did make citizen participation a routine and important part of most governmental programs.

One of the most far-reaching governmental programs relating to housing and urban renewal was the Community Development Block Grant (CDBG) program. Debated in Congress during the presidency of Richard M. Nixon, it was signed into law by President Gerald R. Ford in 1974.

Congress melded several community development and housing programs, which previously had been separately administered, into the Housing and Community Development Act of 1974. A major provision of this legislation was the Community Development Block Grant program to be administered by HUD. Among the objectives of the program were the elimination of slums and blight, improvement of public services, rational land use, desegregation of housing according to income, and increased economic opportunities for low- and moderate-income people. Although funds would come from the federal government, the goal of the legislation was to delegate to state and local governments responsibility for functions that the Nixon Administration believed could best be performed at that level. Communities were to develop their own programs and decide how to spend the funds they receive, a change from earlier programs that required extensive approval procedures by the federal government.

Although its primary emphasis was on the low- and moderate-income populations, it aimed to revitalize the entire community. The grants provided under this act were intended to be flexible, and funds could be used to aid in economic development in nonresidential areas. The greatest portion of funds granted were to benefit low- and moderate-income persons, however, and were not intended to be used in areas of a city that did not meet those income standards.

The Housing and Community Development Act of 1974 also established the Section 8 rent assistance program. The existing housing program of this legislation allowed low-income residents to select the housing they wished to live in, frequently their current homes. If landlords wished to take part, the local housing authorities would inspect the dwellings and negotiate for necessary repairs and fair market rents, according to HUD standards. The tenants agreed to pay one-quarter of their incomes toward the rents, and the agency would pay the balance. In this program, the tenants could take their Section 8 certificates if they chose to move. The new construction program was the second part of Section 8, in which HUD selected the dwellings by arranging contracts with developers of rental housing and guaranteeing payments for low-income tenants enrolled in the program. As a result of increasing development and financing costs, this program required higher subsidies than the existing housing program.

During the 1980's, relatively little attention was paid to building or maintaining public housing, and many of the existing units fell into worse condition than had previously been the case. This housing is referred to as severely distressed public housing. Many people believe it is more costly to repair these units than to demolish them and build new public housing. In a statement of objectives for fiscal year 1994, HUD planned to reduce the number of distressed public housing units partially through demolishing them and building low-density, small-scale developments scattered throughout communities. One objective was to decrease the segregation of people according to race and income, which had been a result of earlier public housing projects.

During the 1980's and early 1990's, largely as a result of a decrease in government spending on social programs, many people became homeless. By 1994, there was a greater number of homeless persons in the country than at any time since the Great Depression. Unemployment, mental illness, alcoholism, and drug addiction all contributed to homelessness. In 1993, under the administration of President Bill Clinton, HUD proposed to unify the existing fragmented system to coordinate services to homeless people, in an attempt to ensure that the different groups that make up the homeless population receive the appropriate services.

Context

Housing and urban renewal are complex, multifaceted concerns of the United States government that affect all Americans both directly and indirectly. Providing housing and directing rational urban development are ongoing activities of government, and are affected by the country's changing social, economic, and political conditions.

Relieving one problem often causes other problems to worsen. For example, as central city neighborhoods are improved by new business development or by the rehabilitation of old buildings, former occupants who might have been able to make a living or afford the rents of the buildings in their previous, perhaps dilapidated, condition, are forced to relocate to areas that might be less desirable or affordable for them. By eliminating what might have been considered slum conditions, areas are gentrified, displacing the previous tenants.

The reality of limited tax dollars forces federal, state, and local governments to prioritize spending. Other programs and problems that are funded at a higher level than housing and urban renewal programs may still affect housing and the urban environment. For example, when buildings are demolished to make way for a federally funded transit project such as light rail construction, the inhabitants of those buildings are forced to relocate. As long as citizens require housing and cities continue to change and deteriorate, housing and urban renewal issues will be part of the government agenda.

Bibliography

Greer, Scott. *Urban Renewal and American Cities: The Dilemma of Democratic Intervention.* Indianapolis: Bobbs-Merrill, 1965. Although dated, contains a valuable history and discussion of urban renewal efforts and problems in the United States.

Jacobs, Jane. *The Death and Life of Great American Cities.* New York: Random House, 1961. Conversationally written book offers detailed discussion of the causes of urban degeneration and renewal, and of what contributes to the livability of a city.

Salins, Peter D., ed. *Housing America's Poor.* Chapel Hill: University of North Carolina Press, 1987. Compilation of scholarly, yet readable, articles about federal housing policies and history.

Schwartz, David C., Richard C. Ferlauto, and Daniel N. Hoffman. *A New Housing Policy for America: Recapturing the American Dream.* Philadelphia: Temple University Press, 1988. Discusses U.S. housing problems and policies, and state and federal programs. Advocates possible changes and solutions. Indexed. Bibliographical notes.

Smith, Neil, and Peter Williams, eds. *Gentrification of the City.* Boston: Allen & Unwin, 1986. Compendium of articles discussing urban rehabilitation, gentrification, and displacement in the United States and elsewhere. Although scholarly, is a good source of information on the subject.

Welfeld, Irving. *Where We Live.* New York: Simon & Schuster, 1988. Highly readable social history of U.S. housing policies. Discusses impacts of economic conditions on urban development and suburbanization in the United States.

Willmann, John B. *The Department of Housing and Urban Development.* New York: Praeger, 1967. Straightforward history of HUD, its precursors, and early activities.

Debbie Schiedel

Cross-References

Budgets of National Governments, p. 158; Business and Government, p. 177; Entitlements, p. 610; Federal Mandates, p. 662; Funding of Government, p. 724; Government Agencies, p. 765; Government Roles, p. 778; Grants-in-Aid, p. 791; Land Management in the United States, p. 1045; Policy Development and Implementation, p. 1414; Public Policy, p. 1633; Public Utilities, p. 1640; Race and Ethnicity, p. 1654; Resource Management, p. 1718; The Supreme Court: Role in Government and Law, p. 1935; Urban Governments, p. 2052; Urban Policy, p. 2057; Urbanization, p. 2071.

URBANIZATION

Field of study: Economic issues

Urbanization is the development of cities, which alter their region's social, cultural, and economic structures as they grow. Urbanization began thousands of years ago with improvements in agriculture that led to the possibility of supporting large nonrural populations with agricultural surplus. Cities have also developed as a result of technological and other advantages.

Principal terms
> COMPARATIVE ADVANTAGE: ability of a region or a company to produce and export a good more cheaply than another region or company
> ECONOMIES OF SCALE: general principle that unit costs decrease as the number of units produced increases
> EXTERNALITY: cost or benefit that the actions of a person or organization creates for others who are not directly involved with the person or organization
> GRADIENT: percentage change in price or market value per mile as rents, population densities, or wages
> LOCATION THEORY: use of economic principles to explain where various activities take place
> VOTING WITH YOUR FEET: demonstration of one's preferences by moving from one jurisdiction to another

Overview

The trend toward urbanization can be measured and observed in all parts of the world, but it has been especially dramatic in many of the world's developing nations, particularly during the twentieth century. There are both costs and benefits to urbanization. The expansion of urban areas and the continued growth of large metropolitan cities has largely redefined the lives of the world's population. In cities one finds the clustering of firms, more expensive land, the substitution of capital for land as a measure of wealth and status, and congestion. One also finds enhanced business, social, and cultural opportunities.

Throughout its colonial era and over more of its early national period, the United States was overwhelmingly agrarian and rural, with few significant urban areas. Even the principal colonial cities of Philadelphia, New York, and Boston—large by eighteenth century standards—would be considered small by twentieth century standards. In the years since the mid-nineteenth century, however, the United States has become increasingly industrialized and urbanized. During the late nineteenth and early twentieth centuries the newest residents of American cities were, more often than not, the grown children of American farmers and other rural people or newly arrived immigrants from Europe. By the late twentieth century almost every region of the United States was urbanized. Oddly enough, the western region is, in relative terms, more urban than the earlier-settled eastern region.

Prior to 1950, the U.S. Census Bureau classified as an urban area any city or incorporated place with at least 2,500 inhabitants. By this definition, the first national census, in 1790, found that nearly 95 percent of the nation's population resided in rural areas. Sixty years later, in 1850, the nation was only 15.3 percent urban. Although the country was three times more urban than it had been in 1790, it was still overwhelmingly rural.

In the late nineteenth century the United States began to become a truly urbanized nation. It became more urbanized despite the fact that the nation's rural population continued to expand. The urban population grew much more rapidly, however, in both absolute and relative terms. The 1890 census found that the United States was just over 35 percent urban, in 1900 nearly 40 percent, in 1910 nearly 46 percent, and by 1920 the Census Bureau reported for the first time that a majority of the nation's population, 51.2 percent, resided in urban areas.

Beginning with the 1950 census, the Census Bureau expanded its definition of an urban area to include unincorporated areas around incorporated areas with 2,500 or more inhabitants. In the 1990's, slightly more than 75 percent of U.S. residents inhabited urban areas, even though after the end of World War II an increasing number of people and businesses shifted their residences from the central cities to suburban areas. If a more restrictive definition of an urbanized area is applied—a large central city with a minimum of 50,000 residents—then in 1990 there were nearly 400 urbanized areas in the United States that contained roughly 64 percent of the nation's total population.

An urban area is much more than a place with a large population within its boundaries, and a city is more than an aggregation of buildings. Urban areas are zones or regions that are defined by the organization, distribution, and use of economic and social resources. A city may be more accurately defined by its role as a market area than by its political boundaries. A market area is that area within which factory and shop production can be sustained efficiently. Within the imprecise and extensive boundaries of a market area, people and firms come together to exchange not only goods and services but also ideas and innovations. The clustering and diversity of consumers and producers nourish and encourage innovation. Along with competitive pressures, people and resources can also complement one another and thereby allow firms to become more efficient. An extensive market area also makes it easier for firms to specialize and consequently achieve economies of scale that tend to reduce their production costs.

The size of cities has long been constrained by a community's transportation system. Preindustrial cities were built to fit the scale of pedestrians. Shops, factories, and residential dwellings all had to be within reasonable walking distances of one another in order to be economically feasible. This scale began to change with the electrification of street railways (first used in Richmond, Virginia, in 1888), which were widely adopted during the 1890's. With improvements in both internal and external transportation systems, communications, fire protection, and disease control, the boundaries of cities rapidly expanded. Rapid expansion has also blurred the line between urban and rural areas, as it became feasible to reside outside the political boundaries of a city and still be within its economic boundaries.

Cities exist because there are enough economic and social incentives to justify their existence. There were and are sufficient rewards for people and firms to settle in urban areas. The specific site of a city can often be traced to its proximity to some intrinsic or constructed advantage. Intrinsic advantages include such things as natural harbors or access to navigable waterways. Cities such as Philadelphia, Boston, New York, Pittsburgh, Chicago, New Orleans, and San Francisco all owe their location to the advantages of natural water routes. Constructed or acquired advantages might include concentrated financial districts or ready access to railways or highway systems.

Cities may also exist or grow as a result of direct government promotion. For example, the Nevada cities of Reno, Lake Tahoe, and Las Vegas all owe much of their existence and growth to the state government's liberal divorce and gambling laws. The choice of Washington, D.C., as the U.S. capital was also the result of political choice rather than geographic advantage.

Other complexities regarding cities include how they grow or shrink and how their economic activities are arranged. Easy answers to such questions are not to be found, since a variety of circumstances combine to produce particular explanations for individual cities. Every city has its own unique attributes with respect to demography, technology, social customs, economic conditions, and geographic setting.

Applications

Analyses of urbanization often turn to the interactions between households and firms. The clustering of households and firms provides for a larger and thus more efficient market, but it also creates problems with externalities, the provision of local public goods, and other related market failures. Unfortunately, in a densely populated community there are bound to be neighbors and other third parties who indirectly benefit or suffer because of the behavior and decisions of others. How effectively an urban area deals with these issues can to a large extent determine the quality of life for its residents.

One externality in any large urban setting is traffic congestion. It has exasperated the Romans, for example, from the time of their empire to the modern age. Simple remedies for alleviating congestion are not often found. Whenever too many users crowd a network of roads, the consequence will be lost time, frustration, and added costs for all commuters. An efficient flow of transportation reduces costs and increases benefits throughout the community, but there are few incentives for any individual to undertake road improvements. Thus a person may complain about traffic but vote against increased taxation to build better roads. There is also the question of whether it is more efficient for the community to construct roads that satisfy average demand or that satisfy peak demand. Moreover, if the community decides to allocate public funds for the construction of new and improved roads it may turn out to be counter-productive, since better roads might encourage more cars and trucks to use the system, thereby creating a larger traffic jam on the new roads.

Housing is an important issue since housing structures are relatively permanent and since the price of land varies greatly by location. Housing structures can be replaced but for many years they are important in defining an urban area. There is also an external effect to housing since property values depend not only on the condition and location of a particular structure but also on the value of nearby properties and the perceived status of the neighborhood. The neighborhood effect of property values demonstrates the advantages and disadvantages of clustered structures.

Since firms and households all need land, they must bid for it at different locations. If this is done in a free market then the highest bidder, presumably the one who attaches the greatest value to use of the land, will acquire land in competition with other potential users. More remote parcels of land will be cheaper but of less interest to users such as retail stores or other commercial users. The process of bidding for land largely determines the form of a city and can be described by a gradient, which shows the percentage change in price or market value per mile. Most, but not all, communities also impose various zoning laws and restrictions in an attempt to control the form of the city.

The provision of local public advantages can be a useful determinant of in which jurisdiction a person or firm chooses to locate, particularly in a large metropolitan area with several distinct and bordering suburbs. For example, a family with school-age children may elect, if it can afford it, to live in a community with higher property taxes if those tax dollars are used to finance high-quality schools. When the children graduate from the schools, the family may then decide to relocate to a suburb with lower taxes. The family has voted with its feet, revealing its preferences by moving in or out of one community depending on its needs. Having such choices encourages diversity and permits communities to develop their own comparative advantages in form and structure. By providing residents with alternative packages of public goods and tax schedules to pay for those goods, the overall allocation of public goods may be made more efficient.

Context

Cities have existed for five millennia. The first cities were settled around 3000 B.C.E. in Mesopotamia in the Near East. Cities and urbanization have had their greatest effect on the lives of the world's people, however, only in the last few centuries. In the years since the Industrial Revolution, generally agreed to have begun in the mid-eighteenth century, the number and the size of urban areas has grown dramatically, while the relative inhabitation of rural areas has declined. By the late twentieth century, most of the world's population was employed in urban or suburban markets.

The governing and operation of cities necessitate some collective action by their residents. If all the residents of a community have the same or similar values and preferences, then the allocation of public funds for public uses will be relatively straightforward. With a diverse array of needs and preferences, however, problems inevitably arise.

Any town, city, or metropolis is dependent on the availability of rural agricultural surpluses, so there has always been a critical relationship between urban and rural communities. Not until the modern era have rural surpluses and transportation been generally adequate to sustain large urban populations. Industrialization and urbanization progressed together, but this progress was made possible by an agricultural revolution that dramatically increased crop yields and decreased the required number of farm laborers. By freeing up resources, thereby allowing resources to find their most productive use, the total level of output increased markedly. This increased output was used to feed an expanding population and facilitated the accumulation of capital and profits that could be used to foster new innovations and growth. Consequently, the history of urbanization mirrors the emergence of the modern industrialized world. It is a world that is clearly not without danger and costs, but it is also a world that provides more opportunities, more goods, and more services than was possible in the preindustrial age.

Bibliography

Cronon, William. *Nature's Metropolis: Chicago and the Great West*. New York: W. W. Norton, 1991. Exploration of the settlement and growth of a major American city and region, with analysis of the critical connections between cities and their hinterland regions.

Girouard, Mark. *Cities and People: A Social and Architectural History*. New Haven, Conn.: Yale University Press, 1985. Illustrated history of the structures and functions of cities from the Middle Ages until the late twentieth century.

Hohenberg, Paul M., and Lynn Hollen Lees. *The Making of Urban Europe 1000-1950*. Cambridge, Mass.: Harvard University Press, 1985. Economic, social, and political history of the emergence of modern urban Europe.

Hoover, Edgar M. *The Location of Economic Activity*. New York: McGraw-Hill, 1948. Introduction to the factors that define the spatial dimensions of economic activity.

Jacobs, Jane. *The Economy of Cities*. New York: Random House, 1969. Discusses the idea that rural economies are built upon urban economies, rather than the other way around.

Monkkonen, Eric H. *America Becomes Urban: The Development of U.S. Cities and Towns, 1780-1980*. Berkeley: University of California Press, 1988. Examination of the diversity and evolution of large and small American cities.

Mumford, Lewis. *The City in History: Its Origins, Its Transformations, and Its Prospects*. New York: Harcourt, Brace & World, 1961. Sweeping narrative of the nature, the forms, and the functions that cities have had.

Toynbee, Arnold. *Cities on the Move*. New York: Oxford University Press, 1970. Study of the issues that link cities with surrounding regions, as well as the forces that have led to the formation of capital cities for economic, political, and social reasons.

Timothy E. Sullivan

Cross-References

Business and Government, p. 177; City Government in the United States, p. 266; The City-State, p. 272; Civil Unrest and Rioting, p. 317; Fire Protection, p. 700; Immigrants and Politics, p. 861; Industrialization, p. 916; Political Machines and Bosses, p. 1468; Public Utilities, p. 1640; Urban Governments, p. 2052; Urban Policy, p. 2057; Urban Renewal and Housing, p. 2064.

UTILITARIANISM

Field of study: Political philosophy

In utilitarian philosophy an action is good if its consequence provides the greatest good for the greatest number. The names most closely associated with the development of utilitarianism are those of its founder, Jeremy Bentham, his faithful disciple, James Mill, and their critic, John Stuart Mill.

Principal terms

FELICIFIC CALCULUS: Bentham's arithmetical procedure for calculating amounts of pleasure and pain

FICTIONS: words that refer to abstract entities, not real ones

NATURAL LAWS: universal moral rules, known by reason alone

NATURAL RIGHTS: basic rights and liberties that all human beings by nature possess

PHILOSOPHICAL RADICALS: utilitarian disciples of Bentham

SOCIAL CONTRACT THEORY: view that the state is created by the consent of its members

Overview

The basic principle of utilitarianism is that the moral result to be sought in all that one does is the greatest balance of good over evil. Disagreement over how to apply this principle has produced two variants of the general theory: act-utilitarianism and rule-utilitarianism.

Act-utilitarians appeal directly to the utilitarian principle to judge the morally correct action suitable to a given situation. In the case of truth telling, for example, an act-utilitarian would ask, "What effect would my telling the truth have on the general balance of good over evil in this particular situation?" For act-utilitarians, there are no universal rules of morality like that of always telling the truth; rather, their emphasis is upon the consequences of the act in the specific case under consideration. Rule-utilitarians, on the other hand, would ask, "What would happen if everyone were to lie in similar situations?" For rule-utilitarians, it may be right to obey a rule always to tell the truth in circumstances in which telling the truth does not lead to the best consequences, if truth telling serves the greatest general good in the long run.

Jeremy Bentham (1748-1832), an act-utilitarian, maintained that the rightness or wrongness of any action is determined by the amount of happiness or pleasure produced. This leaves unanswered the question of how the quantity of pleasure and pain associated with any given act is to be determined. Bentham turned to science for the answer. He believed the time had arrived for the methods of the natural sciences to be employed by social scientists. Aware that the theoretical mainstay of science is mathematics, with its vocabulary of measurement and calculation, he sought to erect a science of politics upon the firm bedrock of a "mathematical ethics." Pleasure, he contended, may be said to be of lesser or greater value depending upon seven measurable variables: intensity, duration, certainty, distance, fecundity, purity, and the number of people affected. For any act, simply add up the pleasure and pain; if the sum of pleasure is greater than the sum of pain, the act is good; if the sum is less, the act is bad. This arithmetic is Bentham's famous felicific calculus.

Bentham assumed that felicific calculus reflected a fundamental fact of nature. All people have desires and seek to gratify them. Problems arise when desires conflict, as they frequently do, and very often the primary responsibility for conflict resolution falls upon government. When this occurs, Bentham claimed, the directing principle that should be employed by public officials for deciding which gratifications are to be suppressed and which are to be satisfied is no different from the one that ought to guide private decision—the principle of utility. The goal of both citizens and lawmakers ought to be the greatest happiness of the greatest number.

Bentham's act-utilitarianism bristles with problems. First, there are technical problems associated with the felicific calculus. The notion that pleasure and pain can be quantitatively calculated by a moral thermometer capable of measuring pleasure, similar to the way a thermal thermometer measures heat, is mathematically implausible. No real units of measurement exist for the precise calculation of the pleasure and pain. Furthermore, it is impossible to know what is to be measured. One may know that felicific calculus is designed to sum and compare pleasure and pain; the problem is there is no way to determine the various and remote consequences of any act.

Bentham's identification of the pleasurable with the ethical is also problematical. Even assuming that it is true that people everywhere always seek to maximize pleasure and minimize pain, this cannot, by itself, justify the principle of utility. To argue, as Bentham does, that because it is the case that individuals always seek pleasure maximization, therefore they ought to, is to fall prey to the logical fallacy of deriving an ethical principle solely from matters of fact. Put another way, Bentham errs by attempting to develop a theory of morality of what humankind ought to do based upon what they in fact do.

Finally, Bentham considers pleasure solely in quantitative terms. More than any other factor, this restriction accounts for the difference between act-utilitarians such as Bentham and rule-utilitarians such as John Stuart Mill. In ethical theory, Mill pointed out, quality matters. Failure to take into account the fact that some pleasures are qualitatively superior to others, no matter how intense the others might be, makes it possible to proclaim the life of a satiated pig morally preferable to that of a dissatisfied Socrates.

Mill, however, did not reject the utilitarian principle of the greatest good for the greatest number, rather he was convinced that recognizing some pleasures to be more valuable than others is compatible with the principle of utility. This introduction of quality, however, subverts the methodological centerpiece of Bentham's utilitarianism—the felicific calculus. Quantity and quality are no more comparable than trees and operas.

For Mill, the deciding factor regarding which qualities are to be deemed qualitatively superior is the collective wisdom of humankind. This wisdom comes to be embodied within the commonsense rules of everyday morality—truth-telling, paying one's debts, self-sacrifice, and so forth. These rules for directing moral behavior are subject to the supreme principle of utility in two ways: An act that contradicts the overarching rule of the greatest happiness of the greatest number can never be right, and in cases where two "secondary rules" conflict, appeal must be made to the ultimate rule or principle of utility.

Applications

Jeremy Bentham seemed destined for a legal career. Shortly after graduation from the University of Oxford, however, he attended a series of lectures on the British constitution delivered by the celebrated English jurist Sir William Blackstone (1723-1780). In listening to Blackstone, Bentham claims to have suddenly realized his own theory of law and to have made the decision to devote his life to philosophy and social reform. His intent was to use the utilitarian principle of the greatest happiness for the greatest number to provide a general framework of social conditions that would advance the well-being of the people of England first and then the world. In pursuit of this aim, he wrote a large number of works. Those most important for his political theory are *A Fragment on Government* (1776), and *An Introduction to the Principles of Morals and Legislation* (1789).

A Fragment on Government was written in response to Blackstone's *Commentaries on the Laws of England* (1765). Bentham's primary interest was reform of the legal system; in *A Fragment on Government* he attacked Blackstone for providing a justification of the legal status quo under the guise of merely explaining it. Bentham focuses his criticism on Blackstone's defense of the natural law and natural rights theory of traditional philosophy and the corollary idea of the social contract.

Bentham had come to view the English legal tradition as ambiguous, disorderly, and burdened with historical irrelevancies. The root of much of this confusion he believed was the natural law and natural rights tradition. He dismissed as mere fictions, natural laws (universal rules of obligation known by reason), natural rights (the liberties derived from them), and social contracts (in which certain powers are granted to the government in return for the promise to provide the condition under which the citizens might enjoy their natural rights). A problem arises when people mistakenly conclude that there is a corresponding reality for these fictitious abstractions. The problem is the confused mumbo jumbo that characterizes English jurisprudence. To correct this, Bentham recommended replacing natural law theory with the simple and clear principle of utility.

The importance of Bentham's *An Introduction to the Principles of Morals and Legislation* for political theory is that in this book Bentham spells out the implication of utilitarianism for lawmakers. Specifically, the legislator in a democracy is nothing less than a social scientist who utilizes felicific calculus to restructure society for the greatest happiness of the greatest number. It was the journalist James Mill who defined utilitarianism for the public. Though he added almost nothing original to Bentham's philosophy, his "Essay on Government," written for the *Encyclopedia Britannica* in 1820, is regarded as the definitive statement of early utilitarian political thinking. Moreover, it was James's son, John Stuart Mill, who was destined to become the most illustrious of all the utilitarians.

Educated at home by his father, the younger Mill was a staunch act-utilitarian, until, at the age of twenty, he suffered a severe bout of depression, a condition he attributed to the failure of his early education to attend to the emotional side of his personality. The attempt to correct this imbalance led him to the works of poets such as Samuel Taylor Coleridge and William Wordsworth. This interest in romantic poetry represented the death of his commitment to the relentlessly rational act-utilitarianism of Bentham and his father. By the time he emerged from his melancholia, he was convinced that he had discovered the key to a more humanistic utilitarianism—the appreciation of the qualitative superiority of intellectual over sensual pleasures.

Individual liberty is the centerpiece of John Stuart Mill's most famous essay, *On Liberty* (1859). Its general theme is that the government's power to interfere in the lives of its citizens ought to be severely limited. Neither the state nor society has the right to interfere in a person's liberty unless the exercise of that liberty harms others. Mill justifies this rule of limited government interference on utilitarian grounds: Personal liberty encourages the personal responsibility and moral improvement upon which the advancement of civilization depends.

On Liberty was Mill's manifesto on the importance of freedom of expression. His great fear was that the psychology of majority opinion would suppress dissent. In an impassioned plea for unlimited freedom in the realm of ideas, Mill cites his three celebrated reasons for why unlimited expression serves the principle of utility: If majority opinion is false, dissent serves the truth; if true, debate authenticates this fact; and if partially true, truthfulness can be more closely approximated.

Considerations on Representative Government (1861) provides Mill's prescription for protecting individual liberty within the framework of representative democracy. From his perspective, the purpose of government is to promote the advancement of civilization through the moral improvement of its citizens. Self-government, he thought, provides the individual freedom and responsibility necessary for moral maturation. Furthermore, this progress is dependent upon the intellectual excellence of a few select geniuses. In order to protect the "intellectual elites" from the danger of majority tyranny, Mill proposes a unique blend of democracy and elitism. He advocates that legislative and administrative functions of government be left to the "intellectual elite." To further protect these superior intellects from the uninformed demands of the general public, he recommended a proportional system of representation to ensure minorities a voice in the legislature, as well as a scheme for weighted voting that would allow the intellectual elites to cast more than one ballot.

Mill's attempt to humanize Bentham's act-utilitarianism is not without its own problems. For example, in claiming that some pleasures such as individual liberty are superior in kind or yield a higher quality of pleasure than others, it is hard to see how the utilitarian standard of the greatest good for the greatest number is to be gauged.

Mill never does make this clear. Moreover, it is difficult to justify such distinctions on strictly utilitarian grounds. This leaves Mill open to the charge that in the process of showing that utilitarianism need not be limited to Bentham's narrow version of utility as simple self-interest, he tacitly abandons utilitarianism.

Context

Early utilitarianism was as much a reform movement as it was a philosophy. As a philosophy it dominated the political climate of Great Britain for more than a century. A major contributing factor to its widespread acceptance was its simplicity. It was not only the easy-to-understand ethical and political direction provided by the idea (that the morally good action is one that produces the greatest good for the greatest number) that accounts for this popularity. The nineteenth century followers of Bentham and the two Mills were more interested in correcting the shortcomings of society than they were in fictions—abstract political doctrine. Early utilitarianism advocated a program of reform: better food, better working conditions, better schools, better laws, better and more representative government, laissez-faire economics, and reform of the criminal justice system in order to deal more effectively with crime, an issue which in the mind of the public had come to be associated with the social dislocations produced by the capitalist system. The political agitation of the philosophical radicals, as the reform-minded utilitarians called themselves, made them a potent force in politics. In short, the utilitarians believed, as their name indicates, in taking useful, practical steps toward the good.

By the twentieth century, utilitarianism as a political philosophy had dissipated. Perhaps the primary reason for this subsidence of utilitarian political theory is that the early utilitarians begged one of the perennial questions in the history of political thought: How can every individual seek her or his own self-interest without tearing apart the social fabric of society?

Neither Bentham nor the two Mills provided a way out of the conflict between individual welfare and the social good, but Henry Sidgwick (1838-1900), another English philosopher, recognized the dilemma, and he attempted to resolve it by integrating the utilitarian principle with the categorical imperative articulated by Immanuel Kant, the great German philosopher. Kantianism and utilitarianism are fundamentally opposed to each other, however, so much so that Sidgwick was forced to consider theological principles for uniting the two. This attempted union of Kantian theory and theology with utilitarian doctrine makes almost meaningless Sidgwick's use of the term "utilitarianism" as a name for his philosophy.

At the beginning of the twentieth century, there was a revival of utilitarian thought, spearheaded by two British philosophers: George Edward Moore (1873-1958) and Hastings Rashdall (1859-1924). These men held that morally right acts are not limited to those that give pleasure but consist of conduct that produces the best possible consequences for all involved. At first, their impact upon political theory was marginal, but gradually this changed. The names of political theorists associated with one or another version of utilitarianism has grown into a long list. Some names from the list include Sir Karl Popper, Stephen Toulmin, J. J. C. Smart, and Richard Brandt.

As a practical criterion for legislation in democracies, the maximization of pleasure and the minimization of pain for the greatest number is very much alive. Most, if not all, policy debates in democratic nations are framed in rhetoric that can easily be translated into the language of the utilitarian principle. It is important to note also that the autonomous individual—one who can decide an act on the basis of one's own calculation of self-interest—remains both the vision and hope of liberal democratic theorists. The spirit of utilitarianism lives on.

Bibliography

Anschutz, R. P. *The Philosophy of J. S. Mill*. Oxford, England: Clarendon Press, 1953. Time-honored classic on the political thought of John Stuart Mill.

Bentham, Jeremy. *A Fragment on Government and an Introduction to the Principles of Morals and Legislation*. Edited by Wilfrid Harrison. Oxford, England: Basil Blackwell, 1967. The audacity of Bentham's masterful attack upon Blackstone's ideas is in no small way responsible for the *Fragment*'s appeal, but the *Principles* is the more important work.

Halevy, Elie. *The Growth of Philosophical Radicalism*. Translated by Mary Morris. Winchester, Mass.: Faber & Faber, 1949. Comprehensive historical account of early utilitarianism.

Long, Douglas G. *Bentham on Liberty: Jeremy Bentham's Idea of Liberty in Relation to His Utilitarianism*. Toronto: University of Toronto Press, 1977. Long is generally critical of the tendency toward social engineering that he sees in Bentham's utilitarianism.

Mill, James. *Political Writings*. Edited by Terence Ball. New York: Cambridge University Press, 1992. Comprehensive sample of the elder Mill's political writings. Ball's introduction is superb.

Mill, John Stuart. *Autobiography of John Stuart Mill*. New York: Columbia University Press, 1960. Provides insights into the structures of Mill's thought.

_____. *Considerations on Representative Government*. London: Parker, Son, and Bourn, 1861. Elaboration of J. S. Mill's political theory.

_____. *On Liberty*. London: J. W. Parker, 1859. Impassioned plea for individual liberty and freedom of expression.

_____. "The Subjection of Women." In John Stuart Mill and Harriet Taylor Mill, *Essays on Sex Equality*, edited by Alice Rossi. Chicago: University of Chicago Press, 1970. Argues that women should be granted equal status in the family, the workplace, and the political arena.

_____. *Utilitarianism*. London: Parker, Son, and Bourn, 1863. Readable depiction of humanistic utilitarianism.

Thomas J. Mortillaro

Cross-References

Civil Liberties Protection, p. 291; Civil Rights and Liberties, p. 298; Civil Rights Protection, p. 304; Deism, p. 495; Epicurean Political Philosophy, p. 624; Equality and Egalitarianism, p. 630; Feminist Politics, p. 682; Kant's Political Philosophy, p. 1025; Legal Systems in Anglo-American Governments, p. 1085; Liberalism, p. 1118; Mill's Political Philosophy, p. 1204; Neo-Idealism, p. 1287; Positivism, p. 1557.

UTOPIANISM

Field of study: Political philosophy

Utopianism is the imaginative description or advocacy of a nearly perfect society, which generally would be characterized by social harmony, contentment, just institutions, and the absence of poverty and suffering.

Principal terms
ANARCHISM: theory that a society can achieve justice and equality by abolishing a centralized state

ANTI-UTOPIA (DYSTOPIA): nightmarish opposite of a utopia

COMMUNISM: idea that the communal ownership of the means of production will result in greater equality, justice, and cooperation

MARXISM: ideas of Karl Marx, including his goal of a future communism without class conflict, crime, poverty, or political coercion

PHILOSOPHER-KING: wise, authoritarian ruler in the utopian society envisioned by Plato

REFORMISM: idea that practical and significant improvements can be made in social and political institutions

UTOPIA: Thomas More's term derived from Greek words meaning "no place"; closely related to *eutopia*, which means "good place"

Overview

Although the term "utopia" was not coined until the sixteenth century, utopian conceptions of an ideal society can be found in early civilizations. Forerunners of this tradition include myths of a golden age or a benign state of nature in the remote past. About 2000 B.C.E. in ancient Mesopotamia, the *Epic of Gilgamesh* gave an account of a legendary king who went in search of such a paradise, but his quest turned out to be futile. About 750 B.C.E., the Greek writer Hesiod looked back to a golden age characterized by abundance and peace, and this mythical view of the past became deeply entrenched in the Western imagination. Likewise, the Hebrew Bible told of a lost paradise in the Garden of Eden, and many thinkers of the Judeo-Christian tradition have envisioned a messianic kingdom in which the harmony and virtue of the lost paradise would be regained.

Plato's *Republic* (written about 360 B.C.E.) is the first great work that gives an extended description of an ideal social order. Plato's utopia was based on a division of labor into four classes: the rulers would have complete control over legislative and deliberative functions; under them, the auxiliaries would have executive and military responsibilities; the majority of citizens would have productive duties in agriculture and industry; slaves would perform the most menial of tasks. The guardians of the society would have authority to determine what the common citizens were expected to read and think, and the guardians would also control eugenic breeding in the interest of the common good. The philosopher-king would stand at the apex of society and would exemplify the virtuous and wise guardian; presumably his training in philosophy would prevent any abuse of power. Plato argued that a division into social classes was just since it was based on the natural capabilities of different people, and that this division would promote the general happiness based on the virtuous exercise of natural gifts. To ensure that members of the ruling class would promote the common good rather than pursue their private interests, they were not to be allowed to be members of private families or to possess private property. It is uncertain to what extent Plato believed these utopian conceptions were practical and achievable.

From Plato to Thomas More, a number of utopian schemes appeared from time to time. Plutarch's life of Lycurgus (written about 100 C.E.) tells of the mythical founder of a communal society of ancient Sparta, and portrays Lycurgus as an enlightened legislator who redistributed property, abolished gold, eliminated great wealth, and organized a system of selective breeding and communal education, all on behalf of the common good. St. Augustine's *The City of God* (written about 426 C.E.) looks upon the Christian Church as God's representative on earth; this assumption prompted later Christians to speculate about a future millennium of happiness within a theocratic kingdom. In the twelfth century, Joachim of Fiore prophesied a future "Age of the Spirit" when Christians and infidels would unite in harmonious brotherhood.

Thomas More's imagination was stimulated by the European voyages of discovery as well as the climate of opinion of the Renaissance. His famous book, *Utopia* (1516), purported to describe an ideal society found on an island in the Americas. More used a number of Greek puns to let informed readers know that he was not describing an actual place: The island "Utopia" means "no place," the river Anider means "no water," the city Amanote means "dream town," and the name of the narrator, Raphael Hythloday, means "dispenser of nonsense." To add realism, it was said that Hythloday had traveled to the island Utopia on a voyage with Amerigo Vespucci. Hythloday often compared Utopia to Plato's ideal society, and claimed that the Utopians did not have any poverty or scarcity, were not interested in private wealth, practiced a form of primitive communism, lived in houses that were simple and lacking in luxury, and ate their meals in groups of thirty households. The society was cooperative rather than competitive, and the young were always respectful of the old. Some aspects of Utopia, however, were less than perfect. The legal system was often harsh, and slave labor was widely used. While it is clear that More was writing a critique of many aspects of European society that he disliked, it is often uncertain when More was advocating his social preferences. For example, the Utopians practiced religious toleration, but when he became chancellor of England thirteen years later, More did not show any interest in such a policy.

During the seventeenth century, utopian works tended to glorify the increasing progress in science and technology. Tommaso Campanella's *The City of the Sun* (1623) envisioned a society in which scientific knowledge benefited humanity, and in spite of his experiences with the Inquisition, he looked forward to a universal Christian monarchy. Campanella combined astronomy with the scientific theories of Galileo, and, in contrast to More, he did not see any need for the family. Sir Francis Bacon's *New Atlantis* (1627) gave a less fanciful picture of a society improved by advances in science and technology, and his description of the House of Solomon, a research institute that advanced knowledge through cooperation among scientists, was partially realized with the organization of the Royal Society in 1660. James Harrington's *Commonwealth of Oceana* (1656) was an even more realistic version of a good society; attacking ideas of divine-right monarchy and religious intolerance, he advocated limits on land ownership, a division of political power, a written constitution, and the principle of rotation of office.

In the nineteenth century, the two more prominent utopian writers were Edward Bellamy and William Morris. Bellamy's best-selling book *Looking Backward* (1888) gave an account of how Julian West slept from 1887 to the year 2000, to awaken to a new world of political and economic equality based on socialism and brotherly love. Capitalists and workers had managed to settle their differences in a peaceful, orderly, evolutionary manner. *Looking Backward* was one of the most influential books ever published, and Bellamy's followers organized Nationalist Clubs in many countries. William Morris, a talented artist and agrarian socialist, was in agreement with many of Bellamy's goals, but he strongly disagreed with Bellamy's positive view of urbanization and modern industry. Morris' alternative vision in *News from Nowhere* (1891) described a largely pastoral community without large cities or large industrial organizations. In Morris' utopia, people had gradually learned to make goods in enjoyable and satisfying ways, and this return to craftsmanship had produced a renewal of art.

While there have been many utopian writings in the twentieth century, they generally have not had the influence of the works of earlier centuries. H. G. Wells's *A Modern Utopia* (1905) looked to the utopian ideas of the past, and envisioned the possibility of a world state in the hands of an elite called the Samurai, a highly educated group required to lead a Spartan way of life. His other utopian work, *Men Like Gods* (1923), was more optimistic about the prospects that a peaceful utopia could be built on the foundation of universal education. Probably the most famous utopian work of the twentieth century, B. F. Skinner's *Walden Two* (1948), presents a vision of a harmonious community in which the behavior of its members has been psychologi- cally conditioned according to the principles of positive reinforcement. Although their behavior presumably was determined by Skinner's methods, the members of the community had the illusion of exercising freedom and autonomy. The protagonist of the book, Frazier, explained that the key to utopia was to train members to wish to do what was in their common interest.

In much of the twentieth century, positive utopias appear to have been less prominent than nightmarish visions of anti-utopia, or dystopia. Aldous Huxley's *Brave New World* (1932) pictured the twenty-fifth century as a time in which industrial production and inhumane efficiency had replaced almost all notions of human freedom and justice. Even humans were mass-produced to serve the needs of the state, and sentiments of love and altruism had become a distant memory. George Orwell's *1984* (1948) described a totalitarian order in which every room had a two-way television so that Big Brother would be able to monitor every conversation. The government exercised strict control over personal lives and culture, including selective breeding and the rewriting of history. Orwell, a liberal, was warning about the modern dangers that he believed were most clearly exemplified in Nazi Germany and Stalinist Russia.

Applications

The term "utopianism" usually refers to a form of imaginative literature rather than concrete attempts to apply utopian ideas, but over the years there have been social projects that can be described by the term. Many such projects have been inspired by religious ideas, such as the simple communism practiced by some early Christians. Medieval monasteries, for example, were attempts to build communities that practiced altruism and cooperation, without the distraction of private property or family attachments. In the early fifteenth century, the radical followers of John Huss organized a form of communism in the Bohemian town of Tabor, until they were defeated by an army of noblemen and business leaders. Two centuries later in England, a radical group known as Levelers advocated an extreme form of equality, and the followers of Gerrard Winstanley, called the Diggers, organized several communities that practiced communism until mob violence put an end to the experiment in 1650.

The nineteenth century witnessed numerous attempts to create utopian communes, both secular and religious. Robert Owen, author of *A New View of Society* (1813), provided good housing and education for the workers of his textile business at New Lanark, Scotland. In 1827, Owen purchased the large facilities built by the followers of George Rapp in Indiana, but this idealistic enterprise, called New Harmony, failed after numerous disagreements among the members. Many people were shocked by Owen's opposition to organized religion, the nuclear family, and private property. Despite its failure, New Harmony became an inspiration for later attempts to found utopian communities. One of Owen's followers, Joseph Warren, formulated a doctrine of "Individual Sovereignty," which emphasized individual freedom from restraint and the use of vouchers in place of money. Warren organized two small communities, one called Utopia in Ohio and another called Modern Times on Long Island. In spite of their lack of organization, they appeared to operate fairly successfully for a number of years.

Among the religious communities, the most successful were those organized by the Shakers, followers of Mother Ann Lee. By the middle of the century, there were some six thousand members organized into eighteen communities. The Shakers renounced private property, practiced celibacy, conducted ecstatic religious ceremonies, and worked diligently at producing simple but beautiful furniture. More controversial were the Perfectionists, who were disciples of John Humphrey Noyes. Noyes taught that humanity's original innocence could be regained through a religious experience, and he organized a communal society without private property or individual families at Oneida, New York. The most publicized aspect of the Oneida community was its practice of complex marriage, a form of free love based on mutual consent. For many years the community's silverware business was a success, but by 1879, internal dissension and outside hostility had become so strong that Noyes fled to Canada.

In the twentieth century, the various Marxist-Leninist forms of government can be considered as utopian experiments. Both Marx and Lenin wrote of an advanced stage of communism in which there would be a classless society based on the principle, "from each according to his ability, to each according to his needs." Marx described this society as based on an economy of abundance in which all work was voluntary, and with the workers themselves in control, the state would wither away. Spokespeople for the Soviet Union never claimed that they had progressed beyond the stage of mature socialism, but as late as the 1970's, Leonid Brezhnev spoke of moving toward communism and building a just and free society. Even more, Mao Tse-tung looked to a rapid realization of communism when he launched the Cultural Revolution in 1966. By the 1980's, however, the economic realities under Marxist-Leninist systems were increasingly bleak, resulting in compromises with private property and other nonsocialistic practices. By 1991, the Soviet Union and all of Eastern Europe had repudiated the Marxist-Leninist approach to government and economics, and most socialist countries appeared to be headed in the same direction.

Context

At least since the beginning of recorded history, visionaries have dreamed of a world without poverty, suffering, or conflict. Among such visionaries, many utopian thinkers have tried to formulate their dreams into a systematic account. The many different forms of utopian vision have had little in common with one another, except that most have included the values of equality, harmony, and prosperity. All social reformers have a vision for a better future, and it is often impossible to make a sharp distinction between the practical reformer and the unrealistic utopianist. In the eighteenth century, for example, people often looked upon opponents of slavery as utopian dreamers, but from the perspective of the twentieth century, the abolitionists appear to have been advocates of idealistic reform that was in step with the forces of history.

It is often said that a document such as the Declaration of Independence of 1776 expresses a utopian vision, because no society has ever achieved the optimum realization of social equality or the rights of "life, liberty, and the pursuit of happiness." A close reading of the declaration, however, reveals that Thomas Jefferson understood that these ideals would never be fully realized, and that in writing the document, he referred to these ideals primarily to justify the fact that the thirteen states were seceding from the British Empire. Although Jefferson was a man with a moral vision for improving the status quo, he was never a utopian thinker. One can contrast Jefferson's call for modest change with Marx's vision of a communist society in which liberated citizens during a single day would have unlimited freedom to move from one profession to another, to go fishing or hunting, and then to engage in after-dinner discussions of social philosophy. While Jefferson's call for change was always grounded in the reality of his day, Marx's utopian fantasies often have the same flavor one encounters in Thomas More's *Utopia*.

There is controversy about whether utopianism has been good or bad in its consequences. Those who agree with the first position usually argue that improvements in social relations do not occur without the inspiration of high ideals, and that imagination can provide a stimulus for progress. Those who fear the dangers of utopianism point out that utopian thinkers have often been unwilling to make compromises with their vision of the good, and that many utopian thinkers minimize the concept of human freedom, especially the freedom for anyone who might wish to promote an alternative vision of a good society. Generalizations on both sides tend to minimize the great diversity among the utopian thinkers over the centuries. Although most utopian thinkers have tended to accept some degree of stifling conformism, there have been many exceptions. Utopian fantasies of the past have yielded both good and bad results, and it is likely that the same will be true in the future.

Bibliography

Berneri, Marie Louise. *Journey Through Utopia*. London: Routledge & Kegan Paul, 1950. Excellent description and assessment of the most important utopian writers from Plato to Aldous Huxley. Raised as an anarchist, Berneri emphasizes the intolerant and authoritarian aspects of utopian visions, especially in Marxism.

Bowman, Sylvia, et al. *Edward Bellamy Abroad: An American Prophet's Influence*. New York: Twayne, 1962. Good analysis of Bellamy's life and work, with much material about the Nationalist Societies and their influence throughout the world.

Levitas, Ruth. *The Concept of Utopia*. Syracuse, N.Y.: Syracuse University Press, 1990. Scholarly study in the history of ideas, with an emphasis on visionaries of the twentieth century. Levitas views utopianism as a positive inspiration for a better way of life.

Manuel, Frank, and Fritzie Manuel. *Utopian Thought in the Western World*. Cambridge, Mass.: Belknap Press of Harvard University Press, 1979. Monumental and scholarly study of intellectual history from the ancient Greeks to Herbert Marcuse. Recognizes both the positive and negative aspects of utopianism.

Mumford, Lewis. *The Story of Utopias*. New York: Boni and Liveright, 1922. With this pioneering but still useful work, Mumford looks at both the contributions and dangers of utopian visions of escape and reconstruction, arguing that reconstructionist visions often have been beneficial influences for change.

Negley, Glenn, and J. Max Patrick, eds. *The Quest for Utopia: An Anthology of Imaginary Societies*. New York: Henry Schuman, 1952. Collection of excerpts with good introductory essays to about thirty works. The editors write that utopian visions are noble aspirations that have promoted progress.

Popper, Karl. *The Open Society and Its Enemies*. 5th ed., 2 vols. Princeton, N.J.: Princeton University Press, 1966. Classic attack on the utopian theories of Plato and Karl Marx, with Popper's plea for piecemeal reform rather than utopian engineering.

Tod, Ian, and Michael Wheeler. *Utopia*. New York: Harmony Books, 1978. Concise and interesting account of both literary works and utopian experiments. The writers emphasize architecture and anticipations in the past that have occurred, and include many excellent illustrations.

Thomas T. Lewis

Cross-References

Anarchism, p. 66; Anarchism in Marxist Thought, p. 72; General Will, p. 745; Idealism, p. 855; Marxism-Leninism, p. 1155; Neo-Idealism, p. 1287; Plato's Political Philosophy, p. 1396; Political Philosophy, p. 1505; Positivism, p. 1557; Postmodernism, p. 1570; Radicalism, p. 1661; Religion and Politics, p. 1685; Revolutionary Governments, p. 1725; Totalitarianism, p. 1987.

THE VATICAN

Field of study: Religion and government

As the official residence of the pope, who is the supreme authority of the Roman Catholic church, the Vatican is the center of Roman Catholic government throughout the world. It also exists as an independent political entity that is represented by diplomats throughout the world, and it is an important player on the international stage.

Principal terms

COLLEGE OF CARDINALS: assembly of cardinals of the Roman Catholic church, who elect the new pope upon the death of the reigning one

CURIA: curia romana (literally the Roman Court), the administrative arm of the Vatican

PAPAL STATES: secular territories ruled by the popes until the unification of Italy in 1870

POPE: supreme leader of the Roman Catholic church; technically, the pope's official title is bishop of Rome

SEE: territory of a bishop; the Holy See is the title given to the territory ruled by the bishop of Rome, so the term is often synonymous with the Vatican

Overview

Nestled on 109 acres in the heart of the city of Rome, the Vatican is a small, independent nation and the headquarters of the Roman Catholic church. In theory and tradition, although not always in practice, the Roman Catholic church is an absolute monarchy, with the pope, an elected monarch, having final decision on matters both spiritual and temporal. The organization and operation of the Vatican reflects this view, as tempered and refined by the millennia.

According to ancient tradition, the first bishop of Rome was Peter, regarded as the leader of the twelve Apostles who had accompanied Christ during his ministry. According to Catholic interpretation of Matthew 9:18, Peter was singled out by Christ to be the leader of the church. Martyred during the reign of the Emperor Nero, Peter is considered to have been the first pope, and successive popes have continued what is known as the apostolic succession—an unbroken line that connects today's pope to the original apostles.

Over the course of centuries, it has become the doctrine of the Roman Catholic church that the election of the pope by the college of cardinals is divinely inspired and directed by the Holy Spirit, the third personage of the Trinity. It is thus assured that the supreme pontiff, as the pope is sometimes known, has a power and authority beyond those of merely secular monarchs or other heads of state. In this sense, the Vatican is an absolute monarchy, one in which the concepts of "church" and "state" are indissolubly intermixed.

From late classical times onward, the growth of the power of the pope and the church necessitated the expansion of church government and bureaucracy. The church's loss of secular territory and power, which took place in the nineteenth century, did not reduce the need for this bureaucracy so much as change it. Much of the bureaucracy is contained in the Vatican, which is both the physical location of the government of the Catholic church and an independent nation.

The centerpiece of the ruling structure of the Roman Catholic church is the college of cardinals, formally established during the 1100's. According to church law, the cardinals of the Holy Roman church constitute the senate of the pope and aid him as his chief counselors and collaborators in church government. The college has two main duties: the election of a new pope upon the death of the incumbent and the administration of the church. Cardinals within the Vatican play an immensely important part in church operations.

Upon the death of a pope, the cardinals of the church are summoned to Rome to meet in order to select his successor. This meeting, known as a conclave, is held in the Sistine Chapel, famous for Michelangelo's frescoes, and there the cardinals from around the world are locked away until they have elected a new pope by a two-thirds plus one majority, with no cardinal permitted to vote for himself. The office of the papacy is for life, and, with only one known exception, no pope has ever abdicated.

The power of the Roman Catholic church and the Vatican resides, ultimately, in the pope himself. Since the late nineteenth century the pope has been held, officially, to be infallible when speaking *ex cathedra* ("from the chair") in matters of doctrine, and papal encyclicals and other documents have a profound impact not only on the activities of the faithful but on secular governments as well, especially regarding their social policies and laws.

Actual administrative operations of the church in general and the Vatican in particular are conducted by another institution, which dates to the eleventh century, the curia romana, most often known simply as the curia. The curia is divided into a number of departments that handle various interests of the church, including diplomatic, administrative, doctrinal, and professional.

The most important of these departments is the Secretariat of State, with the cardinal secretary of state serving the pope as a sort of prime minister and chief of staff, as well as acting as the head of the Vatican's diplomatic service. The Vatican plays a major role in international relations, and its representatives in nations throughout the world often conduct behind-the-scenes roles in sensitive negotiations.

Under the Secretariat of State are ten congregations, which are essentially cabinet-level departments handling the operations of the Vatican. Some of these congregations are concerned with religious and doctrinal issues. Others tackle administrative and procedural subjects, such as those that deal with bishops, clergy, religious and secular institutions, and Catholic education. Finally, there are departments established to meet specific situations, such as the Congregation on Oriental Churches, which deals with those churches that hold to the Eastern rite version of Catholicism.

The curia also includes a number of courts, or tribunals, which adjudicate matters that fall within church or canonical law. The Sacred Apostolic Penitentiary, which began sometime before the twelfth century, is concerned with special cases falling under church law, such as favors, absolutions, dispensations, and the use of indulgences, especially among the clergy. The Sacred Roman Rota is the best known of these, and is almost exclusively occupied with reviewing cases regarding dissolving marriages, which is necessary since the Catholic church does not accept the concept of divorce. Finally, there is the Supreme Tribunal of the Apostolic Segnatura, which functions as a version of a Vatican Supreme Court, hearing appeals from the other tribunals.

Much work of the Vatican is accomplished through an array of councils, commissions, and committees, established by the popes and lodged within the curia. Some of these groups include nonclergy, including some at the executive level. They often have considerable influence on church policy.

Administrative duties are handled by the offices of the curia. The Prefecture for the Economic Affairs of the Holy See, for example, corresponds to the treasury departments of other nations. It supervises the influential Vatican Bank. The Prefecture of the Papal Household is the largest of these offices; it conducts the daily business of the Vatican. Finally, there is an important office, technically outside the curia and answerable only to the pope: the Palatine Administration, which oversees the Vatican Library, the Secret Archives, the Vatican Printing Press, and the *L'Osservatore Romano*, the Vatican's highly respected semiofficial newspaper.

Applications

World War II was a period of great delicacy and danger for the Vatican. Set in the very heart of Fascist Italy, which, along with imperial Japan, was one of Nazi Germany's two principal allies, the Vatican was officially neutral. Its physical integrity and moral authority supposedly was respected, or at least recognized, by both sides in the struggle. In actuality, while the Vatican had reached an accommodation with the Italian government through the Concordat of 1929, it was at odds with Adolf Hitler's Germany, and in 1937 the reigning pope, Pius XI, had published his encyclical *Mit brenneder Sorge* ("With Burning Concern"), which condemned Nazi attacks on the church, clergy, and believers.

The successor of Pius XI, Eugenio Pacelli, took the name of Pius XII upon his election to the papacy in 1939. Equally opposed to the horrors of Nazi brutality and the threat of Communist atheism, Pius XII recognized, at the outbreak of the war, that the Holy See would have to steer a difficult course of political neutrality to achieve its goal of moral redemption among the belligerent nations. Accordingly, the entire structure of the Catholic church was placed in the difficult, often dangerous, position of aiding those most injured and endangered by the conflict, especially the Jews. This assistance, while ordered by the pope, was given largely in clandestine or unofficial fashion, and this, coupled with the fact that official church commentary on the struggle was usually cautiously phrased, caused many to accuse the pope and the church government of ignoring the plight of those suffering under Nazi tyranny.

In truth, during the war, the widespread diplomatic corps of the Vatican gathered vast amounts of information about prisoners of war, refugees, and missing persons, and passed this information along to governments, relief agencies, and families. In addition, it mounted unprecedented efforts in cooperation with international voluntary agencies to provide medicine, food, and clothing to the millions displaced by the global conflict. All of these were the result of the policy adapted and implemented under the direction of Pius XII, and provide clear indications of how the government of the Roman Catholic church still functions, in many ways, in the fashion of an absolute monarchy.

While the courage of the policy of Pius XII can be debated, there is clear evidence of its effectiveness. During the war, 90 percent of the Roman Jews were saved—many of them hidden in Church facilities, others spirited away to safety in the countryside. By contrast, in The Netherlands, where the Catholic clergy courageously, even boldly, spoke out against the Nazi atrocities, almost 80 percent of the Dutch Jews were eliminated. This would seem to suggest that the pope's clandestine approach, combined with quiet diplomacy, might have been the better of the two approaches.

Diplomacy is traditionally one of the strongest and most important aspects of Vatican activities, and its official representatives, who serve in countries throughout the world, are respected as among the most professional and effective in their field. The hallmarks of Vatican diplomacy include a high degree of intelligence and tact, a well-honed skill at dealing with difficult situations (such as those that existed during the reign of the Communist Party in eastern Europe), and small delegations whose abilities and influence are greater than their size would suggest.

True to church tradition, Vatican diplomats, known collectively as legates, are divided into a variety of ranks, with subtle distinctions between them. A nuncio, which comes from the Latin word for "announcer," is a permanent diplomatic officer, with the rank of ambassador, stationed at the capital of a country. In nations in which Catholicism is the predominant religion, the nuncio is automatically and traditionally accorded the rank of dean of the diplomatic corps.

In non-Catholic countries, the Vatican's representative is known as a pronuncio. The office and service are essentially the same, except that a pronuncio is not automatically the leader of a capital's diplomatic corps. Internuncios have the status of ministers, appointed to represent the Vatican at a nation, often with a specific mission to be accomplished.

For nations that do not have official diplomatic ties to the Vatican, apostolic delegates can be assigned to act as channels of communication and as unofficial liaisons. Until the United States opened formal diplomatic relations with the Vatican in 1984, relationships between the two nations were conducted through the apostolic delegate in Washington, D.C.

Context
During the early days of Christianity, when the faith was small, scattered, and insignificant, the role of the papacy was primarily pastoral and religious. As the church

grew in adherents and strength, however, the bishops of Rome began to assert their primacy, especially in matters of church doctrine and belief. By the time of the reign of Emperor Constantine the Great (288?-337 C.E.), who made Christianity the official religion of the Roman Empire, the church was a significant influence in official public life as well as religious activities. When Constantine left Rome to establish Constantinople (modern Istanbul) as his capital, the popes were left as de facto rulers of Rome.

According to some historians, the Donation of Pepin, a grant from the French King to Pope Stephen II in 754, established the Papal States. These were specific areas in Italy, centered about Rome, where the pope ruled as a secular monarch. During the Middle Ages and even more so during the Renaissance, the pope took on a dual role as both a spiritual leader and as a secular prince who ruled over subjects, collected taxes, raised armies, and waged wars. Some popes of the Renaissance, such as Julius II (1503-1513), became more renowned for their military exploits and diplomatic coups than their spiritual leadership. The Reformation was, at least in some part, a reaction against the church's involvement in secular affairs.

Later developments over the course of centuries diminished the church's overtly secular powers and reduced its territory. By the time of Italian reunification, the Papal States were a relatively small territory immediately adjacent to Rome, and in 1870 they were forcibly incorporated into Italy. In protest, the popes retreated into the Vatican, and it was not until 1929 that a concordat between the church and Italy established Vatican City as the world's smallest independent state. The pope obtained a secular territory minute in relationship to its international importance.

The influence of the Vatican is immense because the power and authority of the Roman Catholic church, a truly global institution, is felt on both the spiritual and political planes. The pronouncements of the pope on secular matters such as labor relations, economic fairness, and race relations are considered as carefully as his religious and doctrinal considerations. The Vatican news media has influence throughout the world, while representatives of the Vatican, traditionally the dean of the diplomatic corps in predominantly Catholic countries, are everywhere recognized as skilled and knowledgeable diplomats. Although small in territory, the Vatican remains large in influence.

Bibliography

Hebblethwaite, Peter. *In the Vatican*. Bethesda, Md.: Adler & Adler, 1986. Informal but informative volume about the inner workings of the Vatican, with a focus on the time after the second Vatican council.

Holmes, J. Derek. *The Papacy in the Modern World, 1914-1978*. New York: Crossroad, 1981. Contains much relevant information for the period it covers. As might be expected, it emphasizes the decisions of the popes rather than the bureaucracy that implemented those decisions.

Murphy, Francis X. *The Papacy Today*. New York: Macmillan, 1981. Provides insight into the relationship between the pope and the organizations that translate his will into action.

Nichols, Peter. *The Politics of the Vatican*. New York: Praeger, 1968. Reviews the influence that the Roman Catholic church has had in world affairs from the time of Constantine to the middle of the twentieth century.

Packard, Jerrold M. *Peter's Kingdom: Inside the Papal City*. New York: Charles Scribner's Sons, 1985. Overview of the operations of the Vatican as a religious body and as a government. Useful starting place for the student of Vatican affairs.

Michael Witkoski

Cross-References

Church and Government in History, p. 230; Church Government, p. 241; Liberation Theology, p. 1124; Religion and Politics, p. 1685; Theocracy, p. 1968; Thomas Aquinas' Political Philosophy, p. 1974.

VETO POWER

Field of study: Politics

Veto power is the constitutional authority that the president of the United States uses to prevent congressional enactments from becoming law.

Principal terms
BICAMERAL: having two houses or chambers
LINE-ITEM VETO: power to veto individual sections or lines of a bill; some state governors have this power
OFFICE OF MANAGEMENT AND BUDGET: presidential staff agency, part of the Executive Office of the White House; gives bill-signing advice to the president through its central legislative clearance process
POCKET VETO: if Congress has adjourned for the term during the ten-day period within which the president has to consider a bill, it does not become law if he does not sign it
PRESENTMENT CLAUSE: every bill passed by Congress must be "presented" to the president before it can become a law, as stated in Article 1, section 7, clause 2, of the Constitution
SINE DIE: final adjournment at the end of a congressional session; from the Latin for "without day"

Overview

"Veto" is a Latin word that means "I forbid." The veto power is one of the checks and balances found within the United States Constitution, in this case, a partial check on the power of Congress. The earliest known formal governmental use of this power was in the Roman Empire, in which the tribunes of the people could nullify decrees of the senate or the proceedings of the magistrates by saying the word "veto."

The delegates to the U.S. Constitutional Convention of 1787 were anxious to prevent any of the three principal branches of the proposed new government from encroaching on the independence and powers of the other branches and from exercising oppressive or authoritarian power. At the convention, James Madison urged that each branch of the government be given both constitutional and political means of restraining the others. The Constitution's granting of veto power to the president establishes the single most important limit on the exercise of power by the United States Congress. Alexander Hamilton commented in Federalist No. 73 that the veto power "not only serves as a shield to the Executive, but it furnishes an additional security against the enaction of improper laws. It establishes a salutary check upon the legislative body. . . ." Madison, also an author of the Federalist Papers, believed that the legislative branch with its broad lawmaking powers would inevitably attempt to encroach on the independence of the executive, both politically and constitutionally. Thus the primary purpose of the veto was to help maintain the independence of the executive branch from Congress. That the veto also furnished the president with a useful political tool was an additional benefit.

The veto provisions of the Constitution were carefully drafted. The Constitution explicitly prevents Congress from avoiding or evading the president's veto power. The "presentment clause" requires that bills be presented to the president, as well as "every order, resolution or vote to which the concurrence of the Senate and House of Representatives may be necessary (except on a question of adjournment)." The president is constitutionally empowered to consider and pass on any congressional measure that has the potential to become law.

The actual operation of the veto power is simple. If the president approves the bill or resolution that has been presented, the president signs it and it becomes law. If the president disapproves of the measure, it may be returned to the house of Congress in which it was initiated, with a separate veto message setting forth the president's objections to the bill. Congress may then reconsider it, and if both houses pass it again by a two-thirds majority it becomes law. In this case, the president's veto is said to be overridden. If the president does not act on a measure within ten days, Sundays excepted, it becomes a law without a signature. If, however, Congress has adjourned *sine die* in the interim, it does not become a law. In this case, the bill is said to be "pocket vetoed."

There have been few important constitutional issues regarding the veto or the pocket veto. One issue that arose several times was whether the president can pocket veto a bill when Congress is in a short recess or only at the final adjournment at the end of the congressional session. The United States Court of Appeals for the District of Columbia settled this question in *Kennedy v. Sampson and Jones* (1974). President Richard M. Nixon had refused to sign the Family Practice of Medicine Act of 1970 and instructed the Administrator of General Services not to publish it as a law. He claimed that the bill was pocket vetoed because Congress had recessed for the Christmas holidays during the ten-day constitutional period immediately after the bill had passed. Both courts that considered the issue decided against President Nixon's claim. By the time the Court of Appeals rendered its opinion in the case, Nixon had already resigned and his successor, President Gerald Ford, declined to appeal to the Supreme Court.

The Constitutional Convention expected that Congress would be the dominant branch of the government. As the representative or popularly elected branch, Congress was supposed to reflect the public's political will better than the other two branches. Consequently, there was some doubt in the early years of the republic whether the veto power should be used unless the president believed a bill to be unconstitutional. This issue was fought out during George Washington's presidency. Although Washington established the precedent that a bill could be vetoed for political reasons alone, vetoes were infrequent until the administration of President Andrew Jackson. The first six presidents vetoed six bills altogether. Jackson vetoed twelve, strengthening his administration's political influence with Congress. Jackson's most celebrated veto was that of the bill to recharter the Second Bank of the United States in July, 1832. This veto, together with the withdrawal of federal funds the following year, effectively brought the bank down. Jackson's free use of the veto established it as a powerful tool of presidential leadership. Later presidents followed Jackson's example. Often the mere threat of a presidential veto can influence policy.

The most important reason for the veto's political potency is that Congress can rarely muster the two-thirds majority required in each chamber to override a veto. Franklin D. Roosevelt, president from 1933 to 1945, vetoed 635 bills—more than any other president. Only nine of his vetoes were overturned by Congress, in part because Roosevelt was very popular and always had Democratic majorities in both the Senate and House of Representatives. Even a less popular president such as Richard Nixon was able to make his veto stick most of the time. During his five and a half years in office, Nixon vetoed forty-three bills. He was only overridden seven times, despite facing opposition party control of both houses and, after the unveiling of the Watergate scandal, growing unpopularity and distrust. President George Bush, a Republican, was able to sustain forty-four of his forty-five vetoes, again in spite of Democratic control of both houses during all four years of his administration. Presidents John F. Kennedy and Lyndon Johnson issued fifty-one vetoes between them; not one was overridden.

The difficulty of overriding the veto is a decided political asset for a president. Yet the veto power is negative in character; it can prevent but not create. Although the president may prevail on a particular issue and make Congress shape a bill in accordance with his or her views, the president has no power to force Congress to pass a bill that it does not want. When President Bush threatened to veto the Civil Rights Bill of 1991 if it contained employment quotas, Congress left quotas out despite majority support for the quota plan. On the other hand, President Bush entirely failed to persuade Congress to pass several key elements of his domestic program: The veto power did not help him get his legislative program through Congress.

Some political scientists argue that the veto is actually a sign of presidential weakness, not strength. The power is only used when Congress has refused to accept a president's views on an issue. For example, the frequency with which President Gerald Ford used the veto from 1974 to 1976 was a strong indication that Congress did not accept Ford's leadership. Ford vetoed sixty-six bills and was overridden twelve times.

Another important limitation on the veto power is its relative uselessness on fiscal and budgetary issues. Congress normally passes a single comprehensive appropriations bill and a few supplemental appropriations bills for each fiscal year. The president is unlikely to veto an entire bill simply because of dislike for one part of it. This weakness of the veto is all the more galling to presidents when Congress attaches irrelevant "riders" to appropriations bills. For example, after President Jimmy Carter vetoed a bill providing for increased salaries for Public Health Service physicians, Congress added the pay raise to mental health services legislation, a pet project of First Lady Rosalyn Carter. The president then signed the bill.

For these reasons, some presidents have argued for a line-item veto—the power to strike out particular parts of a bill that has passed. To establish such a power for the president might require a constitutional amendment, although it may be constitutionally possible for Congress to make most federal spending discretionary for the president, rather than mandatory. Yet as the twentieth century neared its end, Congress showed little disposition to grant the president either of these powers.

Applications

The first purpose of the veto for the Framers of the Constitution was to give presidents a tool to defend their office and themselves from encroachments on their power by the legislature. Congress has made many attempts to limit presidential power, especially in the areas of appointments, budgeting, and military powers. The veto power has been used, successfully on the whole, to prevent encroachment on the executive office. There have also been some dramatic examples of congressional attempts to limit presidential power in which the veto has been overridden. During the struggle over Reconstruction policy after President Abraham Lincoln's death, Congress passed the Tenure in Office Act in 1867. This act provided that the president—then Andrew Johnson, Lincoln's successor—needed the approval of the Senate to dismiss from the administration any officer who had been appointed with the consent of the Senate. This act would have crippled the president's ability to impose his policy on his own executive branch. President Johnson vetoed the act, but his veto was overridden. Johnson immediately dismissed Secretary of War Edwin Stanton, thus openly violating the act. For this "crime" Johnson was impeached, but the effort to convict him in the Senate failed by one vote. The struggle's outcome confirmed the president's control over his own administration. The veto itself had not been enough to protect the presidency, but Congress's inability to enforce the act in the subsequent impeachment proceedings produced the same effect.

The War Powers Act of 1973 was another congressional attempt to restrain presidential power. It had been learned in 1971 that presidents Johnson and Nixon had systematically distorted facts to put the Vietnam War in a more favorable light. Congress then passed the War Powers Act to prevent future presidential wars. President Nixon vetoed the act, but Congress overrode his veto. Every U.S. president from Nixon to Clinton has claimed that the act violates his constitutional powers. Nearly all these presidents have actually refused to obey the act's requirement that Congress be formally consulted before the commitment of U.S. troops to hostilities. In the absence of the political will in Congress to enforce the act, it will remain meaningless.

The veto also has been widely used by presidents attempting to protect their political programs. Most have been successful. From 1789 to 1993, presidents vetoed 1,476 bills; only 104 of these vetoes were overridden—about 7 percent. In addition to Andrew Jackson's veto of the bank recharter, another notable policy veto was President Harry S Truman's rejection of the Taft-Hartley Labor Relations Act of 1947. The veto was overridden by Congress. Truman's subsequent refusal to invoke the Taft-Hartley Act during the Korean War set the stage for an important test of the president's constitutional authority in wartime in *Youngstown Sheet and Tube Company v. Sawyer* (1952).

In practice, presidents cannot be familiar with all the legislation before Congress. They are assisted in their study of bills that have passed or are about to pass by the Office of Management and Budget (OMB), which is part of the Executive Office of the White House. This office circulates copies of all enrolled bills to the executive branch units that are affected by them. The agencies have forty-eight hours in which to make a recommendation to the president. These recommendations, accompanied by draft signing or veto statements, are presented by the OMB to the president within the first five days of the ten-day period within which the president must act. Presidents most often accept OMB recommendations to approve bills, but are much less likely to accept a veto recommendation. Most bills that pass have a substantial constituency of some kind supporting them.

Context

The veto power is one of the essential balances that maintain the system of separation of powers in the United States. This incomplete check on legislative power has served to prevent most congressional encroachment on the executive, although its negative nature has prevented presidents from dictating the content of the laws to Congress. Thus, maintenance of the executive's independence from legislative domination has been the great success of the veto power. In the political sense, however, presidents face an uphill battle in dealing with Congress. Their two formal powers—recommending legislation to Congress and vetoing bills—help set the legislature's agenda and prevent some of what presidents oppose from passing, but Congress's law-making power is so formidable that the president's prerogatives are only marginally useful. Conflict between the two political branches of the government is inherent, because of the overlapping powers and differing constituencies of the two institutions. Presidents can influence Congress but can rarely dominate it. The power they need most—a lever to persuade Congress to pass the bills that support their program—does not exist except in the most unusual political situations. It was the emergency of the Great Depression that gave Franklin Roosevelt his initial mastery of Congress. In normal times, the public wish for dramatically successful political leadership from the president seems bound to be unfulfilled.

Bibliography

Cronin, Thomas E. *The State of the Presidency*. 2d ed. Boston: Little, Brown, 1980. Excellent, clear discussion of presidential powers and limitations.

Edwards, George C., III, and Stephen J. Wayne. *Presidential Leadership: Politics and Policy Making*. 3d ed. New York: St. Martin's Press, 1994. General survey of presidential politics with excellent coverage of presidential-public relations and presidential-congressional relations.

Farrand, Max, ed. *The Records of the Federal Convention of 1787*. New Haven: Yale University Press, 1966. Includes all the important records of the Philadelphia convention; especially useful for understanding the range of opinion on the new governmental structure.

Hamilton, Alexander, James Madison, and John Jay. *The Federalist Papers*, edited by Clinton Rossiter. New York: New American Library, 1961. The eighty-five essays of *The Federalist* were originally published in 1788 to promote ratification of the proposed constitution. They are among the most brilliant expositions of U.S. political theory ever published. Numbers 73 through 75 are particularly relevant to understanding presidential powers, including the veto.

Neustadt, Richard E. *Presidential Power: The Politics of Leadership from FDR to Carter*. New York: John Wiley & Sons, 1980. Classic discussion of the limits and potentialities of presidential power.

Spitzer, Robert J. *The Presidential Veto: Touchstone of the American Presidency*. Albany: State University of New York Press, 1988. Discussion of the U.S. president's use of the veto as a policy tool.

Robert Jacobs

Cross-References

VICO'S POLITICAL PHILOSOPHY

Field of study: Political philosophy

The eighteenth century Italian philosopher Giambattista Vico developed a theory about the rise and fall of states that explains how governments come into being through their elaboration of socioeconomic relationships and their development of religious consciousness. A central feature of these processes is the forging of political myths that support law and order and promote the allegiance and obedience of their citizens.

Principal terms

AGE: in Vico's view, a historical cycle or stage characterized by a dominant feature (such as the "Age of Heroes")

BARBARISM: stage of social and cultural development preceding civilization that is characterized by relative disorder

CIVILIZATION: advanced stage of social and cultural development characterized by a high level of political organization

MYTH: narrative about gods or heroes that explains a society's origins, customs, or laws and reveals the society's collective consciousness, particularly through its use of language

MYTHOPEIA: creation of myths

PHILOLOGY: literally the love of literature; a branch of philosophy that seeks to understand culture through language

RECURRENCE: Vico's term for a cyclical historical development that follows the same general patterns in every civil society

Overview

Giambattista Vico (1668-1744) was a native of Naples, Italy, where he lived and died. One of the purest thinkers of his time, his brilliant work went unappreciated until after his death. Even today there is considerable ignorance about the importance of his contributions to the philosophies of history and government. Many people admire Vico, however, for the broad intellectual range, originality, and imaginative penetration that he displayed in his master work, *Principii Scienza Nuova . . . d'intorno alla Comune Natura delle Nazioni (Principles of New Science . . . concerning the Common Nature of the Nations)*, which he published in 1744.

Vico's philology is seen in his persistent search for the origins of social phenomena through words and the ideas that they express. In his own use of words he often preferred their etymological meanings to broader scientific or philosophical interpretations. He liked to focus on the etymon of a word or phrase. For example, in *New Science* he uses the word "principles" to refer to the beginnings of cultural periods or social institutions. His phrase "common nature" designates the fundamental universal characteristics of tribes or nations that are associated with their "births." To Vico, these are the foundations on which civilizations rest. He sees the myths and fables of the folk as their natural languages, which are poetry that he regards as valid accounts of their makers' customs and institutions. In this way he links philology to history and to a culture's social institutions, including government.

Vico was the first philosopher before Johann Gottfried von Herder (1744-1803) to regard mythology as an expression of a nation's wisdom. Other thinkers of the Enlightenment, such as Voltaire, Diderot, and Montesquieu, regarded mythology as born of ignorance and delusion. Vico believed that a mythology represented the collective mind of a folk and revealed important truths about their civilization and culture. His views not only anticipated those of Herder, but also those of the German historian Karl Lamprecht (1856-1915). Lamprecht held that the historical development of any age could only be understood from its collective psychology. Vico thought that a mythology was the product of a peoples' "poetic wisdom" and thus represented their creative genius.

Vico's reconstruction of history is based on the postulate that words and myth are integrally related to the narrative quality of myth and thus operate in the same discourse as language. Myth thus is poetry and a reliable source of history and of the origins of social institutions. The language of myth is a mental construct that expresses the collective mind of a people in the age of gods or heroes during early linguistic development. As such, the language used could not be other than "poetic," and its recorders "poets." Their vocabularies might be small, but their thoughts were sublime. They had to use figurative devices such as metaphor, simile, metonymy, and synecdoche to expand their thoughts. Enhancing their words by the power of imagination, ancient writers originated "poetic characters" (such as gods and heroes) and were mythopoeic, their mythmaking being a product of their "collective intelligence" and their narratives the result of their "poetic wisdom." Hence, according to Vico, history is based mainly on written texts (such a text might actually be a record of oral testimony) rather than on an empirical process dependent on an accumulation of facts.

To Vico, human nature consists of matter and mind. The frontispiece of *New Science* presents an illustration of civil institutions in symbolic form. In the upper-left corner is a seeing eye inside an illuminated triangle, which represents the eye of God, or Providence (this can be compared to the Great Seal of the United States, on which the eye of Providence appears over a pyramid in a triangle surrounded by radiant light; this icon also appears on the reverse of the one-dollar bill). On the lower-right side of Vico's icon is a woman (Lady Metaphysics) contemplating Providence while standing on a celestial globe (Earth), which is supported by an altar (sacrifices to Heaven) on one side only; on the left side is a statue of the theological poet Homer (imaginative power and poetic wisdom). Rays from the eye of God connect with Lady Metaphysics' heart, from which they rebound to connect with Homer. Vico explains that Lady Metaphysics looks upon Providence as above the order of things, which she oversees. He wishes to show the important role God or Providence plays in world history, but without detracting from the exercise of humanity's free will. He believes that only Providence can check people's excessive desires, fiery temperament, and selfish self-love to prevent them from destroying the world.

Vico's "new science" is based on the axiom that theories must start where their subjects begin. It is thus concerned with genesis, or becoming, as reflected by the collective mind of a society. Vico believed that he had to come to terms with how the oldest civilizations emerged from their barbarous origins. To perform this task he tried to penetrate the minds of protomen, who were like wild beasts in the forest, rather than civilized human beings. What caused these primates to become human and civilized? Vico concluded that the minds of these creatures developed a religious consciousness and began to think about divinity or the gods. This religious experience humanized them and allowed them to step across the threshold into civilization. They then began to socialize together in caves and grottoes; they developed sign language, speech, and eventually writing; they entered into contractual marriages and started organized families; and they sacrificed to their gods and buried their dead. Eventually, government and law followed.

As a result of his analyses, Vico proposed that history shows that all nations pass through cycles of birth, maturity, decline, and death. To Vico, human societies neither are mechanisms nor are like organisms; they are organisms—"living organisms." If the key to humanism and civilization is religious myth, the keys to the operation and survival of cultural institutions, such as government and law, are myths that support these institutions through the various cyclical periods of social history. Vico's view of myth includes a "philosophy of authority." This concept is based on the origin of property because the original founders of society also founded property, laws, and customs.

Vico's first cycle of civilization is the "Age of the Gods." It began after protomen developed a sense of divinity and religious worship. In their state of barbarism protomen were stateless and existed as tribes, clans, or hordes until religious consciousness entered their minds. Then their language spoke of the gods and engaged in supplication and oracular discourse.

Vico's second cycle, the "Age of Heroes," began with contractual marriages and the establishment of patriarchal families. Bloodline families were extended when single men wandering alone sought the protection of patriarchs and became their attendants, or *famuli*. When the *famuli* became the *plebs*, or common people, signs of possible revolt were detected by members of the patrician class and they joined together in mutual defense to form the first aristocratic commonwealths. Later the landed-estate "fathers" merged to form the first monarchical government. Language spoke of heroes and courage and of heraldic ceremony and armorial bearings.

Vico's third cycle, the "Age of Men," began when the common people (*plebs*) gained sufficient power to influence the monarchy by the threat of class conflict and possible revolt or revolution. At this point, limited monarchy may result or a revolution may replace the monarchy with a republic and a democracy. The language of men is colloquial and tends to be loose, inexact, ungrammatical, and shoddy. Vico traces the typical course of the gentile nations through these three stages of civilization. The irony is that the Age of Men not only rises to glory for a considerable time, but it inevitably sinks into decadence ending in dissolution and barbarism. Vico considers each of his three ages a "seed time" for the age that follows, but revolution, civil war, foreign invasion, plague, or self-inflicted economic collapse can disrupt or terminate the progress of a cycle.

Applications

In *New Science* Vico accomplishes several important tasks that contribute to human knowledge and speculation. First he lays down an organic cyclical theory of historical processes that recognizes the transcendental power of Providence, whose existence has prompted a religious consciousness in the collective mind of the human race that will serve to curb immorality and prompt people to seek social justice, instead of normal self-interest. Vico's historical organicism and cyclicalism anticipated similar concepts in the German historian Oswald Spengler's remarkable *The Decline of the West* (originally published in German, 1918-1922), which holds that all cultures follow the same patterns of growth and decay, and do so within similar lengths of time—about a thousand years. Spengler also argues that each culture has a unique "soul" and expresses its own forms of art, thought, and action, and that the stages which cultures pass through are marked by identical crises. Spengler, however, does not discuss the role of religion in respect to human morals or survival. That is done by the English historian Arnold Toynbee in his monumental *A Study of History* (ten volumes, 1934-1954), for although Toynbee rejects Spengler's biological concept of civilizations as organisms, he emphasizes the importance of religion in the regulation of human immorality. He attributes the decline of civilizations to their moral transgressions and holds that only a return to some form of catholicism or the invention of a new syncretistic religion can halt such declines.

Vico's respect for mythology and his preference for "*mythos*" (story) over "*logos*" (dictum) led him to produce what *New Science* calls "the first comprehensive study of myth." His genealogical method of investigation allowed him to discover the important function that political myth performed at the beginning of a civilization in sanctioning law and government and the continuing impact that it exercised in the cyclical stages of history. This discovery anticipated the work of the modern French economist and political scientist, Francis Delaisi, whose *Political Myths and Economic Realities* (1925) sees human society as a "living organism." Delaisi proposes that during the course of history various political myths have been invented that sanction the forms of government by guaranteeing legal authority, thus inducing willing obedience among the governed. The myths that Delaisi discusses are the polytheistic, the Christian, the feudal, the papal, the monarchical, and the democratic.

Vico's linkage of language and myth in some ways anticipates the theories of the German linguist Max Müller. Müller's *Essay on Comparative Mythology* (1856) and *Contributions to the Study of Mythology* (1897) see myths as personifications of natural phenomena, with the gods being adjectives that become "names." In this way, Müller conceives of mythology as a "disease of language." Vico's idea that mythology is closely related to language was revived in another form by the German philosopher Ernst Cassirer. Cassirer's *The Philosophy of Symbolic Forms* (1923) proposes that myth, language, and science function together as "symbolic forms" of "mythic thought" that enables people to understand their own nature—and even to understand the order of nature. Although Vico did not follow this latter idea, his researches into myth have led to the most recent view that myth not only constitutes a narrative but is also a mode of apprehending reality. If so, myth may prove to be a structural form of consciousness intersecting the structure of language as an internalized system of rules for expressing an ultimate and comprehensive view of reality.

Context

Vico's *New Science* is wide-ranging, complex, sometimes obscure, and seldom without ambiguities. It is a great intellectual achievement and well worthy of study. It boldly invents the cyclical theory that has been carried on in the modern age by several outstanding thinkers. Vico's notions of "monumental history" and "recurrence" were fundamental to Friedrich Nietzsche, although "recurrence" was conceived of by him in a purely materialistic way. The Russian Nicolai Danilevsky (1822-1885), botanist, economist, and political scientist, presented a theory of the repetition of three sociocultural patterns (historico-cultural type, negative agency, and ethnographic material). Each of his historico-cultural types has unique features not transmissible to peoples of other types. In this connection Danilevsky lays down the important law that a people must enjoy political independence if their potential civilization is to develop. In *The Decline of the West*, Spengler protests against rationalism and linear progressivism, holding that as organisms, cultures are subject to birth, growth, maturity, decline, and death and that decline had already set in in the Western European world. As organisms, too, cultures are morphologically determined, and Spengler proves himself a master at reading the meaning of their forms. Much maligned by academicians, he proved too perceptive, too imaginative, and too unscientific for their liking.

As a political scientist, Vico has shown a people moving from the anarchy of barbarism to political organization and government control. If Vico as a historian respects the concept of the unity of world history in terms of cultural cycles, as a political scientist he has contributed a methodology that extends the field of inquiry to include human nature and to investigate origins and providential destiny.

The many philosophers whom Vico's *New Science* has influenced include Montesquieu, Rousseau, Goethe, Herder, Comte, and Marx. The English poet-philosopher Samuel Taylor Coleridge introduced Vico's work to England, but it was actually the French historian Jules Michelet whose partial translation of *The New Science* saved Vico from obscurity. No doubt astonishing to many, it has been noted that Vico's theories of poetry and language are incorporated in James Joyce's linguistically complex novel *Finnegans Wake* (1939), in which Joyce attempts "a reconstruction of the 'heroic' thought processes."

Bibliography

Adams, Henry P. *The Life and Writings of Giambattista Vico*. London: George Allen & Unwin, 1935. General biography of Vico and critical exposition of his thought, excellently done.

Bedani, Gino. *Vico Revisited: Orthodoxy, Naturalism, and Science in the Scienza Nuova.* Oxford, England: Berg, 1989. Assessment of studies of Vico in English and Italian that concerns principally the topics of the subtitle.

Haddock, B. A. *Vico's Political Thought.* Brymill, Swansea, Great Britain: Mortlake Press, 1986. Examination of how Vico applied technical terms that he learned from rhetoric and law books to his critique of political philosophy, and places him in the broader realm of political theory.

Mali, Joseph. *The Rehabilitation of Myth: Vico's "New Science."* New York: Cambridge University Press, 1992. Argues convincingly that Vico tried to defend myth against the charge that it was false to reality.

Moran, Robert Paul. *Philosophy of History: An Introduction.* New York: Bruce, 1970. Excellent survey of the principal kinds of philosophies of history, with examples of their chief representative—all discussed plainly and accurately.

Richard P. Benton

Cross-References

Commonwealths, p. 364; Democracy, p. 513; Feudalism, p. 688; Government Types, p. 785; History of Government, p. 829; Jurisprudence, p. 1019; Locke's Political Philosophy, p. 1142; Monarchy in History, p. 1221; Montesquieu's Political Philosophy, p. 1228; The Nation-State, p. 1241; Nietzsche's Political Philosophy, p. 1300; Political Myths and the Philosophies of Mosca and Pareto, p. 1474; Political Philosophy, p. 1505; Polity, p. 1545; Religion and Politics, p. 1685; Rousseau's Political Philosophy, p. 1756; The Social Contract, p. 1827.

VOTING BEHAVIOR IN THE UNITED STATES

Field of study: Politics

Voting is the most fundamental political activity in democratic systems. By voting, citizens select representatives and make policy choices to govern themselves. Studies of American voting behavior examine both the act of voting and the policies, attitudes, and behaviors that are behind it.

Principal terms
ELECTORATE: those members of a society who have the right to vote, whether they exercise it or not
LEGITIMACY: feeling within a society that its political leadership and constitutional order are proper for that society
MASS SUFFRAGE: situation in which the right to vote is accorded to most adult members of a society without regard to class status, race or ethnicity, gender, or other demographic characteristics
PARTY IDENTIFICATION: expressed sense of belonging to a political party
VOTER TURNOUT: rate of participation of eligible voters in an election

Overview

Modern scholarship on voting behavior in the United States tends to focus on two areas of inquiry: the causes of voting and the factors that influence the choices made by American voters. Explorations of American voting behavior also attract much debate, about the importance of voting to democratic political systems.

Voting in public elections serves several purposes, not the least of which is to provide for the peaceful transfer of power among political elites. Voting is often seen as the expression of a mandate for governing according to a political platform or agenda, but it is also a measure of political strength among competing political groups. Voting confers legitimacy upon governing elites. It also strengthens the legitimacy of the constitutional order within which political competitions occur. This is particularly true in political systems whose governing elites have expanded mass access to the vote, thereby allowing more elements in a society to make psychological investments in the political system. Finally, within electoral systems characterized by mass suffrage, voting is the single most important peaceful mechanism by which the people as a whole can exercise their self-determination.

While political attitudes of voters and nonvoters within societies do not appear to differ greatly, several other characteristics distinguish voters from nonvoters in the American electorate. For example, individuals with higher levels of education vote at higher rates than do those with lower levels of education. In theory, at least, education allows a person to overcome certain systemic barriers to voting, and it improves a person's ability to deal with complex and conflicting campaign discourse. Furthermore, while individuals with high income levels are more likely to vote than those with low income levels—owing to the wealthy's greater economic stake in the political system—some of the impact of income is diminished by educational differences.

Older Americans tend to vote at higher rates than younger Americans—particularly voters under twenty-five years of age. One explanation for this is that younger voters have yet to establish and appreciate their own stake in the political system. The same argument may partially explain the impact of race and ethnic background on voting behavior. White voter turnout is generally higher than that among African Americans and Hispanics. This may be attributable to a sense of apathy among nonwhites who doubt that their voices will be heard. More important, black voter turnout has yet to overcome the latent effects of past discrimination in civil and voting rights, especially in the South, where the stigma of discrimination is greater and African American voter turnout is lower than in other regions of the country. At the same time, nonwhite turnout is affected by lower levels of socioeconomic status.

Voter turnout generally tends to be lower in the South than in other parts of the country. Among the factors that play a role are the generally lower educational and income levels of Southerners and the history of more restrictive registration require-ments, particularly those affecting African Americans and poor whites. In addition, the traditional paternalism of Southern culture has tended to discourage the involve-ment of women in the electorate.

The 1980's and 1990's have provided some evidence of a gender gap in voter turnout nationwide. During this period women were slightly more likely to vote than were men. This trend is partly explained by increasing levels of education and income among women, by the heightened interest in feminist issues, and by the increasing success of women in winning elective offices and influencing policy decisions.

Party identification appears to have an impact on voter turnout. Citizens who decline to register with any party are the least likely to vote, followed by Democratic identifiers and then Republicans. Whatever advantages the Democratic Party is perceived to enjoy because of its status as the largest party within the electorate are partially nullified by the fact that its partisans are less likely to vote in presidential elections than Republicans are.

Once Americans decide to vote, several factors help determine how they will vote. Using national surveys of individual voters since the early 1950's, students of American voting behavior have divided the determinants of the vote into long-term and short-term forces.

The most prominent long-term force determining voting choices is the party identification of individual voters. While public opinion polls indicate that the Ameri-can electorate has grown less partisan since 1952, party identification still plays a strong role in the voting decisions of those voters who identify with a political party. Those who identify with, or lean toward, either the Democratic or the Republican party tend to vote for their preferred party's candidates. Republican voters exhibit greater loyalty to party candidates than do Democrats, while the partisan preferences of independent voters fluctuate over time.

Another long-term factor in American voting patterns, particularly since the 1960's, is race. While whites have generally tended to vote Republican, by far the most loyal sector of the Democratic electorate includes blacks and other nonwhite voters.

Despite the impact of long-term forces, it is clear that other forces of short-term duration also play important roles in determining American voter choices. Among these short-term forces are voters' perceptions of individual candidates and important issues. Several studies of voter attitudes from the 1950's point to an increase in candidate-centered voting, particularly in the 1980's. Republicans have dominated most presidential elections since the 1950's largely because of positive popular perceptions of their candidates, not because of increasing Republican identification in the electorate or widening acceptance of Republican policy agendas.

While democratic theory focuses upon the importance of voters making decisions on the basis of issues, the reality is that issues are generally less important to predicting the choices of American voters than are either party identification or perceptions of the candidates. Issues cannot affect the vote unless voters are aware of them and regard them as relevant to their own interests. Unfortunately, the content of American campaigns is increasingly focused on personality issues rather than policy debates. While the increased education of the American electorate makes it more capable of dealing with complex issues, the reality is that most citizens obtain news about political campaigns primarily through television and other electronic media, whose campaign coverage emphasizes "newsworthy," rather than substantive, issues.

Finally, changes in the partisan loyalty of certain groups give some clues as to the impact of other variables on voter choices. Much, for example, has been written about the coalitions of groups that have made up the Democratic and Republican parties since the 1930's. Generally, the "New Deal" coalition of the Democratic Party has combined voters with low incomes, African Americans, union members, Roman Catholics and Jews, Southerners, and residents of central cities. By contrast, Republican Party supporters are mostly voters not defined by these characteristics. Since the 1950's, group loyalty within both coalitions has been lacking. Yet the greatest loyalty to either party came from the loyalty to the Democratic Party of poor people, blacks, and central-city residents. These people, however are the elements of the electorate who are among those least likely to participate in elections, thereby reducing the advantage that the Democrats enjoy from their support.

Applications

Public opinion research in many U.S. states provides examples of how knowledge of national voting behavior can be applied at the subnational level. A case in point is the 1991 gubernatorial election in Louisiana.

In presidential elections, Louisiana has gone the way of most Southern states since the 1960's, voting mostly for Republican Party candidates. In statewide politics, however, Louisiana has remained stubbornly attached to the Democratic Party. Nevertheless, in 1979 Dave Treen became the first Republican governor of Louisiana since Reconstruction, only to be voted out of office four years later in the landslide reelection effort of his two-term predecessor, Democrat Edwin Edwards. In party identification as well, the Democratic Party retains a majority in Louisiana.

Since the early 1970's, Louisiana has operated under a blanket primary system in which all candidates—regardless of party affiliation—are listed on one ballot. When Edwards ran for reelection in 1987, he placed second behind another Democrat, U.S. Congressman Buddy Roemer. Edwards had been indicted and tried on racketeering charges during his third term as governor. Although he was not convicted, public opinion polls indicated that most voters thought that he was indeed a crafty "crook" who knew how to evade the law. By promptly withdrawing from the runoff election to which his second-place finish in the primary entitled him, Edwards gave Roemer the governor's office without a majority mandate.

By 1991 Louisiana's political climate was different, and to Edwards' benefit. Roemer had switched parties, and former Ku Klux Klan leader and neo-Nazi David Duke had won a seat as a Republican member of Louisiana's House of Representatives in 1989. In 1990 Duke had attracted worldwide attention when he lost a U.S. Senate race against Democratic incumbent J. Bennett Johnston in which he won 44 percent of the vote. Waging a "mainstream" white rights and anti-welfare campaign, Duke got more than 60 percent of the white vote in that election, and he announced that he would run for governor in 1991.

Edwards' decision to challenge Roemer in the October, 1991, primary was predicated on his knowledge of Louisiana electoral patterns. First, the blanket primary system tended to produce runoff elections between candidates representing the extreme left and extreme right, while the numerous moderate candidates drew votes from each other. The October primary had at least seven gubernatorial candidates, including a third Republican who drew votes from the incumbent Roemer. As the candidate of the left, Edwards understood that his most loyal supporters were black voters. Since the mid-1960's black voter registration in Louisiana had more than doubled, to represent 27 percent of the state's registered voters in 1991. Edwards accurately predicted that he would meet and defeat David Duke in the November runoff election.

With Edwards and Duke in the runoff, and with worldwide media speculating on the possibility of a fascist governor in Louisiana, pollsters were nervous for two reasons. While the black vote for Edwards was a certainty, what would be its level of turnout? Also, in previous polls many Duke supporters refused to tell pollsters what their preference was, resulting in his voter support being seriously underestimated. The keys to Edwards' victory were ensuring a high black voter turnout and convincing whites that Duke was a racial extremist who would cause economic damage to Louisiana.

Within the first two weeks after the primary one poll gave Edwards a four-percentage-point lead, statistically too close to call. Expert speculation supported that contention. Then on November 5, eleven days before the runoff, Southeastern Louisiana University released a poll projecting that Edwards was heading toward a landslide victory with a margin as large as 14 percent. Edwards was expected to receive 97 percent of the black vote, but for him to win, black voter turnout had to be as high as white turnout;

he also needed continued defections of white voters from Duke. Over a two-week period between the primary and the runoff Duke's share of the white vote dropped from 59 percent to 49 percent. Nevertheless, pollsters worried about the accuracy of their projections on Duke.

On November 16, 1991, Edwards defeated Duke by 61 percent to 39 percent, and statewide voter turnout was a record 77 percent of registered voters. For the first time in the state's history black turnout exceeded white turnout. Among white voters, Duke received about 55 percent of the total vote, less than in his 1990 Senate race. The 1991 race was a dramatic example of democracy at work, and of the importance of accurately understanding the dynamics of voter turnout and electoral decision making.

Context

Voter participation is at the heart of democratic theory. Limits on voting, whether legal or cultural, are seen as damaging to the health of a democracy. Historically, the United States has led the world in the expansion of voting rights, but not without fierce struggles and setbacks. Most property ownership and tax paying requirements for voting were eliminated in the early nineteenth century. National voting rights were not extended to women, however, until the Nineteenth Amendment was adopted in 1920, and the full force of federal protection for African American voting rights did not occur until Congress passed the Voting Rights Act of 1965. Finally, the Twenty-sixth Amendment in 1971 forbade states to discriminate in voting rights against citizens who were eighteen years of age or older.

While the electorate in America has expanded and become less selective, voter turnout has recently dropped. Average voter turnout in American presidential elections since the 1960's has been in the 50th percentile, dropping from 63 percent in 1960 to about 50 percent in 1988. Voter turnout rates among European democracies over roughly the same time period have ranged between 75 percent and 95 percent, with little comparable slippage.

Factors depressing voter turnout in the United States, in comparison to other democracies, include measurement differences; lack of automatic voter registration; lack of negative incentives for nonvoting (such as fines); holding elections on workdays; overly complex ballots; only vaguely different agendas between the major parties; and a shift of vote-generating resources away from the parties. Voter turnout in America has also been affected by markedly higher levels of political cynicism and apathy among voters, and it is affected in specific elections by the dynamics surrounding controversial candidates or issues, if controversy exists at all.

Voter turnout in U.S. national elections is generally measured as a percentage of the voting-age population, as opposed to a percentage of registered voters. Since the responsibility for voter registration in America rests with individuals, many people in the United States never register to vote and, therefore, cannot vote on election days. Most other Western democracies make voter registration automatic upon the attainment of either legal age or a certain educational status. Some democracies require voting or penalize nonvoting. Most European democracies make voting a national holiday or hold elections over full weekends. Voting in other democracies is generally less complex, requiring fewer decisions on ballots, and it occurs less frequently than in the United States. Thus, the psychological costs to the voter are lower than in the United States.

While the American two-party system entails campaigns around somewhat competing national agendas, the multiparty politics of most other democracies is more ideological, more diverse, and more competitive. In addition, American parties appear to have lost much of their access to resources previously available to get out the vote. Instead, parties compete for such resources with personal candidate campaign organizations, interest groups, and political action committees. At the same time, there has been a shift away from personal contact with voters and toward more contact through paid and free mass media.

There are those who argue that comparatively low or declining voter turnout is a sign that democracy in America is in critical condition. On the other hand, there is a line of argument that high voter turnout is a sign of political conflict and instability. If this is true, low turnout would be a sign that people are generally satisfied with the status quo. It is hard, however, to reconcile democratic theory and its goal of widespread self-determination with the notion that it may be healthier for democracy if people do not vote.

Bibliography

Asher, Herbert B. *Presidential Elections and American Politics*. 5th ed. Pacific Grove, Calif.: Brooks/Cole, 1992. Excellent review of the impact of attitudes, candidates, issues, and electoral strategies on American voters in every presidential election since 1952.

Campbell, Angus, et al. *The American Voter*. New York: John Wiley & Sons, 1960. Seminal study of the dynamics of political attitudinal development and its impact on the voting behavior of the American electorate. Calls into question the rationality of the American voter.

Nie, Norman H., Sidney Verba, and John R. Petrocik. *The Changing American Voter*. Enl. ed. Cambridge, Mass.: Harvard University Press, 1979. Revisionist work arguing that since the 1960's voters increasingly made voting decisions on the basis of their evaluations of candidates and issues.

Niemi, Richard G., and Herbert F. Weisberg. *Controversies in Voting Behavior*. 3d ed. Washington, D.C.: Congressional Quarterly Press, 1993. Excellent collection of essays on voting behavior. Particularly helpful are the chapter introductions, which give nontechnical overviews of their subjects.

Piven, Frances Fox, and Richard A. Cloward. *Why Americans Don't Vote*. New York: Pantheon Books, 1988. Examination of the impact of voting regulations on voter turnout.

Rosenstone, Steven J., and John Mark Hansen. *Mobilization, Participation, and Democracy in America*. New York: Macmillan, 1993. Broad examination of the dynamics of political participation in the United States.

Wattenberg, Martin P. *The Rise of Candidate-Centered Politics: Presidential Elections of the 1980s*. Cambridge, Mass.: Harvard University Press, 1991. Examines the 1980's as a decade marking the decline of political parties and the rise of candidates as influences on American electoral politics.

Wolfinger, Raymond E., and Steven J. Rosenstone. *Who Votes?* New Haven, Conn.: Yale University Press, 1980. Much-cited exploration of the determinants of voter turnout in the United States.

Michael Kurt Corbello

Cross-References

African American Politics, p. 28; Asian American Politics, p. 115; Democracy, p. 513; The Democratic Party, p. 520; Elections, p. 578; Gender Politics, p. 738; Initiatives and Referendums, p. 923; The Media and Elections, p. 1161; Multiparty Systems, p. 1235; Political Participation, p. 1479; Political Party Roles, p. 1499; Political Science, p. 1532; Presidential Elections in the United States, p. 1596; Public Opinion Polling, p. 1627; The Republican Party, p. 1699; Voting in History, p. 2116; Voting Processes, p. 2123; Woman Suffrage, p. 2141; Women in Politics, p. 2147.

VOTING IN HISTORY

Field of study: Civil rights and liberties

Voting is the process by which a group reaches a decision in choosing among alternatives, using a show of hands, voice, or written ballot. In modern democratic governments, voting is the right of all citizens, using the secret ballot, to select public officials at all levels of government.

Principal terms

BALLOT: a piece of paper on which candidates or proposals appear for voter selection

ELECTORAL SYSTEM: the portion of a political system concerned with electing candidates for office

FRANCHISE: the right to vote; also called suffrage

PROPORTIONAL REPRESENTATION: electoral system in which multiple members are elected from a single electoral district according to the proportions of the total vote that they receive

SECRET (AUSTRALIAN) BALLOT: ballot cast in such a way that only the voter knows what choices he or she has made

UNIVERSAL SUFFRAGE: situation pertaining in a political community that gives all citizens the right to vote; in practice, such communities attach age requirements to the franchise

Overview

As a means for citizens to choose the leaders of their government, voting is a universal practice in modern democracies. Voting in this sense is a creation of Western civilization, which was responsible for its spread throughout the world. The earliest records of the exercise of political power by voting come from ancient Greece and Rome. In Homeric Greece, priests were chosen by lot. By the fifth century B.C.E., the city-state of Athens chose many of its political officers by lot, but the vote was used only for special offices. Voting was common in law courts. When Socrates was tried for subversion in 399 B.C.E., he was convicted by a vote of Athenian citizens. He was sentenced to death by a separate vote.

In the city-states of ancient Greece only male citizens were allowed to vote, and all votes counted equally. Women, aliens (noncitizens), and slaves were excluded from holding the franchise. The Greek view of citizenship was strictly hereditary and had no provision for naturalization (the process of making citizens of aliens). Thus, aliens were permanently excluded from voting and other rights of citizenship. Of the approximately 200,000 inhabitants of ancient Athens, only about 40,000 were eligible to vote.

In Rome at the end of the republican period (just before the birth of Christ) all male citizens had the right to vote either in local municipalities or in Rome itself. The earliest form of voting in Rome was probably no more than group acclamation. By the fifth century B.C.E., however, Roman citizens elected officials by a process that resembled modern voting. At the end of the republican period the city of Rome had several electoral assemblies. One of them, the "Comita Tributa," gave the common people the opportunity to elect a variety of public officials.

Voting in early times was not restricted to the great ancient civilizations. In his essay *On the Germans*, the late first century Roman historian Tacitus describes voting in assemblies of the Germanic tribes that bordered Roman lands. Like the Romans, voting in the Germanic tribes was the right of all male members. The word of elders could carry more weight, but only because of their age and reputed wisdom, not because of inherited social status. Their views could be overridden by a vote of the whole assembly. When a decision was to be taken, matters were first discussed by a smaller group of chieftains, then brought before the whole tribe. Agreement was indicated by shouting approval; disapproval was registered by the noisy banging of weapons.

The view that the right to vote should be attached to membership, or citizenship, in the political community passed from the ancient world to the medieval cities of Europe and then to the north Italian city-states of the Renaissance such as Siena and Bologna. Citizens, however, were few in number and tended to be confined to the wealthy few. The usual medieval view was that ownership of land should be the basis for representation in royal courts and therefore for voting. This view became the basis of the various forms of property requirements for suffrage that the modern world inherited from the Middle Ages.

The feudal view that only great landowners could vote in advisory assemblies did not please the merchant class that arose as medieval cities gained a measure of prosperity. Dissatisfied by their exclusion from power, cities constantly sought ways to gain control over their own affairs. Monarchs often granted cities various liberties in exchange for much-needed favors, such as loans by wealthy merchants to finance royal wars. Further struggles for political power took place within the cities themselves. The associations or "gilds" of wealthy merchants took control of civic affairs, granting the vote only to their own members. The less prosperous craft gilds that were excluded from power agitated, sometimes successfully, for redress of their grievances.

At their height in the late Middle Ages, many European cities were centers of rich civic life, but they never enacted universal manhood suffrage. What is called the "gild democracy" of the era is something of a misnomer, since the gilds excluded most of the populace. By the seventeenth century, elections in countries in continental Europe, such as France and Germany, had become little more than empty ceremonies. Across the English Channel in England, however, history was taking a different course.

England was the place where the representative bodies of government that are now so familiar truly began. The English assemblies go back to the old German practices of elective gatherings that were recorded by Tacitus. They had been preserved by England's Anglo-Saxon people, whose early kingdoms adapted Teutonic ideas of government centering on popular assemblies. The first of these Anglo-Saxon assemblies—that of the "wise men" or Witan—had the right to elect the king. King Canute, for example, was elected by such a gathering.

The representative assembly that eventually became England's Parliament gradually emerged under Norman rule after 1066. The council of barons envisaged by the Magna Carta of 1215 to check the powers of kings was no more than a feudal council, based on large-scale land ownership. The earliest version of Parliament, however, was founded at the end of the thirteenth century, when King Edward I called the "Model Parliament." Its members included the clergy and great landed magnates, as well as knights and "burgesses" who represented counties and towns, respectively. Gradually, these latter two groups sat in a separate assembly, which became the House of Commons. It was not intended to represent landed interests, but the people of the realm as a whole. At first, election to these offices was considered a burden, and an "election" was little more than a crowd's acclamation of a prearranged nomination. As the powers of the House of Commons increased, however, the right to vote for its members took on added significance. By the eighteenth century, voting was carefully controlled by a system that gave effective power to a handful of the aristocracy.

The aristocracy's power was not cracked until 1832, when the Great Reform Bill passed Parliament. After decades of popular agitation, parliamentary seats were redistributed from rural areas to populous cities, and about 200,000 voters were added to the roles by reducing how much property one had to own in order to vote. Many newly enfranchised voters, however, regarded their vote as a commodity for sale, and corrupt election practices abounded. In 1867, after more agitation, Parliament passed the Second Reform Bill, which added another million voters. Further reforms of the 1880's moved Britain closer to an electoral democracy, though many undemocratic practices, such as plural voting, remained. Not until well into the next century was universal suffrage established.

In America, the Revolution of 1776 was not at first the democratic affair it is often imagined to have been, so far as voting was concerned. Colonial America had imitated many of the restrictions of its mother country, England. Property qualifications for voting were less restrictive, however, since land was much easier to obtain than in England. Also, personal property could be substituted for land in some colonies. Religion, however, was often used to exclude Jews, Catholics, and nonbelievers from the franchise. At the end of the colonial period, voting remained a highly restricted affair.

After the Revolution, property, religious, and other qualifications for voting were still prevalent and, with few exceptions, the franchise remained exclusively male. The initial period of restricted voting, however, was succeeded by increasingly democratic practices. The new states found themselves competing with one another for immigrants, so they often offered the franchise to newcomers. In time, all males who paid taxes were allowed the vote.

By the era of Jacksonian Democracy of the 1830's, a broad segment of white males could vote, though the franchise was not universal until after the Civil War. Yet other groups, notably women and African Americans, were barred from suffrage. The

Fifteenth Amendment to the U.S. Constitution guaranteed the right to vote to former slaves in 1870, but in the South this right proved short-lived. After African Americans began voting during the Reconstruction period, the rise of "Jim Crow" laws spelled an end to black voting in the South. While blacks could usually vote in the North it was not until after World War II that a movement would arise to abolish all legal and social barriers to black citizens enjoying full political and civil rights.

Meanwhile, women were organizing to press their claims to political equality. In 1848 a group of women leaders met at Seneca Falls, New York, and issued a declaration of grievances against male oppression. Prominent among their complaints was the assertion that women had an "inalienable right to the elective franchise." Under the leadership of women such as Susan B. Anthony, Elizabeth Cady Stanton, and Lucy Stone, woman suffrage organizations rallied women, as well as sympathetic men, to the cause of expanding the franchise. In 1869 Wyoming Territory accorded women the vote; and by 1917 female suffrage had been granted throughout a patchwork of states and local communities. World War I finally saw the breakdown of the last serious opposition to woman suffrage in the United States. In 1919 both houses of Congress passed a constitutional amendment, to guarantee women the right to vote. In 1920 it was passed as the Nineteenth Amendment.

Across the Atlantic and Pacific oceans, the same cause was already winning support. Women achieved the right to vote in national elections in New Zealand in 1893 and in Australia in 1902. In Europe a host of nations, beginning with Finland in 1906, granted women the right to vote. A few nations in Asia and South America did so in the 1920's and 1930's. In Great Britain, where demands for woman suffrage were heard from the 1840's onward, victory was finally achieved in 1918, when women over age thirty were allowed to vote; in 1928, the age was lowered to twenty-one. By the early 1990's, few democratic nations in the world still formally barred women from voting. Even Switzerland, long a holdout with regard to national elections, finally agreed to universal suffrage. Countries that continued to exclude women from the franchise included various traditionalist Arab states on the Persian Gulf, such as Kuwait and Saudi Arabia.

In the United States, the struggle for universal suffrage did not end in 1920, because African Americans remained effectively disfranchised in the South. Only after the successful Civil Rights movement of the 1950's and 1960's, led by the Reverend Martin Luther King, Jr., and others, was universal suffrage a reality in the United States. Finally, arguments for lowering the voting age in the United States were finally successful in 1971, when the Twenty-sixth Amendment lowered the voting age to eighteen.

Applications

By the end of the twentieth century, the question of who should be allowed to vote appeared to have been settled in favor of a universal franchise. Questions about voting revolved around how, not whether, the vote should be exercised.

Several general systems of voting for legislative representatives are practiced among modern world democracies, and each system has its adherents. In the representative system practiced in countries such as the United States and Great Britain, voters within a delineated electoral district choose a single member, who is elected on the basis of receiving more votes than any other candidate. When more than two candidates run, one may be elected with only a plurality, not a majority of votes. Since the candidate with the most votes wins, this system is known as "first past the post" or "winner take all."

In a second system, which is a variation on the first, a single member is also chosen in an electoral district; however, he or she must receive a majority of the votes cast in order to be elected. When no candidate achieves a majority, a second, or "runoff," election is held—usually a week later—between the top two candidates. This is often called a "majority" electoral system.

A third system known as "proportional representation," or PR, is somewhat different. Several variations of this system are in use around the world, but all have in common the practice of electing several members—not only one—from each electoral district. The key feature of this system is that parties win seats in proportion to the number of votes they receive. Thus, small parties can be represented in the legislature in accordance with the size of their electoral following. Under the single-member district systems, small parties rarely receive representation because the only candidates elected are those with a plurality or majority of the votes cast.

The most prevalent form of PR is the "list system," which is practiced in several forms. In all of them, voters choose from among lists of candidates drawn up by the various parties. Although voters may have some choice among the individuals on the lists, in the main, they vote for parties, not for individual candidates. This version of PR accordingly gives political parties maximum influence. Versions of the "list system" are used in many European countries and in Israel. In most PR systems, parties must receive a minimum, or "threshold," percentage of the votes cast in order to remain on the ballot in the next election. (Alternatively, parties may get on the ballot by presenting a required number of signatures of voters who support them.) This requirement has the advantage of keeping very small parties, which tend to fragment legislative bodies, from electoral consideration.

Each of these different electoral systems has special advantages and disadvantages. The principal argument for proportional representation, for example, is that it is more "democratic." That is, it is more likely to allow representation of minorities. Adherents of PR in the United States often make this argument. Under the plurality and majority voting systems, minority parties gain few, if any, legislative seats. On the other hand, a disadvantage of PR is that it fosters the expression of social division by allowing small, sometimes divisive, parties to elect members. Under non-PR systems, racial and ethnic groups must seek allies among other groups to form majorities; under PR systems, these groups can more easily ignore others, thereby increasing alienation among social groups. Opponents of PR in the United States point out this potential for "Balkanization" if such a system were adopted.

A second problem of PR systems is that they may yield unstable governments in parliamentary governments. Since coalitions are necessary to govern where no majority party exists, small parties must be included. The greater the number of partners within a coalition, the more likely it is that they will disagree, resulting in the government's "fall." Further, in order to satisfy the demands of small partners in coalitions, minorities may force unpopular practices on the majority. Small religious parties in Israel, for example, have sometimes had this effect. When majorities must follow policies of minorities, the central democratic tenet of majority rule is thwarted.

Context

Voting is a central component of democracy. Those who participate in selecting their political officeholders by voting in elections are putting into practice the idea of popular sovereignty that underlies modern democracy. Voters apply the ultimate democratic sanction against rulers by removing them from office. The centuries-old struggle for the extension of the franchise to ever wider segments of society and the demand for the secret ballot so that suffrage could be exercised without reprisals from the powerful are among the most powerful human dramas of modern times.

While voting by small elites had a place in medieval practices in Europe, it began to spread to lower ranks of society in the seventeenth and eighteenth centuries in England and colonial North America. During this period, the authority of crowned heads and aristocrats was undermined by the independent thinking of new, reformist religious leaders, who were followed by the secular philosophies of the Enlightenment. The Protestant practice of the self-government of religious congregations combined with the new philosophies of consent as the basis of obligation to authority. In the end, the vote was the principal form in which this consent could be expressed; one group after another declared that it would peacefully obey authority if it had an active voice in choosing the leaders through the franchise. In much of the world today, the election of officials through democratic voting is the sole means of establishing legitimacy to political authority. The power of the idea of electoral democracy is such that authoritarian and totalitarian regimes have long held "elections" to justify their existence, even if only one candidate stood for office or the results were known to be rigged. For the foreseeable future, the demand for universal suffrage is likely to be a feature of every modern state.

A remaining question is what form "universal" suffrage should take. With the widespread, large-scale migration, many people live in countries where they have no effective say in their governance. Even when they enter other countries illegally, demands are heard that they be given the vote. Opposition to such proposals by citizens is often vocal, but it is unlikely that in the long run any large population segments can endure life in the modern state without a voice in choosing their rulers.

Finally, after centuries of struggle to gain the franchise, it is ironic that so many citizens of Western democracies ignore this hard-won right and avoid the polls on election day. Moreover, certain critics of modern democracy devalue voting as a form of political participation. Nevertheless, voting remains a vital aspect of modern democracy, which cannot function without free, regular elections.

Bibliography

Campbell, Angus, et al. *The American Voter*. New York: John Wiley & Sons, 1960. Classic study of the individual voter in the United States by scholars of the Michigan school.

Lakeman, Enid. *How Democracies Vote*. London: Faber and Faber, 1970. Detailed study of several European election systems, comparing majority systems with proportional representation systems.

Nie, Norman, Sidney Verba, and John R. Petrocik. *The Changing American Voter*. Cambridge, Mass.: Harvard University Press, 1976. Examines changes in the attitudes of American voters after 1960.

Seymour, Charles, and Donald Paige Frary. *How the World Votes: The Story of Democratic Development in Elections*. 2 vols. Springfield, Mass.: C. A. Nichols, 1918. Despite its age, this work remains the most comprehensive history of voting and election practices in English. Contains important analyses and much fascinating information and data about its subject.

Smith, T. E. *Elections in Developing Countries*. New York: St. Martin's Press, 1960. An examination of variations in voting and electoral practices in the Third World.

Charles F. Bahmueller

Cross-References

Activist Politics, p. 7; Citizenship Rights and Responsibilities, p. 260; The City-State, p. 272; Civil Liberties Protection, p. 291; Constitutional Governments, p. 432; Democracy, p. 513; Elected Versus Appointed Offices in the United States, p. 572; Elections, p. 578; The Electoral College, p. 584; Feminist Politics, p. 682; History of Government, p. 829; Multiparty Systems, p. 1235; Political Participation, p. 1479; Town Meetings, p. 1993; Voting Behavior in the United States, p. 2109; Voting Processes, p. 2123; Woman Suffrage, p. 2141.

VOTING PROCESSES

Field of study: Civil rights and liberties

Citizens of a political system participate in the decision-making process of government by voting. Voters may make decisions directly in direct democracies; however, people are more likely to be part of a political system in which they elect representatives to make the decisions.

Principal terms

AUSTRALIAN BALLOT: ballot form that allows the voter to vote in secret

LITERACY TEST: requirement that prospective voters be literate in order to register to vote

POLL TAX: payment required as a condition for voting; formerly used in some parts of the United States

PROPORTIONAL REPRESENTATION: system in which legislative seats are allocated proportionally to each party's share of the popular vote; frequently used in European countries

SINGLE-MEMBER DISTRICT: system in which a candidate is elected to office by the voters of that district; commonly found in the United States

Overview

Voting is one of the many forms of political participation by which citizens in a democracy can attempt to influence public policy. The emphasis on citizen participation is the distinguishing characteristic of a democratic society, and the extent to which a society's population participates in its political arena is one method of evaluating how democratic it is. A truly democratic political system will place few barriers between its citizens and the process of voting. All democracies, however, have some restrictions that limit access to suffrage.

To have truly democratic elections, it is generally agreed that several crucial conditions must be satisfied. Substantially the entire adult population must have the right to vote for candidates for office and elections must take place within prescribed time limits; no substantial group in the adult population may be prevented from forming a party or putting up candidates; all the seats in the legislative chamber may be contested, and normally are; campaigns must be conducted fairly, and neither the candidates nor the voters may be prevented from presenting or discussing their views through legal restrictions, violence, or intimidation; votes must be cast freely and in secret, and must be counted honestly; the candidates who receive the proportion of votes required by law must be installed in office for their proper terms of office until new elections are held. Within these guidelines, there is a great diversity of election systems. No two countries have identical arrangements in terms of voter qualifications and election procedures.

Historically, the concept of "one man, one vote" in a democratic political system had little support. The propertied or educated classes seldom supported the idea of giving electoral equality to the masses. In the American colonies and in the early years of the United States, suffrage was limited to white, male property owners. The amount of property required to participate in the electoral process varied; however, over time, property requirements were removed and suffrage was extended to all white males. Following the Civil War, suffrage was effectively extended to African American males by the Fifteenth Amendment; however, by the end of the nineteenth century several devices had been adopted in the South to either prevent African American participation or limit its impact. The most prevalent was the literacy test, which required prospective voters to be able to read, write, and interpret the constitution of the state or the U.S. Constitution. The white registrar administering the test had considerable flexibility in deciding the standards of literacy. Whites might be required only to sign their names, while African Americans could be expected to interpret constitutional provisions. Literacy tests were later eliminated in the United States.

Some Southern states also required the payment of an annual poll tax of one dollar or two dollars in order to register to vote. In some states, the poll tax was cumulative, requiring the tax to be paid for all previous years in which the person had been eligible to vote but had not. At one time, the maximum state cumulation was thirty-six dollars in Alabama and forty-seven dollars in Georgia. Payment dates ranged from three to eighteen months in advance of an election. The poll tax disfranchised large numbers of white voters as well as blacks, and where it was used, only a small percentage of the potentially eligible electorate actually participated in the electoral process. The poll tax was eliminated for national elections in 1964 with the enactment of the Twenty-fourth Amendment. A 1966 Supreme Court decision eliminated the poll tax for state elections.

Some Southern states prevented African Americans from having a meaningful impact on the election process through the white primary. In these states, only whites were allowed to participate in party primaries, under the rationale that primaries to nominate candidates were internal functions of a private organization. The white primary was declared unconstitutional in 1944, on the grounds that selecting candidates for election is a public function.

Other restrictions on suffrage included sex and age. Wyoming, in 1869, was the first state to allow women to vote. It was followed by Utah in 1870 and Colorado and Idaho by the end of the nineteenth century. In 1902, women received the universal right to vote in Australia; however, universal suffrage for women did not occur until 1920 in the United States. In Portugal women's suffrage was not adopted until 1975, while in Spain it did not occur until 1977.

Most countries also have a minimum voting age. In the 1990's, the most common minimum voting age was eighteen, although some democracies required individuals to be twenty or twenty-one years of age in order to vote. In the United States, the legal age to vote was universally set at eighteen by the Twenty-sixth Amendment in 1971.

While the world's major democracies have provided for universal adult suffrage, all have some minimum requirements that must be met in order to participate. For example, most democracies, including the United States, restrict the vote to citizens by birth or naturalization.

Another restriction on suffrage is residency in the constituency or country for a specified period of time, which can vary from thirty days to a year. At one time these requirements were much greater. In the United States, the state of Mississippi had a two-year residency requirement. The Voting Rights Act of 1970 set a maximum residency requirement of thirty days for presidential elections. Two years later, the Supreme Court expanded the requirement for a reasonable residency requirement to all elections.

Registration is another prerequisite for voter participation in many democracies. Before citizens are allowed to vote, their name must appear on an official list of eligible voters maintained by the government. In the United States, states began to require registration at the beginning of the twentieth century in order to prevent election fraud. Registration in the United States is the individual's responsibility. As a result, turnout in elections has declined since it was instituted. In contrast, most democracies place the responsibility of registration on government. In most U.S. states, voters must be registered thirty days prior to an election. Several states, including Maine, Minnesota, and Wisconsin, allow voters to register at their polling place on election day. One state, North Dakota, does not require voters to register. These four states are generally among the states with the highest voter turnout in the United States. In 1993, the United States Congress enacted a "Motor Voter" registration law that required states to permit individuals to register to vote when they apply for a driver's license, at certain state welfare offices, or by mail. The intent of the legislation, which was to take effect in 1995, was to increase participation by making registration easier.

Some democracies disqualify persons from voting for other reasons. These reasons include having a recognized mental illness; having been convicted of a crime; holding certain public offices, such as judge, police officer, or member of the armed services; being a parent who has lost rights over his or her children; or being a conscientious objector, vagabond, vagrant, undischarged bankrupt, prostitute, or drunkard.

Applications

An examination of the range of participation in democratic governments throughout the world reveals a checkered pattern. In some countries, including the United States, the chief executive is popularly elected. In others, there is a hereditary monarch or an executive chosen by the legislature. Some countries have bicameral legislative bodies with both houses being elected by the people, as is the case in the United States. Other countries have either unicameral legislative bodies or have upper houses that are either appointed or indirectly chosen without direct popular participation.

The different levels of government in a country also impact on voting opportunities. The levels of elected governments within a country is generally either two, such as in New Zealand, or three, as in the United Kingdom. In the United States, there are at least four levels of elected offices: federal, state, county, and municipal.

The frequency of elections varies widely. On the average, voters in twenty-two democracies that have existed since the 1940's have the opportunity to vote for representatives to the lower house of the government once every 40.7 months, with the range being from twenty-four to sixty months. In the United States, voters vote every two years for the lower house, the president has a four-year term of office, and members of the Senate serve for six years.

The frequency and variety of elections is greatest in the United States. In addition to national offices, voters in the United States elect a wide variety of officials at the state and local level. Two-thirds of the states elect governors in nonpresidential election years. Approximately 60 percent of U.S. cities select municipal officers in odd-numbered years. U.S. voters also have the opportunity to elect a number of officials to nonrepresentative offices, including judges, law enforcement officials, attorneys general, treasurers, comptrollers general, superintendents of education, and even the head of the National Guard.

U.S. voters in the late twentieth century used the Australian or secret ballot to select their elected officials. This, however, was not always the case. Until the end of the nineteenth century, voters in the United States did not have a secret ballot. The earliest colonial elections required voters to appear in person before election officials and orally vote for their candidates. This could constrain a voter from supporting a candidate different from that of others who were listening. Later, parties printed the ballots, which were frequently differentiated by color or design so people could easily see how individuals voted.

With the advent of the Australian ballot, the party's ability to influence voting choice was diminished; however, parties still can try to influence the ballot's form. In general, the dominant party in a state has advocated the use of a party column ballot. In this form, all candidates of a party are listed in a column on the ballot. Voters may vote a straight party ticket by marking a circle at the top of the ticket. This type of ballot makes it easier to vote for all candidates from one party. In the United States, approximately thirty states use this form.

States with weaker party organizations frequently use the office-block ballot form, in which candidates are grouped by the office they are seeking. Because voters must vote for each office separately with this ballot, they are more likely to split their ticket or vote for candidates from different parties.

Some countries, including Italy, Belgium, and Australia, have compulsory voting statutes. Citizens who do not vote may be subject to fines. Their average voter turnout has ranged from 94 percent in Italy to 88 percent in Australia and Belgium. Although actual prosecution of violators has been limited, the compulsory voting laws seem to increase turnout. When The Netherlands abolished compulsory voting in 1967, turnout in that country declined by approximately 10 percent.

Another factor that impacts on voter turnout is the administrative arrangements that govern voting. For example, in Italy the polling stations are open for two days, for as long as sixteen hours a day. Election days are public holidays in Italy and a number of other countries, which makes it easier for citizens to vote. The ease with which voters can cast absentee ballots can also affect turnout. Some countries, including Canada and New Zealand, allow any citizen to vote in advance. Others, including Australia and Germany, allow voters to vote by mail in advance. Other countries allow for proxy voting, whereby one person can vote on behalf of another. Special polling stations in such places as hospitals, old-age homes, and embassies abroad are allowed in still other countries. Finally, some countries facilitate participation by allowing voters to vote in a different polling station from that for which they are registered. In the United States, absentee voting requirements are determined by individual states. Most states allow absentee voting by mail for members of the armed forces and government employees. A few states allow for proxy voting. Overall, however, the United States does not facilitate the voting process as much as other democracies. As a result, only 55 percent of the eligible electorate voted in the United States in 1992.

The method of translating votes into representative seats varies by country. The winner-take-all system is used in most English-speaking countries. When suffrage was expanded to include the masses on the European continent, however, traditional parties, faced with the prospect of domination by socialist parties, objected to this system. There were also objections from minorities who were represented by small parties. As a result, proportional representation systems began to be used in Europe, beginning with Denmark in 1855. There are a number of methods by which votes can be translated into representative seats in a proportional system, but the end result is the same: Proportional representation encourages a multiparty system, because more than one candidate is elected from each voting district.

Context

Democratic societies are distinguished by the fact that ordinary citizens have the right to participate in the selection of public officials and in the affairs of the government. In the late twentieth century, democracy was a widely accepted form of government, representing a triumph over arbitrary power exercised by a few over the many. Supporters of democracy argue that the citizens are the most appropriate judges of their own interests.

Voting is the most common form of political participation in a democracy. Historically, many countries, including the United States, limited the suffrage. Although most barriers to participation have been removed, voter turnout varies significantly in different countries. In general, European countries have had turnout rates of 80 percent or higher. By contrast, the United States has ranked near the bottom among the world's democracies in voter turnout. Between 1920 and 1992, the level of turnout in a U.S. presidential election never exceeded 63 percent; in 1988, it was only 50 percent of the eligible voters. In nonpresidential election years for the same period, the turnout rate never exceeded 50 percent.

The more privileged elements of the population are most likely to participate in the political process. In countries with a near-universal turnout, however, participation of all classes is the rule. Citizens can offset their lack of financial resources with numbers. In countries such as the United States, where close to half of the population does not participate, the influence of the privileged classes over the political system can be inordinately high.

Voting is an important factor in the public policy process. Elected officials risk being voted out of office if their policies fail to satisfy a majority of the electorate. The extent of participation is a measure of how fully democratic a society is. Without significant participation by its citizens, a political system may cease to function in the interest of the public. Voting is the mechanism through which people can ensure that government remains responsive to its citizens.

Bibliography

Butler, David, Howard R. Penniman, and Austin Ranney, eds. *Democracy at the Polls: A Comparative Study of Competitive National Elections*. Washington, D.C.: American Enterprise Institute for Public Policy Research, 1981. Cross-national comparisons of general elections in twenty-eight Western democracies.

Delury, George E. *World Encyclopedia of Political Systems and Parties*. 2d ed. 2 vols. New York: Facts on File, 1987. Describes the institutions of government, level of party activity, and election systems of the world's countries.

Flanigan, William H., and Nancy H. Zingale. *Political Behavior of the American Electorate*. 8th ed. Washington, D.C.: Congressional Quarterly, 1994. Short analysis of voting in the United States, which includes sections on laws, partisanship, ideology, political communication, voter choice, and survey research.

Teixeira, Ruy A. *The Disappearing American Voter*. Washington, D.C.: Brookings Institution, 1992. Analysis of the decline in voter participation in the United States, with proposals for increasing participation.

Verba, Sidney, Norman H. Nie, and Jae-on Kim. *Participation and Political Equality: A Seven Nation Comparison*. Cambridge, England: Cambridge University Press, 1978. Cross-national analysis of political participation.

William V. Moore

Cross-References

Citizenship Rights and Responsibilities, p. 260; Democracy, p. 513; Elected Versus Appointed Offices in the United States, p. 572; Elections, p. 578; The Electoral College, p. 584; Nomination Processes, p. 1312; Political Participation, p. 1479; Political Parties, p. 1485; Political Party Conventions, p. 1492; Political Party Roles, p. 1499; Political Platforms, p. 1512; Political Representation in the United States, p. 1525; Primary Elections, p. 1603; Public Opinion Polling, p. 1627; Two-Party Systems, p. 2033; Voting Behavior in the United States, p. 2109; Voting in History, p. 2116; Woman Suffrage, p. 2141.

WAR

Field of study: Military

War is a nation's use of violence in an attempt to achieve an end. The word is also used figuratively to describe other hostile and extreme acts by governments: trade war, the Cold War, the war on crime, and so on. Universally decried as inhuman and evil, it has been practiced universally.

Principal terms

COUNTERPOPULATION BOMBING: concentrated bombing of enemy targets, civilian and military, which usually causes heavy casualties among noncombatants

FIRST STRIKE: initiation of war by one country upon another, regarded as an illegal act in international law

JUS AD BELLUM: regarding the question of whether resorting to war is justified

JUS IN BELLO: regarding the question of whether a particular form of force is justified

NONCOMBATANT (CIVILIAN): nonparticipant in war

RIGHT AUTHORITY: also referred to as *compétence de guerre*, it refers to the principle that only governments, representing their citizens, have the authority to wage war

SECOND STRIKE: act of war in response to a first strike by an aggressor, considered in international law to be justified under certain circumstances

Overview

A venerable endeavor, war has been with humanity since the beginning of history. War is a frightful and awful enterprise, and because of this, considerable religious and secular thinking over the centuries has been devoted to determining whether governments have the moral right to wage war, and if they do, under what conditions.

In the ancient Christian world, religious violence was generally not condoned. In the Bible, Jesus tells Peter to sheath his sword, and this has been interpreted as Jesus' effectively disarming all Christians. In the early fifth century the Roman Catholic saint Augustine of Hippo wrote on the use of violence. His writings have had a critical influence on the conduct of war in contemporary Western culture. Augustine tried to reconcile Christian teaching against the use of violence with the necessity of defending the then-Christian Roman Empire against invasion from the Vandals. Augustine concluded that under the circumstances, Rome had a moral and ethical responsibility and duty to defend itself from attack by engaging the Vandals in warfare. There were limits, however, to be imposed on the type and extent of harm that could be acceptably inflicted on the enemy.

Augustine used the parable of an onlooker who observes a person unjustly attacking a defenseless victim. The proper action for an onlooker to take is to intervene between the aggressor and victim, even at the risk of the aggressor's or the defender's death or of being attacked by the aggressor. Defense of the victim is required by the observer's love for him as someone for whom Christ died. Since Christ also died for the aggressor, the defender is thus limited in terms of what he can inflict on the aggressor in order to protect the victim. Augustine argued that the appropriate behavior was a proportionate response to the actions of the attacker. The defender is given sanction to counter the attacker's force with a proportionately effective force. This force could include the death of the attacker if the attacker's actions escalated the defensive measures the defender had to take to protect the victim. The defender is obligated to oppose evil and protect the innocent victim.

If this parable is interpreted in terms of war, the aggressor and the defender are enemy soldiers engaged in wartime combat on a battlefield. The purpose of war is to resist and defeat the intentions of the evil forces that exist in the world. The specific nature of this force, however, is circumscribed.

The theme of the right of government to wage war under limited circumstances and the placing of limits on what kinds of violence are acceptable is referred to as the just war doctrine. Over the centuries this tradition of just war has become increasingly secularized and perceived as generic to Western culture. For example, the immunity of noncombatants from war became part of the tradition. The phrase *jus in bello* deals with the limitations on the use of force and literally means what is just to do in war. *Jus in bello* derives from the fundamental ideas of protecting noncombatants during war and that the prosecution of war should be proportionate to the goals of that war. *Jus ad bellum* refers to considerations pertinent to deciding whether to resort to war. *Jus ad bellum* incorporates such concepts as just cause, right authority, right intention, war as a last resort, the costs of war versus the good it will achieve, and that the goal of war is peace.

The concept of right authority, or *compétence de guerre*, legitimizes the use of force by government, which has the authority to wage war, acting on behalf of the citizenry. In the twentieth century, international law (for example, the League of Nations Covenant, Kellogg-Briand Pact, articles 2 and 51 of the United Nations Charter) attempted to define "just cause" by outlawing and condemning aggressive war, while condoning and sanctioning defense as a valid reason for going to war. Religious institutions have generally agreed with this position. Popes Pius XII and Paul VI, for example, condemned offensive use of force while accepting the justice of defense. The American Council of Bishops in 1982 condemned first use of nuclear weapons, a position agreed upon by the Reagan Administration.

War is considered just when conducted for three reasons. The first just cause for war is protection of one's own sovereignty against aggression or protection of one's allies when they are being subjected to aggression. (For example, the United States declared war on Japan after the latter bombed Pearl Harbor in 1941; Great Britain and France declared war on Germany after the latter invaded Poland in 1939.) A second just cause is attempting to recover something that has been taken away by the aggressive actions of another. (For example, a multinational force entered Kuwait in the Persian Gulf War of 1991 in order to expel the invading Iraqi army and reclaim Kuwait's oil fields.) A third just cause is punishing another for previous aggressive actions. (For example, a U.N. peacekeeping force may attack and destroy an outpost in retaliation for that outpost's being used aggressively.) In all these instances, defense against first use of force occurs.

Applications

The doctrine of just war may be applied, for example, to two twentieth century wars, the Falklands War and the Korean War. The Falklands War was fought between Great Britain and Argentina in May and June, 1982. Claiming to recover illegally taken territory and to punish British colonialism, Argentina invaded the Falklands in early 1982 and seized them. In response, Britain claimed that the Falklands had been British territory for the past century and a half, that the inhabitants were British citizens, and that Argentina's military aggression would have to be punished so that it would not set an example for other aggressive countries to seize territory that was not theirs. Both sides, as often happens, claimed just cause and right intent for their actions. Each side, by their argument, was engaging in a second-strike defensive action designed to redress a previous first-strike action that had wrongfully and illegally been inflicted upon it. Both countries were reclaiming territory they believed had been illegally seized from the other. Both sides claimed to be punishing illegal first-strike actions: Argentina was punishing nineteenth century British colonialism, and Britain was punishing Argentina's illegal seizure. Force was the measure of last resort because Argentina would not vacate the Falklands and Britain would not concede the islands to Argentina.

The war was fought by two established military powers for a limited goal (ownership of the islands) and using limited, restrained tactics to fight the war. The war was fought according to the just war rules of conflict. Argentina permitted inhabitants of the Falklands to leave after it seized the islands. Both sides respected the rights of the noncombatant civilians during the war; civilian casualties were light. Although both sides possessed weapons and tactics capable of inflicting much more destruction than occurred, these weapons and tactics were not used. The war was confined to the Falklands. Neither mainland Argentina nor Britain was attacked and neither country engaged in terrorist activities against the other. The war can thus be viewed as a textbook example of fighting a limited conventional war between two similarly armed countries that adhered to the just war doctrine.

The Korean War commenced on June 25, 1950, when more than 100,000 troops of the North Korean army crossed the thirty-eighth parallel separating North from South Korea. The South Korean army resisted, but, in the face of a superior force, quickly disintegrated. On June 27, the North Koreans occupied the capital of Seoul.

To the United States and President Harry S Truman there was no doubt that the invasion was instigated by either the Soviet Union or China as a probing action to see how easily and far it could extend its sphere of influence into Asia.

The secretary general of the United Nations, Trygvie Lie, believed that North Korea had violated the United Nations Charter. In no way could the invasion by North Korea be viewed as a second-strike defensive action against a perceived South Korean first-strike invasion. North Korea's invasion was a first-strike aggressive action, which was condemned and outlawed by the United Nations Charter. It was thus the clear duty, by this interpretation, of the U.N. Security Council to take measures to reestablish peace and security in Korea by providing whatever assistance was necessary to South Korea to repel the invasion. Only Yugoslavia (a Communist bloc country) voted no. Communist China voted yes, and India and Egypt abstained. Just cause and right intent resided with the allied forces.

The stated intention of the United Nations was to expel the North Korean invaders from South Korea in order to reestablish the status quo. The war was to be a limited conventional action (no use of atomic weapons was seriously considered) involving limited goals (removing North Korea from South Korea). The United Nations response was thus proportional to the action taken by North Korea. By the end of September, the goal of forcing the North Koreans out of South Korea was accomplished. One crisis was resolved but now another consideration, acceptable according to the just war doctrine, presented itself: Should North Korea be punished for its aggressive act of invading the South? An appropriate proportionate response would be to invade North Korea. It was argued that the North Korean attack destroyed the sanctity of the thirty-eighth parallel and that North Korea had been intent on destroying South Korea. Crossing into North Korea with the intention of totally defeating the invaders could be viewed as an entirely appropriate response and punishment. On the other hand, the original mission of the United Nations as stated in the Security Council resolution (which Communist China supported) was only to repel the armed invasion. In this light, invasion of North Korea would have been a disproportionate and inappropriate response.

Unlike the similar situation in the 1991 Persian Gulf War, in which allied forces expelled Iraq from Kuwait but did not invade and take over Iraq, the United Nations forces did invade North Korea. The invasion resulted in the entry of Communist China into the war, believing that it had just cause and right intention to prevent the U.N. forces from invading China via North Korea. The Chinese intervention resulted in the inflicting of huge numbers of casualties and mass destruction on both sides that otherwise would not have happened if North Korea had not been invaded. The war eventually settled into a stalemate that was finally ended at the negotiating table in 1953, on the same terms that would have occurred had the United Nations stopped at the thirty-eighth parallel.

Context

There exists a long precedent that governments have the right to engage in wars as a method of last resort so long as the wars are just and right and are conducted appropriately. Specifically, these conditions are as a second-strike defensive action of last resort to protect oneself or an ally from a first-strike aggression, to recover lost territory, or to inflict punishment.

What appears to be most problematic in the prosecution of such wars are considerations of *jus in bello* regarding the issue of restraints, limits, and justification of use of a given force. In particular, difficult considerations arise regarding appropriate proportional retaliation and the protection of noncombatants. The example of the Falklands War presents a textbook case in which *jus in bello* was strictly observed. In many instances, however, what constitutes appropriate *jus in bello* is much more difficult to decide. In the case of the Korean War it has been argued that the U.N. invasion of North Korea was a disproportionate response to the original mandate. That the invasion resulted in no tangible gains and needless tragedy bolsters the argument in this case. Others have argued that the invasion was an entirely appropriate proportional response, punishment for the North's invasion of the South.

During World War II, in September, 1940, the German Luftwaffe commenced seventy-six nights of bombing London, with devastating effects. More than sixty thousand civilians were killed and 25 percent of all homes were destroyed. In February, 1942, Albert Harris became commander in chief of Britain's bomber command. An advocate of concentrated bombing on selected targets, he oversaw the bombing of Cologne, Germany, by more than one thousand planes in May, 1942, during which an average of thirty-one tons of bombs per square mile were dropped and a third of Cologne was devastated. In 1943, Harris oversaw the concentrated bombing of Berlin in which large numbers of civilians were killed but Germany's war-making abilities were not diminished. Finally, early in 1945, Harris oversaw the firebombing of Dresden, a city that had not yet been bombed because of its lack of military value. A firestorm resulted, as intended, utterly destroying the city and causing thousands of civilian casualties. Harris' policies were supported by Prime Minister Winston Churchill at the time, but after the war Harris was the only British war leader not to receive a peerage.

Germany's devastation of London clearly violated noncombatant immunity. Could the same be said of the retaliatory counterpopulation strikes on Germany? These strikes were in part an expression of rage against the Germans but were also part of a strategic total war doctrine. Great Britain clearly believed itself to be just and Germany unjust, and the country was faced with a supreme emergency.

Similarly, the dropping of the atomic bombs on Japan caused terrible death and destruction but undoubtedly shortened the war and saved many American soldiers from death; the alternative was invading Japan. Could the Japanese have been given a demonstration of the atomic bomb's power and given the opportunity to surrender? Would they have accepted such an offer? The right to engage in just wars is an unambiguous right of governments, but the prosecution of wars in the appropriate manner is rife with ambiguities and conflicting interpretations. In this age of nuclear weapons, these ambiguities become especially chilling.

Bibliography

Arnold-Forster, Mark. *The World at War*. Briarcliff Manor, N.Y.: Stein and Day, 1973. Discusses many aspects of World War II that bear directly on war as just.

Blainey, Geoffrey. *The Causes of War*. New York: Macmillan, 1973. Blainey draws thirty-three conclusions on war, peace, and neutrality in the areas of causes of war, varieties of war, and theories of war. Many of these conclusions bear directly on the issue of just war.

Fussell, Paul. *Thank God for the Atom Bomb, and Other Essays*. New York: Summit Books, 1988. A soldier in World War II who likely would have participated in an invasion of Japan, Fussell argues that dropping the atomic bombs on Hiroshima and Nagasaki was moral and just.

Johnson, James Turner. *Can Modern War Be Just?* New Haven, Conn.: Yale University Press, 1984. Thorough consideration of the just war concept, covering ancient times through the late twentieth century, and considers religious, military, and civilian perspectives.

_____. *Just War Tradition and the Restraint of War: A Moral and Historical Inquiry*. Princeton, N.J.: Princeton University Press, 1981. A scholarly, readable consideration of the just war concept.

Ramsey, Paul. *The Just War: Force and Political Responsibility*. New York: Charles Scribner's Sons, 1968. A thoughtful, scholarly, and thorough consideration of the topic.

Russell, Frederick H. *The Just War in the Middle Ages*. New York: Cambridge University Press, 1975. Thoughtful discussion of the just war concept as it was addressed in the Middle Ages. Provides a useful comparison with the just war concept in the modern era.

Stoessinger, John G. *Why Nations Go to War*. 3d ed. New York: St. Martin's Press, 1982. Discusses seven modern wars in an attempt to understand the various causes for wars.

Laurence Miller

Cross-References

Alliances, p. 47; Armed Forces, p. 89; Arms Control, p. 95; Augustine's Political Philosophy, p. 121; Civil Wars, p. 325; Imperialism, p. 889; Initiatives and Referendums, p. 923; Insurgencies and Coups d'État, p. 930; International Law, p. 956; Military Conscription and Conscientious Objection, p. 1185; Military Governments, p. 1192; Military Structure, p. 1198; National Security, p. 1261; Patriotism, p. 1384.

THE WELFARE STATE

Field of study: Political philosophy

The welfare state is a political system designed to provide economic security for citizens in the context of the tensions and dislocations found in industrial societies. While all welfare states embody responses born of practical necessity, they also reflect the ideological predisposition of their societies, and, therefore, display a wide range of characteristics.

Principal terms

CONSERVATISM: ideology that stresses tradition and elitism

ENTITLEMENT: benefits that are viewed as a right, either because they have come to be rooted in society's view of citizenship, or because citizens have paid for them

KEYNESIAN ECONOMICS: economic theory that spending should exceed tax revenues during recessions to stimulate demand and preserve employment levels

LIBERALISM: in its classical sense, an ideology that stresses individual freedom, the free market, and minimum state intervention in social and economic life

SOCIAL DEMOCRACY: form of socialism that seeks to use democracy to implement social or political control of the economy and relatively egalitarian standards of living

Overview

Welfare states are political systems that provide economic security in a continuing and systematic fashion. They are often viewed as a policy safety net that catches those who have fallen on hard economic times, but this view is too restrictive and ignores many key welfare state features. Welfare states are perhaps better understood as an entire political and economic system, because, in addition to their safety net function, they also provide security by enhancing and stabilizing the economy, and often provide goods and services at levels far beyond those of a safety net. While any state exhibiting these characteristics could conceivably be called a welfare state, the term is usually applied only to industrial capitalist democracies. Virtually every country in this category has some form of public welfare system, although there are significant differences in their characteristics and the values and beliefs underlying them.

Most scholars link the common theme of welfare protection found among these states to the logic of industrial society itself. Prior to industrialization, most people lived in close-knit farming communities, in which the individual had greater personal control over the means of subsistence and where shortfalls in economic security were addressed through combinations of support by friends and the extended family, charity by churches, and limited support by local notables. This system was undermined by industrialization. Families were uprooted and moved to cities, where the sources of employment were concentrated. Individual security became dependent on impersonal market forces over which the average individual had little control, such as the factory. If sickness, old age, or the business decisions of employers brought unemployment, the average citizen would lack the means of subsistence. States were forced to intervene at some level, because large numbers of impoverished workers constituted a threat to the social order. There were also humanitarian reasons for providing some measure of security.

Industrialization had effects beyond simply generating the need for an organized welfare effort. Perhaps most important, industrialization brought increases in education, communication, and information, even among its poorest citizens. These skills and resources gave the rank and file of society a greater capacity for political activity, thus allowing them to demand improvements in their living conditions. Industrialization also fostered new political philosophies, such as socialism, among those who were already educated. The combination of poor conditions, a working class that was increasingly active politically and capable of using its electoral strength to demand reforms, and the emergence of a number of ideological oppositions to free-market capitalism laid the groundwork for governmental intervention.

In spite of these early pressures and efforts, the modern welfare state did not emerge until after World War II. The years between the initial reforms of the nineteenth century and the postwar expansion of the welfare state played an important role. World Wars I and II required enormous state direction of economic activity, which served as a powerful precedent, and the Great Depression that occurred between the two wars resulted in further criticisms of the free market, increased concerns about economic security and stability, and further established the precedent of intervention in the market by democratic governments. Finally, the Cold War rivalry between communism and democratic capitalism that emerged after World War II reinforced attempts by the democracies to provide secure living standards in an effort to avoid social unrest and instability, and also to provide proof that democracy better satisfied the needs of its citizens.

The resulting welfare states' first line of defense against economic insecurity is management of the overall economy. This is accomplished primarily through the application of Keynesian economics, which came into extensive use after the Depression and World War II. This theory suggests that governments should run budget deficits, that is, spend beyond the amount of taxes they collect, when the economy is in recession, thereby increasing economic demand and maintaining employment. When the economy is growing too quickly, thus producing inflation, governments should incur budget surpluses, which reduce demand by taking money out of the economy, thus helping to contain inflation. The Keynesian approach to management, therefore, provided security by maintaining high levels of employment and economic growth without high rates of inflation, which erodes the real value of wages and savings. The Keynesian emphasis on the budget also provided a framework for direct supplements to the incomes of individuals through policies that compensate for the loss of income as a result of changes in circumstances, such as sickness and retirement, or the inability to earn sufficient income in the first place. Indeed, these items typically constitute 40 percent or more of most industrial democracies' budgets.

Direct support for individuals is provided through two basic types of policies. The first is social insurance. These benefits are generally financed through special taxes, which are used for old-age pensions, health care, and unemployment and disability insurance. In the United States, for example, Social Security is financed through the compulsory Federal Insurance Contributions Act tax withheld from workers' paychecks, and public health care for the elderly (Medicare) is financed through a similar deduction. Although each worker pays into social insurance systems and benefit levels may vary by the amount paid, all citizens of the welfare state are entitled to some level of benefits, whether they have contributed or not. Social insurance is supplemented by public assistance programs. These usually are financed through general tax revenues and are designed primarily to supplement the incomes of persons, or households, falling below certain prespecified income levels, or means tests. These benefits include welfare assistance, income supplements for low-income families with children, and the provision of free or subsidized housing and health care to those in need. While some form of means testing is usually applied, this is not always the case. Countries such as Sweden and Great Britain provide health care financed through general tax revenues to all of their citizens.

The policies underlying the welfare state were highly successful from the 1950's through the mid-1970's. Most democracies experienced general affluence, and the standards of living of most of their citizens increased substantially. Ideological tensions between the working class and the upper and middle classes virtually disappeared, as the working class came to enjoy essentially middle-class lifestyles. With the economic disturbances of the mid- and late 1970's, the welfare state entered a period of critical rethinking and experienced some partial reversals. Keynesian economics proved unable to cope with the supply-side disturbances that plagued the industrial economies following the oil crises of the 1970's, and social security systems were impacted by the growth of the aged population relative to workers paying into the system. Politicians were unable to sustain the budget deficits central to Keynesian economic management; citizens decried chronic deficit problems but refused to part with their benefits, which were viewed as entitlements either because they had paid for them or because they had come to be viewed as a right of citizenship. At the same time, citizens were increasingly critical of the high rates of taxation demanded by the welfare state and refused to shoulder additional tax burdens to finance it. As a result, through the 1980's and early 1990's, domestic politics in the industrial democracies centered on identifying new policy approaches capable of restoring economic performance with little or no increase in taxes, and without sacrificing the lion's share of benefits, although in Great Britain and the United States the attack on spending was fairly aggressive.

Applications

While all welfare states embody responses to the problems of industrialization and demands for protection from their citizens, they vary considerably in size and character. Welfare states' policies provide different degrees of independence from the market and, consequently, different levels of security. Because the policies of different welfare states embody different degrees of egalitarianism, they can reinforce inequality as well as eliminate it. Variations in the size, equality, and independence from the market of different welfare states are associated with dominance of particular ideologies. In liberal welfare states, such as the United States, policies are chosen to reinforce market activity. As a result, the overall size of the welfare state relative to the economy is small in comparison to other systems, and the benefits themselves are meager and are based on stringent means tests in order to discourage reliance on them. The chief exception to this rule is Social Security, because the benefits are "purchased" in a manner similar to private insurance. Countries such as Germany have a more conservative character, based on strong traditions of state intervention in the economy, as well as an acceptance of social privilege. As a result, their welfare states are somewhat larger and provide substantial security, but do not make a great effort at creating socioeconomic equality. Social insurance is even more important in this system, and benefits tend to be tied to the income of the head of the household, typically the father. Germany's pensions and benefits to families with children are high, but single-parent households are treated less generously. Other welfare states are distinctly social democratic. Social democrats believe in using democracy to achieve a socialist society. As a result, they tend to produce the largest welfare states. They are more egalitarian and provide greater security and independence from the market. While social democracies rely heavily on social insurance, they also provide extensive public assistance programs that are not means tested, such as national health and day-care systems, or that have high income thresholds as qualification for the program.

A brief comparison of the Swedish, German, and U.S. welfare states clearly illustrates the nature of the differences and their connection to varying ideological tendencies. The first issue to consider is size, which is captured at least crudely by government spending as a percentage of gross domestic product (GDP). In 1989, government spending constituted 57.3 percent of GDP in Sweden, 41.6 percent in Germany, and 34.6 percent in the United States. Rates of taxation followed a similar pattern. Thus, welfare state size is related to ideology, with social democracies producing the largest systems, and market-oriented liberal regimes the smallest.

These countries also vary in the degrees of security that they provide. One aspect of security is the likelihood of unemployment. Using the average percentage of the labor force unemployed during the 1980's, a striking pattern emerges, with Sweden averaging 2.3 percent unemployed, Germany 6.1 percent, and the United States 7.0 percent. The U.S. emphasis on participation in the free market actually results in lower levels of employment. Research strongly suggests that levels and patterns of welfare spending are the single most important factor in reducing poverty; therefore, one might also consider the security provided by welfare states in terms of the percentage of their populations living in poverty. Using the official United States poverty line for 1979 to 1982 as a benchmark, 6 percent of Sweden's population lived in poverty, 8 percent in Germany, and 13 percent in the United States.

These three welfare states vary in terms of the equality of protection and benefits that they provide. One way of comparing this aspect of welfare states is to compare the level of guaranteed benefits against the legal maximum possible within a system. In Sweden, guaranteed benefits constitute 82 percent of the maximum. The corresponding figures for Germany and the United States are 56 percent and 22 percent, respectively. Thus, in Sweden the benefits of the welfare state are almost universal, whereas in the United States they are highly influenced by income. The reduction of poverty among specific groups by government programs provides another example. The Social Security program in the United States more than closes the gap between the average incomes of elderly families and the poverty line, but the modest public assistance programs in the United States fail to do so for families with working-age adults. Sweden's programs, on the other hand, close the gap for both groups.

Context

Society's ambivalence toward the welfare state is perhaps best illustrated by considering the debates within two theoretical traditions that are typically opposed to one another: liberal theories of capitalist democracy, and theories of socialism. These debates occasionally make allies of philosophical enemies and serve to underline the welfare state's status as a hybrid system of political economy.

Some theorists of capitalist democracy emphasize freedom from state control and the rights of individuals to act as they see fit, that is, liberalism. For these theorists, the free market is the preferred mechanism of social coordination and is far superior to collective human decision making. They believe that the free market will produce optimal outcomes, if left unfettered. This group opposes the welfare state, because the taxes and regulations that it embodies limit individuals' freedoms to dispose of their property as they see fit, and its benefits encourage dependence rather than giving individuals incentives for self-development. The welfare state also distorts market mechanisms and is likely to further bureaucratic, rather than democratic, government.

Theorists who support the welfare state counter these charges by pointing out that markets often fail, and that their adjustments often produce great social hardship and instability. Indeed, the welfare state may be critical to the survival of market capitalism itself. They point to the success of Keynesianism in the 1950's and 1960's as proof that market outcomes can be improved through political management. These theorists also point out that freedom from restriction and unhindered property rights mean little if individuals are locked systematically by the market in a struggle for subsistence, and that individuals must have sufficient economic foundations if they are to engage in self-development, or effectively exercise their political rights under democracy. The welfare state itself was enacted by democratic majorities, and its continued survival depends on their support.

An intense debate over the welfare state also exists among various kinds of socialist theorists. This debate is far easier to characterize. Revolutionary socialists and communists are opposed to the welfare state precisely because it protects capitalism by producing a better environment for the lower classes, thereby producing a favorable view of capitalism and limiting unrest, instability, and the chances of a revolution. Social democrats, on the other hand, view the welfare state as an early form of socialism that places greater and greater portions of the economy in the hands of the society and weakens dependence on market forces.

Bibliography

Clark, Barry. *Political Economy: A Comparative Approach.* New York: Praeger, 1991. Thorough but highly readable discussion of the ideological underpinnings of the market and political intervention. Considers how these philosophies are reflected in nine different policy areas, seven of which are key elements of the welfare state.

Friedman, Milton. *Capitalism and Freedom.* Chicago: University of Chicago Press, 1962. Statement by a Nobel Prize-winning economist as to why the welfare state, and government intervention in general, are undesirable in both political and economic terms.

Heidenheimer, Arnold J., Hugo Heclo, and Carolyn Teich Adams. *Comparative Public Policy: The Politics of Social Choice in America, Europe, and Japan.* 3d ed. New York: St. Martin's Press, 1990. Excellent survey of the variations in policy and policy outcomes found among the welfare states. Extensive bibliography for each policy-based chapter.

Schwarz, John E., and Thomas J. Volgy. *The Forgotten Americans.* New York: W. W. Norton, 1992. Account of the failure of the market and social programs to provide for the subsistence of working families. Contains a number of family histories, and also draws on Volgy's experiences as mayor of Tucson, Arizona.

W. David Patterson

Cross-References

Budgets of National Governments, p. 158; Capitalism, p. 197; Citizenship in World Governments, p. 254; Debts and Deficits in the U.S. Federal Budget, p. 489; The Democratic Party, p. 520; Entitlements, p. 610; The Family and Politics in the United States, p. 649; Government Roles, p. 778; Industrialization, p. 916; Keynesianism, Monetarism, and Supply-Side Economics, p. 1032; The Left and the Right, p. 1079; Liberalism, p. 1118; Political Economy, p. 1455; Scientific Humanism, p. 1784; Social Democracies, p. 1839; Social Democratic Parties, p. 1846; The Social Security System, p. 1852; Social Services, p. 1858.

WOMAN SUFFRAGE

Field of study: History of government and politics

Woman suffrage refers to the movement to secure the right to vote for female citizens in various nations. Suffrage movements incorporated calls for other social and political reform, including the abolition of slavery, improved workplace safety, and changes to marriage and property laws governing women's position in the community.

Principal terms
FEMINISM: advocacy of the rights of women and their social, political, and economic equality with men
SENECA FALLS CONVENTION: meeting held in Seneca Falls, New York, in 1848, that marked the beginning of the women's rights movement in the United States
SUFFRAGE: the right to vote in elections; also known as the franchise
SUFFRAGETTE: derisive term applied to activist female supporters of woman suffrage

Overview

The woman suffrage movement was a political and social reform movement that sought the extension of the franchise to women. In the United States, the first call for a woman's right to vote took place at the Seneca Falls Convention. In Great Britain, the suffrage movement grew out of middle- and upper-middle-class women's work in philanthropic activities, and by the 1860's, it had attracted sufficient exposure to force consideration of the issue by the House of Commons. The movement also gained strength from women's work in the abolitionist movement in the United States, and the gradual acceptance of democratic principles that led to widening the male franchise in Great Britain.

Prior to the emergence of an organized suffrage movement in Britain and the United States, the legal and political status of women was not at all clear. Political rights were granted on the basis of a number of factors, including birth, property ownership, and religion. In the seventeenth and eighteenth centuries, there was no consistent or widely accepted barrier per se to women's participation within political systems. Few women voted, however, and no women held any elected office in either Britain or its American colonies.

It was not until the American Revolution that women were expressly denied the right to vote. State constitutions were drafted that completely denied women the opportunities to vote and hold public office. Because the states had the authority to regulate elections, the barriers preventing women from voting also extended to local and national political offices. The situation of female political participation had shifted from one based on custom or local tradition to one rooted in the law. The legal systems of the United States and Great Britain did not recognize women as citizens and therefore denied them the right to vote.

With few exceptions, Western political thinkers did not view women as full participants in political life. The significant exceptions to this rule were the ancient Greek philosopher Plato (427-347 B.C.E.), Mary Wollstonecraft, and John Stuart Mill. Plato's dialogue, *The Republic*, concluded that the best political system was one based on the most efficient use of people's different natural abilities and talents. The political system contained three classes of persons: those who produced goods and services necessary for the material survival of the community, soldiers, and those who would rule the polity. The third class of persons were called philosophers, and their ability to rule was based on virtue, or excellence of character. The issue for Plato was whether women were capable of exercising virtue that would permit them to rule as philosophers. Plato reasoned that men and women were equal in political ability, and the ideal, or best, political system would be one ruled by equal proportions of men and women. Women had similar natures to men; therefore, it would be unnatural for women to be considered inferior to men when determining who was best fit to rule the political system.

Mary Wollstonecraft's *A Vindication of the Rights of Woman* (1792) focused on the natures of men and women concerning their participation in political matters. Wollstonecraft argued from the premise that distinctions among persons based on wealth, birth, and sex were not sufficient to prevent individuals from exercising their rights. Her political thought was shaped by the French Revolution and its calls for liberty and equality among male citizens. Wollstonecraft advanced the idea that differences in female and male natures resulted from the different educations each received, and she called for a radical rethinking of the educational system. Boys and girls should be educated together, and both sexes should be subject to a disciplined program of mental and physical exercise. Social interaction between boys and girls would lead to a sense of enlightenment concerning male-female relationships, and the equal education of boys and girls would advance the cause of human freedom. Wollstonecraft's arguments have been criticized by feminists because she strongly supported the family unit, and viewed the ideal woman as both wife and mother. Nevertheless, Wollstonecraft's treatise focused philosophical and political attention on the inequality of political participation between men and women and on the unequal education given to children based on sex.

The foremost advocate for woman suffrage among Western political thinkers was John Stuart Mill. An early supporter of woman suffrage in Great Britain, Mill was elected to the House of Commons, where he introduced legislation in 1865 that would have given women the right to vote. His efforts to secure the franchise for women were part of a larger struggle to expand the right to vote to members of the British working class. The House of Commons took up debate on expanding the vote in 1867 and subsequently passed the Second Reform Act. The act granted a substantial portion of the working class the right to vote, but it only applied to male citizens.

In his essay *On the Subjection of Women*, Mill argued against the prohibition of women in Parliament and in support of extending suffrage to women to utilize their political talents. First, Mill argued that if a woman's nature made her unfit for public office, it was redundant to pass legislation preventing her from seeking such offices because a woman would not be likely to seek an office for which her nature made her unfit. Mill further stated that if a woman did seek public office, competition among several candidates would, in all probability, prevent the woman's election. If an unfit woman managed to be elected, Mill suggested that the situation would not be horrible, given the fact that many unfit males were elected to Parliament. Mill's second position was that if women have special political skills that could be used to improve the situation of the community, it was unjust to fail to benefit from their service. Mill extended his analysis further by arguing for changes to the legal system. Under British law, a husband could seize his wife's property and wages, and engage in domestic violence against his spouse without being punished. The final authority in terms of child care was with the father, not the mother. For Mill, legal equality between women and men was the necessary first step for ending the sex and class domination of women in the most private aspects of people's lives—the home and family. Mill's analysis of women's emancipation was based on three arguments. First, legal changes were required, especially the right to vote. Second, since legal reforms could not, by themselves, transform the way men treated women, Mill argued that the movement toward emancipation would need to be extended to the home and family. Finally, Mill placed these prior arguments within the context of economic reform, where the family would act as a cooperative economic unit that would eventually raise the status of women within society. In the end, Mill argued for complete female participation in all aspects of public life and was a strong supporter of women's suffrage.

Applications

In Great Britain, the woman suffrage movement was founded in the mid-nineteenth century, but women did not receive the right to vote until 1928. The suffrage movement reflected the gradual acceptance of democratic theory and the rising pressure for equal rights for women in the 1860's and 1870's. In the 1860's, a small group of women in London formed a committee to lobby for the vote. The time was ripe for such an effort, because Parliament was debating legislation designed to expand the male franchise. The committee persuaded John Stuart Mill to propose that any changes in the voting law should include the right to vote for women. Although Mill's proposal was defeated, the issue of suffrage was placed on the political agenda. A number of suffrage committees were formed throughout Britain.

Until the early twentieth century, suffrage committees sought changes in women's legal status through constitutional means. In 1897, a number of local committees joined to form a national organization, the National Union of Women Suffrage Societies (NUWSS). Initially, most of the women who joined were from the middle class, but by the 1900's, working-class women participated in larger numbers because they believed the only way to press the government to address their economic and social problems was to gain the vote. In 1903, a new group emerged to challenge the

NUWSS. The Women's Social and Political Union (WSPU), founded by Emmeline and Christobel Pankhurst, was formed to focus attention on the suffrage question by using more militant tactics. The motto of the WSPU was "deeds, not words." Members sought public attention by employing militant tactics, including disrupting political meetings, holding outdoor demonstrations, and engaging in various acts of civil disobedience. These tactics led to an increase in public attention, which directly resulted in an increase in financial contributions to carry on the struggle for the vote. As a result of the intransigence of the Liberal government in the 1900's, many suffragists were jailed for destroying property. The struggle continued until the outbreak of World War I in 1914. Suffrage activity came to a halt, and women's groups threw their energy into the war effort. Since millions of women were required to enter the labor force to make up for the shortfall of male workers as a result of the war, many public officials came to realize that women had earned the right to vote through their contribution to the war effort. In 1918, Parliament passed the Representation of the People Act that granted the right to vote to women 30 years of age or older. Politicians feared that if women had the vote from the age of 21, they would outnumber men in the electorate. A decade later, Parliament granted the right to vote to all women 21 years of age and older with little debate.

In the United States, the suffrage movement originated with the Seneca Falls Convention. Prior to the Civil War, suffrage was a key component of the reform agenda of the women's rights movement. This consisted of women who were active in the abolitionist movement, and who argued that there were parallels between the enslavement of African Americans and the subordination of women. Following the Civil War, the Republican Party and the abolitionist movement initiated a series of constitutional amendments designed to grant the former slaves legal and political rights. Many in the women's rights movement argued that women should also be given full legal and political rights. The Republicans argued that civil rights for former slaves was a higher priority than suffrage for women, and the efforts to grant rights to African Americans could not be jeopardized by simultaneously pursuing the goal of woman suffrage. This emphasis caused a split within the women's rights movement. Both Henry Blackwell (1825-1909) and his wife, suffragist Lucy Stone (1818-1893), supported the Republican Party's position on the suffrage issue. Opponents, including Susan B. Anthony (1820-1906) and the women's rights movement founder, Elizabeth Cady Stanton (1815-1902), split from the movement to form the National Woman Suffrage Association (NWSA) in 1869. The same year saw the formation of the American Woman Suffrage Association (AWSA), led by Blackwell and Stone. The two groups did not oppose each other simply as a result of the Republicans' emphasis on African American suffrage. There were ideological, personality, and strategic differences between the groups. The NWSA linked the suffrage question to other grievances held by women. The AWSA remained more moderate and adopted the strategy of pursuing suffrage as a single issue distinct from other concerns. The NWSA favored the adoption of a constitutional amendment so that all women would receive the right to vote, while the AWSA followed the state-by-state approach that would build enough momentum to force woman suffrage onto the political agenda. The lack of success in securing the right to vote for women finally prompted the two groups to join forces in 1890, forming the National American Woman Suffrage Association (NAWSA). The union was not amicable. NAWSA gave in to the racism of Southern suffragists who were determined not to allow African American women the right to vote. The organization became more moderate in ideology and adopted the strategy of pursuing suffrage as a single issue. The group also broadened its base of support by bringing in working-class women, as well as upper-class women associated with the Progressive reform movement. By 1917, when the United States entered World War I, several states had passed laws granting women the right to vote. The Sixty-sixth Congress passed the Anthony Amendment in 1919, which stated that the right to vote could not be abridged on account of sex. Fifteen months later, on August 26, 1920, the Nineteenth Amendment was ratified by three-fourths of the states, and women in the United States had finally won the right to vote.

The woman suffrage movement was successful for a variety of reasons. First, it took place during the Progressive Era, when numerous changes to social and economic institutions prompted calls for suffrage. Second, women's contributions to the war effort won them credibility and legitimacy within society at large. Third, the hard work and dedication of the suffragists, as well as their political strategy, allowed the movement to flourish based on a broad alliance of women and men from all walks of life. This broad base of support allowed the movement to exert legislative pressure that ultimately resulted in the right to vote for women.

THE GRANTING OF WOMAN SUFFRAGE IN MODERN NATIONS

1893	New Zealand	1944	France
1901	Australia	1945	Italy
1915	Denmark		Japan
1917	Russia	1946	Liberia
1918	Canada	1948	Israel
	Great Britain	1949	China
	Poland	1950	India
1919	Germany	1952	Argentina
	The Netherlands	1953	Mexico
1920	United States	1956	Egypt
1921	Sweden	1963	Iran
1931	Spain	1971	Switzerland
1934	Brazil	1980	Iraq
	Cuba		
1939	Philippines		

Context
The woman suffrage movement is significant for a number of reasons. In ideological terms, granting women the right to vote was supported by those who argued that women would have a calming influence on political life and would be less susceptible to corruption upon entering the political arena. Suffrage was supported on the basis of societal benefits. By allowing women to compete for political office, the quality of leadership would be increased and better public policy would be the end result. Perhaps the most persuasive argument for suffrage was the legitimacy of the political system. Denying women the right to vote denied representation to one-half the population. This was clearly unjust, because women paid taxes but were not represented in the legislature. In most nations, suffrage was granted in the period following World War I when the contribution of women to the war effort was recognized as being important.

Bibliography
Barber, James David, and Barbara Kellerman, eds. *Women Leaders in American Politics*. Englewood Cliffs, N.J.: Prentice-Hall, 1986. Useful, thorough collection of short articles by historical figures and scholars on numerous topics related to women in politics and society.

Darcy, Robert, Susan Welch, and Janet Clark. *Women, Elections, and Representation*. New York: Longman, 1987. Excellent study of past and current activities relating to women in the political process. Excellent bibliography and historical discussion of representation and suffrage.

Flexner, Eleanor. *Century of Struggle: The Woman's Rights Movement in the United States*. Rev. ed. Cambridge, Mass.: Harvard University Press, 1975. Definitive work on the struggle for women's suffrage in the United States. Often-cited work in this area.

Kraditor, Aileen. *The Ideas of the Woman Suffrage Movement, 1890-1920*. New York: W. W. Norton, 1981. Focuses on the efforts of American women to secure the right to vote, from the merger of the two main women's rights organizations to the ratification of the Nineteenth Amendment.

Tierney, Helen, ed. *Women's Studies Encyclopedia*. 3 vols. Westport, Conn.: Greenwood Press, 1989-1991. Excellent source for a variety of issues in the arts, sciences, social sciences, and culture relating to women.

Jeffery L. Jackson

Cross-References

WOMEN IN POLITICS

Field of study: Politics

As public officeholders, women are the most underrepresented social group in the United States. The fact that women constitute more than half of the population gives them a unique role in politics.

Principal terms
EQUALITY: having the same rights or status
FEMINISM: advocacy of full legal and social equality for women
FRANCHISE: the right to vote in public elections
GENDER GAP: measurable differences in voting behavior between men and women
SUFFRAGE MOVEMENT: historical struggle to win women the right to vote

Overview

In colonial America, political rights were granted largely on custom and usage, which implied that politics was for men only. This was rarely specified, however. Where specifications existed, they tended to be based on property, wealth, age, and religion, not gender. Land ownership was a particularly important qualification. Propertyholders generally were male, but conditions existed in which property could be held by women. Daughters and widows could inherit, divorced women could leave a marriage with their property, and women could even own property in their own names. Therefore, under certain circumstances, women were eligible to vote while many men were not. Few women, however, had the franchise and fewer exercised it. While colonial America was not a political golden age for women, it did not bar them completely from participation, either. That came after the American Revolution.

When the former colonies became the United States, each had separate written constitutions, which specified the qualifications required for the franchise. Before the American Revolution, local governments were essentially private spheres. Local rights of political participation and the ability to hold elective office were lost when the national government began including local governments under the national system. This was accomplished by first specifying who had national or state political rights, and then limiting participation to those persons.

The American Revolution led to a general loss of status for American women. Two reasons for this loss were the shift from custom, which allowed for conditions under which women could vote, to written constitutions, which did not; and the move from a property-based franchise toward universal manhood suffrage.

The process of restoring and expanding the female franchise was complex, because suffrage was controlled by individual states and because of the distinctive electoral bases of various local governmental units. Nevertheless, the movement toward women's suffrage began at the local level.

Political participation for women has been more readily available at the local level for two reasons. One concerns the functions and activities of local government, which include caring for the poor, education, sanitation, and the regulation of activities that affect the health and welfare of citizens. These fit within the scope of traditional roles and concerns of women. One reason advanced for female suffrage was women's concern for protecting and advancing the health and welfare of their families. A second reason was that local government was conducted close to home and required only part-time commitments. Women traditionally were tied to household and family obligations that permitted only a limited amount of free time and forced them to remain close to home. Women could participate in local government while still fulfilling their other roles.

In the United States, the period when no woman is known to have voted lasted thirty-one years, from 1807, when New Jersey withdrew suffrage, to 1838, when Kentucky granted it on a limited basis. Even in states where the local franchise was not available, women were elected and appointed to local offices and positions in relatively large numbers. In nonsuffragist states, women were elected to school-related positions in roughly equal numbers as in suffragist states. In 1906, women were elected to the position of county supervisor in 18 of 53 South Dakota counties, and 9 of 102 Illinois counties, although both were nonsuffragist states.

On August 26, 1920, the Nineteenth Amendment became part of the United States Constitution, giving the right of suffrage to women. Suffragists had campaigned for the vote; they did not particularly want, nor did they seek in large numbers, to gain public office. Having the vote would facilitate two different strategies. First, women would have more influence over male politicians and would be able to lobby more effectively for needed reforms. Second, women could use their votes through direct legislation, which allows citizens to petition to overrule legislation or initiate new legislation. As for holding public office, there was little difference after national suffrage from the situation beforehand. In 1929, 122 women served in state legislatures; that number increased to only 140 by 1937.

The early leaders of the suffrage movement believed that with the vote, women would become the cutting edge of social change. They claimed that women would have a morally uplifting, life-enhancing, and liberalizing effect on the nation. They believed, too, that women could prevent wars. James D. Cox, the unsuccessful 1920 Democratic presidential candidate, greeted ratification of the Nineteenth Amendment by declaring that the civilization of the world was saved, because the mothers of the world would stay the hand of war. Although women tended to be more antiwar than men, even with the right to vote, they lacked the political power to prevent war.

This view echoed the rhetoric that suffragists had employed for reasons of expediency as well as personal conviction. In the early days of the suffrage movement, many suffragists had focused on the sexual and social liberation of the individual woman as the key to equality. Suffrage was only one necessary reform in a long agenda that they hoped would revolutionize male-female relationships and society as a whole.

Suffrage leaders gradually began to emphasize women's roles as wife, mother, and homemaker. Women were the guardians of the family's spiritual values, while man's domain was the public world of commerce, work, and power. In arguing for the vote, suffragists asserted that women would bring their home-nurtured morality to the public sphere, and the reforms that they sought would preserve and protect the welfare and stability of the family. "Enlarged housekeeping" was the term temperance leader Frances Willard used to describe politics, and depicted women in aprons wielding brooms, cleaning up public messes.

After gaining suffrage, women's organizations established a joint congressional committee to lobby for and monitor the progress of legislation affecting women and children. Their first victory was a controversial 1921 maternity and infancy bill that appropriated $1.25 million annually for educational instruction in the health care of mothers and infants. This was the forerunner of the late twentieth century Maternal and Child Health Block Grant, which serves nearly twelve million low-income women and children, and the Women, Infants, and Children (WIC) Program, which provides dietary supplements and health care to about 2.4 million needy pregnant women, nursing mothers, and children under five years of age.

In the mid-1920's, many male politicians quit trying to win women's political favor. It had become clear that no female voting bloc existed, and women generally voted like their husbands, if they voted at all. Millions of women voted, but in far fewer numbers than men. Only about one-third of the eligible female electorate voted in 1920. Acquiring the habit of voting proved to be a slow process, particularly in what was still a hostile climate.

With the passage of the suffrage amendment, the energy seemed to drain out of the movement for women's political rights. Gaining the right to vote had been a single dramatic issue that unified and compelled women to action. Having won the vote, women could not find any comparable simple and universal issue around which to mobilize. Disillusionment set in when they found that winning the vote had not changed their lives significantly.

Some contemporary political scientists have concluded that the early suffragists were right: The real obstacle to equality was not the vote, but the division of lifestyles between men and women. It was not until women became self-supporting equal partners with men that women began to vote in large numbers. It was not the right to vote, but changes in the structure of society, that brought about changes in the political role of women.

Applications

Beginning with the 1980 presidential election, when Ronald Reagan won the presidency with eight percentage points less support from women than men, a new phenomenon started to appear in voting patterns. In the 1982 elections, more women than men voted Democratic in thirty-three of forty-four Senate and gubernatorial races, although the White House was controlled by a Republican president. Women provided the winning difference in the election of three governors and turned some Democratic victories into landslide mandates for progressive change. Edward J.

Rollins, President Reagan's chief political adviser, warned that the party with the women's vote would be the majority party, while the party of men would be the minority party. By the end of 1982, the phenomenon was termed the "gender gap."

The women's vote tends to reflect the values of the organized women's movement in responding to candidates' positions on important policy matters more than on their party affiliations or personal attributes. Being a Democrat does not guarantee votes for a candidate who is a war hawk, or who favors increased military spending or cutting such domestic programs as job training, family planning, and Social Security. Increasingly, these are the issues about which women care.

The reason that the gender gap took so long to appear reflects the nature of U.S. society. Social changes that have worked to the benefit of women had a long gestation period. Women's political and social gains have been won only by expending considerable amounts of energy to eliminate the barriers to full equality.

As political strategists continue to ponder the long-term meaning of the electoral gender gap, two other gender gaps have remained entrenched in the political and social structures of the nation. First, women are a majority of the population, but they hold only a small percentage of elective and appointive offices. Women may vote for what they hope will be compassionate and peaceful governmental policies, but they do not occupy the seats of power where the real decisions are made. Another gender-related gap deals with pay equity. During most of the last half of the twentieth century, working women averaged only fifty-nine cents of pay for every dollar that men earned. Both of these issues have complicated women's attempts to achieve political and social equality.

As late as 1939, bills were introduced in state legislatures to prohibit married women from working in state or local government if their husbands earned equal to or more than a base income. At the time, a majority of both men and women favored such legislation. The shortage of workers during World War II brought millions of women into the workforce, and they have remained ever since. In 1940, only 25 percent of all working-age women had jobs outside of the home. By 1945, that figure had jumped to 36 percent. In the early 1990's, more than 53 percent of all working-age women were employed outside the home.

Women in the 1990's earned less than men in every job category. Even more disturbing is the fact that women college graduates, on the average, earned less than male high school graduates. According to the *United States Department of Labor Dictionary of Occupational Titles*, which lists 427 occupations with their wage levels, 80 percent of all working women were employed in twenty-five generally low-paying jobs, including secretaries, clerks, wait staff, household service persons, salespersons, elementary school teachers, and librarians. Only 1 percent of American women earned $25,000 per year; three out of five working women earned less than $10,000 annually. The wage gap was even greater for minority women. For African American women, the average salary was fifty-four cents for every male dollar; for Latino women, forty-nine cents for every male dollar.

In the 1990's, one out of every two married women with children under six years of age worked outside of the home, as compared to only 19 percent in 1960. By the 1990's, nearly two-thirds of women with children over the age of six held jobs outside the home.

In 1983, the Women's Equity Action League reported that 77.7 percent of poor people were women and children, and 74 percent of the elderly poor were women. Thirty-three percent of all single-parent families maintained by women lived in poverty. Female-headed families represented 50 percent of the nation's 6.4 million poor families, though they made up only 16 percent of all families.

In 1982, more than one-third of all minority families were headed by women, and more than one-half lived below the poverty level, despite the fact that 56 percent of minority women who headed households were in the labor force. Among poor families with children under eighteen, the poverty rate was 68 percent for African Americans, 67 percent for Latinos, and 43 percent for whites.

For millions of American women who live in poverty or on its edge, the feminization of poverty leads directly to the feminization of politics. They are determined to have a greater say over the political, economic, and social forces that dictate the way that they live.

Political scientists have developed a model of the factors that increase voting in the United States. The model suggests that voter turnout increases along with employment, education, income, age, interest in the campaign, and concern with the outcome of the election. Since 1920, when education began being measured in median years of education completed, women have been slightly better educated than men. While only 18 percent of American women earned college degrees in 1900, more than 50 percent of American women in the 1990's have earned theirs. Women make up just over half of all students enrolled in higher education.

These demographic changes have had a radical impact on women's role in society, how women perceive themselves, and how they seek solutions to their individual and family problems. Millions of educated single women are placing higher values on personal independence, satisfying work careers, and pay and job equity. These changes in society have caused changes in the political role of women.

Context

The year 1992 was dubbed the "year of the woman" when female membership in the Senate and House of Representatives increased dramatically. It was also a year in which newly elected president Bill Clinton appointed women to 30 percent of the top jobs in his administration. Most women believed, however, that it would be at least another decade before any lasting political and electoral gains were made by women. First-term U.S. senator Dianne Feinstein (California), part of an electoral surge that increased the number of women in the House from twenty-eight to forty-seven and in the Senate from two to seven, was reportedly stunned by the prediction that she would probably be in her grave before the number of female senators reaches twenty, and that her granddaughter will probably be dead before women reach parity with men in the United States Senate.

Redistricting and retirements had opened up many congressional seats that women captured. Twenty-two of the twenty-four newly elected women in the House won in open-seat races, as did four of the five new female senators. The 1993 races were more difficult for women than those of 1992. In 1992, women ran primarily for seats in Congress, but in 1993, women sought the offices of governor and mayor. Results indicate that fewer voters prefer women in executive offices than in legislative posts.

Voters have been found to worry that women are not tough enough to be governors, yet feel uncomfortable when women come across as too tough. Women have to strive constantly for a comfortable middle ground of appearing strong enough to lead, but not so tough as to appear threatening. The issue agenda is also difficult for women. The economy and crime are two dominant political issues. Voters seem to have less confidence in women than men on both issues.

On the other hand, many voters view women as more in touch with their constituents and caring more about people. They think women certainly know the price of a gallon of milk—an advantage in an environment where 86 percent of voters consider themselves middle class and three-fourths think that the middle class is having a difficult time. Overall, voters think women are more in touch, care more about the average person, are better listeners, and are better negotiators than men—all legislative traits. They also believe that women are not as good as men in handling crises, supervising big budgets and staffs, being tough, and managing—all executive traits.

Bibliography

Abzug, Bella, with Mim Kelber. *Gender Gap*. Boston: Houghton Mifflin, 1984. Useful, highly readable account of the history of the women's movement. Includes a directory of organizations active in gender-gap politics.

Darcy, Robert, Susan Welch, and Janet Clark. *Women, Elections, and Representation*. New York: Longman, 1987. Comprehensive examination of the history and status of women in state and local governments.

Githens, Marianne, Pippa Norris, and Joni Lovenduski, eds. *Different Roles, Different Voices: Women and Politics in the United States and Europe*. New York: Harper-Collins College, 1994. Multifaceted reader that examines the women's movement for electoral rights from United States' and European perspectives.

Allison L. Hayes

Cross-References

Civil Rights and Liberties, p. 298; Feminist Politics, p. 682; Gay and Lesbian Politics, p. 732; Gender Politics, p. 738; Reproductive Politics, p. 1692; Voting in History, p. 2116; Woman Suffrage, p. 2141.

THE WORLD BANK

Field of study: International government and politics

A *publicly owned financial intermediary, the World Bank is the foremost international development agency that lends money for development projects to member countries.*

Principal terms

BRETTON WOODS SYSTEM: consists of the International Monetary Fund, the World Bank, and the General Agreement on Tariffs and Trade, the first two of which were created at Bretton Woods, New Hampshire, in 1944

GENERAL AGREEMENT ON TARIFFS AND TRADE (GATT): international agreement made in 1947 to encourage reductions in trade barriers; its central tenet of nondiscrimination is implemented through the most-favored nation principle

INTERNATIONAL MONETARY FUND (IMF): international agreement made in 1944 in order to ensure exchange rate stability through the use of short-term loans

SECTORAL ADJUSTMENT LOAN (SECAL): loan to support economic reform within a particular sector

STRUCTURAL ADJUSTMENT LOAN (SAL): loan made on the condition that the recipient country will adopt specified economic or financial reforms

Overview

The World Bank is a quasi-autonomous group comprising two agencies: the International Bank for Reconstruction and Development (IBRD), founded at the Bretton Woods Conference in 1944 along with its twin, the International Monetary Fund (IMF), and the International Development Association (IDA), created in 1960 to provide concessional loans to developing nations. Although the IBRD stands at the center of the World Bank group, the two agencies are administered as a single institution and are virtually indistinguishable. They share the same staff and follow the same policy guidelines. The IDA is essentially a "legal fiction" in that it is not a truly autonomous institution, despite the fact that it formally has its own constitution. The two affiliates in the World Bank group—the International Finance Corporation (IFC), created in 1956 to assist economic development in poor countries through private investment, and the Multilateral Investment Guarantee Agency (MIGA), created in 1988 to encourage the flow of direct investment to the Third World through the lessening of noncommercial investment barriers—are independent of the World Bank. Both are run as separate institutions. The World Bank is therefore generally understood to include both the IBRD and IDA—a definition followed herein.

The World Bank, which began operations in 1946, was designed (essentially by American officials) to be an efficient intermediary for the transfer of resources at the global level. It has emerged as one of the three pillars of the postwar international economic order. The other two are the IMF, created to ensure monetary stability through the use of short-term loans, and the General Agreement on Tariffs and Trade (GATT), created in 1947 to encourage negotiated reductions in trade barriers and to foster free trade.

During its first fifty years, the IBRD membership (which is a prerequisite for membership of the IDA and IFC) more than quadrupled: from thirty-eight in 1946 to 178 in 1994. A rapid increase in its membership during the 1990's was caused by the historic changes in Europe: the collapse of communism in Eastern Europe and the Soviet Union, and the region's adoption of a market economy. Most new members of the bank in the 1990's were former Communist countries or the constituent parts of the former Soviet Union that became independent—for example, Mongolia, Croatia, Albania, Russia, Latvia, Lithuania, Moldova, Belarus, Tajikistan, and Ukraine.

According to its Articles of Agreement, the World Bank's objectives are "to finance reconstruction, to promote foreign investment and international trade, and to guarantee lending by others, or to lend itself, for the more useful and urgent projects." The bank was conceived primarily as a source for long-term loans on near-commercial terms to member countries. At its beginning, the IBRD provided loans to European countries devastated by World War II. Yet it soon became involved in lending to developing countries. With assets worth more than $100 billion, a yearly lending program of about $24 billion (in 1993), and an annual administrative budget of more than $1 billion, the bank is the leading international agency that is concerned with development. As the single largest provider of loans to developing nations, it exerts considerable influence in those parts of the world.

The stockholders of the bank are its member governments, who control votes in the organization proportional to their subscriptions. About 43 percent of its voting shares are held by the five largest shareholders: the United States, Japan, Germany, Great Britain, and France. By controlling the largest share of votes (37 percent in 1947; 17.59 percent in 1992), the United States exerts significant influence over World Bank decisions. The bank is administered by a board of governors, composed of all member countries who meet once a year; an executive board consisting of twenty-two elected and appointed directors who approve all loans; a president, who is chairman of the executive board; a chief operating officer; and a staff of economists, engineers, and other professionals, all with impressive technical and intellectual reputations, who are drawn from developed and developing nations. The bank's professional staff issues influential research publications, notably the annual *World Development Report*, on issues such as trade liberalization and debt. With more than 6,200 regular staff in 1991, the bank has developed into a large bureaucracy. The location of the bank in Washington, D.C., and an unwritten understanding that the bank presidents (eight so far) will be American citizens appointed by the United States president, make American influence in the institution preeminent.

The IBRD obtains its funding through paid-in contributions from member countries (10 percent of the share capital), commercial borrowing, and loan repayments. The bulk of its funding, however, is obtained from bond sales on the capital markets in the industrial countries. These bonds are backed by the capital put up or callable capital (90 percent of the share capital) by member governments, giving bank bonds first-class status in the American ("Triple A rating"), European, and Japanese markets. The bank borrows at extremely favorable rates because its creditors have the guarantee that its callable capital is committed to meeting its obligations.

The IBRD lends money at rates that are significantly more favorable for most borrowers than those they can obtain on commercial rates—despite the fact that the bank itself raises most of its funds on the capital market. Its loans are repaid over periods lasting ten to fifteen years, and it lends to countries that it regards as creditworthy. Almost all of its loans are either to, or guaranteed by, governments. Founded on sound financial principles, the World Bank has never suffered a default on a loan. Latin America has been the region that has benefited most from IBRD loans.

The International Development Association (IDA) is the concessional finance wing of the World Bank. It is an integral part of the bank, and its organizational structure replicates that of the IBRD. It was created in response to the developing nations' demands during the 1950's (especially of India) for a Special United Nations Fund for Economic Development. Its creation in 1960 transformed the World Bank into a development agency. Unlike the IBRD, the IDA is funded primarily by grants made by its richest member countries from their own aid budgets. The IDA terms are concessionary. Its loans, referred to as credits, are interest-free and carry an annual service charge of 0.75 percent. They mature in thirty-five to forty years with a grace period of ten years, and repayments begin ten years after the credit is signed. They are restricted, however, only to the poorest countries—those with an annual per capita GNP of $610 (in 1990 dollars) or less. Because of this criterion, IDA credits have gone to sub-Saharan African countries, Bangladesh, Indonesia, and the two largest developing countries—India and China. As a region South Asia has received the most IDA credits over the years.

Although the IDA credits are reserved for the poorest countries, there are a few "blend countries" that receive both IDA and IBRD loans. Countries "graduate" from the IDA to the IBRD as they gain in economic strength. Eventually, the IBRD lending itself is phased out and the countries move to commercial borrowing when their per capita income exceeds $2,850. In 1994 the IDA had 157 members—twenty-one fewer than the IBRD. While IBRD membership is required for being a member of the IDA, not all IBRD members have joined the IDA.

Applications

The IBRD's initial priority, after it became operational in 1946, was reconstruction of the war-ravaged economy of the European states. Between 1947 and 1953 it committed $753 million to Europe, which was more than it lent to any other region. It was overshadowed in this role, however, by the Marshall Plan, which supplied

Europe with about twenty times as much money during the same period. Thereafter, the bank's focus shifted to Third World development. While its lending policies and approaches to development have changed over time, primarily in response to the changing international environment and priorities established from time to time by its presidents, the bank has played an important role in promoting development in the Third World.

During its first three decades, both IBRD and IDA loans were made to finance projects, and the bank's lending was overwhelmingly to the governments, government agencies, and state-owned enterprises. Under President Eugene Black (in office, 1949-1962) the bank concentrated on large-scale infrastructure projects in transportation, power, and ports—for example, the Indus River Basin project on the border of India and Pakistan. Though George Woods (president, 1963-1968) sought to extend the bank's lending into new areas such as small-scale agriculture, education, and water supply, it was under Robert McNamara (president, 1968-1981) that the bank became highly visible and its combined lending increased dramatically: from $953 million in 1968 to $12.4 billion in 1981.

The World Bank's mission under McNamara was highly idealistic and moralistic, focusing on helping the poor in the developing world. McNamara committed the bank to poverty alleviation programs and deepened its concern for issues relating to population pressure, social and economic inequality, and rural development. IDA financing, in particular, gave priority to irrigation facilities and agricultural credit during the 1970's. The bank, in fact, acted as a lender of "last resort" to developing countries.

Under McNamara's successors—A. W. Clausen (1981-1986), Barber Conable (1986-1991), and Lewis Preston (beginning in 1991)—the bank shifted its priority to adjustment lending. The 1980's and 1990's witnessed an explosion of two forms of policy-based lending—structural adjustment loans (SALs) and sectoral adjustment loans (SECALs). SECALs (loans to support economic reform within particular sectors, such as agricultural price reform or trade liberalization) were the main form of adjustment lending between 1984 and 1991. SALs (which look beyond projects to the economy as a whole and impose conditions such as price reforms, removal of subsidies, liberalization of internal and external trade, privatization, export promotion, deregulation, wage restraint, and contraction and restructuring of government institutions) emerged as the main form of loans after 1992. SALs are therefore given on the condition that recipient countries will adopt designated economic or financial reforms.

Policy-based lending was the World Bank's response to the international debt crisis in the 1980's. By influencing national economic policies at the highest level, the bank sought to stabilize economies and succeeded in bringing about structural adjustments in many loan recipient countries. Yet the adjustment lending policy became highly controversial in the 1990's. A number of critical studies published on the eve of the bank's fiftieth anniversary in 1994 pointed to the negative impact of the bank's policy on the living standards of the poor in countries implementing structural adjustment programs. Critics also charged that the bank has become a de facto policymaker in many developing countries.

Context

The planners who met at the United Nations Monetary and Financial Conference at Bretton Woods in July, 1944, tried to design a postwar international economic order by creating multilateral institutions that would help bring about stability in international trade and investment—which had collapsed in the wake of the Great Depression of the 1930's. They erected the World Bank on the premise that it would promote self-sustaining economic development by facilitating the flow of private investment capital. It was not, however, created with the problems of the modern Third World in mind. Nevertheless, the bank's priority shifted from reconstruction to development in the context of the changing international environment. The beginning of the Cold War and the decolonization of Asia and Africa provided the context in which the bank's priorities changed. With the onset of the Cold War, development assistance began to be viewed by many in the West as a check on the spread of communism in the Third World. The search for ways to provide development assistance led to the creation of the IDA, which transformed the bank into the leading development agency.

The bank's lending policy was heavily influenced by the neoliberal theory of economic growth, popular in the West in the early postwar period. Central to this theory was a belief in the desirability of economic growth that was expected to alleviate poverty through a trickle-down effect. As a result, the bank focused on growth-related sectors such as infrastructure development, transportation, and energy. Under McNamara the bank adopted a new theoretical approach to development: redistribution with growth. After McNamara committed the bank to poverty-oriented projects in the early 1970's, the bank's lending focused on agricultural and rural development, basic needs, primary and nonformal education, and alleviation of urban poverty. This radical shift in policy was McNamara's response to the dramatic changes in the international system in the early 1970's—the oil crisis of 1973-1974, the Third World demand for the creation of a new international economic order, the failure of development in the Third World in the 1950's and 1960's, and the emergence of a radical critique and a Latin American alternative (dependency theory) to the Western development theory, which provided a better explanation for poverty, backwardness, and underdevelopment in the Third World.

Under the leadership of A. W. Clausen, who emphasized economic growth and free-market principles, the bank's focus shifted from basic needs to SALs in the early 1980's. This policy change was the bank's response to the balance-of-payment difficulties experienced by many developing countries—notably Mexico, Argentina, and Brazil—in the wake of the debt crisis of 1982. Borrowing from the bank thus became conditional on the recipient government's undertaking to implement bank-imposed reform programs. The bank also responded to the growing concern expressed by nongovernment environmental organizations (NGOs). It instituted a new environmental policy in 1989 and required countries to prepare comprehensive environmental action plans in order to be eligible for IDA loans. In 1990 President Conable re-introduced poverty alleviation as a major focus of the bank's activity in response to the human suffering and degradation in Africa. Two years later the *World Development Report* committed the bank to the concept of sustainable development.

During the 1980's and 1990's the bank became a much more visible institution as its lending policies came under serious scrutiny and attack from critics on the left and right. Those on the left—Cheryl Payer and Teresa Hayter, for example—advanced the thesis of "aid as imperialism" and argued that the bank has been an instrument of Western private capital in the underdeveloped world. On the other hand, market-oriented conservative critics such as Peter Bauer, David Stockman, and Milton Friedman claim that the bank has promoted state planning and socialism in the Third World at the cost of private enterprise. They question whether the bank should lend at all to the qualified member countries.

Much of the criticism in the early 1990's focused on the shift from project- to policy-based lending, the greater collaboration between the bank and the IMF, and the apparently negative ecological effect of the bank's projects in many developing countries. The critics also point to the bank's "pervasive preoccupation with new lending" as pointed out in the 1992 Wapenhans Report. This report, written by a former bank vice president, criticized the bank's lending culture—the rush to get money out the door—which has allowed it to grow continuously in spite of the "unsatisfactory" results of its projects. The number of unsatisfactory projects, according to the report, increased from 15 percent in 1981 to 38 percent in 1991.

Notwithstanding these criticisms, the bank has addressed many concerns expressed by the Third World governments, local peoples, and international and national NGOs. In 1993, for example, the bank decided to drop the controversial Sardar Sarovar and Narmada Sagar dam project in India because of the publicity given by international NGOs to the negative effect of the dam on the local population—especially the problem of resettlement of the displaced people. Likewise, the bank developed a new forestry policy in 1991, adopted a water resources policy in 1993, and committed $2 billion for twenty-three projects specifically designed to improve environmental quality and preserve natural resources.

The bank's shareholders disagree about the priority and role of the institution in the late 1990's and beyond. While the United States and Great Britain emphasize promoting the private sector, continental European countries worry more about the poor and the environment. Nor is there an agreement among bank staff: Some still see it primarily as an aid institution; others think it should become more of a commercial one. Though the World Bank's role as a lender to developing countries has been partly usurped by the markets—as witnessed by the net private capital flows to developing countries, which reached $88 billion in 1993, compared to the bank's total lending of $24 billion—private capital is not yet available to many developing countries, especially in Africa, nor can it meet needs in areas such as education and health, where returns to private lenders are uncertain.

Despite their criticism of the institution, the developing countries consider the bank's lending, which has totaled nearly $300 billion in loans and concessional aid since the 1950's, to be a positive contribution to Third World development. They do not, therefore, support the goal advanced by some critics that the bank should work itself out of a job. The bank's huge and powerful bureaucracy will prevent it from going out of business. The World Bank will therefore continue to exist as a major multilateral institution well into the twenty-first century, though its priority may change in response to the changing international environment.

Bibliography

Bandow, Doug, and Ian Vasquez, eds. *Perpetuating Poverty: The World Bank, the IMF, and the Developing World*. Washington, D.C.: Cato Institute, 1994. The sixteen essays in this volume analyze the impact of the multilateral lending institutions, such as the IMF and the World Bank, and regional development banks on the living standards and sustained economic prosperity in the Third World.

Danaher, Kevin, ed. *50 Years Is Enough: The Case Against the World Bank and the International Monetary Fund*. Boston, Mass.: South End Press, 1994. The three dozen brief essays in this volume provide highly critical, polemical, and often unsubstantiated evaluation of the two multilateral institutions.

de Vries, Barend A. *Remaking the World Bank*. Washington, D.C.: Seven Locks Press, 1987. An insider provides an analysis of the issues and problems facing the institution in the 1980's.

Gibbon, Peter, Kjell J. Havnevik, and Kenneth Hermele. *A Blighted Harvest: The World Bank and African Agriculture in the 1980s*. Trenton, N.J.: Africa World Press, 1993. Provides a detailed analysis of the effects of agricultural adjustment in six African countries: Ghana, Kenya, Mozambique, Tanzania, Uganda, and Zambia.

Mason, Edward S., and Robert E. Asher. *The World Bank Since Bretton Woods*. Washington, D.C.: Brookings Institution, 1973. Monumental history of the origins, policies, operation, and impact of the IBRD and other members of the World Bank Group.

Osterfeld, David. "The World Bank and the IMF: Misbegotten Sisters." In *The Collapse of Development Planning*, edited by Peter J. Boettke. New York: New York University Press, 1994. Critical study of the Bretton Woods twins, arguing that both institutions have failed in accomplishing the original goals of their founders.

Payer, Cheryl. *The World Bank: A Critical Analysis*. New York: Monthly Review Press, 1982. Provides a detailed and critical analysis of the World Bank's typical industry-oriented and people-oriented projects and argues that the bank is a huge public subsidy to private profit.

Williams, Marc. *International Economic Organisations and the Third World*. New York: Harvester Wheatsheaf, 1994. Perceptive analysis of the impact of the IMF, the World Bank, GATT, and the United Nations Conference on Trade and Development (UNCTAD) on Third World development.

Sunil K. Sahu

Cross-References

THE WORLD COURT

Field of study: International government and politics

The World Court, or International Court of Justice, is the primary judicial organ of the United Nations. When called upon, the court offers legal opinions and renders judgments in matters of international disputes.

Principal terms
ADJUDICATION: process of making legal decisions; the final decision of a court after a trial

COMPULSORY JURISDICTION: World Court's ability, in theory, to compel nations to obey its judgments

INTERNATIONAL LAW: rules and principles of law that regulate the interrelationships of nations and their conduct toward one another

JURISDICTION OF THE COURT: court's authority to hear and judge a case or enter a decree

LITIGANT: person, nation, or other party engaged in a lawsuit

PLEADINGS: formal written or oral statements by a plaintiff who brings a lawsuit and a defendant who answers the charges

Overview

In 1945, the Charter of the United Nations established the World Court as one of six major organs within that body. The charter formally referred to the court as "an International Court of Justice," whose mission was to help settle disputes among nations peacefully and provide advisory opinions for those with legal questions. The charter also indicated that all U.N. members were automatically parties to the Statute of the Court. On a case-by-case basis, nonmembers could become parties as determined by the General Assembly upon the recommendation of the Security Council.

Each year, the General Assembly of the United Nations must approve, by a two-thirds vote, the budget for the World Court. Expense items include salaries for court members and staff, building and maintenance costs, operational costs, *per diem* travel, subsistence allowances, and even pensions. These are all free from taxation. Although the court's annual budget is in the millions of dollars, its expenditures have been less than 1 percent of the total outlay for the United Nations.

The World Court's headquarters is the Peace Palace at The Hague, The Netherlands. Within its labyrinthine hallways and cavernous confines, the court's fifteen judges deliberate in the Great Hall of Justice. The fifteen judges, each from a different country, are elected by majority votes in the Security Council and the General Assembly of the United Nations. They serve nine-year terms and may be reelected. One-third of the terms expire every three years. Vacancies resulting from death or resignation are filled by replacement judges who go through the same election process as that of their predecessors. Presiding over the other judges of the court are the president and vice president, who direct the work of the court for a three-year term. Judges do not have to step aside on cases that involve their own countries; they are considered able to render independent judgments and remain unbiased. In fact, if a nation involved in a case has no judge on the bench, it may appoint an ad hoc judge of its own choosing.

The judges listen to legal arguments about such issues as territories, treaties, money, murder, and violence. The litigants are neither individuals nor corporations; they are entire nations. The law these judges render is not of local or even national origin, but rather international law.

Court proceedings are usually conducted in one of the two official languages, French or English. If litigants orally plead in a language other than one of the official languages, they must provide written translations in French or English.

Litigants normally argue their cases before the entire bench of fifteen judges. Under special circumstances, however, they may plead their cases before a special chamber with three or more judges in attendance.

The court follows specific procedures in processing cases. First, each case is assigned a number. All U.N. members are notified of the impending proceedings so as to alert any nation that might have a stake in the deliberations. Next, written pleadings by the contending parties are submitted to members of the court and to other interested persons. Then the oral hearings take place. The applicant state—the nation that instituted the suit—pleads first, followed by the respondent state—the nation against whom the action was brought.

After oral arguments are closed, the court withdraws to deliberate and to make its decision. Sitting in private chambers, the judges state their opinions and provide a rationale for their positions. A vote is then taken, with majority rule. No detailed minutes of the deliberations are prepared, only an abstract of the essentials of the debate: the votes taken, the judges who voted for or against the applicant state, and any statements the judges wish to enter into the record.

The decision of the court is read at a public meeting. Copies of the decision are distributed to all parties concerned and to all members of the United Nations, and a sealed copy is deposited in the court's archives. The text of the case is made available to media personnel. It also appears in an annual report distributed by the court. Although the court may award costs in its judgments, normally each party involved in the litigation bears its own costs.

Although the World Court is said to have compulsory jurisdiction in the matters it hears, it cannot force a judgement on either of the contending parties if either finds the decision unacceptable. The United States, Russia, Iran, England, and France are among the nations that have on occasion refused to carry out the court's judgments. Some nations have even refused to appear before the court or to participate in the deliberations. The court can only use moral persuasion and possibly the fallout of bad publicity within the world community to prod contending parties to abide by its decisions.

Applications

The World Court has attempted to settle a number of wide-ranging international disputes and has offered a variety of advisory opinions to interested parties. Between 1947 and 1990, approximately two cases per year were submitted to the court. During that time, sixty-one contentious cases were adjudicated by the court, with twenty advisory cases on the docket.

The cases heard by the World Court fall into several broad categories. Some cases, for example, deal with issues such as reparations for deaths, injuries, and damaged properties. In 1947, Great Britain sought damages from Albania when British destroyers and lives were lost because Albania had mined the Corfu channel in the Ionian Islands off Greece. In 1948, the court rendered judgments in the killings of several agents of the United Nations in such trouble spots as Palestine, Israel, Jordan, and Egypt.

Many other court cases have involved territorial disputes. For example, in 1951 the court adjudicated the claims of France and Great Britain as to which country controlled the Channel Islands in the English Channel. In 1955, it ruled in Britain's dispute with Argentina and Chile over their claims to the Falkland Islands Territories and certain portions of Antarctica. It determined the boundaries of Honduras and Nicaragua in 1960. In 1962, the court rendered judgement as to whether Thailand or Cambodia had rightful claim to the temple of Preah Vihear.

The World Court also has heard arguments over territorial waters, the various continental shelves, and fishing and mineral rights. In 1951, the court presided when Great Britain disputed the baselines drawn by Norway in calculating its territorial waters, which Britain asserted favored Norwegian fishermen. After mineral resources were discovered and exploited in the bed of the North Sea, friction arose in 1969 among West Germany, Denmark, and The Netherlands over who controlled the mineral rights; the court defined a method to determine where the sea ends and the continental shelf begins. In 1974, the court resolved a treaty dispute between Britain and Iceland over fishing rights, reducing tensions in the so-called "cod war." During the 1980's, the court dealt with continental-shelf boundary disputes between Libya and Tunisia, Libya and Malta, and Canada and the United States.

International incidents involving aircraft have also occupied the court. It investigated the destruction of a U.S. plane near Japan in 1952 and another forced down in Hungary in 1954. When an Israeli commercial airliner was shot down over Bulgaria in 1955, Israel instituted court proceedings. In 1983, a South Korean Boeing 747 was blown out of the sky after violating Soviet airspace. In 1988, a U.S. Navy warship mistakenly shot down an Iranian Airbus. All these incidents resulted in cases undertaken by the World Court.

Other cases before the World Court have centered on disputes concerning imposed blockades, types of intervention permissible in civil wars, the proliferation of nuclear testing and the making of atomic bombs, protection of human rights, political asylum, hijackings, and environmental concerns.

The World Court's handling of these diverse cases has resulted in several concerns about the court's operations and effectiveness. Litigants commonly complain that the World Court is slow and cumbersome, often taking several years to hear a case because of delays, and going through a complicated process before rendering a judgment. To expedite urgent cases, a five-judge panel called the Chamber of Summary Procedures is available. Although using this panel would speed up the process, the procedure has never been used by any nation.

The court's slowness in rendering judgments may be partly attributed to the fact that each case usually presents a unique set of circumstances, requiring the court to evolve new principles of international law. Without precedents and with clear guidelines seldom available, nations have tended to be wary of bringing cases before the World Court. Critics have claimed that widely accepted legal norms often are lacking in the court's considerations.

A more serious issue is that adjudication is entirely voluntary: Nations are not required to bring their disputes before the World Court, nor are they forced to abide by the court's decisions if they consider the rulings to be unacceptable.

Although the Statute of the Court [Article 36] focuses on compulsory jurisdiction in the court's decision-making process, the wording is subject to various interpretations. The Security Council of the United Nations, which has enforcement powers, had never (as of the mid-1990's) attempted to enforce the court's decisions. Therefore, the court has no power to initiate legal actions; it can only react to the initiatives of the sovereign nations that bring cases before it.

A famous case that illustrates the problem of compulsory jurisdiction of the World Court was that of Nicaragua's dispute with the United States in the mid-1980's. Nicaragua charged that the United States had violated its bilateral Treaty of Friendship, Commerce, and Navigation, and accused the United States of laying mines in Nicaraguan harbors and training and financing the paramilitary Contra insurgents to overthrow the legitimate government of Nicaragua. Nicaragua believed that the United States had violated its sovereignty and political independence.

The court found in favor of Nicaragua and awarded damages. The United States, which had advocated compulsory jurisdiction of the court since 1946, abruptly renounced the court's findings and refused to pay compensations. Critics from the United States and elsewhere charged the court judges with national and political bias, especially against the United States. U.S. officials claimed the court had overreached its jurisdiction because, they reasoned, the case should have been resolved by political and diplomatic means, not by legal means.

The United States has not been alone in ignoring some of the World Court's decisions. Iran did not obey the court in the Iranian hostage case in 1979. France ignored the court's judgment in the nuclear test cases in 1974. Albania refused to carry out the court's ruling in the Corfu channel incident.

In the large majority of cases, however, the nations have gone along with the court's instructions. In the late twentieth century, more nations—including the United States—have simply become more selective about deferring to the opinions of the World Court.

Context

The dream of establishing a world supreme court to settle international conflicts peacefully and avoid the butchery of war goes back to biblical times. In the United States, the beginnings of legal and judicial means to settle international squabbles peacefully can be traced to the Jay Treaty of 1794 and the Washington Treaty of 1871. Both treaties came about after bloody conflicts between U.S. and British forces, involving basic questions on regulating commerce and on developing the principles of international maritime law. Commissions and tribunals were created as a result of these treaties, which led to a heightened interest in the possibility of a true judicial arbitration system for settling international disputes, using rudimentary models of court procedures familiar to both the United States and Britain, employing the principle of neutral judges, and applying rules of law to render decisions peacefully rather than engage in war and bloodshed.

In Europe, the Hague conferences of 1899 and 1907 furthered the realization of international judicial arbitration by establishing the Permanent Court of Arbitration. Although it did not function as a court, it developed a model for conducting arbitration proceedings and created a series of general rules in codifying international law.

After World War I, the arbitration court declined in importance. The League of Nations, established in 1919, organized its own international court, the Permanent Court of International Justice, in 1920. For the first time, a real court existed for settling international disputes. Technically, the Permanent Court of International Justice (also popularly known as the World Court) was not an official organ of the League of Nations. Belonging to the League did not automatically make a nation a party to the court or vice versa. While the league was headquartered in Geneva, Switzerland, the court was located in The Hague, The Netherlands. The court rendered judgments and gave advisory opinions independent of the league's authority. Although the United States was never a party to the Permanent Court, the court had a U.S. judge as a member for the entire twenty-two years it was in existence.

When the League of Nations ceased operating in 1946, the Permanent Court disappeared with it. In their places arose the United Nations and a newly reconstituted International Court of Justice, minus the word "permanent."

The framers of the charter of the United Nations believed that the court should be an integral part of the United Nations, not an independent entity as the old Permanent Court was in its relationship with the League of Nations. The framers viewed the court as equal to the other five principal organs of the United Nations: the General Assembly, the Secretariat, the Security Council, the Economic and Social Council, and the Trusteeship Council. They reasoned that making the World Court an integral part of the United Nations would elicit better cooperation and coordination, because the court would have ties with the specialized agencies under the complex umbrella of the United Nations and thus would gain more respect from member nations.

Throughout the existence of the U.N. World Court, critics have complained that nations seldom use the court because it is too slow to respond and is unable to compel nations to obey its judgments. The court's advocates counter that it has been and will continue to be essential in sorting out legal liabilities after acts of violence and wars. Advocates also foresee the court's playing an increasingly significant role in international adjudication as the world becomes the so-called "global village." They see it as the best hope for nations to secure peace and stability in a contentious world.

Bibliography

Damrosch, Lori F., ed. *The International Court of Justice at a Crossroads*. Dobbs Ferry, N.Y.: Transnational Publishers, 1987. Position papers by international law experts focusing on compulsory jurisdiction of the World Court. Somewhat technical, but useful in understanding the special problems of the court.

Franck, Thomas M. *Judging the World Court*. New York: Priority Press Publications, 1986. Argues that the United States should be committed to compulsory jurisdiction of the World Court. Highly readable and informative on the role of the court in settling disputes.

International Court of Justice Yearbook. The Hague: International Court of Justice, 1946-. Annual publication of the World Court, discussing its activities and providing data about its organization, jurisdiction, and administration. Valuable when seeking the most recent information about the court.

Luard, Evan. *The United Nations: How It Works and What It Does*. Revised by Derek Heater. New York: St. Martin's Press, 1994. Depicts the World Court as an integral part of the United Nations. Chapter 4 focuses on the activities of the court. Succinct and lucid discussion.

Rosenne, Shabtai. *The World Court: What It Is and How It Works*. 4th ed. Norwell, Mass.: Kluwer Academic Publications, 1989. A definitive work on international law and the World Court. Detailed history of the court, its role, and how it operates. Interesting case briefs.

Yearbook of the United Nations. Dordrecht, The Netherlands: Martinus Nijhoff Publishers, 1946-. Annual summary of the United Nations' activities, including a review of the judicial work of the World Court. Useful when seeking current materials.

Richard Whitworth

Cross-References

Conflict Resolution, p. 397; International Agreements, p. 949; International Law, p. 956; International Relations, p. 969; Legal Systems in Anglo-American Governments, p. 1085; Superpowers and World Politics, p. 1916; Treaties, p. 2020; United Nations, p. 2045; World Government Movements, p. 2174; World Political Organization, p. 2186.

WORLD GOVERNMENT AND ENVIRONMENTAL PROTECTION

Field of study: International government and politics

Because environmental problems do not respect national borders, international cooperation is essential for effective environmental protection. The United Nations is at the center of international efforts to protect the environment, but many other organizations also play important roles. The major problems are enforcing compliance to agreements and obtaining funding.

Principal terms

DEVELOPED NATION: country with a strong industrial base, which may require importation of raw products from developing nations

DEVELOPING NATION: country with a limited industrial base; usually poor, but may be rich in exportable natural products

ECOLOGY: complex of interrelationships among living organisms (including humans) and their environment

ENVIRONMENT: entire complex of water, land, climate, and living organisms that provide natural resources, habitats for survival, and aesthetic benefits

OZONE LAYER: fragile layer of the upper atmosphere whose high ozone content blocks most of the sun's ultraviolet radiation from entering the lower atmosphere

POLLUTION: waste put into the environment above the levels that the environment can absorb or recycle

Overview

In an increasingly globalized world, there is no problem more in need of international cooperation and governance than environmental protection. Environmental problems are inherently international. Carbon dioxide released from automobiles and factories in the northern hemisphere adds to the greenhouse potential of the atmosphere worldwide, as does the carbon dioxide that is released when the rain forests of Amazonia, Indonesia, and Africa are destroyed. Atmospheric pollutants produced in one country are carried to all corners of the globe. The ozone layer is thinnest over Antarctica in winter, not over the states that produce and release the ozone-thinning chemicals; however, the ozone hole mixes with and thins stratospheric ozone worldwide at other times of the year. Pollutants dumped or seeping into rivers flow from one jurisdiction to another. Toxic substances, dumped into oceans or lakes by one nation, wash onto the shores of others. Migratory birds poisoned by insecticide in their winter home fail to return to their summer breeding grounds. Waterfowl incapable of finding nesting sites in their summer breeding areas send no offspring to their winter haunts. Nuclear reactor accidents send radioactive materials into neighboring countries, and nuclear war could decimate all the world's ecosystems.

An 1870's Swiss attempt to protect migratory birds was one of the first organized efforts to deal with international environmental problems. The need for international cooperation has grown ever since, and recognition of this fact has driven governments to cooperative interactions on a number of fronts. As with most international actions in the late twentieth century, the United Nations has played a central role in the effort to generate effective laws and agreements protecting the global environment. Many environmental programs are administered by the U.N. Environment Program (UNEP) and U.N. Development Program (UNDP). The United Nations also organizes meetings on international environmental concerns. Two of the best known and most far-reaching were the U.N. Conference on the Human Environment, held in Stockholm, Sweden, in 1972; and the U.N. Conference on Environment and Development (UNCED), often called the Earth Summit, held in Rio de Janeiro, Brazil, in 1992. Conferences with more restricted agendas also have been organized by the United Nations. These include the Vienna Convention on chemicals that deplete ozone in the stratosphere (1985), and a follow-up meeting in Montreal in 1987, which led to the Montreal Protocol restricting production and use of the chemicals.

The United Nations, through UNEP and UNDP, cooperates with other organizations to develop international environmental programs. The proliferation of organizations involved with environmental problems may be a problem in itself, because it tends to preclude continuity of international efforts. Some organizations, such as the World-watch Institute and the World Resources Institute, function as watchdogs; both of these produce regular reports on the state of the world's environment. The National Wildlife Federation and the National Audubon Society also perform watchdog functions in their publications, and lobby vigorously for environmental action. The Nature Conservancy finds and buys land of ecologic value in many parts of the world, often turning it over to the appropriate governmental body for management. Other international organizations concern themselves more directly with the management of a particular resource. The International Whaling Commission attempts to manage whale stocks by international agreement among whaling nations. The World Conservation Union works to gather and apply scientific information to the conservation of living resources at all levels, from species to ecosystems; it also drafted the Convention on International Trade in Endangered Species. The World Heritage Convention lists important cultural and biological sites, and helps to fund their maintenance.

International economic organizations such as the World Bank, General Agreement on Tariffs and Trade (GATT), and the International Monetary Fund (IMF) are important in funding international environmental projects. In the past, they often released funds for environmentally unsound projects, ignoring the connections between ecological and economic well-being. International organizations made up of groups of neighboring countries, countries surrounding a body of water, or countries related environmentally in some other way also play important roles in international environmental management, as they negotiate the management of the resources they share. The Organization of American States, the countries surrounding the North and Baltic seas, and the Asian Development Bank are examples.

The major problems with international environmental governance are the same as with all international governance: assuring sustained compliance and financing the programs. International laws and agreements almost always depend on the cooperation of the nations involved. If an agreement stands in the way of national goals, many nations will disregard it, secretly or openly. There is little the other members of the international community can do to enforce the agreement. International censure and trade sanctions are the common weapons and are sometimes effective.

Applications

The history of the International Whaling Commission (IWC) demonstrates some of the problems of international regulatory attempts. Established in 1946 to study whales and regulate whaling worldwide, the commission comprises the nations that have, or once had, whaling fleets. In 1986, it declared a ban on commercial whaling, permitting only subsistence hunting and collection for scientific research. Increased efficiency of the subsistence hunters and increased interest in whale research in several countries, some of it questionable, countered some of the protective effect of the ban. In 1991, Iceland declared its intention to withdraw from the commission to resume whaling; in 1993, Norway declared its intention to resume hunting Minke whales. The nonbinding, unenforceable nature of international agreements is exemplified by the IWC's problems; on the other hand, whaling was slowed by the ban. Evidence exists that some whale populations have increased in parts of their ranges, indicating that the ban, even without full compliance, gave some whale species a useful reprieve.

The United Nations Conference on the Human Environment, held in Stockholm, was a landmark in international environmental governance. Held in response to increasing concern with environmental problems and their international nature, it led to widespread recognition of the link between environmentally destructive development strategies and increased poverty, and reinforced the idea that international cooperation and coordination were essential to alleviate both environmental degradation and poverty. The importance of the conference is shown by the fact that more than 67 percent of all the international environmental treaties adopted before 1992 were adopted after the 1972 meetings.

International meetings in Vienna in 1985 and Montreal in 1987 resulted in the Montreal Protocol on ozone-depleting substances. It called for scheduled reduction in chlorofluorocarbons (CFCs), chemicals that had been used widely as refrigerants, but that interact destructively with stratospheric ozone. Because replacing CFCs used in industry is an expensive proposition, provisions were made in 1990 to assist developing nations in that replacement. Approved projects were funded using UNEP funds transferred to the Global Environmental Facility (GEF), an organization set up to help developing countries fund environmentally critical projects. The World Bank then dispensed the funds to the ozone projects. This indirect approach left some observers suspicious that the funds involved were already committed to environmental development, rather than the new funds that were needed. Despite the funding problem, the

Montreal Protocol is an example of successful international governance, as shown by the decrease in the use of CFCs.

The 1992 Earth Summit in Rio de Janeiro (UNCED) set the stage for future international environmental efforts. Eight thousand delegates, nine thousand media representatives, and three thousand persons representing nongovernmental organizations attended. The five most important agreements that came out of the conference are as follows: The Rio Declaration on Environment and Development is a nonbinding statement of the environmental responsibilities of nations, which also expressed the need for economic development to progress in the context of sound environmental policy. The forest convention is a set of nonbinding, general principles to be used in generating an international forestry policy. Agenda 21 is an action plan for environmentally sound, sustainable development, including problems, goals, implementation procedures, and cost estimates. The climate convention drew up plans for countering the greenhouse effect, although it set no binding target dates. The biodiversity convention outlined strategies and regulations for conserving living things and their habitats, and for apportioning the profits from the use of living resources between the developing nations, who often have the resources, and developed nations, who exploit the resources.

None of the conventions was accompanied by enforcement mechanisms, and fierce negotiations resulted in compromises that many believe took the teeth out of some statements. Still, the broad agreement on such important environmental and developmental issues has been seen as a hopeful sign. The major problem with implementing UNCED is funding. The UNCED secretariat estimated that more than $600 billion would be required to implement fully the program suggestions. The largest part of the funding ultimately must come from developed countries, which historically have not funded such programs to the level suggested by international organizations. Developed nations would need to contribute 0.7 percent of their gross national product to fund properly the UNCED initiative; in 1991, the average actual contribution was only 0.33 percent of gross national product.

A second aspect of the funding problem involves the mechanisms for obtaining and dispensing the funds. They have been so convoluted and disorganized that it is difficult to determine the efficiency of aid efforts. UNDP, UNEP, and the Development Assistance Committee of the Organization for Economic Cooperation and Development all have been suggested as organizations to oversee the use of funds for environmentally sound development. Most observers contend that none of them has performed such duties satisfactorily in the past. Perhaps because of this poor track record, less than 20 percent of development assistance funding has flowed through the United Nations, leading some observers to believe that multilateral funding will be required to accomplish the goals of UNCED. Multilateral funding, however, has had a checkered history. The World Bank and other financial institutions through which much of the funding has been channeled are thought to be too willing to fund big projects at the expense of smaller ones. They also have ignored environmental considerations in awarding funds in the past, although there is some indication that these institutions are increasing their environmental awareness.

The Global Environmental Facility (GEF) was created in 1991 as a three-year pilot project to solve some of these funding problems. It was jointly administered by the World Bank, UNDP, and UNEP, and was designed to disperse funds in a manner that would ensure efficient and environmentally sound development. The funds involved were to be new contributions, not redistributions from other programs. How well that has worked is not easy to determine, because of the manner in which funds are dispersed. The UNCED climate change and biodiversity conventions agreed to use a mechanism like the GEF, but arguments over representation and operational procedures have delayed agreement on specific funding mechanisms.

These examples of attempts at international environmental governance illustrate the significant problems, but also show that considerable progress was achieved in the last quarter of the twentieth century. It is not yet clear whether international agreements can work to achieve sustainable development or whether the global system will continue being degraded by nationalistic misuse of the world's resources, perhaps to the ruin of all the world's nations.

Context

The problems associated with international environmental treaties and agreements are the same as those involved with many international programs: how to ensure compliance and how to finance the programs. Disagreements often occur between the developing countries and the developed nations. Developing countries are the recipients of funding, which is often accompanied by restrictions. They work to maintain control of their resources, to reap a fair profit from the use of those resources, and ultimately to achieve the economic status of a developed nation. The developed countries that donate the funds want input into their use. They seek to have the funds used efficiently to maximize international environmental benefit, and they often want the funds to contribute somehow to their own economic growth. The two groups' interests and interpretations of benefits and costs often differ, and consensus is difficult to obtain. Most observers agree that in the past, treaties have generally favored the developed countries.

There is one difference between environmental and other international development questions, however. Most people, on both sides, recognize the need for action on many environmental problems. Climatic change attributable to the greenhouse effect, the thinning ozone layer, the extent of oceanic pollution, and the biodiversity crisis are not universally accepted as problems, but most serious scientists, government officials, and increasing numbers of citizens throughout the world recognize the potential for serious consequences in all these situations. Most people have seen the consequences of human misuse of resources and abuse of technology in the form of environmental problems such as smog over cities, nuclear reactor accidents, and chemical leaks from industrial plants and toxic waste dumps. Given these observable problems, it is possible to imagine one or more environmental problems escalating into an event of global proportions. Many people also believe that, even if global catastrophe is not imminent, local and national problems can become international problems because of technological advances and the increasing interdependence of the world's economies.

Despite the difficulty of generating an environmentally sound, sustainable development agenda, the need for international cooperation has been increasingly recognized. Cooperation in environmental matters has created a climate of international discussion that may carry over into economic and political realms. International economics is so tightly associated with environmental problems that the environmental discussions have affected international economics. The environmental problems of developing countries are more clearly shared with the developed nations than are the developing countries' economic and political problems, although all are intertwined. Much remains to be done, however, to secure the essential goal of international cooperation in the solution of urgent environmental problems.

Bibliography

Brown, Lester R., Hal Kane, and Ed Ayres. *Vital Signs 1993: The Trends That Are Shaping Our Future*. New York: W. W. Norton, 1993. Excellent annual report on trends in environmentally sensitive areas, such as food, agriculture, energy, atmosphere, and the economy. References for each topic; graphs.

Chen, Victor. "Crisis of a Crowded World." *Audubon* 96 (July/August, 1994): 50-77. Report on global population problems leading up to the United Nations 1994 International Conference on Population and Development.

French, Hilary F. *After the Earth Summit: The Future of Environmental Governance*. Worldwatch Paper Number 107. Washington, D.C.: Worldwatch Institute, 1992. Published just before UNCED, it is an excellent introduction to international government and environmental problems. Notes provide a number of references.

Stackhouse, John. "A Tale of Two Sisters." *International Wildlife* 24 (July/August, 1994): 16-25. Compares the results of a large World Bank loan to Bangladesh with a small loan made from a local bank with local needs in mind.

World Resources Institute. *World Resources 1994-95: A Guide to the Global Environment*. New York: Oxford University Press, 1994. Superb source of information on the state of global resources and interactions of international agencies governing these resources. New reports are published every other year. Extensive notes and references, index, graphs, and extensive tables.

Worldwatch Institute. *State of the World 1993*. New York: W. W. Norton, 1993. Excellent annually produced report on the ecological state of the world. The first chapter outlines the status of most problems and other chapters consider certain problems in more detail. Extensive notes and references, index, some illustrations, graphs, and tables.

Carl W. Hoagstrom

Cross-References

Developed and Developing Nations, p. 533; Diplomacy and International Negotiation, p. 552; Environmental Protection, p. 617; Foreign Relations, p. 718; International Agreements, p. 949; International Law, p. 956; International Monetary Fund, p. 963; International Relations, p. 969; Resource Management, p. 1718; Trade with Foreign Nations, p. 2000; United Nations, p. 2045; The World Bank, p. 2153.

WORLD GOVERNMENT MOVEMENTS

Field of study: International government and politics

World government movements from the 1930's to the 1990's stressed creating a strong central government with its own military force to reduce the possibility of war.

Principal terms
AGGRESSOR: nation that starts a war
CONSTITUTION: written document containing the broad description of a government's powers and structure
FEDERATION: organization of states giving power to local governments and limiting the power of the central or national government
LEAGUE OF NATIONS: first world organization of national governments, organized in 1919 after World War I; collapsed in 1939
UNITED NATIONS: second world organization of national governments, organized in 1945 after World War II

Overview

Movements for a world government have a history dating back far beyond the 1930's. Alexander the Great, for example, may have been the first leader to try to organize a world community through military conquest. In the modern world, however, the key impetus to new ideas about world government came from the failure of the League of Nations to maintain peace in the 1930's. Most criticisms of the league, which was organized in the aftermath of World War I for the purpose of collective security (an attack against one member was presumed to be an attack against all), stressed its failure to win the cooperation of its members for any type of military action. A stronger charter or constitution was needed, one that required nations to act in case of aggression, or one that created an international army that could be sent into battle against aggressors.

H. G. Wells (1866-1946), the famous British author of *The Outline of History* (1920), criticized the league from its beginning. It simply was not strong enough. He called for scientists, technicians, and intelligent people to organize a new order based on a strong world state. Wells wanted an "open conspiracy" of supporters to fight "particularistic governments" that showed uninterest for anything more than local, narrow issues. Only the acceptance of global values by all people would put an end to war and conflict. Wells wanted an elite of industrialists, bankers, scientists, journalists, and writers to lead this new state after overthrowing the old one. In a book titled *The Open Conspiracy* (1928), he described how this elite would attain power and totally reform society, not by violent revolution but by spreading word of the need for a stronger world government to citizens throughout the world. An ordered society governed by an educated elite would be created by human beings when they recognized how dangerous the old system of national states had become. Many of the proposals initiated by Wells would be developed more fully by the designers of world governments after World War II.

In 1940, Wells sent a letter to *The Times of London* describing a draft for a new declaration of rights that would cover all humanity. Wells had the declaration translated into forty-eight languages and called for a worldwide debate on the issues he raised. In late 1941 a committee of experts reported the results. The Declaration of the United Nations issued in January contained much of the same language as Wells's document in its call for a world without war and a dedication to human rights. The list of rights developed by Wells and later included in the Universal Declaration of Rights adopted by the United Nations in 1948 included the right to live; the right to knowledge; freedom of thought and worship; the right to work; the right to property; freedom of movement; freedom from violence; and the right to be ruled by the will of the majority through law. Variations on these themes would be found in almost every world government design issued in the future.

Applications

Clarence Streit adopted Wells's ideas in his book *Union Now* (1939). Streit's book proved very popular and went through fourteen reprintings in two years. Streit called for a new world constitution modeled on the U.S. Constitution. Any nation that was self-governing and respected individual freedom could join. The founding nations would be the United States, Great Britain, Canada and other British dominions, the nations of western Europe (except Germany and Italy), and the Union of Soviet Socialist Republics. The new organization would have a union defense force made up of soldiers from all member nations. All tariffs and customs duties would be eliminated and an international postal and communications system would be created.

Member states would retain home rule in most domestic matters, as long as human rights were respected, and could keep their traditional system of government. There would be a two-house legislature with a lower house based on population and an upper house with equal representation for each nation regardless of size. Presidential power would be held by a five-member executive board elected by the legislature. Streit organized a group, the Inter-Democracy Federal Unionists, to lobby for his plan in Washington, D.C. In 1940 he changed the name to the Federal Union, Inc. It had sixty chapters in the United States before the end of 1940. Critics of Streit's plan objected to its reliance on European nations to lead the new government and said it would create just another form of Anglo-American domination. Another criticism was that although the U.S. Constitution worked for the United States, this did not mean a similar structure would work elsewhere, especially in the age of Hitler.

In 1943, Ely Culbertson (1891-1955), the world's leading authority on the game of contract bridge, published a detailed plan for world government. Culbertson's book *Total Peace* (1943) offered a solution to a major problem—how to create a government strong enough to keep peace without taking away the freedom and sovereignty of nations. Culbertson's plan was to divide the world into eleven regions, with the most powerful country in each region serving as a local police officer. A world federation government, composed of a two-house legislature, a supreme court, and a world president, would have the power to interfere in any region to stop a war. The legislature would consist of a world senate, with each country having one vote, and of the world trustees, elected by region on the basis of population.

Nations belonging to the federation would renounce war as an instrument of policy and contribute troops to an international police force. This force would have twelve units, eleven made up of troops from the eleven dominant nations in the world, and the twelfth composed of soldiers from smaller nations. The international force would consist of about 22 percent of the total world army, larger than the forces contributed by any single great power, but not big enough to be dominant. Since no single power contributed more than 20 percent, none could become dominant. The international military force outnumbered the contributions of any single state. Each nation would have an army large enough to defend itself from attack but not big enough to start a war. As had happened to Streit's plan, the one offered by Culbertson received criticism from many internationalists, who believed his scheme was simply another example of imperialism, because the eleven big powers would be able to control the rest of the world. Small nations would have little influence in their regions or in the central world government.

Later, in 1942, Harold Stassen, Republican governor of Minnesota and a future presidential candidate, offered a much simpler plan for the creation of the United Nations of the World. Stassen called for creation of a seven-member executive council representing seven geographical regions of the world, an international court of fifteen to settle most disputes between nations, and an international legion to enforce court decisions and keep peace. He called for citizens of the world to give up their national allegiances and work together for peace. The Stassen plan resembled that of another Republican leader, Wendell Willkie, who ran against President Franklin D. Roosevelt in 1940. Willkie published a book called *One World* (1943) calling for a United Nations Council to govern the world. He gave few specifics, however, on how the council would be organized or how an international government would function. Willkie's key point was to get moving as quickly as possible to create a world federation. The rest of the book described his travels around the world.

The movement for world government received support. Five thousand delegates gathered in New York City in 1943 to launch a Christian mission on world order (CMWO). John Foster Dulles, who served as secretary of state from 1953 to 1959 during the administration of Dwight D. Eisenhower, addressed the crowd and said Americans faced a critical period and that if they failed again to support world government, as they had in 1919 when the Senate rejected membership in the League of Nations, the world would fall apart into anarchy and ruin. The CMWO delegates adopted a Six Pillars of Peace platform and set up study groups in local churches across the nation to discuss the importance of creating a world federation.

In 1944, Philip Nash, president of the University of Toledo, published *An Adventure in World Order*, which described a government representing all nations of the world.

The government would feature a unicameral parliament that elected an eight-member executive board whose job was to enforce peace. The four great powers—the United States, Great Britain, the Soviet Union, and China—would have permanent seats on the board but only one vote each, and no veto power. A majority vote was needed to take action and, unlike the procedure established in the Security Council of the United Nations, a "no" vote by a great power did not kill a resolution. Nash believed collective security was the key, the idea being that an attack against one member of the world state would be seen as an attack against all. A small international army would be established, but no nation was required to furnish troops. Each nation could act voluntarily, and Nash hoped that the use of economic sanctions would be the best way to restrain aggressors. Military force would only be used as a last resort. Nash believed his plan avoided the problem of domination by the world's great powers that had afflicted previous ideas about world government.

James T. Shotwell, an international lawyer, described his vision of world government in *The Great Decision* (1944). Shotwell saw prevention of war as the key job of the world assembly he proposed. It included an international court to settle most quarrels between states. If a nation refused to abide by the court's decision it would be hit with economic sanctions. If this action failed to halt the offending behavior, the aggressor state would be bombed by an international air force. Shotwell's plan received good reviews from newspapers and journalists, but Norman Thomas, leader of the American Socialist Party and an avowed internationalist, criticized it and other such plans because they failed to deal with the true causes of aggression—the economic and social ills that drove nations to war.

After World War II ended and nations reflected on their recent experience, a continuing series of proposals came forth to make sure such a disaster never occurred again. In 1947 the United World Federalists (UWF) were organized in France and the United States. The group's charter called for strengthening the United Nations, created in 1945, by giving it the power to make and enforce laws for the whole world. The UWF issued a new constitution in 1948, hoping it would be adopted by the United Nations. It called for a one-house legislature with ninety-nine members elected by voters with one delegate for each million people in a country's population. The legislature would establish an international army, limit the sale and manufacture of weapons, and create agencies responsible for developing the world's natural resources. This new government would collect taxes directly from all citizens of the world and create a world bank and a world court. It would also write rules for immigration and migration, commerce, and business activity. Robert M. Hutchins, president of the University of Chicago, played a major role in writing this constitution. The UWF rewrote the constitution in 1968 and 1977 to reflect new attitudes toward the environment and economic inequality.

Context

Throughout the 1950's and 1960's interest in world government remained high, though almost every new proposal mirrored the United World Federalists' constitutional creation. In 1966 the World Order Models Project (WOMP) began developing computerized models of an ideal world state. It called for drastic disarmament, an end to nuclear development, and the dismantling of nuclear bombs and missiles, as well as an effective program to eliminate poverty. It also called upon people to become aware of the dangers of pollution and the threat to the world's environment resulting from industrialization. Indefinite economic growth simply could not continue, WOMP scientists concluded, and they called for a worldwide effort to save the planet from an ecological catastrophe.

In a series of publications, WOMP authorities outlined their vision of a new constitutional system for humankind. A central world administration would protect the world's health, environment, oceans, and natural resources. This government would make economic decisions based on the welfare of all the world's peoples and safeguard their human rights and dignity. World security would be based on solving problems of poverty and discrimination.

A similar solution to the world's problems came from the World Constitution and Parliament Association, founded in 1977. This group proposed a constitution for the "Federation of the Earth" aimed at preserving natural resources and protecting humanity against pollution and ecological disruption. The world federation would have as its first objective protecting and improving the quality of life of all peoples. The new constitution divided the world into five regions, one for each inhabited continent, each having a local government. All people would be governed by world law, however, made by a world legislature elected from each region. Representation would be based on population. A world supreme court, along with regional district courts, would have jurisdiction in all criminal and civil cases. Human rights would be guaranteed, and decisions by the courts would be binding on all parties. An international army would be available to enforce court decisions.

The One World Movement (OWM) launched a campaign in the 1970's and 1980's to promote another style of world government. Headquartered in Colorado, the OWM called for a "World Council" of two bodies, a House of Experts and a House of Commons. There would be 400 experts, mainly engineers, scientists, lawyers, and environmentalists, selected by the 1,000-member Commons. Seats in the Commons would be apportioned by population. Members would represent "the highest good of all the people of the earth." Legislation would begin with the Experts, and if approved by a majority, go to the Commons. The Commons would then consider the measure, but it could be rejected only by a two-thirds majority. The Commons would also elect a president from three candidates nominated by the Experts. The president would have few powers, however, beyond signing laws and appointing a cabinet of advisers. All officials would take a pledge of service to humanity. The OWM proposal called for world citizenship and the abolition of traditional national governments.

In 1992, Richard Falk, a lawyer and teacher, published *Explorations at the Edge of Time: The Prospects for World Order.* Falk's work calls for a world government dedicated to denuclearization, demilitarization, depolarization, development, and democratization. Falk's proposed system of government also calls for the abolition of nations and the rule of world law. The world would be safe from war, he concludes, when problems of poverty, discrimination, and exploitation had been solved.

Bibliography

Center for the Study of Democratic Institutions. *A Constitution for the World*. Santa Barbara, Calif.: Center for the Study of Democratic Institutions, 1965. Proposal, in pamphlet form, for world government.

Clark, Grenville, and Louis B. Sohn. *World Peace Through World Law*. 2d ed. Cambridge, Mass.: Harvard University Press, 1960. Describes some of the early proposals for world government, provides recommendations of its own, and has extensive information on older works about world government.

Divine, Robert A. *Second Chance: The Triumph of Internationalism in America During World War II*. New York: Atheneum, 1967. Discusses various proposals and movements made in the United States in the 1930's and early 1940's. Thoughtful analysis of the systems proposed by Streit, Shotwell, and Culbertson.

Falk, Richard A. *A Study of Future Worlds*. New York: Free Press, 1975. Brief criticisms of previous designs and a call for new approaches to international law and peacekeeping.

Kiang, John. *One World: The Approach to Permanent Peace on Earth and General Happiness of Mankind*. Notre Dame, Ind.: One World Publishing Company, 1984. Guide to world government movements, with notes and discussion of almost every modern idea concerning world government.

Leslie V. Tischauser

Cross-References

Confederations, p. 391; International Agreements, p. 949; Leagues, p. 1072; Sanctions, p. 1777; Supranational Government Institutions, p. 1922; United Nations, p. 2045; World Government and Environmental Protection, p. 2167; World Political Organization, p. 2186.

THE WORLD HEALTH ORGANIZATION

Field of study: International government and politics

The World Health Organization (WHO) was established under the auspices of the United Nations in 1948, to encourage and assist governments in fulfilling their responsibilities for the health of their peoples, and to secure the active participation of the public to that end.

Principal terms
ASSOCIATE MEMBER: territory not responsible for its international relations, which is admitted to WHO as a nonvoting member
MEMBER: government that has entered into alliance with WHO; each member has one vote in matters of policy and procedure that come before the board
PANDEMIC: epidemic of, for example, a particular strain of influenza that covers a wide area and affects a high proportion of the population
SECRETARIAT: staff of WHO, which is appointed by the director-general and carries out the tasks of the organization
UNITED NATIONS: international organization established during World War II to promote international peace and security

Overview

The World Health Organization (WHO) is an international alliance of governments and territories that operates under the direction of the United Nations to improve global health. Its primary functions are to promote the development and improvement of health services throughout the world, to collect and disseminate information on all matters pertaining to the public health, and to further biomedical research and the application of new findings.

WHO's public health ideology, set forth in the preamble to its constitution, is as follows: Health is not merely the absence of disease, but a state of complete physical, mental, and social well-being; every person has a fundamental right to the highest attainable standard of health; worldwide health is intrinsic to world peace and security, and is contingent upon cooperation between people and countries; and the progress made by any country in the promotion and protection of health is of value to all. Operating within this ideology, on April 7, 1948, WHO began the lofty task of eradicating diseases that threaten nations, large and small, across the globe.

WHO has its headquarters in Geneva, Switzerland, and is part of the supporting umbrella network for a number of international organs and agencies commonly referred to as the United Nations system. WHO is a specialized agency within the system, however, and is not subordinate to the United Nations. Instead, WHO has formal agreements with the United Nations and other international agencies to share information and use common administrative practices. WHO has its own governing bodies, its own membership, and its own budget.

The members of all organizations of the United Nations system, including WHO, are either governments or government-sponsored territories. WHO operations are financed by annual contributions from its member nations. The amount of these contributions is determined by the World Health Assembly, WHO's governing body, and is based primarily on each government's ability to pay. The United States, for example, contributes approximately one-third of the WHO budget. Each member has only one vote, regardless of the size of its contribution. Associate members (territories not responsible for their international relations, but who have been admitted on the application of the responsible member) do not have a vote, but may participate in the deliberations of the World Health Assembly.

WHO is a three-tiered organization, consisting of the World Health Assembly, an executive board, and a secretariat. The main tasks of the assembly, which includes delegates from each member nation, are to approve the proposed annual program and budget and to decide upon major questions of policy. The assembly also elects twenty-four delegates to select the executive board. Appointees of the board are not merely administrators, but are technically qualified in the field of health. The board acts as the executive organ of the assembly, prepares the agenda for each session of the assembly, and submits to it a general program of work covering a specific period. The board acts on behalf of the whole membership of WHO, not on behalf of those countries elected to designate its members. The executive board also nominates the director-general, who is appointed by the assembly to serve a five-year term. The director-general is the technical and administrative head of the secretariat, which is the staff of WHO. The director-general recruits these internationally representative workers and stations them around the world to carry out WHO's mission.

Although its headquarters are in Geneva, WHO has organizations located in six continental regions: the Eastern Mediterranean, Africa, Europe, Western Pacific, Southeast Asia, and the Region of the Americas. WHO also has offices in forty-six countries, and regularly deploys personnel and health specialists to perform hands-on instruction to areas in need. WHO has established fifty-nine influenza centers throughout the world where virus strains are isolated and identified, vaccines are developed, and data are analyzed by specialists.

Despite the humanitarian nature of WHO, international health care does not operate outside of an economic and political climate. If the policy is to emphasize comprehensive health and well-being, WHO must consider health promotion, health protection, disease prevention, medical care, and physical, mental, and social rehabilitation, not only for the health sector, but also for other social and economic sectors. Organizers must consider the international dimensions and ramifications of the education of the physician, the health team, and the various bureaus of policies and exchange, which often involve negotiating a complicated maze of international communications, persons, policies, politics, and power.

A progressive provision was written into WHO's constitution that gave its legislative body the authority to adopt, by simple majority vote, international regulations that would become binding automatically on the member states, except for those who notified that they rejected, or had reservations about, the regulations. The intent was to streamline international legislative techniques and to consolidate previous international health conventions and agreements. WHO regulatory powers were expressly limited, however, covering only requirements and procedures to prevent the international spread of disease, the international comparability of reporting for statistical purposes, and standards relating to drugs and vaccines. This circumscribed regulatory scope covered primarily traditional matters that had been the subject of international legislation since the middle of the nineteenth century.

Since its constitution was written, WHO has adopted only two international regulations using its formal legislative process: the Nomenclature Regulations, which deal with the statistical classification of morbidity and mortality; and the International Health Regulations, which cover quarantinable diseases, such as plague, cholera, yellow fever, and smallpox. WHO regulations are revised approximately every ten years to incorporate global improvement in the knowledge and control of epidemic diseases. For example, smallpox was removed entirely from the scope of international quarantine control in 1981 as a consequence of the global eradication of this disease— a result of WHO's eradication program.

Although WHO as a legislative body has ratified only two international health regulations, it has undertaken substantial international regulatory activities in collaboration with the United Nations and other specialized agencies. WHO advises the United Nations on the administration of instruments to control the distribution and use of dependence-producing drugs. It also collaborates with the Food and Agriculture Organization (FAO) to advance food standards aimed at protecting consumers' health and ensuring fair practices in the food trade. Using the procedure of consensus rather than formal legislation for the approval of international norms has accelerated the legislative process and avoided balking by member states.

Applications

By 1965, the conceptual understanding of a need for preventive instead of curative medicine in developing countries had led to improved management practices, information gathering, knowledge generation, and enhanced communication and technology education and training directed by communication. WHO has been in the forefront in providing encouragement and background documentation to technical discussions on education and the role of universities in the strategies of international health. Since the early 1970's, there has been a growing interest in the relationship between educational programs for the health professions and the actual practice of health care. Team care has been a vital concept. Under the guidance of WHO, critical attitudes and progressive reviews have been made of health care and strategies for better management. Improved health and workforce training have been devised through collaboration with major universities and technical schools across the globe.

In 1977, motivated by the gross inequality in the health status of various populations, particularly between developed and developing countries, the World Health

Assembly decided that the main social target of governments and WHO in the coming decades should be for all people to attain a level of health that would permit them to lead socially and economically productive lives. This goal has been the basis of a revolution in public thinking on matters of world health. In 1978, an international conference was held in Alma-Ata, in what was then the Soviet Union. The principal result of this conference was a declaration that primary health care was the key to attaining health for all by the year 2000.

Primary health care as defined at Alma-Ata includes, at the least, education concerning prevailing health problems and the methods of preventing and controlling them; promotion of adequate supplies of food and safe water, proper nutrition, and basic sanitation; maternal and child health care, including family planning; immunization against major infectious diseases; prevention and control of locally endemic diseases; appropriate treatment of common diseases and injuries; and provision of essential drugs. The conference also urged all governments to formulate national health policies and strategies with a view toward developing health systems based on primary health care, and to cooperate with one another to this end.

This declaration was expanded upon and put forth as a formal document entitled "Health for All by the Year 2000." Members of WHO pledged to support this global effort to foster world health, which is based on the view that development must build on self-reliance, community involvement, and social justice. WHO promoted education and primary health care as the means to the goal of improved world health and quality of life.

Prevention is a key component of primary health care. To promote prevention, WHO allocated resources to encourage governments to provide universal immunization of children against the common infectious diseases of childhood by the year 1990. In 1994, this goal had yet to be achieved, even in the most developed nations such as the United States.

In its role as educator, WHO publishes a variety of publications, such as the *International Digest of Health Legislation*, a quarterly journal delineating the national and international legal instruments on a wide range of subjects, from control of AIDS (acquired immune deficiency syndrome) to environmental protection and management. WHO also publishes the *Weekly Epidemiological Record*, which contains health travel information, including vaccine and documentation requirements, and the incidence of disease. WHO technical publications include scientific articles reporting the results of research sponsored by the organization or relevant to its activities, and reviews of relevant subjects by international groups of experts. WHO also issues daily bulletins informing health specialists of the trends and courses of major diseases, and publishes brochures dealing more fully with important health questions, bibliographies, directories, books of specifications and standards, and periodicals devoted to health statistics and health legislation. There are publications for the public at large, as well as official publications that place on record the discussions and decisions of WHO's governing bodies. WHO also holds conferences to share scientific knowledge and to structure campaigns to fight a specific disease.

Context

Many contributing factors and events led to the establishment of WHO as an instrument of securing global health. International health cooperation began in Paris in 1851, with the first International Sanitary Conference. These conferences took place periodically with little result until 1903, when the various European quarantine requirements for plague, yellow fever, and cholera were combined into a single International Sanitary Convention. At that time, the principal players in Europe agreed that a permanent international health bureau should be established, especially as the American republics had already joined forces to form what later became the Pan American Sanitary Bureau.

Between 1907 and the end of World War I, various regional alliances were formed to combat the international spread of disease, the most prevalent of which at that time was cholera. After the war, in an optimistic universal desire to build a better world, the League of Nations was established. One of its tasks was to facilitate prevention and control of disease, incorporating all existing international bureaus under its direction. This incorporation proved problematic, however, resulting rather in consultative and cooperative arrangements among the primary existing organizations: the International Public Health Office, based in Paris; the Health Organization of the League of Nations, also in Europe; and the Pan American Sanitary Organization, based in the United States.

The league soon concerned itself with such broad subjects as nutrition, housing, and cancer. It pioneered the establishment of international committees of medical experts and designated national medical research centers to carry out international responsibilities on its behalf. The league created a new dimension in international health work: It opened up direct communication with the international biomedical community instead of acting solely through senior public health officials.

By the time of World War II, the league was defunct and little progress was made toward international health. When the war ended in 1945, however, a United Nations conference was held in San Francisco, and a proposal to establish an international health organization was unanimously approved. On April 7, 1948, the World Health Organization officially came into being with the ratification of its constitution.

Before the twentieth century, health care was considered to be a private matter between individuals and physicians. After pandemics of malaria and influenza, it became evident that many environmental, economic, social, cultural, and educational factors affect the health of people and communities and influence the delivery of health care. Increasing awareness of the political effectiveness and economic benefit of government involvement in improving health made such action politically popular. Health policy has become an accepted concept in the twentieth century, and the formulation of health policy a normal function of government.

Since its inception, WHO's role has broadened from that of a clearinghouse for statistical data and a mobilizer of resources, to that of a world health conscience, a consultant, and a helper giving visible expression to progressive ideas and decisions within national social policies.

Taking this more hands-on approach, WHO has entered developing and underdeveloped countries to combat the poverty-malnutrition-infection cycle and the inequitable distribution of national health resources. These problems go to the heart of the social and political structures of member states, and their solutions are contingent upon mutual confidence and common objectives among members. Over time, this confidence has grown, becoming less diluted by fear or threat of loss of national sovereignty and responsibility. Thus, WHO has been able to fill in the gaps of technical expertise required to complement national efforts toward health for all.

Bibliography

Basch, Paul F. *Textbook of International Health.* New York: Oxford University Press, 1990. Not a textbook in the standard sense, this engaging and easy-to-read guide presents a comprehensive overview of the origins, applications, and future of international health systems.

Evaluation of the Strategy for Health for All by the Year 2000: Seventh Report on the World Health Situation. Geneva: World Health Organization, 1987. Provides a thorough evaluation of the strategy for Health for All and a detailed account of the development of health systems and the patterns and trends in health status.

Goodman, Neville M. *International Health Organizations and Their Work.* 2d ed. Edinburgh: Churchhill Livingstone, 1971. The standard source for the history of international health organizations, with a primarily administrative orientation.

Hoole, Francis W. *Politics and Budgeting in the World Health Organization.* Bloomington: Indiana University Press, 1976. Comprehensive exploration and conceptualization of the budgeting and policy-making processes of WHO. Straightforward text and numerous illustrations, charts, and tables.

Introducing WHO. Geneva: World Health Organization, 1976. Directed toward the general public, this introduction to WHO aims to clear up misunderstandings as to the organization's basic activities.

Lambo, Thomas A., and Stacey B. Day, eds. *Issues in Contemporary International Health.* New York: Plenum Press, 1990. Essays by health care experts, focusing on the relationship between international health and preventive medicine, emphasizing education and technology.

Leslie Pendleton

Cross-References

WORLD POLITICAL ORGANIZATION

Field of study: International government and politics

Sovereign states dominate global decision making and ongoing societal interactions across borders, but their activities are increasingly impacted by the growth of international treaties and multinational organizations. Whether these expanding governmental and societal links will ultimately be stabilizing or destabilizing is unclear.

Principal terms
GOVERNMENT: individuals and institutions responsible for making binding rules for a state
INTERNATIONAL ORGANIZATION: group of people or states exhibiting some sort of leadership and bureaucratic structures organized across state borders to pursue common objectives
NATION: group of people who identify with each other on the basis of some common characteristic such as religion, race, culture, or language
POLITICS: interaction between government and the people who are governed
SOVEREIGNTY: legal characteristic of a state that enables its leaders to make rules independent of any higher political authority
STATE: organized community occupying a geographical area, and providing authority, security, laws, and a system of justice
SUPRANATIONALITY: characteristic of an international organization possessing at least some of the decision-making power of its member states, and thereby able to impose organizational decisions on them
TREATY: agreement among sovereign states establishing international law for those who have signed and ratified

Overview

Politics is the process by which society is given order and direction. At the global level, the main political actors since 1648 have been states. States possess people, territory, borders, and a government exercising sovereignty. Sovereignty, the legal characteristic of a state that enables its leaders to make rules independent of any higher authority, gives each state theoretical equality and also makes each state responsible for its own security. Sovereignty thereby defines the political framework and establishes the possibilities for organization globally.

Interaction among sovereign states at the global level can be based on either conflict or cooperation. The international arena is usually portrayed as anarchical, with the emphasis on conflict and rule by the strongest states through the use of force, since there is no global government to make and enforce decisions. While the most powerful states do carry disproportionate weight, over time a primitive political system has evolved that recognizes that states cannot exist in isolation from one another and emphasizes the need to cooperate to pursue common interests. Building on the process of interaction and the need to order relations with each other, states first developed international law and later international organizations to manage their common needs.

International law arose out of the practices of states that were involved with each other but lacked rules to govern their interactions. Habits or customs evolved that established norms that were generally followed in matters such as trade and sea travel. Recognizing the advantages of clearly defined rules, such customs were often later written down or codified as treaties by states that wanted to establish more regularized patterns of interaction. Treaty-making is a voluntary activity, in which all states that sign a treaty agree to take on the obligations contained within the treaty vis-à-vis the other signatories. While both custom and treaties can be sources of international law, states prefer treaties that spell out obligations more precisely. As the number of states has expanded, so too has the number of treaties dealing with the rules of diplomacy and other social and commercial issues. While not used as often, additional sources of international law include widely recognized general principles, or judicial decisions by national or international courts that have a bearing on interstate activity.

Critics claim that international law does not exist, because there is no international legislature to make the law, there is no international police force to enforce it, and it is not always obeyed. Such views overlook the reality that laws at the domestic level are not always enforced and obeyed, and that conformity to the law is never complete. States obey most of their legal obligations in the vast majority of cases, because they made the laws and it is in their interests to obey them. When states violate international law, there are provisions for retaliation and sanctions but it is up to the states involved to determine enforcement or adjudication. Because international law has facilitated interstate interaction, it has mushroomed in the twentieth century to deal with such questions as trade, finance, travel, and communication.

States also have used their treaty-making powers to join together to form international organizations when their interests correspond. Early international intergovernmental organizations grew up in the nineteenth century in Europe to deal with issues such as river traffic on the Rhine and Danube. Such governmental organizations expanded in scope and complexity in the twentieth century, as first the League of Nations and then the United Nations sought universal membership among states to try to promote international peace. While the league failed with the coming of World War II, the United Nations has seen its role wax and wane depending on the ability of its sovereign member states to coordinate their interests. Since the founding of the United Nations, most members have been behind in paying their dues and hesitant to support actions with which they disagreed.

A variety of regional intergovernmental organizations have been formed. Typical are alliances such as the North Atlantic Treaty Organization and the Organization of American States, formed for common defense; economic groupings such as the North American Free Trade Area and the Asia-Pacific Cooperation forum; and others with varied purposes, such as the Conference on Security and Cooperation in Europe, and ASEAN, a grouping of a number of Southeast Asian states. Each of these organizations is limited by the sovereignty of its members and can only act when enough members agree to a common action. Such organizations can provide mechanisms for ordering global society, but they are not always effective. The one exception is the European Community, in which the state members are in the process of transforming a customs union into an economic and monetary union, with the possibility of a common foreign and security policy. The unique feature of the European Community is its supranationality, that is, states have transferred some of their sovereignty or decision-making power to the organization, allowing its officials to implement policies for member states. Even here the surrender of sovereignty is not complete, since member states still are able to expand or contract the scope of the decision-making power of the European Community, and some member states have expressed reservations about increasing its power at the expense of states.

Applications

Although sovereign states are still the main political actors globally, their actions are conditioned by the presence of international law and international organizations that must be factored into foreign policy decision making. Powerful states usually dominate, but the weak are not completely at the mercy of the strong and both jockey for position in this increasingly complex global arena. Iraq's invasion of Kuwait in August, 1990, is illustrative. Saddam Hussein's forces had clearly violated Kuwait's sovereignty, and U.S. President George Bush said such aggression would not be allowed to stand. Bush worked through the Security Council of the United Nations to secure an immediate condemnation of the invasion, and in November, 1990, the Security Council authorized the use of force against Iraq if it did not meet the January 15, 1991, pullout deadline. While Bush was securing United Nations backing, he also was working to build a united coalition of sovereign states including Arabs, a North Atlantic Treaty contingent, some Asian representatives, and even a group of soldiers from Poland. The United States never surrendered command of its forces, operating through a joint command run by an American and a Saudi Arabian general, but Bush used the legitimizing force of the U.N. resolutions and Saddam Hussein's disregard of international law to build a global coalition against Iraq.

A closer look at the Persian Gulf War reveals the complexity of a situation in which sovereign states working through international organizations were the main actors, but important nongovernmental international organizations and less well-organized nationality groups also complicated both the war and its aftermath. While nongovernmental organizations possess no sovereignty, their actions shape the international landscape, providing increasing interdependence across state borders and additional focal points for popular loyalties that may conflict with people's allegiance to the state. A nongovernmental international organization is a private group formed when people join together across state borders to establish leaders and organizational structures that pursue objectives that impact on interactions of states. One type of nongovernmental organization is the Palestine Liberation Organization, a group of Arabs who came together in 1964 to push their claims to the land of Israel, supported Saddam Hussein throughout the Persian Gulf War, and helped to organize pro-Iraqi popular demonstrations in many Arab countries. Another type of nongovernmental organization also helped to set the stage for the Persian Gulf War: multinational corporations, which are private enterprises with subsidiaries operating in more than one state to serve a global market. Multinational corporations had helped Saddam Hussein build up his military, and possibly even nuclear and chemical weapons, capabilities. Several German and U.S. companies legally sold Iraq goods that had both civilian and military functions. Iraq also obtained such materials indirectly through the black market or illegal operations of unauthorized suppliers.

Although not as well organized, the Kurds, a nation of people living in Turkey, Iraq, Iran, Syria, and Armenia, represent another type of nongovernmental organization. They have attempted intermittently to establish an independent Kurdestan for many years, and in the wake of the 1991 war, they rebelled again. While the United States, Great Britain, and France were willing to intervene to stop Iraqi attacks on the Kurds, the three powers were not willing to champion the Kurds' desire for an independent state for fear that it would jeopardize the regional balance of power.

Thus, although the withdrawal of Iraq from Kuwait demonstrated President Bush's diplomatic skill in leading a coalition of sovereign states against Saddam Hussein, his task was made easier by the aid of United Nations Security Council resolutions and the clear-cut violation of international law that helped to rally support. His task was complicated, however, by the actions of the Palestinian Liberation Organization, various multinational corporations, and national groups such as the Kurds, all of whom were pursuing their own international agendas. The Persian Gulf War shows that states are not the only international actors, and that global society is characterized by the activities of an increasingly interconnected web of governmental and nongovernmental organizations pursuing their own interests, which may be in political conflict with one another.

Context

Sovereign states remain the preponderant international actors. Their number has grown from about a dozen in 1648 to nearly two hundred in the mid-1990's, with new states especially desirous of exercising their sovereignty to the fullest extent possible. Large numbers of new states came into existence at the end of World War I, and after the demise of colonialism in the mid-1950's and 1960's. New states also have been created from the union of formerly separate states, such as the joining of the Federal Republic of Germany and the German Democratic Republic in 1991, or the disintegration of states, such as the dissolution of the Soviet Union into fifteen successor states in 1991 or the splintering of Yugoslavia in the early 1990's. Such changes have marked the evolution of the state system since its beginning.

States have not always been the main global actors. Prior to 1648, global political authority was exercised by the Roman Empire and later by the Roman Catholic church working through local principalities and fiefdoms. Such groups laid the groundwork for the organization of the state in the 1600's and the transition in terms of organizational authority. Some analysts contend that a similar evolution is under way with the power of the state being challenged from two opposing directions. Economically the state is too small to provide for the larger markets needed to be competitive; according to this argument, the state ultimately will have to cede authority to international economic organizations such as the International Monetary Fund and the General Agreement on Tariffs and Trade, and to growing numbers of regional free trade areas and customs unions. The European Community and its move toward supranationality is seen as the foremost example of what states must do to remain viable economically. An opposing view argues that states are too big to provide a focal point for popular loyalties, with people generally finding it easier to identify with smaller units that can be more responsive to local needs. The reemergence of nationalism and growing demands of various groups for their own nations, the splintering of large states such as the Soviet Union, and the hesitancy of various nongovernmental groups in Western Europe to support the European Community's move to a common currency are cited as evidence for this critique of the state.

Neither side can dismiss the growing number of international organizations. In the early 1900's, there were fewer than one hundred; by the late 1980's, more than three hundred intergovernmental organizations and more than twenty-five hundred nongovernmental organizations had grown out of the increasing technological, ecological, communications, and commercial ties proliferating throughout the world. On the other hand, it is hard to argue with what has been labeled the retribalization of global politics as cultures, peoples, and tribes clash with one another on the basis of their particular beliefs and faiths. Analysts also disagree about whether this increasingly complex global network will be more or less stable: Some argue that states can coexist peacefully because of supranational and subnational organizations, while others maintain that such global complexity is likely to degenerate into anarchy. What does seem clear is that governments and peoples are more tightly linked than ever before and such links are likely to increase, further complicating the role of the state.

Bibliography

Barber, Benjamin R. "Jihad vs. McWorld." *Atlantic Monthly* 269 (March, 1992): 53-63. Two global tendencies operating at cross purposes, one driven by narrow hatreds and the other by expanding markets, are presented as the main forces at work globally.

Baylis, John, and N. J. Rengger, eds. *Dilemmas of World Politics: International Issues in a Changing World*. Oxford, England: Clarendon Press, 1992. Articles by British and U.S. scholars discussing the theories, institutions, and issues that characterize international politics of the early 1990's; suggested guide to further reading on various topics.

Bennett, A. LeRoy. *International Organizations: Principles and Issues*. Englewood Cliffs, N.J.: Prentice Hall, 1991. Pessimistic overview of the League of Nations,

United Nations, and various regional organizations and their prospects.

Claude, Inis L., Jr. *Swords into Plowshares: The Problems and Progress of International Organization*. 4th ed. New York: Random House, 1984. Classic treatment of the theoretical basis, evolution, problems, and prospects of international organizations with a concentration on the United Nations network.

Huntington, Samuel P. "The Clash of Civilizations?" *Foreign Affairs* 72 (Summer, 1993): 22-49. Argues that the dominating source of international conflict will increasingly be cultural, based on civilizations separated from each other by their religion, history, language, and tradition. Subsequent issues carried comments and counterarguments by other experts.

Keohane, Robert O., and Joseph S. Nye. *Power and Interdependence*. 2d ed. Glenview, Ill.: Scott, Foresman, 1989. Explores the anticipated beneficial implications of increasing interdependence, with case studies of the oceans, monetary issues, and United States' relations with Australia and Canada.

Lodge, Juliet, ed. *The European Community and the Challenge of the Future*. 2d ed. New York: St. Martin's Press, 1993. Overview of the structures, policies, external relations, and future implications of the common activities of the European Community.

Slomanson, William R. *Fundamental Perspectives on International Law*. St. Paul, Minn.: West Publishing, 1990. Survey of the basics of international law and the key areas it covers, and a chapter on how to research international law topics.

Judy Bell Krutky

Cross-References

Empires and Empire Building, p. 597; Federations, p. 675; Geopolitics, p. 759; History of Government, p. 829; Imperialism, p. 889; International Law, p. 956; International Relations, p. 969; Isolationism and Protectionism, p. 1000; North Atlantic Treaty Organization, p. 1332; Peace, p. 1390; Supranational Government Institutions, p. 1922; World Government Movements, p. 2174.

ZIONISM

Field of study: Politics

Zionism originated in the nineteenth century as a Jewish nationalist movement with the goal of creating a Jewish homeland in Palestine, the ancestral home of the Jewish people. Since the creation of Israel in 1948, the term has evolved to mean the acceptance of the Jewish state.

Principal terms
BALFOUR DECLARATION: 1917 declaration of British support for a
    Jewish homeland in Palestine
HASKALAH: secular Jewish movement that paralleled the Enlightenment
POLITICAL ZIONISM: concept of political recognition of a Jewish
    homeland in Palestine
PRACTICAL ZIONISM: movement to establish Jewish settlements in
    Palestine, encouragement of immigration to Palestine
ZION: biblical term referring to Jerusalem, ancient capital of Israel

Overview

The term "Zionism" was first coined in 1890 by Nathan Birnbaum. Birnbaum was a member of an organization, in reality a loose collection of societies, collectively referred to as Hoveve Zion (lovers of Zion). The association had been founded in Russia during the early 1880's and advocated the emigration of Jews to Palestine. Birnbaum published a biweekly journal, *Selbst-Emanzipation* (self-emancipation), that served as a vehicle for dissemination of his ideas. Zionism, in Birnbaum's viewpoint, was meant to serve as a political philosophy for the advocates of practical Zionism, or the actual emigration to Palestine. Like many of the early Zionists, Birnbaum was a socialist, arguing for the establishment of egalitarian agricultural settlements in Palestine. By the mid-1890's, Hoveve Zion societies had been established through much of Europe and extended to the United States. The influence of the group was such that at the First Zionist Congress in 1897, nearly all delegates were associated with the group.

Jewish tradition had always retained the memory of the ancestral home in Israel. According to this tradition the coming messianic age would result in the return of the Jews to the biblical Holy Land. Liturgy and prayers, many of which could be traced back for centuries, formed the roots of what became Zionism. For many Jews, Palestine was not merely a dream. By the 1890's, thousands of Jews had already immigrated.

The Enlightenment, which began in Europe during the eighteenth century, had its counterpart in Judaism. Liberalization of religious practice in Europe brought greater toleration of Jews as full citizens within their respective countries. The result was a reduced emphasis on Jewish tradition, and assimilation within the dominant Christian population. This new freedom from religious tradition spawned the development of a more secular movement among younger Jews that came to be known as Haskalah, or enlightenment. The response was as diverse as the countries in which the movement flourished, ranging from complete assimilation to a renewed study of Jewish tradition.

In Russia, liberalization appeared only under the rule of Czar Alexander II, which began in 1855. Alexander ordered the repeal of many of the existing restrictions on Jews. In consequence, literature, associated with Haskalah, emphasizing the cultural emancipation of Russian Jews, began to supplant traditional messianic belief among its followers.

Emancipation of Russian Jews came to an abrupt halt following the assassination of Alexander II in 1881. Putting the Jews in their traditional role of scapegoat, Alexander's son, Nicholas II, reestablished many of the earlier restrictions, ushering in a long period of bloody pogroms and seizure of Jewish property. Among those reacting to conditions was Leo Pinsker, an Odessa physician, who published an essay called *Auto-emanzipation* (auto-emancipation) in 1882. In his essay, Pinsker argues that hatred of the Jews was not simply the result of economic backwardness, but was inherent in the gentile population itself. Further, if the Jews were to be liberated, they must do it themselves. Pinsker appealed to the richer Jews of Western Europe to aid their fellow Jews of Russia. Borrowing from the European ideas of nationalism, Pinsker argued for the concentration of Jews in their own land, using the economic support of the West. Not surprisingly, Pinsker found little support from the relatively comfortable Jews in Western Europe. In Odessa, however, a group of followers formed around Pinsker, calling themselves the aforementioned Hoveve Zion. Members of this group, with the financial aid of Baron Edmond de Rothschild in France, established the early settlements in Palestine that became the forerunners of later colonization.

Though the Jewish humanism associated with the Haskalah movement in Russia ultimately proved a failure, some of its most important tenets were to be the basis of the Zionist movement. One tenet was the secularization of Judaism and another the importance of physical labor in production.

Into the mid-1890's, Zionism remained the dream of only a small number of groups. Its transformation into a popular movement was the direct result of a small booklet written by a popular playwright and journalist, Theodor Herzl. Herzl was born in Budapest in 1860, into a socially prominent family that had discarded most of the trappings of Judaism. Herzl was at first a strong supporter of the concept of assimilation, but events were to convince him of the impossibility of the process. First, Herzl observed the emergence and success of political parties based on anti-Semitism. Herzl also served as the Paris correspondent for a Vienna newspaper at the 1894 trial of Alfred Dreyfus, a Jewish officer in the French army falsely accused of treason. The trial, which quickly became a farce, and the subsequent rioting against the Jews of France, convinced Herzl that Jews could only find a home in their own state. His 1896 publication of *Der Judenstaat* represents the official beginning of political Zionism. In the booklet, Herzl argued that the political forces of the world should be encouraged to support formation of a Jewish homeland. (It is not clear in the booklet where that homeland should be. Argentina was a possibility, but Herzl came to support Palestine as the ideal answer.)

In June, 1897, Herzl began publication of *Die Welt* (*The World*), which served as the major means for dissemination of Zionist information until World War I. Shortly after, Herzl arranged for the convening of the first Zionist Congress, which met in Basel, Switzerland, in August, 1897. The purpose of the congress was to take steps necessary for the formation of a Jewish state. Speakers dealt with a variety of topics: the emergencies faced by Jews in the face of local hatreds, the economic justification for Zionism, and of course the possibility of settlement in Palestine.

Colonization was to be based on agricultural settlements, including farmers, laborers, and other tradespeople. Herzl believed that the people were not ready for a purely democratic form of government; his own bias was toward a democratic monarchy, with politics shaped by the upper echelon of the society. All would be equal, however, in the eyes of the law. Further, Zionism was to become an international movement, mobilizing and encouraging support from the Jewish population in various countries and from their respective governments.

Zionist congresses continued to meet each year until 1901, with meetings held every two years after that time. Herzl developed severe heart disease, dying in 1904 at the age of forty-four.

Applications

With Herzl as the major spokesman for Zionism, the center of the movement was established in Vienna. The meetings of the Zionist Congress established the political forum for the movement. Herzl was aware that despite these promising beginnings, only the support of governments would enable the eventual establishment of a Jewish state, wherever that might be.

Herzl envisioned a sovereign state to be the home of the Jews. Sovereignty would be the first major objective of Herzl's political Zionism. He believed the piecemeal settlements that were slowly being established in Palestine by advocates of practical Zionism were too limited. In pursuit of his goal, Herzl carried out negotiations with the Turkish government with the hope of receiving a charter establishing Jewish autonomy in Palestine. That these negotiations failed was not the result of resistance by the Arab population already in the land; only some half million Arabs were living in that part of the Middle East at the time, and there was no organized movement in support of an Arab nationalism. Rather, the question of monetary compensation for the Turkish sultan, Abdul Hamid, became the major source of contention.

Herzl did find a measure of success in London. In 1903, the British government offered land in the East African territory of Uganda for a Zionist state. Herzl's view of the need for a Jewish state was founded less on reliving history than on the need to find a solution to the plight of his fellow Jews. For this reason, he seriously considered the British offer. Most of the Zionists, however, were Russian Jews, who would settle only for a homeland in Palestine. Herzl died in 1904, and the Ugandan offer was rejected by the seventh Zionist Congress in 1905.

As a movement, Zionism never represented more than a small proportion of Jews worldwide, but it was a well-organized and highly vocal minority, willing to put its plans in action. With waves of pogroms continuing in Russia, becoming more violent each year, young Jews from that country continued to emigrate to Palestine. By the beginning of World War I, about 90,000 Jews had established themselves in settlements. With Germany and Turkey allied in the war, the center of the Zionist movement moved to London, where it was led by Russian Jews living in that city, most notably Chaim Weizmann and Nahum Sokolow.

During the first decades of the twentieth century, many of the proponents of Zionism had been involved in the socialist movement in Russia. It was no surprise, therefore, that Zionism evolved into a socialist movement. Its leaders in Palestine believed the movement to be rooted in the need for people to have land of their own, and in the dignity of physical labor. It was the romantic figure of Jewish youth tilling communal land that became the dominant feature of early practical Zionism. Many of those youth would become the leaders of the state of Israel after 1948.

In the second decade of the twentieth century, the movement evolved into what Weizmann called synthetic Zionism, with emphasis placed on a cultural renaissance of Judaism. The Hebrew language was reborn and the Hebrew University founded in Jerusalem. Money was collected through the worldwide Jewish National Fund with the goal of buying land and animals for the settlers. Weizmann, a chemist by trade who contributed significantly to the British war effort, became the natural leader of the movement.

Weizmann was instrumental in the British publication of the Balfour Declaration in 1917, in which the British government declared its support for a Jewish national homeland to be established in Palestine. Though the publication had several motives, not least of which was the attempt to rally worldwide Jewish support for the British, its existence was the first tangible evidence that the Zionist dream might become reality.

After the defeat of the Central Powers in World War I, the Zionist movement was shifted to Paris. Weizmann and Sokolow led the fight to guarantee rights for all minorities in countries established after the war. Jews were defined as a separate people, entitled to the rights and protections of other minorities. Zionism was therefore able to work within defined institutions among the population in order to emphasize Jewish culture, at the same time opposing assimilation. The period between the wars saw a jump in the Jewish population of Palestine to more than 600,000 persons. The settlers practiced their own form of self-government. The most powerful of the political parties remained the Socialist Zionists, which included members of the labor unions and those from agricultural settlements. The goal was that of a socialist, egalitarian, secular, and Jewish society that would also include members of the Arab population.

The development of a strong Arab nationalist movement precluded any easy solution. In 1929, the first Arab riots against the growing Jewish population occurred, and would continue throughout the period of the British mandate. The murder of most of Europe's Jews during the Holocaust, made worse by the exclusion of many of these Jews from Western countries (including the United States) where they might have found safety, catalyzed the movement for a Jewish homeland. In 1947, the British, tired of being caught between the fighting Jewish and Arab factions, announced a pullout from Palestine. In November, 1947, the United Nations voted for partition of Palestine into separate Jewish and Arab lands that would remain economically linked. Though partition was not accepted by the Arab population, on May 14, 1948, the state of Israel was declared.

Context

The intellectual appeal of Zionism has two major roots. First, there was the attachment by Jews after the Diaspora for the land of their heritage: Israel. Though by the time of Herzl it had been some 1,800 years since the Jewish people had had a land they could call their own, the attachment to Zion was never lost. The Jewish liturgy contains deeply felt expressions of longing for a return. Indeed, much of the concept of the coming messiah was centered on his role in leading the Jews back to Israel.

The second root for the Zionist movement began in the liberal movements in Europe that followed the French Revolution of the 1790's. The Enlightenment, which began during the latter half of the eighteenth century in Western Europe, and which allowed for the growth of the liberal ideal, included within its tenets that of religious toleration. For the Jews, it turned out, this meant primarily the ability to assimilate into the predominantly Christian population, not the free expression of Jewish culture. Furthermore, only in Western Europe was the possibility of cultural assimilation open to the Jews.

Liberal ideas found little sympathy in Eastern Europe, where the largest populations of Jews were found. Dominated by czarist Russia, the Jews of Eastern Europe were a population separate from the region's gentiles. Jews had their own language, Yiddish, and their own community structure. Jews were excluded from the Russian political and legal systems, such as they were. With the assassination of the reform-minded Alexander II in 1881, a wave of persecution swept over the Jews in Russia, eliminating any chance for the Jews to play a role in a more tolerant society. As a consequence, Eastern European Jews began to emigrate to Western Europe and to the United States. A small number emigrated to Palestine, where they established several agricultural communities.

Palestine of the late nineteenth century was largely unoccupied, devoid of either Arab or Jew. Part of the Ottoman Empire for centuries, much of the land was empty wilderness. Much of the large-scale Arab immigration into the land paralleled that of the Jews; that is, it occurred primarily during the early twentieth century, following World War I.

During World War I, Palestinian Jews played an important role in the British liberation of the area from Turkish domination. A Jewish legion was established, which formed part of the British force. The Jewish role in the war, including that of Chaim Weizmann, resulted in the Balfour Declaration of 1917.

The British government initially hoped to establish a joint government in the region, including members of both the Zionist and Arab populations. Arab leaders, however, refused to acknowledge any promises made by the British to members of the Zionist movement. The Jewish community in the 1920's established a Jewish agency, with the intent of aiding new immigrants and playing a more active role in governing the region. Arab leaders refused any attempt at cooperation. In August, 1929, the first major attacks were made by Arabs against Jews, setting off what was, in effect, a civil war, which ended only with the war of liberation after the establishment of Israel in 1948.

Since 1948, Zionist organizations have played a strong role in maintaining financial support for Israel. This has included both foreign aid from the United States and direct financial support from citizens of Western countries. In addition, Zionist organizations have continued to support the immigration of Jews to Israel.

Bibliography

Bein, Alex. *Theodor Herzl*. Translated by Maurice Samuel. New York: Atheneum, 1970. Early biography of one of the major influences in development of Zionism. Provides a broad synopsis of Herzl's short life and work.

Elmessiri, Abdelwahab. *The Land of Promise: A Critique of Political Zionism*. New Brunswick, N.J.: North American, 1977. Controversial book, written and distributed by the Arab Information Center. The author contends that Zionism as a political movement has reinterpreted Jewish history.

Herzl, Theodor. *The Jewish State*. Mineola, N.Y.: Dover, 1988. The book from which the concept of political Zionism has its origin. Herzl discusses the failure of assimilation and argues that only through establishment of a Jewish state would Jews find a land in which they could live at peace.

Laqueur, Walter. *A History of Zionism*. New York: Holt, Rinehart and Winston, 1972. Detailed history of Zionism, from its roots to establishment of the Jewish state. An excellent political analysis of the movement.

Mandel, Neville. *The Arabs and Zionism Before World War I*. Berkeley: University of California Press, 1976. Examines the role played by Zionism in Palestine. Emphasis is placed on Arab-Jewish relations during the period, including aborted attempts at establishment of Arab-Jewish entente.

Pawel, Ernst. *The Labyrinth of Exile: A Life of Theodor Herzl*. New York: Farrar, Straus, & Giroux, 1989. One of several excellent biographies of Herzl. Included are more recent ideas on the role of the Dreyfus trial and other events of Herzl's time.

Sachar, Howard. *A History of Israel: From the Rise of Zionism to Our Time*. New York: Alfred A. Knopf, 1976. Thorough discussion of the historic role of Zionism in the formation of Israel. Stressed is the period between 1917 to 1948. A discussion of the politics of early Zionism and socialism within the Jewish settlements of Palestine is also detailed.

Segre, Dan Vittorio. *A Crisis of Identity: Israel and Zionism*. New York: Oxford University Press, 1980. Discusses the effects that the concept of Zionism has on the politics of the Jewish state. The question of what constitutes a Jewish identity is addressed in the light of Jewish immigration.

Richard Adler

Cross-References

Church and Government in History, p. 230; Independence Movements and Transitions, p. 896; International Relations, p. 969; Liberalism, p. 1118; Nationalism, p. 1268; Religion and Politics, p. 1685; Russian Political History, p. 1770; The State, p. 1878; Theocracy, p. 1968.

GLOSSARY

Abortion: Medical procedure that terminates pregnancy, usually before the fetus is viable.

Absolute monarchy: Centralized government ruled by a monarch with complete control over the people and property within the nation—particularly in Europe in the seventeenth and eighteenth centuries.

Accountability: Requirement that public officials be answerable for their actions through elections, impeachment, or other mechanisms to enforce the public will.

Adjudication: Application of existing laws or rules to special situations through case-by-case decision making.

Administration: Managing the tasks of government with economy and efficiency.

Administrative law: Area of law dealing with the powers and procedures of government agencies.

Affirmative action: Government policies that promote and require preferential treatment of minorities to redress the effects of past discrimination or to promote diversity in workplaces, schools, and other sectors.

Alien: Person who is not a citizen or a national of the country in which the person physically resides.

Alliance: Agreement between states in which each pledges to assist the others in security matters.

Ally: State that coordinates its defense policies with those of one or more other states, frequently on the basis of formal treaties.

Ambassador: Highest-ranking diplomatic representative appointed by one country to represent it in one or more other countries.

Anarchism: View that all forms of government are oppressive and intolerable to free and rational people.

Anarchy: Absence of rule, lawlessness; associated in classical thought with direct democracy.

Antifederalists: Those who opposed ratification of the new U.S. Constitution from 1787 to 1789.

Apartheid: A social and political system of racial segregation; practiced in South Africa from 1948 until 1991, during which time a white minority held privileged status and blacks were denied equal rights.

Appellate court: Court of review to determine the validity of the rulings of lower courts.

Appropriation: Spending or obligation of public funds for authorized purposes.

Arab League: League of twenty-two Arab states and organizations formed in 1945.

Arbitration: Method of resolving a disagreement between two parties in which a third party makes a decision after hearing both sides of the dispute.

Aristocracy: In classical thought, rule of the best or of the virtuous; in contemporary life, commonly associated with rule of the rich or a hereditary upper class.

Arms control: Attempts to reduce the risk of war—especially nuclear war—by regulating arms competition among nations and by reducing incentives for war.

Arms race: Rivalry among countries to outdo one another in the level or quality of their weapon systems.

Articles of Confederation: Agreement ratified by the thirteen original U.S. states in 1781, forming a government in which the states retained important powers while the national government received only limited power; replaced by the Constitution in 1789.

Australian ballot: Ballot form that allows the voter to vote in secrecy.

Authoritarianism: Government by arbitrary authority that ignores fundamental rights of individuals and rules through force rather than consent.

Authority: Legitimate rule of a government over its citizens.

Autocracy: Government by one person wielding absolute authority.

Autonomy: Self-rule of a nation or of a community or group within a state.

Balance of power: Condition in which the military and economic strength of competing countries or alliances is approximately equal.

Ballot: Piece of paper on which the names of candidates or proposals appear for voter selection.

Bargaining: Actions and negotiations in which two or more parties seek to resolve conflicts while pursuing their interests.

Bicameralism: Having two houses or chambers, particularly in a legislative body.

Bill of rights: Constitutionally specified restraints on the powers of government, often involving social as well as civil rights.

Bill of Rights: First ten amendments to the U.S. Constitution, listing basic liberties that the federal government cannot abridge; these include freedom of speech and religion, protection against arbitrary searches and seizures, and certain rights guaranteed to citizens accused of crimes.

Bloc: Alliance characterized by comparative homogeneity and ideological commonalities among allies.

Block grant: A grant of funds usually from a higher level of government to a lower that specifies a range of activities for which monies may be used, with recipients allowed broad discretion to spend within these limits.

Bond: Certificate of indebtedness, tendered by a unit of government (the borrower) to a lender, that provides written recognition of the legal obligation to repay the loan plus interest.

Bourgeoisie: In Karl Marx's philosophy, the capitalist economic class that owns and controls business firms and industries and derives its income from profit.

Bretton Woods system: International monetary control system that comprises the International Monetary Fund, the World Bank, and the General Agreement on Tariffs and Trade, the first two of which were created at Bretton Woods, New Hampshire, in 1944.

Budget: Document that describes a government's plans for spending and specifies taxation and deficit policies for a single fiscal period.

Budget deficit: Amount by which expenditures exceed receipts within a fiscal year, an amount the government must borrow.

Bureaucracy: Administrative organization usually staffed by career employees and characterized by a division of labor, specialization of tasks, hierarchical chain of command, standard operation procedure, and formal record keeping.

Bylaw: Local ordinance passed by town meeting and having the force of law.

Cabinet: Heads of the major government departments, who advise the president or prime minister.

Campaign: Various activities—such as speeches, television advertising, and rallies—engaged in by a candidate seeking public office, or by others active on the candidate's behalf.

Capitalism: Economic system that allows private property and open competition between businesses in a free market.

Caste system: Social hierarchy of India in which people are born into one of four castes.

Categorical grant: A grant provided for a specific purpose, with recipients allowed little discretion in how funds will be spent.

Caucus: Meeting of key political party leaders, usually to decide party policy or select a candidate; also, meeting of registered party members to select representatives who will attend conventions at which delegates will select the party's presidential candidate.

Censorship: Suppression of the publication or dissemination of any form of expression regarded as objectionable.

Central bank: Government entity that functions as a "bankers' bank" and acts to influence the money supply and interest rates as part of monetary policy.

Charismatic leadership: Term describing a leader with great personal magnetism able to attract a large following.

Charter: A legal document granted by a state that creates a municipality and defines its legal status.

Checks and balances: Principle that the judicial, legislative, and executive branches of government have the power to limit and counteract one another's decisions.

Chief executive: Top officer in the executive branch of a government.

Chief of state: Ceremonial and symbolic leader of a nation (also called the head of state), such as the king or queen of England; in the United States the chief of state and the actual head of government are the same—the president.

Citizen: Member of a state or nation by birth or naturalization.

City manager: An appointed officer who carries out the executive duties of a municipality in a council-manager form of government.

City-state: Small, independent political entity composed of a city and the surrounding countryside, as in ancient Greece.

Civic education: Education of the members of a nation in the rights and responsibilities of citizenship.

Civil disobedience: Refusal to obey a law that one considers morally unjust or unconstitutional.

Civil liberties: Freedoms or rights guaranteed to all individuals by law, custom, or judicial interpretation.

Civil rights: Explicit acts of government, either constitutionally derived or promulgated as statutory law, that protect citizens from unfair, arbitrary, and discriminatory treatment at the hands of government or other citizens.

Civil Rights movement: Predominantly black-led movement of the 1950's and 1960's based in churches and legal-action groups that worked to extend full social and political rights to all Americans.

Civil service: Body of individuals chosen by merit and protected from improper political interference who administer a government's programs.

Civil war: War within a country, rather than between countries.

Class: Group sharing a common economic or social status.

Class conflict: Marxist notion that society tends to polarize into two dominant conflicting groups, impoverished workers and wealthy capitalists.

Closed primary: Election in which only citizens who registered as party members before the election are permitted to vote.

Cloture: Procedure used to close off debate so that a legislature can move to a vote on a bill.

Coalition: Temporary alliance or association of groups to advance a common cause.

Coalition government: In a parliamentary system, government in which two or more political parties share control because no one political party won a majority of seats in the most recent election.

Cold War: Period of conflict and competition between the United States and the Soviet Union, and their allies, which lasted more than four decades after World War II.

Collective bargaining: Negotiations between employees, through their labor unions, and their employers regarding wages and working conditions.

Collective security: System in which nations agree to defend one another against attack; an attack against one is considered an attack against all.

Collectivism: System in which people as a group share in the ownership, production, and distribution of property.

Colonialism: System whereby a country exploits economic and political control over a foreign country for self-serving reasons.

Commander in chief: Ultimate governor of a military entity, usually a highly placed civilian executive officer.

Common law: The legal system in use in the United Kingdom and many former colonies of Britain, called "common" because it is expected to be uniform across an entire nation, and distinguished by a relatively greater reliance on "judge-made" rather than legislatively enacted law.

Commonwealth: Republic or democratic state.

Communism: In theory, a classless society managed by the dictatorship of the working class, and with most property owned by the state.

Confederation: Compact, or league, among sovereign political states to serve mutual interests and provide mutual support; the central government usually lacks the ability to make and enforce binding decisions on the member states.

Congress: Lawmaking branch of the U.S. government, consisting of the House of Representatives and the Senate.

Conscientious objection: Refusal to serve in the military on grounds of religious beliefs or conscience.

Consent of the governed: Agreement of those being governed to a form of government or political system.

Conservatism: Political belief that stresses individual freedom, the free market, and minimum state intervention in social and economic life (also called classical liberalism). Modern conservatives also emphasize political and cultural traditions as well as personal virtue and character formation.

Constituency: Citizens whom a political leader formally represents.

Constitution: Basic or fundamental law of a politically organized body, such as a nation, it defines the structure and powers of government; it may include limitations on governmental powers, such as descriptions of individuals' civil rights and liberties.

Constitutional democracy: Form of democratic government in which the majority is limited by rights assured to all, such as freedom of speech and religion.

Constitutional law: Area of jurisprudence in which laws, governmental actions, and judicial decisions are examined to determine whether they violate constitutional principles that are intended to limit governmental abuses.

Constitutional monarchy: Political system in which a monarch is restrained by constitutional limitations or that has a monarch as ceremonial head of state, but assigns political power to the leader of a majority within parliament.

Constitutionalism: Belief in limited government guaranteed through a written or understood contract.

Consulate: Extension of an embassy serving to protect its citizens abroad and to perform administrative tasks.

Containment: U.S. policy adopted in 1947 to limit the expansion of the Soviet sphere of influence.

Convention: Gathering of delegates representing members of a political party, who adopt a party platform and nominate candidates for office.

Corporatism: Political system in which principle economic functions (such as banking, industry, labor, and government) are organized as corporate entities.

Cost-benefit analysis: Technique by which the costs and benefits of proposed actions are identified, assigned dollar values, and compared to calculate net results.

Counterinsurgency: Military and polinical action taken by a government to defeat insurgents.

Counterrevolution: Revolution led by past leaders attempting to regain control.

Counterterrorism: Methods used to combat terrorism.

County: Large territorial division of local government.

Coup d'etat (coup): Sudden illegal takeover of government control, often violent but need not be ("bloodless coup")

Courts: state and local: Judicial branch of state governments; as the systems that try most civil and criminal cases in the United States, they apply state laws and local ordinances in individual cases and issue decisions that control the acts of local authorities, state officials, and all the citizens within their jurisdictions.

Courts: U.S. federal: As the major components of the judicial branch of the United States government, federal courts operate independently of state judicial systems and are responsible for hearing cases and administering justice respecting federal law; they are organized in three levels that include district courts, courts of appeals, and the Supreme Court.

Cultural Revolution: Power struggle in China launched by Mao Tse-tung, his wife Jiang Qing, and her radical allies against the pragmatists led by Liu Shaoqi and Deng Xiaoping, resulting in widespread chaos from 1966 to 1976.

Decolonization: Replacement of colonial empires by politically independent states.

Demagogue: Political figure who achieves personal power by appealing to the baser instincts of the masses through a rhetoric of ethnic or racial hatred or class envy.

Democracy: Government of, for, and by the people of a political unit, usually through elected representatives.

Democratization: Transition from authoritarianism to democracy and the consolidation of democracy.

Deregulation: Removal or restricting governmental regulation usually of economic or business activity.

Despotism and tyranny: Synonymous terms for governments that are uncontrolled by law or custom in which power is typically concentrated in the hands of a single authoritarian ruler.

Détente: Period of improved relations between rivals.

Deterrence: A strategy that seeks to prevent an adversary from attacking by threatening to retaliate with equal or greater force.

Developed nation: Country with a strong industrial base, or advanced economy, such as Western Europe, the United States, and Japan.

Developing nation: Country with a limited industrial base; usually poor, and agrarian, but may be rich in exportable natural products, such as much of Africa and parts of Asia.

Diaspora: Dispersal of a people and their descendants to places outside their origin.

Dictatorship: Complete control of government power by a single ruler.

Dictatorship of the proletariat: According to Marxist philosophy, the stage following a revolution that overthrows capitalism when a communist government comes to power and exercises dictatorial control in the name of the working class or proletariat.

Dillon's Rule: Legal notion that because American local governments are "creatures of the state," they may exercise only such powers as are granted to them by their state constitutions or state legislatures.

Diplomacy: Communication between states through formal channels according to established rules.

Direct action: Boycotts, marches, and demonstrations undertaken to help force political or legal change.

Direct democracy: Political power exercised directly by the people, rather than exercised for them by elected representatives.

Disarmament: Policies designed to reduce existing armaments.

Discrimination: Unequal treatment of an individual or group based on assignment to a particular category.

Divine right: Claim that a monarch rules by the grace of God, which has been bestowed as an absolute right.

Dual federalism: Form of federal government in which each of the different levels of government is rigidly restricted to the powers explicitly assigned to it.

Due process of law: Principle articulated in the Fifth and Fourteenth amendments of the U.S. Constitution declaring that government cannot deprive citizens of "life, liberty, and property" without following carefully applied legal procedures.

Duty: Responsibility owed by an individual or a group.

Economic development: Process of economic modernization, usually characterized by movement of the rural population to cities and increases in per capita income, education, and industrial production.

Egalitarianism: Belief that attaches utmost importance to the attainment of political, social, and economic equality.

Elections: Process through which citizens select government leaders and rule on issues that may be put before them.

Electoral college: Body of electors chosen by the voters of each U.S. state to select the president and vice president.

Electorate: Set of persons who are qualified to vote in an election.

Elitism: Belief that a small class of superior persons should have the power to rule or dominate the rest of an entire society.

Embargo: Order by a government prohibiting the sale of goods to another country.

Embassy: Permanent mission established by a national government in a foreign country to represent the government's interests in that country.

Emigration: Act of leaving one region or country to establish residence elsewhere.

Eminent domain: Government's power to take private land for public purposes, usually with the owners receiving monetary compensation.

Empire: Political consolidation of vast territories and disparate peoples under one rule.

Empowerment: Movement encouraging average citizens to take responsibility for and control of actions that occur in the public's name; often applied to specific groups, such as women or the disabled.

Enlightened despotism: Form of absolutism during the eighteenth century in which rulers claimed to govern in the interests of the people.

Enlightenment: Western philosophical movement emphasizing reason that arose in the eighteenth century, when its proponents rejected many traditional political, social, and religious ideas.

Entitlement: Governmental benefits to which citizens are entitled because they meet certain criteria specified by law, such as low income or advanced age.

Environmental Protection Agency: U.S. government agency with primary responsibility for environmental and natural resource protection.

Equal protection of the laws: Principle embodied in the fourteenth amendment to the U.S. Constitution that citizens are to be treated equally by government with regard to laws and their application.

Equality of opportunity: Equal chances for all citizens to better their lot in life.

Equality under law: Principle that all citizens are equal before the law.

Espionage: Use of spies to obtain information or steal secrets about the activities of a foreign government.

Ethics: Principles identifying good and bad behavior and promoting moral duties and obligations.

Ethnicity: Racial, national, or cultural characteristics that set a group apart from other groups.

Exclusionary rule: Concept established by the U.S. Supreme Court that prevents evidence obtained in violation of a citizen's civil liberties from being introduced in a court of law.

Executive agreement: In the United States, an international agreement made by the president without the consent of the Senate.

Executive branch: In the United States, the president and the major departments of the government such as state, defense, treasury, and justice; in parliamentary systems, the prime minister and his or her cabinet departments.

Executive order: Rule or regulation issued by the president usually to other administrative officials.

Executive privilege: Implicit authority for the executive to withhold information from the legislative or judicial branches.

Faction: In James Madison's famous formulation, "a number of citizens, whether amounting to a majority or minority of the whole, who are united and actuated by some common impulse of passion, or of interest, adverse to the rights of other citizens, or to the permanent and aggregate interests of the community."

Fairness doctrine: Longstanding requirement in U.S. telecommunications law, no longer enforced, that requires that radio and television stations cover issues of public concern in a manner reflecting divergent relevant viewpoints.

Fascism: Intensely nationalistic ideology that glorifies a corporate, authoritarian state that has the right to control every aspect of citizens' lives.

Federal Reserve: Central bank of the United States, created in 1913 to act as the lender (to banks) of last resort and as the nation's monetary authority.

Federalism: System of government in which a central government and local or subunit governments have separate bases of authority and distinct powers as defined by written constitutions.

Federalists: Americans who supported adoption of the new U.S. Constitution between 1787 and 1789, and who favored a strong central government.

Federation: Governmental system in which some powers are allocated to the central government and others are allocated to the various constituent parts, such as states, provinces, or regions.

Feminism: Advocacy of the rights of women and their social, political, and economic equality with men.

Feudalism: Economic and social order, characteristic of medieval Europe, in which everyone belonged to a fixed strata in an hierarchical chain, from peasant up to lord and king.

Filibuster: Form of legislative obstruction by which a parliamentary minority attempts through continuous talking to defeat or alter a measure favored by the majority.

First strike: Initiation of war by one country upon another regarded as an illegal act in international law.

Fiscal policy: Tax, spending, and debt policies of the government, intended to improve the performance of the economy with respect to employment, inflation, and economic growth.

Fiscal year: Twelve-month period covered by a single budget; the fiscal year of the U.S. government runs from October 1 to September 30.

Food stamps: Credit slips provided to lower-income families to help finance basic food needs.

Foreign policy: Plans and actions that a government undertakes to achieve its goals in the international environment.

Formula grant: Categorical grant distributed automatically according to a preestablished eligibility formula.

Fourteen Points: Principles articulated by President Woodrow Wilson for negotiating an end to World War I, including the goal of self-determination for tha component nations of the former Austro-Hungarian and Ottoman empires.

Fourteenth Amendment: Amendment to the U.S. Constitution that requires states to provide all persons within their jurisdiction "due process" and "equal protection" under law.

Free speech: Right protected by the First Amendment to the U.S. Constitution, guaranteeing the right to speak out politically.

Free trade: Trade in which goods and services can be exchanged without tariff or nontariff barriers.

Freedom: In government and politics the right of individual citizens to decide how to live their lives, including the acquisition of property and involvement in political activities, subject to the necessities of social order and the protection of the rights of others.

Full employment: Situation in which everyone willing and able to work is able to find a job.

GATT: See *General Agreement on Tariffs and Trade*.

General Agreement on Tariffs and Trade (GATT): 1947 agreement among twenty-three nations (including the United States) that reduced tariffs and other trade barriers in order to facilitate global economic growth and development. Now involves more than one hundred nations.

General Assembly, U.N.: Central organ of the United Nations, representing each member state, responsible for discussing questions of international concern and making recommendations for action.

General election: Regular election to choose the holder or holders of an office or offices; contrasts with a primary election, in which political parties chose the candidates who will represent them in a general election.

General revenue sharing: Grants provided by the federal government to state and local governments with few federal limitations.

Genocide: Systematic killing of members of an ethnic or religious group with the intent of eliminating the group entirely.

Gestapo: Secret political police of the Nazi regime, created in 1933 and, under the leadership of Heinrich Himmler, attained a preeminent and feared position.

Gold standard: The value of a nation's currency expressed as a fixed worth in gold.

GOP: Acronym for "Grand Old Party," the popular nickname for the Republican Party.

Government: All the people or institutions that administer or control the affairs of a territorial unit, such as a nation; also, in a parliamentary system, the prime minister and cabinet, who effectively act as an executive branch.

Grant-in-aid: Financial assistance paid by one level of government to another for particular purposes articulated in legislation or administrative regulation.

Grassroots action: Political activity initiated at the lowest level of political systems.

Great Leap Forward: Mao Tse-tung's failed attempt to gain instant modernization and to overtake the Soviet Union ideologically by instituting communes in both urban and rural China and backyard furnaces to make steel during the late 1950's.

Great Society: series of domestic social programs originated by the Lyndon Johnson Administration.

Gross domestic product (GDP): Market value of the final goods and services produced within a nation in one year.

Guerrilla warfare: Violent conflict where at least one side is made up of irregular soldiers engaged in surprise raids and hit-and-run attacks.

Gun control: Regulations or limits on the ownership, manufacture, use, and sale of firearms.

Gunboat diplomacy: Attempt to achieve diplomatic goals by threatening military action.

Head of government: Title frequently given to the political leader in a system of government that has a ceremonial head of state.

Head of state: One who provides ceremonial leadership and continuity in times of governmental transition, and who—within limits—ensures that new governments are formed; often a monarch.

Helsinki Accords: Name commonly given to the Final Act of the Helsinki meeting of the Conference on Security and Cooperation in Europe in 1975.

Holocaust: Systematic mass murder of European Jews by the Nazis during World War II.

Holy Roman Empire: Empire made up of German and Italian territories; regarded as successor to the Roman Empire, it began in the year 800 and ended in 1806.

Home rule: Freedom of local governments to run their own affairs without state interference.

House of Commons: Elected and politically more powerful house of the British Parliament. Effectively, the lawmaking body for the United Kingdom.

House of Lords: One body of the British Parliament, consisting of more than twelve hundred members who serve by virtue of birthright or appointment to the nobility. Formerly a powerful body, but now has little real authority.

House of Representatives: One branch of the U.S. Congress, comprising 435 voting members serving two-year terms who are apportioned among the states according to their populations.

Human rights: Held inherently by each human being, identified as individual civil and political rights, group economic and social rights, and peoples' collective rights.

Humanism: Doctrine that exalts human dignity, particularly that of the individual, and rejects the supernatural.

Ideology: Consistent philosophy or system of beliefs that guides the actions of those who adopt it.

Immigration: Act of entering a region or country of which one is not a native for the purpose of establishing permanent residence.

Impeachment: Legal process by which a legislative body, such as Congress, accuses, tries, and removes government officials (such as the president, vice president, federal judges, or federal officials) who are judged to be corrupt.

Imperialism: Extension of a state's power through conquest and colonialism, with the goal of creating or extending an empire.

Implementation: Process of putting into effect the laws of legislatures and the directives of chief executives.

Impoundment: Choice by a chief executive not to spend certain money that the legislature has appropriated.

Incorporation of Bill of Rights: The process by which the Supreme Court has used the Fourteenth Amendment to make the provisions of the Bill of Rights applicable to the states, also called absorption.

Incumbent: The current holder of an elected office.

Individualism: Concept that each person's interests should take precedence over interests of the state or group, and that people should be free to pursue economic initiative and a personal philosophy.

Industrial policy: Government policies aimed at improving the performance of industry.

Industrial Revolution: Economic, social and scientific changes initiated in England and extended elsewhere, characterized by the replacement of hand tools by power-driven machines.

Information superhighway: Electronic interconnection of thousands of computers and information sources, making vast databases available to non-computer experts.

Infrastructure: Installations or facilities such as paved roads, sewers, piped water systems, and electricity supplies that provide the foundation for economic development.

Initiative: Process by which citizens enact their own laws or constitutional amendments by placing them on the ballot to be approved or rejected by popular vote.

Injunction: Court order that prohibits the execution of certain acts or mandates.

Insurgency: Guerrilla warfare waged against established authority.

Interest group: Organized group that seeks to influence public policy.

Intergovernmental relations: Interrelationships among the federal, state, and local governments.

International agreements: Accords among states and other entities, such as international organizations, that address issues that transcend national boundaries, such as international relations, pollution, and trade.

International law: Rules and principles of law that regulate the interrelationships of nations and their conduct toward each other.

International Monetary Fund: International agreement made in 1944 in order to ensure exchange rate stability through the use of short-term loans.

International organization: Institution created by two or more nations to pursue common objectives.

Internet: Worldwide network of local computer networks, allowing all users to share information resources and to communicate directly with one another.

Iron triangle: Close relationship which is formed among business, regulators, and legislators.

Irredentism: Claim by one country to territory lying under the sovereign jurisdiction of a neighboring country, based on the nationality or ethnic ties of the local population to the claimant nation.

Issue network: People and organizations who share interest in a particular policy issue can include government authorities, legislators, business people, lobbyists, academics, and journalists.

Jacobin: Member of the most radical faction in the French Revolution, used more generally to denote a left extremist.

Jim Crow laws: Laws mandating or supporting the physical segregation of African Americans from other Americans; they were particularly characteristic of Southern states.

Jingoism: Extreme national chauvinism advocating expansionist foreign policy.

Judicial branch: Federal judiciary, headed by the Supreme Court, and including courts of appeals, district courts, and a few specialized courts.

Judicial review: Power of courts to decide whether a statute or executive act is in accordance with the Constitution.

Jurisdiction: Areas in which a court has authority to act.

Jurisprudence: Science of law that deals with ascertaining the principles on which legal rules should be based.

Just war: War or revolution that is justified in terms of its political objectives.

Keynesian economics: Theories of John Maynard Keynes that government should intervene in the economy through fiscal policy, lifting an economy out of recession by spending more and controlling inflation by spending less.

Laissez-faire: Doctrine opposing governmental interference in economic affairs except to protect property rights and to enforce contracts.

Law enforcement: The carrying out of statutes by professionals hired for that purpose, particularly refers to enforcement of the criminal law.

Law enforcement agencies: National, state, and local entities engaged in crime prevention, law enforcement, and apprehension of criminals.

Leadership: Ability of political officeholders to have their positions accepted and adopted as the proper course of action by a group or society.

League of Nations: First world organization of national governments organized in 1919 after World War I, collapsed in 1939.

Left, the: Individuals and political groups seeking progressive political and social change, emphasizing equality over freedom.

Legislative branch of government: Elected or appointed deliberative body with authority to enact, amend, and repeal laws, such as a congress, parliament, kneset, or diet.

Legislative oversight: Monitoring by legislative bodies of the rules and regulations formulated by administrative agencies.

Legislative veto: Power of legislatures to negate or invalidate decisions by members of the executive branch of government without employing the constitutionally required process of lawmaking.

Legitimacy: Widely shared acceptance by a society that those who govern do so with lawful authority; the feeling that the political process deserves public respect.

Less developed countries (LDC): Countries whose per-capita incomes are below those of the developed nations.

Liberal democracy: Form of government characterized by protection for fundamental individual rights, limited government, and free elections coupled with widespread popular participation.

Liberalism: Political doctrine or movement that affirms and seeks social progress and the promotion of the social and political liberties of the individual.

Limited government: Government whose structure prevents official acts that violate the rights of individuals or minorities.

Line-item veto: Power of an official to veto individual sections or lines of a bill.

Literacy test: Requirement that prospective voters be literate in order to register to vote.

Lobbying: Attempting to influence government policy, particularly in legislatures, by applying public pressure or employing professional lobbyists.

Lower house: One of two houses of a bicameral parliament; its members are elected.

McCarthyism: Political style characterized by public hysteria over communism; named after U.S. senator Joseph R. McCarthy, whose broad public accusations that communists were infiltrating American institutions dominated American politics from 1952 until McCarthy's death in 1957.

Magna Carta: feudal English document that recognized the privileges of the English nobility.

Majority leader: Floor leader of the U.S. Senate, elected by the members of the majority party in the Senate, who has little real power and leads through negotiations with fellow senators.

Majority party: Political party holding a majority of the seats within the legislature.

Manifest Destiny: Notion that westward expansion of the United States was inevitable; a prototype of geopolitical thinking.

Market economy: Economic system characterized by private ownership of resources, a limited government role, and competitive markets for goods and services.

Marxism: Doctrine derived from Karl Marx, holding that class struggle is the heart of the historical process and that ownership of the means of production and distribution determines the nature of the social order; collective ownership will follow a class revolution.

Mass media: Organs of mass communication, including newspapers and magazines, radio, and television.

Mayor: Chief executive, normally elected, of a municipality.

Medicaid: U.S. government program that provides health insurance to the poor; administered and partially paid by the states.

Medicare: U.S. government program that provides health insurance to persons sixty-five years of age and older and to others entitled to Social Security benefits.

Melting pot: Common metaphor for assimilation, involving the idea that different ethnic groups melt and blend together to form a uniform American culture.

Mercantilism: Economic system in Europe between the fifteenth and nineteenth centuries by which government strictly regulated the national economy, including wages and prices. Replaced by capitalism.

Merit system: Selection and advancement in public employment based on competitive examinations and ability, knowledge, and skills.

Militia: In early U.S. history, the entire population of adult males who were physically fit and politically eligible for military service.

Ministerial responsibility: The basic requirement of parliamentary government—that the head of government or the entire cabinet is dependent on and responsible to a majority in the legislature.

Mixed constitution: Government charter that combines features of different political types, such as a democracy and aristocracy.

Mixed economy: Direct ownership and operation of specific industries or entire industrial sectors by the state.

Mobilization: Act of bringing individuals together for the purpose of collective political action; usually accomplished through emotional rhetoric and appeals for unity.

Monarchy: Rule by one person, typically a king or queen selected by heredity or arranged marriage.

Monetarism: Belief that the central bank, by regulating the money supply and interest rates, should be the principal tool for maintaining economic stability.

Monopoly: Any economic entity that controls the entire supply of a good or service, thereby destroying free market exchange.

Monroe Doctrine: U.S. policy of opposing European intervention in the Western Hemisphere, articulated by President James Monroe.

Morality: Quality of correct conduct.

Multiculturalism: Movement that promotes the merits of embracing cultural, racial, or ethnic diversity, especially in politics and education.

Multinational corporation: Business with operations in more than one country.

Multiparty system: Political process in which numerous parties compete; frequently produces coalition governments in parliamentary systems.

NAFTA: See *North American Free Trade Agreement.*

Napoleonic code: Civil laws established by French emperor Napoleon I that were eventually adopted in many European and Latin American countries.

Narcoterrorism: Illegal activities linked to drug trade.

Nation-state: Politically organized territory that recognizes no higher sovereignty, and whose population politically identifies with that entity.

National debt: Amount that a national government has borrowed, and not yet repaid, to cover past deficits.

National health insurance: Any health insurance program that a national government organizes in order to guarantee coverage to all citizens for health services.

National liberation movement: Rebellions, often armed, of national or minority groups against colonial governments or native governments under foreign control.

National security: Safety of a government and its society from threats by foreign nations.

Nationalism: Devotion to one's nation and an ideology stressing the unity of a people based on their cultural, linguistic, historical, religious, or ethnic similarity; major movement of the nineteenth century.

Nativism: Cultural and political discrimination against newly arrived immigrants in favor of the interests of citizens who have been in the country for several generations.

NATO. See *North Atlantic Treaty Organization.*

Natural law: System of ethics and political philosophy that sees right and wrong as universal and sees human law as based on morality.

Natural rights: Rights belonging to all human beings, received from nature, rather than a human institution.

Naturalization: Legal process by which a person can acquire a new nationality or citizenship.

Nazism: Ideology of racial supremacy used by the National Socialist German Workers' Party and its leader, Adolf Hitler, to justify totalitarian rule in Germany.

Neocolonialism: Domination of underdeveloped nations by imperialist powers after the former have gained formal independence.

New Deal: Domestic programs of President Franklin Delano Roosevelt, designed to combat the effects of the Great Depression.

New Left: Term used to define the radical youth movement of the 1960's emphasizing economic equality and participatory democracy.

New Right: Advocates of freedom in economic matters and a social order with strong emphasis on traditional moral values.

Nihilism: Literally means "nothingness"; in existentialist thought it typically has the more general sense of a condition in which all cultural values are challenged, that there are no true principles of right or justice.

Nonaligned movement: Movement begun in the 1950's by less-developed states in the tropics and the Southern Hemisphere seeking to avoid political alliance with either of the Cold War's ideological camps.

Nonpartisan: Free from party affiliation, association, or designation.

Nonpartisan primary: Election in which candidates are not permitted to list their party affiliation on the ballot.

Nonproliferation: Preventing the transfer of nuclear weapons or technology to countries that do not have nuclear weapons.

Nonviolent direct action: Method of protest in which the protagonist initiates conflict nonviolently by doing or refusing to do certain things.

North American Free Trade Agreement (NAFTA): 1993 agreement that provides for Mexico, the United States, and Canada to reduce tariffs and other barriers to trade.

North Atlantic Treaty Organization (NATO): Mutual defense alliance among North American and Western European nations.

Nuremberg Trials: Trial of major Nazi war criminals after 1945.

Ochlocracy: Rule by the whole—mob rule.

Oligarchy: Rule by a few.

One-party rule: System in which a single political party runs the government and often suppresses competing parties.

Open primary: Form of direct primary in which any qualified voter may participate, regardless of party affiliation.

Organic theory of the state: Idea, developed mainly by Germans, that the state is a living organism with an inherent need to grow and expand.

Original intent: In constitutional interpretation, the emphasis on what the authors of the U.S. Constitution meant, their original intent, when deciding contemporary constitutional controversies.

Pacifism: Refusal to settle disputes with violence, usually based on moral or religious grounds; often used interchangeably with passive resistance and nonviolent resistance.

Papacy: Office of the pope; system of government within the Roman Catholic church.

Parliament: Body of people's representatives centrally involved in the making of laws and policy; in Britain Parliament is composed of two chambers, the House of Lords and the House of Commons.

Parliamentary system: Political system in which voters select members of a legislative body; the majority party or coalition of parties in that body then chooses the executive branch of government, including the prime minister and the cabinet.

Partisan politics: Behavior of politicians in support of the principles or interests of their own political party.

Party: See *Political party.*

Party platform: Statement of principles and programs that a party is pledged to support.

Party whip: A member of a legislative party who is responsible for party discipline in voting.

Patriarchy: Family-based system of rule dominated by the oldest males.

Patriotism: Political virtue that encourages strong devotion and readiness to make sacrifices for the welfare of one's homeland and fellow citizens.

Patronage: Jobs and other material rewards which are provided in exchange for political support.

Peacekeeping: Interposition of international forces to contain a conflict.

Pendleton Act: Act of U.S. Congress that created the Civil Service Commission in 1883 and gave rise to the modern civil service.

Perestroika: Reforms of Soviet president Mikhail Gorbachev designed to revitalize the Soviet Union, which he led from 1985 until 1991.

Petitioning: Process by which a requisite number of signatures is obtained to initiate a ballot proposition.

Plural society: Society composing distinct racial, linguistic, and religious groups.

Pluralism: The view that democracy and fairness are preserved when a political organization comprises multiple and distinct groups and interests; also condition of society in which diverse cultural, ethnic, racial, religious, and minority groups, and a diversity of private interests, are tolerated.

Plurality: When a candidate or proposition receives more votes than the alternative, but not a majority of the votes cast.

Plutocracy: Oligarchic system in which the ruling minority is chosen on the basis of wealth.

Police power: Right of government to regulate the public health, safety, and welfare.

Police state: A political system in which the police enforce the will of the government's leaders.

Politburo: Body chosen by the Central Committee of the Soviet Communist Party to conduct party business when the Central Committee was not in session.

Political action committee (PAC): Legally constituted committee that can raise and donate money to candidates' political campaigns, subject to the restrictions of federal law.

Political boss: Local or state leader of the party machinery who delivers votes on election day in return for favors.

Political machine: Powerful political organization that operates through a local political party, and dominates the politics of a city or state.

Political party: Association of people who hold similar views and come together to establish their priorities by gaining control of the machinery of government.

Political philosophy: Inquiry into the fundamental concepts concerning political life, such as the nature of the state, justice, law, liberty, authority, community, citizenship, and political obligation.

Political system: Institutions a society uses to run the government.

Politics: Institutions and processes by which laws are enacted, decisions are made, and people are governed.

Poll tax: Payment required as a condition for voting; formerly used in some parts of the United States.

Pollution: Waste put into the environment above the level that the environment can absorb or recycle.

Popular sovereignty: Belief that ultimate authority for government belongs to the people.

Populism, populist: Political ideology that emphasizes the clash between the common peoples and the ruling elites and that promotes greater democracy as well as social and economic equality.

Positivism: Doctrine that holds that human knowledge is based on what is known through actual practice, sense perceptions, and reliance on scientific methods, not on moral values or ideals.

Power: The ability to get what one wants from someone else, by force or by getting someone to think in accordance with one's interests; also, the ability of a state to pursue its strategic interests based on factors such the size of its armed forces, or its industrial capacity.

Power elite: Sociologist C. Wright Mills's term for those who occupy the principal centers of power in the United States whom he believed to act as a single entity.

Presidency, U.S.: Head of the executive branch of government in the United States.

Presidential system: Government in which the executive powers of administering laws are distinct from the legislative powers of making laws, and are carried out by different officials.

Primary election: Election during which the members of a political party cast their ballot for the candidates they wish to represent the party in the general election.

Prime minister (premier): Head of the government (executive branch) and leader of the party (or coalition of parties) holding the most seats in the legislature in a parliamentary system.

Privatization: Assumption of public functions and services by private business enterprise.

"Pro-choice" movements: Umbrella term for organized groups whose aim is to preserve and broaden women's right to choose to obtain an abortion.

Progressive tax: Tax in which people with higher incomes pay a larger proportion of income or wealth as tax.

Progressive movement: Reform movement started in the late nineteenth century in the United States in reaction to the growth of business power in politics and the marketplace; emphasized civil service reform, greater popular control over elections and lawmaking, and regulating industrial activity.

Proletariat: Marx's term for the working class, exploited under capitalism, expected to bring in socialism through revolution.

Propaganda: Information or education systematically provided by governments, often false or misleading, designed to enhance patriotism and foster support for government policies.

Proportional representation: System in which legislative seats are allocated proportionally to each party's share of the popular vote; frequently used in European countries.

Protectionism: Policy of raising tariff and nontariff barriers on products coming from other countries in order to shield domestic industries from competition.

Protest: Expression of dissent from governmental actions or policy.

Public administration: Processes and organizations that carry out the laws and policies of government; also a field of academic study and an area of professional training.

Public good: A good that is provided to everyone at once, and from which no one can be excluded, such as national security or clean air.

Public interest: Shared or common interests of members of a political society, as opposed to private, or individual, interests.

Public policy: Laws and actions taken by authorized governing bodies.

Quorum: Minimum number of members of a legislature who must be present for the valid transaction of business; often a majority of members, but may be lower.

Racism: Belief that one's own racial group is superior to other groups.

Radicalism: In the context of social and political philosophy and practice, behavior or theory that attempts to go to the root of a problem through intellectual analysis or practical policy; also sometimes refers to the degree of departure from previous or familiar practice.

Radicals: Group that seeks great changes in society.

Rationalism: Belief that there are logical principles at work in the universe that are discernible by human reason.

Realpolitik: Traditional perspective for analyzing how states interact, emphasizing national interest and the pursuit of power.

Recall election: Election in which the public decides whether to retain or dismiss an elected official prior to the expiration of the official's term.

Redistributive policies: Policies that take money from one group to allocate to another group.

Referendum: Procedure by which a proposal passed by a legislative body is presented to the voters for approval.

Reform: Fundamental change in the government, constitution, socioeconomic order, or basic values of society that does not involve the violent overthrow of the existing government; also, change within a political system that is consistent with established political rules.

Regime: Type or form of government.

Regressive tax: Tax that places a proportionately larger tax burden on people of lower income or wealth.

Regulation: Rule or procedure made by a governmental agency, usually affecting business activity, and having the force of law.

Relativism: Theory that conceptions of moral values and truth are not absolute, but are relative to the institutions, people, and groups holding such values.

Representation: Standing in for individuals and groups to promote and protect their interests.

Representative democracy: System of governance in which the citizens elect representatives to an assembly or legislative body that is charged with the task of making laws.

Republic: State in which the supreme power belongs to the citizens and is exercised by representatives chosen by them.

Reserved powers: Powers that are held to be exclusive within a specified level of government.

Revolution: Overthrow of an established government, usually in a brief time and often by violence.

Revolutionary government: Regime that claims authority as deriving from its successes in overthrowing an illegitimate regime, and its ongoing efforts to remove counterrevolutionary forces.

Riding: Electoral district for a House of Commons seat in Canada.

Right, the: Individuals and political groups that tend to favor order and stability over change, emphasizing freedom over equality.

"Right to life" movement: Umbrella term for organized groups who advocate restricting or eliminating the right to abortion in order to protect fetal life.

Right-to-work laws: Laws making it illegal to require a job applicant or employee to be a member of a union in order to obtain or keep a job.

Rights: Those things to which individuals, groups, or nations have a just claim, as an individual's right to life, liberty, and the pursuit of happiness as expressed in the Declaration of Independence.

Rights of the accused: Based on the idea that citizens are innocent of crimes until they are convicted, these rights guarantee due process procedures and other protections for those accused of crimes.

Roe v. Wade: Controversial 1973 decision by the U.S. Supreme Court that effectively legalized abortion throughout the United States.

Roman law: The system of law (also called Continental or civil or statutory) most widely used in the European continental states, typified by relatively greater reliance on statutes enacted by legislatures rather than on decisions made by judges.

Rule making: An agency's working interpretation of a law and issuance of binding directives to affected parties.

Rule of law: The general principle that society should be governed by laws, not persons, the laws should be prospective, predictable, as clear as possible, formally written, and enacted through orderly procedures.

School board: Elected or appointed group of citizens who administer school districts.

School prayer: Religious prayers that occur within public schools.

Seat: Right to membership in a legislative body.

Secession: Voluntary separation of a region or a people from a larger polity.

Secretary-general, U.N.: Principal spokesman for the United Nations and its primary mediator in disputes among member countries.

Security Council: Branch of the United Nations responsible for keeping the peace and dealing with emergencies; includes five permanent members and ten states elected for two-year terms.

Self-determination: Right of a people to achieve sovereignty and independence.

Senate: One branch of the U.S. Congress, comprising two members from each state of the union who serve six-year terms.

Seneca Falls Convention: Meeting held in Seneca Falls, New York, in 1848, that marked the beginning of the women's rights movement in the United States.

Separate but equal: Doctrine used by the courts to justify publicly enforcing segregation of the white and black races in Southern states in the U.S. in the late nineteenth and early twentieth centuries. If separate facilities were equal, the courts maintained, they did not violate the "equal protection" clause requirement of the Fourteenth Amendment.

Separation of powers: System in which legislative and judicial powers are placed in different institutions and are exercised by different people.

Shadow cabinet: In parliamentary democracies, the leaders of the opposition political party who would presumably constitute the caucus in a new government if their party won a majority in the parliament.

Single-member district: System in which a candidate is elected to office by the voters of that district; commonly found in the United States.

Slavery: Forced labor of people who are considered property, not free.

Social contract: Implied agreement among people to form a society or government so that they may escape the state of nature.

Social Darwinism: Theory primarily associated with Herbert Spencer that regards human society as an environment within which a ceaseless struggle is waged among social components, including states, with only the strongest surviving.

Social Security system: Basic national American social insurance program, Old-Age, Survivors, and Disability Insurance (OASDI), as well as health insurance (Medicare). OASDI is the largest income maintenance program in the country, covering nine out of every ten labor force participants.

Socialization: Process by which the opinions and behavior of individuals are formed to be consistent with those of a large group.

Sovereignty: Principle that an entity (usually a national government) wields supreme authority over its designated territory.

Spoils system: Granting of government jobs to political supporters by elected officials.

State: See *Nation-state*.

State Department: Department within the executive branch of the U.S. government that is responsible for diplomatic relations with other nations.

State of nature: Condition that humans find themselves in prior to the formation of society and government.

Statesmanship: In the traditional or classical understanding, the high art of political leadership by which certain gifted individuals who possess superior political knowledge and skills promote a nation's comprehensive interests and the common good of its citizens.

Strategic Arms Limitation Talks (SALT): Negotiations held between the United States and the Soviet Union between 1969 and 1985, attempting to limit strategic weapons.

Suffrage movement: Historical struggle to win for women the right to vote.

Suffragette: Derisive term for activist female supporters of woman suffrage applied to suffragists by their opponents.

Sunset law: Requirement that a specified government program periodically demonstrate its effectiveness or be dissolved.

Sunshine law: Requirement that elected officials engaged in official government business do so in public meetings to facilitate public and media oversight.

Superpowers: States whose power exceeds that of other powers in the military, economic, and political spheres, and who therefore exercise enormous influence throughout the world; during the Cold War, the superpowers were the United States and the Soviet Union.

Supply-side economics: Economic theory behind the view that less government and lower marginal tax rates will provide greater opportunities and incentives, thus promoting economic growth.

Supremacy clause: Article 6 of the U.S. Constitution, which states federal law will prevail in cases of conflict with state law.

Supreme Court, U.S.: The highest U.S. federal court, composed of nine members nominated by the president and confirmed by the Senate.

Suzerain: Overlord to whom one is bound by oath or duty.

Tariffs: Tax on the value of a commodity being imported into a country.

Taxation: Compulsory mechanism used by government to acquire money from people by force of law.

Terrorism: Unlawful use of force or violence against persons or property to intimidate or coerce a government or its people in furtherance of the terrorist's political or social objectives.

Theocracy: Government of a state by religious persons who claim to base their authority on God.

Third party: Minor political party that tries to challenge the major parties in a two-party system.

Third World: Developing nations of Africa, Asia, and Latin America; during the Cold War, "First World" and "Second World" referred to the capitalist and communist systems, respectively.

Tory: In British history and politics, one inclined to support royal authority, land-owners, and the Church of England.

Totalitarianism: Form of government in which political leaders exercise centralized and absolute control over all aspects of life, political and cultural expression is suppressed, and individuals, groups, and institutions are not permitted to be autonomous.

Town meeting: The practice in which all citizens of a town meet, discuss issues, and decide on a course of action.

Treaty: Formal agreement among sovereign states on some matter of mutual interest such as trade and defense.

Two-party system: System in which only two parties have a realistic chance of winning control of the government.

Tyranny: Rule by single person maintained in office by force and given to arbitrary conduct.

Underdeveloped country: Nation in which agricultural production predominates over industry and which is usually poorer and less productive than industrial capitalist countries.

Unicameral legislature: Lawmaking body composed of one chamber of elected representatives.

Unitary government: Form of government in which a central authority has final power over all local or subunit governments, which it may alter or abolish at will.

United Nations: Formal association of nations created in 1945 to succeed the League of Nations as an international peacekeeping body.

Universal Declaration of Human Rights: Seminal human rights charter passed by the United Nations on December 10, 1948, annually celebrated as Human Rights Days.

Universal suffrage: Situation pertaining in a political community that gives all adult citizens the right to vote.

Upper house: One of the two houses of a bicameral parliament; its membership may be elected, appointed, or based on heredity; upper houses typically have less power than the more democratic lower houses.

Utilitarianism: Sociopolitical doctrine that utility is the criterion of good or worthy actions, and social or political effort must aim at the greatest good for the greatest number of people.

Utopia: Hypothetical place of ideal perfection, especially in laws, government, and social conditions.

Veto power: Power of an official to prevent authoritative actions by a lawmaking or policymaking body, such as the power of the U.S. president to veto congressional enactments subject to an override by two-thirds of each branch.

Vote of confidence: In a parliamentary system, vote of approval by the Parliament on a bill sponsored by the prime minister and cabinet, who resign if it fails to carry.

Warsaw Pact: Military alliance formed in 1955 between the Soviet Union and her client states in Eastern Europe.

Watergate: Apartment and business complex in Washington, D.C., where a break-in at Democratic campaign headquarters in 1972 led to President Richard Nixon's resignation from office two years later.

Welfare state: Form of government in which the state takes on the responsibility of protecting and promoting the basic well-being of its members through legislation that guarantees support for individuals and families.

Whig: In British history and politics, one inclined to control royal authority and to promote private rights and create democracy.

Whistle-blower: Person who brings public attention to instances of corruption and maladministration in government or business.

World Bank: International financial institution based in Washington, D.C., that lends money to developing nations for economic development projects.

Xenophobia: Suspicion, dislike, or fear of foreigners; often accompanies extreme forms of patriotism or nationalism.

SURVEY
OF
SOCIAL
SCIENCE

ALPHABETICAL LIST

CATEGORY LIST

HISTORY OF GOVERNMENT AND POLITICS

INTERNATIONAL GOVERNMENT AND POLITICS

LAW AND JURISPRUDENCE

RELIGION AND GOVERNMENT

TYPES OF GOVERNMENT

INDEX

Page ranges appearing in boldface type indicate that an entire article devoted to the topic appears on those pages; a single page number in bold denotes definition of a term in the Glossary.

INDEX